W9-AMZ-886

ASTROPHEL

OR

THE LIFE AND DEATH OF THE RENOWNED SIR PHILIP SIDNEY

SIR PHILIP SIDNEY

from the painting sometimes attributed to Zucchero in the National Portrait Gallery

ASTROPHEL

Or the Life and Death

of the Renowned

SIR PHILIP SIDNEY

by

Alfred H. Bill

"The courtier's, soldier's, scholar's, eye, tongue, sword:
The expectancy and rose of the fair state,
The glass of fashion and the mould of form,
The observed of all observers, quite, quite down!"

with 16 pages of illustrations

CASSELL

and Company Limited

London, Toronto, Melbourne

and Sydney

First published in Great Britain, 1938

PRINTED IN GREAT BRITAIN

TO

MRS. WILLIS M. WEST

whose teaching made
History a living narrative
and English Literature
a lifelong delight

This Book

is gratefully dedicated
by one of her old pupils

CONTENTS

CHAPTER		PAGE
	FOREWORD	1
I.	A ROYAL RETROSPECT BY WAY OF PRELUDE	3
II.	"A HAPPY WIFE"	19
III.	"A VERY PARFIT GENTIL KNIGHT"	39
IV.	"WITH HIS SATCHEL AND SHINING MORNING FACE"	60
V.	"BRAVE OXFORD, WONDROUS WELL BELOVED"	80
VI.	LEADING-STRINGS	103
VII.	"A BOW TOO LONG BENT"	129
VIII.	FALSE DAWN	153
IX.	AN INCOMPARABLE PEN	178
X.	ORLANDO INNAMORATO	203
XI.	SETTLING DOWN	234
XII.	MAN OF AFFAIRS	256
XIII.	MY LORD GOVERNOR OF FLUSHING	281
XIV.	"ÆS TRIPLEX"	304
XV.	"A CUP OF COLD WATER"	331
	BIBLIOGRAPHY	355
	INDEX	359

LIST OF ILLUSTRATIONS

SIR PHILIP SIDNEY	Frontispiece
SIR HENRY SIDNEY	To face page 24
LADY MARY, MOTHER OF SIR PHILIP SIDNEY	,, ,, 34
SIR PHILIP SIDNEY AND HIS BROTHER ROBERT	,, ,, 62
FULKE GREVILLE	,, ,, 82
AN ENGLISH ARMY ON THE MARCH	,, ,, 106
THE MASSACRE OF ST. BARTHOLOMEW	,, ,, 106
HUBERT LANGUET	,, ,, 146
QUEEN ELIZABETH AT A PICNIC	,, ,, 168
SIR FRANCIS WALSINGHAM	,, ,, 200
PENELOPE RICH	,, ,, 228
SIR PHILIP SIDNEY	,, ,, 248
MAP OF ZUTPHEN AND SURROUNDING COUNTRY	,, ,, 276
ROBERT DUDLEY, EARL OF LEICESTER	,, ,, 292
MARY SIDNEY	,, ,, 312
TITLE PAGE OF THE FIRST EDITION OF 'ARCADIA'	,, ,, 322
TILTING HELMET OF THE SIDNEYS	,, ,, 322
SIR PHILIP SIDNEY	,, ,, 342

FOREWORD

THIS BOOK HAS BEEN WRITTEN IN THE HOPE OF PLACING before the general reader one of the most brilliant figures of the court of Queen Elizabeth and one that seems to be in danger of being forgotten. Those who desire a scholarly account of Philip Sidney will find it in *The Life of Sir Philip Sidney* by Professor Malcolm William Wallace and in *Sir Philip Sidney* by Miss Mona Wilson, to both of which my indebtedness is gratefully acknowledged. Readers who wish to go still further into the fascinating record of the Sidneys and their times will find much to delight them in the books from which the materials for this volume have been drawn, and of which a list appears at its end.

No apology is made for the somewhat detailed retelling of contemporary events in England and on the Continent. So involved in these were the fortunes of Philip, his family, relatives and friends, that his story would not be understandable without a knowledge of them; and it seemed better to risk being needlessly repetitious to a few than to leave in a state of vagueness the many by whom the history of the period is but imperfectly remembered.

My warm thanks are due to Professor John H. H. Lyon of Columbia University and to Professor Hoyt H. Hudson of Princeton University for their sympathetic interest and wise counsel, to Professor Hudson also for the use of his *Penelope Devereux as Sidney's Stella*, and especially to Doctor James T. Gerould, Librarian of Princeton University, for the cordial hospitality with which he placed at my service all the resources of the Princeton University Library.

ALFRED H. BILL

CHAPTER I

A ROYAL RETROSPECT BY WAY OF PRELUDE

Dispatches from Flanders lay upon the King's desk. There had been some brisk fighting there, fighting in the open field to vary the long succession of siege operations. Not that it could be called a battle in the King's opinion: and his victory at Saint-Quentin twenty-nine years ago gave his opinion some authority, though he had not inherited his father's taste for war. The numbers engaged had been inconsiderable, at least on the side of the enemy. But the bitterness of the encounter and the names on the casualty list gave the affair a certain importance and, to the King, a singular interest.

A score or two of noble English cavaliers and a couple of hundred of English horse had routed and scattered twice their number of the King's light cavalry, thrice charged his Spanish pikemen through and through, and only recoiled before his musketeers when a reinforcement of two thousand men was added to the three thousand already opposed to them. George Crescia, the leader of the King's Albanian mercenary cavalry, had been made a prisoner, the Count Hannibal Gonzaga killed at the head of the Italian mounted arquebusiers. On the English side the renowned Sir Philip Sidney lay dangerously wounded.

The name recalled old memories to the King: strange memories they must have seemed, as he looked back over the many years since he had first heard it. He had been King of England then, the husband of England's queen. Now he was straining all his resources to make England his by conquest.

The King was in his counting-house, but in no such merry mood as the king in the nursery rhyme. To be more precise, he was in his study in the palace of the Escorial; but so pressing were his financial problems that wherever he might be was a counting-house for Philip II of Spain in the late autumn of 1586. He could hardly remember, it is true, when every peso of his enormous revenues was not earmarked long in advance of its receipt. But now, with his great Armada nearly ready for sea, with the tall galleons, the galleys, the supply ships, the galleasses with their three hundred rowers each, assembled at Lisbon and Cadiz; with volunteers pouring in from every Catholic country of Europe; and with the expenses of this stupendous *Empressa de Inglaterra* mounting swiftly toward the staggering figure of twelve thousand ducats a day, he was put to it where to turn for ready money.

The Pope was generously disposed—with promises: a million crowns when a Spanish army should stand on English soil. The English buccaneers had checked and disorganized the flow of treasure from the King's possessions in the New World. They had robbed him of a million and a half in one month of this very year. Only by the mercy of God had the Indian Fleet escaped capture by Drake the year before; and Santiago, San Domingo and Cartagena had been plundered by him. The rich cities of Flanders, which had been like so many gold mines to the King's father, the Emperor Charles V, had turned from an asset to the most expensive of liabilities under the Duke of Alba's Council of Blood; a sales tax of ten per cent upon their commerce had driven them into open rebellion. The extirpation of the Moriscos had changed the once highly-productive province of Andalusia into a waste. The bankers, doubly cautious since the King had repudiated his obligations not so many years ago, were obdurate; and to add a sting to the prohibitive rates of interest which they demanded of him, he had a shrewd suspicion that a Florentine firm almost under the nose of his

Italian viceroy was furnishing the sinews of war to the Queen of England through its London house on quite reasonable terms.

In the half-palace, half-monastery, which he had built to the honour of St. Lawrence, on whose day he had achieved that single military success of his, he wrestled with his difficulties with the laborious and microscopic attention to detail which year after year he had given to the business of his kingdoms. Surrounded with the air of mystery which he loved, his pale face emotionless as a mask of plaster, he had grown more and more mystic, more and more devoted to minutiæ and to this remote retreat. Its granite walls, enclosing an area of almost four hundred thousand square feet, rose four-square to the bitter blasts from the Sierra de Guadarrama. Twelve thousand doors and windows looked out upon the barren plain that surrounded it, or stared at each other across its stony courts. It was well named the Palace of the Slag-heap. Its creator, widower of four queens, father of a son whose death, a homicidal maniac, had been the scandal of Christendom, was a burnt-out old man at fifty-nine. Gout tortured him. A cataract had darkened the sight of one of his eyes. When he came to die, his enemies exulted that he perished like Herod, "eaten of worms" before he gave up the ghost. And after three hundred years his European kingdoms and his vast realms beyond the seas had not recovered from the blight which his rule had placed upon them.

But there was a kind of bleak grandeur in the man, in his single-minded devotion to his duty as he saw it. When his plans miscarried, it was not, in his judgment, because his purposes were not God's purposes, but because he and his assistants were agents unfit in God's sight for so holy a work. Quite lately he had written of a plot to assassinate the Queen of England that a project so much in God's service could only miscarry if its human instruments were unworthy. And nowhere else could he feel so sure of understanding God's will and doing it as in the small, bare rooms of the Escorial which he had appropriated to his private use. They flanked the chancel on the epistle side of the great church that formed the heart of the entire structure. Above it the dome rose four hundred feet into the keen upland air. Through an opening in the partition wall he could see the high altar as he lay in bed, and at any moment could seek refreshment from his labours in the unremitting devotions of the monks of St. Jerome, who formed the garrison of this royal stronghold.

Here in pious pastime he could continue his collection of holy relics. This already included a rib of St. Alban, two bones of the foot of San Diego of Alcala—from which "distilled continually an oleaginous liquor," and a whole thigh of St. Lawrence "with the skin quite burnt and marked with the prongs used in turning him on the gridiron" of his martyrdom, and his foot with a burnt coal still between the toes. Of the saint's head the King was doubtful, believing rather that it belonged to one of the Theban martyrs of the same name. But when the Cardinal de Medici sent him the missing part of the shoulder bone of St. Lawrence which he already possessed, only one of the periodical crises in the affairs of the Queen of Scots distracted him from his pleasure in the gift.

Nothing distracted him from his duties. In a silence broken only by "the blessed mutter of the mass" he laboured through the long hours of the day and night, reading dispatches, passing upon the decisions of his Council, scrawling upon the margins in his abominable handwriting words of caution and rebuke to ambitious generals and ambassadors, whose impetuosity would have far outstripped the slow inexorable "foot of lead" of which their master was so proud. It had worn out many of them, to be sure, the year after year of seeing that "pie de plomo" block plans and enterprises to which they had given their best of brain and blood, because he, Philip, King by the Grace of God, had deemed the time not yet ripe. Don John of Austria, his brilliant bastard brother, ardent, restless and ambitious, had fretted himself to death against it in the Netherlands. Requesens, another of his viceroys there, had ended in the same way. And now Santa Cruz, the commander of the Great Armada, organizer of the fleet that won Lepanto, and destroyer of the hopes of Don Antonio, the Portuguese Pretender, at Terceira, was said to be suffering in mind and body from the endless delays due to his master's minute and continual supervision.

But there were things an old sea-dog past seventy could not be trusted to think of. If God's blessing was to rest upon the expedition, there must be no swearing in the fleet, no gambling, no women. It must be nothing like that army which Alba led over the Mont Cenis into Flanders in '67: ten thousand of the finest troops in Europe and two thousand harlots to serve their carnal appetites. The number, hours and character of the religious services to be held on board must also be designated by the King, and in so important an expedition as this the amount and kind of rations as well. As for the route, conduct, handling and destination of the enterprise, the King had failed through his invariable caution to reap the advantages of his victory at Saint-Quentin; he was moreover always sick at sea; but, since strategy was the mere handmaid of statecraft, must not these matters, too, be prescribed by the supreme statesman?

These admirals, generals, ambassadors and viceroys saw only each his single aim. Their king saw all, for not a document became effective until it had passed his scrutiny. From the slow, broad stream of dispatches, reports and memoranda that flowed across his desk the world was reflected to his eyes with all its multifarious activities. These men forgot things. Everybody forgot things except the King. He forgot nothing. He was quite capable on this particular morning of remembering that Philip Sidney's grandfather had refused knighthood at the hands of the King's grandfather, the great Ferdinand of Aragon, back at the beginning of the century. Nobody now remembered the Turk, for instance, or thanked the King that the Turk had still no foothold in Italy. For Lepanto, which had smashed the Turkish fleet fifteen years before, Don John had got the gratitude as well as the glory. But the King had never been free to dismiss from his mind the threat of the Mohammedan corsairs and the Turkish regular navy.

King of Spain and Portugal, of the Two Sicilies—which included the half of Italy—and of the East and West Indies and the Isles and Continents of the Sea; Archduke of Austria, Duke of Burgundy and of Milan, Count of Flanders, he was the mightiest prince in Europe. But the mere variety of his possessions kept him from moving straight forward with any single enterprise. No one of them could be considered without the rest. The Emperor Charles had found that out in '52, when he was chased out of Innsbruck by Maurice of Saxony and Siena went over to the French. His son had made the unfilial comment that his father had marched into France eating peacocks and had marched out eating turnips.

King Philip had avoided more than one mistake of that kind. When his Mediterranean fleets had been destroyed by the Turk and foul weather, these disasters had not caught him so deeply committed to the task of subjugating his rebellious Flemings that he could not extricate himself. More than once he had shunned the opportunity of removing Elizabeth from the English throne. The half-French Mary, Queen of Scots, who would have succeeded her, would have had her uncle, the Duke of Guise, at her elbow and a French army to support her. Better even the backbiting, feline friendship which he and Elizabeth had maintained between them for a quarter of a century than France in possession of both sides of the water gate that led to his Dutch and Flemish provinces. So clearly from the beginning had he seen the value to him of an English sovereign—a sovereign truly English—on the throne of England that he had strongly supported Elizabeth's succession, although the dying Queen, her sister and his wife, hated her and all she stood for.

Since then he had sat, watching events there through the magic crystal of the correspondence of his ambassadors. He had seen the barons of the North clank into Durham Cathedral, the torchlight red upon their armour, in the last, feeble stand of English feudalism against the power of the crown. He had seen Edinburgh Castle fall before the English cannon, the Catholic Queen of Scots kept a close and closer prisoner by the Protestant Queen of England. He had seen the best blood of the Catholic nobility bought and sold and poured out on the scaffold at York and on Tower Hill. And he had turned a dull ear to the supplications of the persecuted and the incitements of his myrmidons, a deaf one to the appeals of the Irish rebels.

Infrequently he had stretched a shadowy finger to make some small adjustment or to test the strength and direction of opinions. More seldom still he had been annoyingly caught at this, as when his ambassador's secretary had sold out to Cecil, and when the Grand Duke of Tuscany had revealed the details of the Ridolfi plot to that astute statesman. He had supplied the Queen of Scots with just enough encouragement to ensure her being a first-rate nuisance to her royal rival and captor. Less subtly he had allowed the Pope's expedition against the English government in Ireland to base itself on the coast of Spain. He had seized English ships in Spanish ports in times when the pretence of peace between the two countries had been complete, and had turned English mariners and merchants over to the Holy Inquisition to be racked and burnt.

When he had treated as pirates the ships' companies of English vessels that came to trade with his New World colonies, the traders had become pirates in earnest, seizing his ships, plundering his towns and returning to receive knighthood from, and share their plunder with, a sovereign who disclaimed all responsibility for their depredations. He closed his Low Countries ports to English trade, and English trade worked out new routes through Germany, with the result that the Low Countries lost their best customer. English volunteers and English money, privately raised, had poured across the Channel to the assistance of the rebels in arms against his rule.

His ambassador's house had been ransacked, his papers seized, and every person caught hearing mass there, foreigners and English alike, imprisoned in the Fleet by officers of the Queen's own guard. Ships bearing the treasure which was to have paid the King's half-mutinous troops in Flanders had been seized by Elizabeth's order, the money coolly taken out of them, and kept on the flimsiest of pretexts. English pirates openly sold their Spanish prizes in English ports, and Spanish gentlemen had been sold at auction in Devon market-places at a hundred pounds a head. But there had been no war with England.

Piety, patience, modesty and distrust were the principles on which the Emperor Charles had based the upbringing of his son; and the King had still sat, watching until the time should be ripe. Slowly, steadily the Jesuit missionaries had permeated England, cultivating those hardy roots of Catholic thought and Catholic life which still persisted throughout the kingdom after almost thirty years of repression. The doctrine of the laudable assassination of heretic sovereigns, which had been propagated among the English exiles at Douai, had found some fertile soil here and there. At any moment now some shoot of it might burst into crimson flower, and Elizabeth might fall, as William of Orange had fallen, before the pistol of an English Balthazar Gérard.

How time worked for him who waited and schemed to do God's will! France, which once he had had to fear, now weakened by more than twenty years of the wars of religion and torn between the waning power of the crown and the waxing power of the Holy League, was ripe for that partition between Navarre, the Guises and Spain which the King had planned for it. The crown of Portugal had fallen into his lap. The southern provinces of his revolted Netherlands had returned to their allegiance. The Queen of Scots, indignant at her son's neglect, had named King Philip her heir to the throne of England. Elizabeth, committed at last to an alliance with the rebellious Dutchmen, had entangled herself in all the dangerous and expensive business of co-operating with a revolutionary junta which the assassination of William the Silent had deprived of leadership. The Armada would catch her with her best troops beyond the sea and block the Channel while Parma's army landed on her ill-protected shores. Even this young Sidney, the King's namesake, who from the time he became a man had been the shining spear-head of enmity to Spain and Holy Church, seemed unlikely to give further trouble. All in all things promised to be very different from what they were when, two-and-thirty years ago, he had been King of England by virtue of a mere crown matrimonial. "Time and I never fail," said the King.

But Time took its toll of a man while he watched and waited. He had been twenty-seven when he landed at Southampton that July day in 1554, erect, vigorous, with golden hair and a golden beard above his stiff, Spanish ruff. Hair and beard were white now; he was bowed and broken; and the black which he wore was in mourning for his fourth wife. He had worn black that far-off day in England. Of no more than middle stature, it had set off his well-made figure among the gorgeous group of his attendants. The English archers, dressed in the Aragon colours of yellow and crimson, had held the landing. At the trumpets' blare and the cannon's thunder the brilliant throng of English nobles had kneeled before him and Lord Shrewsbury had presented him with the Order of the Garter. Next morning, in a red cloak, his Spanish retinue behind him, he had ridden off in a driving rain to Winchester, where the little neurotic spinster of thirty-eight, with red hair and no eyebrows, awaited her bridegroom with mystical avidity in the belief that like a second Virgin Mary she should bear a son who would bring peace on earth by reuniting all Christendom in the One True Church.

But it had not been without a keen sense of danger at first, that English venture of his. The Spanish marriage had been so unpopular that the Queen had considered surrounding herself with a guard of Catholic Irishmen. An armed insurrection against it six months before had left London grisly with the dangling corpses of rebels. Renard, the Imperial Ambassador, had written to recommend musketeers disguised as lackeys for the suite of the Prince of Spain, a coat of mail under his doublet, and food prepared only by the hand of the Prince's own cook. The six thousand soldiers, destined for service in Flanders, who had formed his escort across the Bay of Biscay, had been firmly shepherded back on board their transports when they attempted to land; and that day on the road to Winchester a courier, bearing to the Prince a ring from his betrothed, spread uneasiness and hesitation among the Spaniards until it could be explained that the Queen's message was only a petition that the Prince should not expose himself further to the storm.

Renard had underestimated the Englishman's reluctance to resort to assassination, however. Wyatt's rebellion had been a sufficient vent for popular dissatisfaction. The new King of England had learned that even he was expected to doff his cap and smile upon the cheering crowds, when he clattered in from Whitehall to hear mass at St. Paul's with his guards, a hundred each of English, High Almans, Swiss and Spaniards, behind him. Of a Sunday afternoon the people had flocked to see him and his nobles flaunting their gay colours in the tilt-yard in the intricacies of the juego de cannas, the javelin game, to the waving of banners and the sound of kettledrums and trumpets. And twenty carts loaded with gold and silver bullion, which had been loaned by the Emperor and was hauled through London streets to the Tower, there to be coined into money to replace the debased currency of the reign of King Edward VI, had done King Philip no harm with his new subjects.

If only that son of Mary, who seemed for so many months to be poised upon the threshold of life, could have been brought to birth; if only the King could have dissuaded the prospective mother from her belief that the birth could be hastened by the smoke of burning heretics as it arose with a savour sweet-smelling to heaven—how different might have been the outcome! Not that the King was mercifully disposed toward the victims of these burnt offerings: he who could sit through an auto-da-fé with an equanimity equal to that with which he watched a review of his troops. But, perfect specimen of the Machiavellian prince that he was, he saw clearly the inexpediency of his wife's headlong method of rooting heresy out of her kingdom. He had caused his chaplain to preach against it in the royal chapel. England was not Spain or even Flanders. But Mary, with a woman's uncompromising devotion to her purpose and her belief that God, if sufficiently assured of her desire to serve him, would give her a son, refused to heed his counsel: and her bishops, smarting from their years of indignity and persecution under her father and her brother, urged her on.

To offenders of another sort—those who would have kept her from her throne—she showed a clemency which Renard regarded as dangerous. Even now the dispatches from Flanders which lay before the King were sprinkled with the names of those whom she had spared and pardoned and who—themselves or their sons—were serving with the English expeditionary forces. The Earl of Leicester, the Commander-in-Chief, was one of them. The King remembered him best as Lord Robert Dudley, a handsome boy in his early twenties, whose father, the powerful Duke of Northumberland, had answered for his treason with his head. Lately released from the Tower, the young man had borne his "corruption in blood" with that swagger which the Spanish grandees wondered at in those attainted of high treason, until it was explained to them that death upon the block in such a case argued the loftiest distinction for the sufferer and his family.

The King had taken him into his own service, had made him the messenger to announce to the dreary Queen his return to England in the spring of '57, and had done his share toward the "restoration in blood" of young Robert, his brother Ambrose, and their sisters. Another brother, John, had hardly survived his liberation from the Tower; and still another, Henry, had fallen, fighting on the King's side at Saint-Quentin. One of the sisters was now the Countess of Huntingdon, unless the King's memory deceived him, which it never did. The other, Lady Mary, had married Sir Henry Sidney, Knight of the Garter, Lord President of the Council of Wales, thrice Lord Deputy of Ireland, and had become the mother of this Philip of whose misfortune the King had just been reading.

Sir Henry Sidney, with his tall, handsome figure, his gallant bearing, and the trenchant humour that spiced his calm, sagacious speech, was a man not easily forgotten. The King had first seen him in the embassy with which the Earl of Bedford had come to escort the Spanish royal bridegroom to his English nuptials. Wise, honest and boldly serviceable, the young knight, who was then only at the beginning of his distinguished career, had been never wanting with a timely word in behalf of the blighted fortunes of his wife's family. His sisters, Mabel and Elizabeth, had shared the Queen's sad life as a neglected princess and died in her service. Jane Dormer, his niece, had been among the Queen's maids of honour whom the Prince of Spain, following what he believed to be still the custom of the country—that custom which had once so delighted Erasmus—had kissed upon the mouth that rainy night when he met his bride at Winchester. The Queen had died in her arms five years later, and Jane, as Duchess of Feria, had become a shining ornament of the court of Spain.

Pleased to show favour to so deserving a family, the

King had stood sponsor for Sir Henry's newborn son. The child, as if in happy augury, had been born on St. Andrew's Day, the festival day of the Order of the Golden Fleece. That day the King, the Duke of Alba and Don Ruy Gomez, in the robes of the Order, with six hundred more of the distinguished cavaliers of Spain, and the Knights of the Garter in gorgeous apparel, had heard high mass sung in the Abbey at Westminster. Not long after, the King had gone down to Penshurst, Sir Henry's place in Kent, for the christening, which was celebrated with a splendour worthy of the royal guest.

The Spaniards, used to the rock-hewn dwellings of their native land, were wont to observe that the English lived in abodes built of sticks and mud; but the old, castellated manor house in the midst of its lordly park, though it had more about it of the feudal stronghold than of the splendid residence which Sir Henry and his son Robert were to make of it years later, had been a noble setting for the occasion. And the other sponsors were suited to such a background: the old Earl of Bedford and the baby's grandmother, the Duchess of Northumberland, whom the death of her husband and son upon the scaffold the year before had turned into an old woman at forty-five.

From time to time in the years between, the stream of inky paper across the King's desk had cast back a shining reflection of this godson of his. The son of a distinguished father, the nephew of four earls, and heir to the richest of them, gifted with a handsome face and a pleasing presence, it would have been strange if the young man had not made a certain figure in his world. But from childhood he had showed the determination to achieve a fame that should be owing to his own efforts. "*Vix ea nostra voco*" ("*Hardly do I call these things ours*") had been the motto that glittered on his shield from early manhood; and the King, though he had neglected his linguistic studies in his youth, could probably supply the Ovidian context. From Paris, Venice and Vienna had come reports of the boy of seventeen whom the King of France had delighted to honour and statesmen and scholars cultivated for the pleasure they took in the sweetness of his nature and the excellence of his understanding.

Courtier, leader in tournaments and revels, consummate horseman and swordsman, writer of masques, romances and verses, the friend and patron of navigators, soldiers, poets and scholars, he had become the model of the young men of his time. He had been twice a member of Parliament, was joint Master of the Queen's Ordnance, had been spoken of as likely to be second-in-command of expeditions led by Lord Howard and Drake. He had been sent on diplomatic missions of great delicacy. There had been a persistent rumour that he was destined for a position more exalted still. And always, as if by an ironical fatality, he had been found in the foremost ranks of those who were bent upon thwarting the will of his royal godfather.

At the age of twenty-two, when Queen Elizabeth had sent him to the Emperor Rudolph with her congratulations on that monarch's accession to his throne, he had wheedled out of her permission to consult with various of the Protestant German princes on his journey, with a view to the formation of a Protestant League against Spain and the Pope. He had entertained the project of marrying the sister of the Prince of Orange and thereby becoming Lord of Holland and Zeeland—a project favourably looked upon by certain Protestant statesmen of the Continent. He had finally married the daughter of Sir Francis Walsingham, of all living Englishmen the King's most able and active enemy.

He had learned war in Ireland under his father in the bitter guerrilla fighting which absorbed so large a part of the time and energy of Elizabeth's viceroys in that unhappy island; and when the acknowledgment of the existence of a state of war with Spain had been wrung from the reluctant Queen, Sir Philip Sidney had been made Governor of Flushing, the fortress that cut off the King's rich city of

Antwerp from the sea. That was now more than a year ago. The King had been reading often of him since, of his wise administration of his charge, of his energetic and prudent leadership in the field, but, most of all, of his tact and wisdom in counsel, when the clashing interests of the Dutch and their English allies, of ambitious English officers and self-seeking soldiers of fortune, were quieted by the gentle strength and honest diplomacy which had won him the love and admiration of his friends and the admiration and liking of his foes.

When, a few weeks after the news of his wound, the report of his death reached the King, all Protestant Europe was ringing with lamentations for him. Even Mendoza, the King's ambassador whom Elizabeth's Council had indignantly expelled from England for his plotting there, wrote to deplore his loss as a loss to the whole of Christendom. But it was of the long, long past that the half-blind old man sat thinking in his bleak chamber in the Escorial. From Zutphen, scene of the fatal combat, had risen that "grand *jammergeschrey*," that wail of a whole town in agony, as Alba's soldiers wreaked their vengeance on the helpless population through the long hours of a Sunday afternoon fourteen years ago. At Flushing the King had bidden farewell for the last time to his beer-guzzling, wine-swilling Flemings, whose endless banquets bored and disgusted their abstemious ruler; and it was there, in one of his rare emotional outbursts, that he had told the enigmatical young Prince of Orange what he thought of him with insulting familiarity. But most sharply the English scenes returned to his mind: Penshurst, the fine, old manor house in its park, with that pleasing blend of magnificence and comfort which he had encountered nowhere but in England; the stately young father and the aged Earl, whose respectful courtesy to their new, foreign sovereign was so different from the servile, Burgundian court etiquette of Spain and Flanders; the indomitable grandmother, whose tired eyes looked out upon her shattered world with a kind of indulgent contempt for what she had suffered; and the pale, beautiful mother of the child, her sorrows forgotten for the time in joy that a man was born into the world.

On an impulse perhaps too complicated to be analysed, an impulse in which there must have been mingled much regret, some sense of righteous retribution, some anger and great pride, the King took his pen and scrawled upon the margin of the dispatch what was all in all the highest tribute among the scores of such that all over Europe were poured out upon Philip Sidney's tomb:

"He was my godson."

CHAPTER II

"A HAPPY WIFE"

BACK IN THE YEAR 1551, WHEN PHILIP OF SPAIN HAD still some time to wait for his kingly crown and was solacing his first widowhood with Doña Isabel de Osorio, a beautiful young English girl sat, reading in Hall and Grafton's *Chronicle*, in a beautiful English country house. She was Lady Mary Sidney, and three years later she was to become the mother of the child whose christening the King of Spain remembered so vividly.

Of few girls in the world could it have been said more truly that she seemed to have been born with a silver spoon in her mouth. Her father, John Dudley, Earl of Warwick, was the most powerful man in England. Her handsome and brilliant brothers, who were his able assistants, shared with her and her lovely sister their hours of leisure. She could not remember a time when the fortunes of her family had not been soaring, her father returning covered with new honours from the successful prosecution of some war or the negotiation of some treaty. And now, to crown all, in her seventeenth year he had married her—privately at Asser in the month of March, and "most publicly and honourably" at Ely Place, Holborn, at Whitsuntide—to young Henry Sidney, whom she dearly loved.

By no means unconscious of her blessings was Mary Sidney. Before she closed the book she wrote on one of its pages:

> Of all thinges the newest is the best,
> save love and frindship, which
> the elder it waxeth is ever the better.

Escript par la maine d'un
femme heuruse assavoir.

But she was not without misgiving as to the permanency of her good fortune. Perhaps already she could see upon the horizon the cloud no bigger than a man's hand, which was to obliterate her sunny sky so that it would never shine again with such pure clarity. More likely she had gathered some sense of the uncertainty of human greatness from the record of human vicissitudes which she had just been reading. For she added:

To whyshe the best and fere the worst
are to points of the wyese.
To suffer then whatt happen shall
that man is happy thryese. 1551.
Mary Sidney
fere God.

And in another set of halting verses she reminded herself that those who strive for too high a goal are alone responsible for their failure. But these, too, she subscribes—in Latin this time—as "written by a happy hand." It is as if she would make her happiness the more precious to herself by thinking of the dangers that might threaten it.

The fate of her paternal grandfather offered her a terrible specimen of them. Minister to King Henry VII, Edmund Dudley, of whom Bacon wrote that he "could put hateful business into good language," had gone to the block, a sacrifice to the popular indignation against his master's greed. Happenings in England during her own infancy and childhood were thick with similar examples. Queen Anne Boleyn, since she could do no better for the dynasty than bring into the world the baby girl who, as Queen Elizabeth, was to become "England's greatest king," had been beheaded in 1536. Gentle Jane Seymour had died of giving birth to the delicate boy who now reigned as King Edward VI. Queen

Catherine Howard had followed Queen Anne up the steps of the scaffold. Queen Katherine of Aragon, mother of the unhappy Princess Mary, had died in the bitterness of neglect. Of the six queens of Henry VIII only two survived him—Anne of Cleves in contented widowhood, and Katherine Parr to become the wife of the turbulent Lord Seymour of Sudely, when at length in 1547 the King died also.

But, though queens might come and queens might go, there had been a court within the court, where little changed. This was the nursery of the small heir apparent; and the Dudley children were frequent visitors there, sharing the studies and the play of the Prince and at least one of his sisters. When the Princess Elizabeth, along with her half-sister Mary, had been reclaimed from bastardy by grace of the failure of their father's later efforts to make the throne safe for legitimacy, she was often about this infantile court. Her little brother, the Prince, called her "sweet sister Temperence," which sounds strangely in the ears of those who have learned to think far otherwise of Elizabeth the Queen.

The atmosphere of the royal nursery was charged with the learning which was held in such high honour at the time. At the age of six the little Edward, "godly and virtuous imp" that he was, could decline any Latin noun and conjugate any Latin regular verb. "Every day at Mass-time," reported his tutor, "he readeth in Solomon's Proverbs in which he delighteth much." At the age of thirteen he was translating Cicero's *De Philosophia* into Greek. Roger Ascham, the great pioneer in education of the day, taught the Princess Elizabeth; and Mary Dudley's education was doubtless benefited by his advice, if she did not actually have a share of his instruction. Certain it is that she enjoyed the excellent education which it was the fashion to give to well-born girls at that time. They spoke French as readily as they spoke English. The Princess Elizabeth was famous for her familiarity with Latin and Greek; her sister Mary was her equal in the modern tongues; and Lady Mary Sidney added a knowledge of Italian and a proficiency in music to her other accomplishments.

Sir William Sidney, father of young Henry Sidney, presided over the Prince's household as Governor, Chamberlain and Steward. His wife, Lady Anne, who was the daughter of Sir Hugh Pagenham, was the Prince's governess; and her sister was, as Sir Henry Sidney expressed it years later, "in such place as among meaner personages is called dry nurse." A granddaughter of Sir William's, little Jane Dormer, the child of his eldest daughter, was one of the Prince's companions in "reading, playing and dancing and such like pastimes answerable to their spirits and the innocence of their years." When Henry was ten, his father had him made Henchman to the two-year-old Prince. He became the lifelong friend of the Dudley boys; and, strong and gentle, gay and kind, handsome and wise, as he was, he must have attracted very early the affectionate admiration of their sister Mary, who was about six years younger than he.

All this while her father had been rising swiftly in his monarch's service. Warden of the Marches of Scotland in 1542, he had borne his part in the taking of Edinburgh and Boulogne two years later, commanded a fleet against the French at the Isle of Wight in 1545 and helped to defeat the Scots at Pinkie. When the dreadful old King—Defender of the Faith by appointment of the Pope and Supreme Head of the Church of England by act of Parliament—carried to heaven's gate an account so mixed of good and evil that St. Peter himself must have been puzzled to balance it, his will provided that until King Edward VI had attained his majority the government of the realm should be vested in a council; and of that council the two leading spirits were those "new men," John Dudley and Edward Seymour.

Seymour, the boy King's uncle, Earl of Hertford and Duke of Somerset, soon made himself Lord Protector of the Kingdom. But Dudley was not less ambitious, selfish and unscrupulous than he. It had been Dudley's foreign policy that triumphed at the peace with France, by which Boulogne was returned to its lawful owners, the French given a free hand in Scotland, and England committed to everything that was opposed to the Emperor and Spain. Earl of Warwick, Lord High Admiral of England, generally admired and popular for his conspicuous bravery in war and the splendour in which he lived, Dudley was not long in taking such advantage of the mistakes of his rival that Somerset found it but a short journey from his place beside the throne to a traitor's scaffold: and Dudley ruled in his stead.

Dudley was a handsome man, of engaging manners, and devoted to his ambitious and resolute wife and to his family of beautiful and intelligent boys and girls. So it would have been strange if he had not been admired and loved in return, especially by his high-spirited elder daughter, to whom he gave such a husband as she might quite naturally have chosen for herself. For between the wish of parents to see their children well provided for and their desire to strengthen their own positions through matrimonial alliances young people were seldom allowed much voice in such matters in that age.

Save that the bridegroom was not of noble birth the match was a brilliant one. The Sidneys claimed descent from a certain William de Sidne, Chamberlain to Henry II, to whom that king granted the manor of Sutton in Surrey. The name was believed to be a corruption of St. Denis, but it was probably derived from Sutton Heath, as Stepney was from Stephen's Heath. John de Sidenie owned a farm in the parish of Alford, about ten miles from Guildford, in the time of Edward I. But from Henry Sidney's paternal grandmother he took the same blood that had gone to the making of the Brandon dukes of Suffolk. Nicholas Sidney married Anne, daughter of Sir William Brandon, and their son William was Henry's father. The Dudley nobility, moreover, though the family could trace descent through the female line from some of the most ancient houses in England, was of most recent creation; and the last two reigns had proved that there was hardly a place so high that it could not be reached by a young man of brains and energy, whose feet were firmly set upon the ladder of court preferment.

William Sidney had won his way with the sword, his service ranging from Spain to Scotland. He held important commands on both land and sea in the wars of King Henry VIII against the French, won his knighthood in arms and was made a banneret for valour. His gratified sovereign made him a Knight of the Garter, a member of the Privy Council, and Lieutenant of the Tower, stood godfather to his only son, giving the child his own royal name, and committed his own son to his care.

King Henry, unlike his parsimonious daughter Elizabeth, who seldom rewarded faithfulness which she was sure she could have for nothing, was prodigal of favours to his devoted servants. Numerous estates and manors were thus added to Sir William's patrimony, notably the Abbey of Robertsbridge in Sussex, including rich iron works, which the King had taken from the monks. King Edward VI was not less mindful of the services of the Governor of his princely household, and the royal benefactions culminated in the grant of Penshurst Place.

Henry Sidney was not slow to follow his father's prosperous fortunes, though his route was necessarily a somewhat different one. Born in 1529, at Baynard's Castle probably, for that was Sir William's usual place of residence in London at that time, he was a student at New College, Oxford, for a term or two when he was fourteen. But his early years were chiefly spent in attendance upon his young master, the Prince and King. By the time he was married he had become one of the four chief Gentlemen of the King's Bedchamber, Chief Cup-bearer, Chief Cipherer, Sergeant of his Majesty's Otter Hounds, and was chief steward of various royal parks and manors. His personal fortune, like that of his father, was continually being augmented by the kingly beneficence.

SIR HENRY SIDNEY

from the painting attributed to Ewoouts, at Petworth, by courtesy of Lord Leconfield

He was "reputed for comeliness of person, gallantness and liveliness of spirit, virtue, quality, beauty and good composition of body" and was generally acknowledged to be "the only odd man and paragon of the court." So his young bride had very good reason to write herself "femme heuruse."

Followed what probably seemed to Mary Sidney always the happiest two years of her life. Honours continued to fall thick about her. In the October after her wedding her father became Duke of Northumberland, and on the same day, in the auspicious company of William Cecil, her husband was knighted for his services in the embassy of the Marquis of Northampton, which carried the Garter to King Henri II of France. A year and a half later he bore his king's offer of mediation between Henri II and the Emperor, and won the praise of the English Ambassador at Paris for his adroitness and discretion. Meanwhile, in the summer of 1552, he served under his father-in-law in the suppression of certain rebels in Northumberland.

All this meant many a long separation for the young lovers. It was irksome to wait for a devoted husband's return, when he must ride post-haste to court with his commander's dispatches before he could seek the longing arms of his impatient wife down in the country. But the best of the nobility and gentry of Tudor times were trained to the rule that they must pay for their wealth and privileges with hard service to their sovereign; and life can have been by no means dull for Lady Mary during these years. Her father had given to her and her husband the manor of Halden in Kent. But in these times of separation she could go to lovely Sion House upon the Thames, where the Duke had established his family since the overthrow of his great rival.

There, when they were not employed in the strenuous duties which he laid upon them, came her five gay, young brothers. Her sister Katherine was her companion; and at near-by Sheen dwelt Henry Grey, Duke of Suffolk, Northumberland's ally, with his three daughters. There were two barges of state to carry the young people from the one house to the other. They fleeted the time with hunting, fishing, tennis, archery, music, and the romping dances of the day, in which one's partner tossed one in the air and excelled if he could twice cross his legs in a pirouette before his feet touched the ground. They had a company of players to amuse them; and on quiet evenings, when he would ease his mind from business and intrigue, Northumberland played at chess with his neighbour Suffolk and made him sulky by defeating him.

Were they troubled in mind at all, one wonders, by certain supernatural warnings of the fate which was soon to overtake so many of that light-hearted group. These appeared: not at Sion House, however, though it had been a Brigittine convent before it became a part of the royal plunder of the religious orders, and carried, too, the sinister implications of having been a part of the ill-gotten possessions forfeited by the Lord Protector at his downfall, but at Suffolk's house, formerly the abbot's buildings of a Carthusian monastery. There, as the Duke and Duchess of Suffolk were pacing the Gothic gallery, a skeleton arm was thrust out of the wall before them, barring their way with an axe that dripped with blood.

At Sion a more reliable prognostication might have been made from the change in the manner and bearing of the Duke of Northumberland himself, as the winter of 1552 drew on toward the spring of 1553. He became anxious and irritable. For the health of the boy King began to show signs of breaking. Always delicate, he grew seriously ill in this, his fifteenth year. If he should die, there would be an end to all John Dudley's greatness. By the will of King Henry the Princess Mary would be the next sovereign of England; and Northumberland, in his desire to outdo even Somerset in binding to himself the Protestant interest, had been so careless of her friendship that he had denied her the privilege of hearing mass in her own house.

If she should become Queen, there were few in England who would support him against her disfavour. Among the country people the continuing evils arising from the enclosure of the commons were laid at his door. More justly the townsfolk—with the content of the shilling three-quarters copper—blamed him that trade was at a standstill and commerce had ceased. The nobles of recent creation envied and distrusted him, as well they might the destroyer of Somerset. The old nobility, Catholic and favouring the Emperor, hated him for an upstart, a Protestant and a Francophile, and shared heartily in the general dislike of his foreign policy, which had conferred substantial benefits upon England's traditional enemy. Recent successes of the French against the Emperor, who, as King of Spain, was England's old-time friend, had sharpened this dislike; and the Duke's own rough and tyrannous behaviour alienated the rabble, which he had attracted by his former frankness and good spirits.

The King grew weaker with the spring's advance, his physicians more puzzled, and the aspect of the Duke's fortunes sicklier still. When all else seemed hopeless, he called in a sort of wisewoman to treat his sovereign, and for his own affairs resorted to a remedy no less desperate. The dying boy was persuaded to sign a will excluding his two half-sisters from the throne and fixing the succession upon the Lady Jane Grey, the eldest of Suffolk's daughters, who, through her mother, derived her title from King Henry VII. Then, to make assurance doubly sure, Northumberland proceeded to marry her to Guilford, the youngest and best beloved of his sons.

Small and freckled, with red hair and eyes of a light hazel colour, the gentle, studious young girl had little that was queenly about her. While the other young folk ran in gay riot beside the Thames, she sought refuge in her books. She loved learning, and the pursuit of it shielded her in some measure from the harsh and unceasing correction of parents who were bent upon preparing her for her high destiny. But a gown of cloth of gold, a mantle of silver tissue, and a head-dress of green velvet set with precious stones made her a charmingly pretty bride. In Northumberland's private chapel at Durham House in London that Whitsuntide she was married. The head of her eighteen-year-old bridegroom, who was so handsome that he was called beautiful, was completely turned: but not by the appearance of his young wife. It was the prospect of becoming King Guilford that elated him.

It was a most splendid occasion. On the same day her sister and Lady Mary Sidney's sister Katherine were married also: the former to Lord Herbert, son of the Earl of Pembroke, and the latter to Lord Hastings, who was to become the Earl of Huntingdon. Jewels and rich robes, spoil of the ruin of Somerset, were drawn from the royal wardrobe to deck the bridal party and their near relatives. But it was the last of pomp and circumstance for any of the Dudleys for many a long year to come, unless one counts the melancholy fiasco a few weeks later, when "Queen Jane" was conducted in royal state to the Tower in preparation for her coronation. Then there were salutes of trumpets and cannon in plenty no doubt; she wore pattens on her little feet to give her a more regal stature; but the thin lines of starers, between which she passed, kept a lugubrious silence as she mounted the worn steps of the grim fortress which was to be her palace for nine days and after that her prison till her death.

For now the Duke's tragedy moved swiftly to its end. Swiftly the young King grew worse. Under the doses of the powerful drugs administered by the female quack who attended him his hair fell out, his nails dropped off. Rumour flew through the country that the Duke had poisoned him to hasten the crown matrimonial that was to shine upon King Guilford's brow. It was whispered that he was already dead and his death kept secret. A crowd filled with suspicious fury gathered in front of the palace at Greenwich, where he lay; and although Sir Henry Sidney carried him to the window to reassure them, many believed that they looked upon a corpse: so terrible was the poor boy's appearance.

The sixth of July came round, the eve of the ill-omened day on which the King's father had sent Sir Thomas More to the block eighteen years before; and that night, in the arms of Sir Henry Sidney, his loved and loving friend since babyhood, Edward VI drew his last, tormented breath. A terrible storm swept through England; there fell torrents of blood-red hail; a monstrous child was born. At the news that her half-brother was dead the wily Princess Elizabeth shammed illness to avoid putting herself in the power of the rapacious Duke. The Princess Mary rode for her life, a hundred miles by daylight and darkness, into Norfolk to the protection of the Howards. And Lady Mary Sidney, at her father's order, fetched the Lady Jane from his house in Chelsea to Sion House, there to be hailed by him and certain of his confederates as their queen.

On Monday, the tenth, the royal barge swept "Queen Jane" past her doubtfully loyal city of London down to the Tower. At Paul's Cross, when the heralds had done proclaiming her, young Gilbert Potter broke the dead silence of the crowd. "The Lady Mary has the better title," he exclaimed. They nailed him by the ears to the pillory for that, and when they thought he had suffered enough to teach him a lesson, sliced them off. There was a rumour abroad that six thousand French troops were about to be landed to support the new queen, and the city lay quiet under the threat.

But by Wednesday night Northumberland and his fellows knew that everywhere else nobles and commons were up in arms in behalf of the Princess Mary. On Friday morning he rode out against them in his scarlet cloak at the head of six hundred men and a train of artillery. But he went with a heavy heart. "The people press to see us," he observed gloomily, as he passed through Shoreditch with his gallant sons Ambrose and Robert beside him, "but not one saith God speed us." Of his soldiers it was said that "their feet marched forward but their minds went backward." They lagged behind; they straggled; near Cambridge they mutinied.

On the Wednesday following his departure his associates whom he had left behind him became so well assured of the failure of their attempt that they proclaimed the Princess Mary queen and took over the Tower in her name. The Duke of Suffolk, hurrying to his daughter with the fatal news, found her seated in desolate grandeur under a canopy of state.

"Come down from there, my child," he cried. "That is no place for you." He took her in his arms, and father and daughter mingled their tears.

"Can I go home?" she asked like a tired little girl.

She could not. She remained, a prisoner, to be joined within a few days by Northumberland, the author of all her woes. His scarlet cloak was tattered and spattered with mud by the hands of the London mob, which would have torn him to pieces but for the heavy guard that surrounded him. It was just two weeks and five days since the death of the King.

So much for "all thinges the newest," to which Lady Mary Sidney had looked forward so bravely two years before. The increasing value which she attributed to "love and frindship" remained for time to prove. What part her husband bore in all this is unknown. Two months earlier he had obtained a royal licence for fifty gentlemen and yeomen above the number of his menial servants to wear his cognizance: which looks as though he planned to take a hand in his father-in-law's coup d'état. He signed as a witness the will of the dying King, thereby making himself guilty of treason as things turned out; and it was not in his nature to desert a cause to which he had promised his support. Perhaps Northumberland had recognized the prudence of keeping him in the background as an anchor to windward in case of failure. At all events the Duke had hardly been arrested before Sir Henry Sidney joined the growing crowd that rushed to seek pardon at Queen Mary's feet. Having received it, and pardon for his wife as well, he went to work to save what he could of life, liberty and fortune for the other members of her family.

The Queen was well disposed to show mercy; and on his side was her memory of those two faithful servants of hers, his sisters, and the influence of his niece Jane Dormer, now a young beauty of twenty-three, who had been for some years her favourite among her attendants. Jane, moreover, came of a family of the most ardent Catholicism. Her grandfather, Sir Robert Dormer, had retired from court in his disapproval of the divorce of Queen Katherine of Aragon; and her grandmother's brother, Sebastian Nudigate, had been one of the Carthusian monks who suffered the horrors of a traitor's death at Tyburn in King Henry's reign. It may be, too, that Sir Henry did not base his efforts solely on the finer feelings of the Queen. He spent ten thousand pounds between the time of King Edward's death and the following spring; it was an age in which great men did not scruple to sell their influence; and some of this money may well have gone into the pockets of those who could drop into the royal ear a friendly word or two in behalf of the young Dudleys.

Their father's case was, of course, hopeless. If the Queen would have forgiven him, the Emperor, through his ambassador Renard, persuaded her not to do so. Her mind made up, she refused even to see the suppliant Duchess. She took the true measure of the cringing servility with which he dishonoured his last days. His conversion back to the faith of Rome failed to move her. He was left for a few weeks to carve the name of his wife, whom he loved, upon the walls of his prison. Then in a suit of swan-coloured velvet he was led out to die. He drew a cross in the sawdust that strewed the scaffold, knelt down to kiss it, and laid his head upon the block.

But in the case of his sons it could be urged that they

had only done what they did in obedience to their father; and the duty of children to obey their parents was held to be absolute in that time. On the other hand, only the desertion of their men at the last moment had saved Queen Mary from falling into the hands of Ambrose and Robert, who had come up with her in her flight; and young Guilford's eagerness for the crown had been notorious. For months their fate hung in a balance that oscillated sickeningly before the eyes of the mother and sister who watched it from the retirement of their disgrace. Renard continued to press for measures of greater severity than the Queen desired to use; and events took such a course as made her doubt whether the policy of mercy, toward which she leaned, were truly a wise one.

Meanwhile, on the last day of September, she made her state entry into London for her coronation. Everywhere were manifestations of the enthusiasm appropriate to such occasions. The five-hundred-foot spire of St. Paul's was rigged with yards like the mast of a ship, a sailor bestriding the weathercock. John Heywood, forerunner of the English drama, made her a speech of welcome in Latin in Paul's Churchyard. The ceremony in the Abbey next day went off in a proper atmosphere of rejoicing. But when the cannon had ceased to thunder, when the joy bells had died away and the bonfires had flickered out, the shouts of the populace grew fainter as it began to be understood that the new reign was to be not merely Catholic but papist in the highest degree and that a marriage with Philip, the Prince of Spain, was the desire dearest to the heart of the new Queen.

An attack was made on the house of Bishop Gardiner, the new Lord Chancellor, and that zealous prelate took to wearing a mail shirt under his robes. There was rioting at the public preachings of the restored religion. Threats and warnings against the Spanish marriage appeared mysteriously on the floor of the Queen's bedchamber, while Parliament was respectfully unobliging. On the day on which the Queen dissolved it a dead dog hurtled through the window of the royal presence chamber with ears cropped, a halter around its neck and a label that recommended hanging for all the priests in England. When Count Egmont at the head of the Spanish marriage embassy slipped across the Channel near the end of December, its members became targets for the snowballs of the boys in London streets. A month later, January 1554, under the leadership of Sir Thomas Wyatt, the smouldering discontent flashed up in arms.

And now a wild hope for the violent deliverance of their dear ones must have shot up in the hearts of the widowed Duchess and her daughter, Lady Mary, with whom she had found refuge. The troops sent against Wyatt deserted to his standard. Southwark fell before him, his fanatical followers trampling knee-deep in the tattered leaves of Bishop Gardiner's sacked library. The citizens of London, though they went dutifully in arms to shop and counting-house, wavered in their loyalty to the new Queen. At Whitehall in her very presence chamber the ladies-in-waiting shivered with apprehension to see the gentlemen pensioners standing guard in armour with pole-axes in their hands.

But Queen Mary had her full share of the Tudor courage. Herself in armour, she rode to the Guildhall. There "in her deep, man's voice" she laid her case before the people and assured them that she would never marry the Prince of Spain without the approval of the Lords and Commons of England. Again the rumour of French intervention on the side of the rebels ran about; and the citizens preferred the prospect of Queen Mary Tudor, even with a Spanish husband, to that of the other Mary, Queen of Scots and betrothed to the Dauphin of France, who would undoubtedly be forced upon them if Wyatt received the support of French soldiers and French ships.

They stood to their allegiance; and Wyatt at length gave up hope of forcing the passage of the long, narrow street, lined on both sides with lofty houses, which was then, and for almost three centuries later, London Bridge. On the night of Shrove Tuesday, which was wild with the weather of an English February, he broke up his quarters in Southwark and stole round by way of Kingston. But for his devotion to his artillery he might have surprised his enemy almost completely in spite of bottomless roads and a broken bridge. Even so it was four o'clock in the morning when the drums of the train bands thundered the alarm through the darkness of the London streets. The ensuing encounter, less a battle than a series of scrambling skirmishes, surged from Hyde Park Corner to Ludgate and back to Temple Bar. There was fighting around the palace of Whitehall, whence the Queen refused to flee. But by the end of the day Wyatt and his lieutenants were prisoners in the Tower. On the day following, the execution of the Lady Jane Grey and Lord Guilford Dudley was resolved upon.

At the news that he was to die young Guilford wept. He had been the spoiled darling of his parents. It was he whom his father had embraced at setting out upon his last expedition. To obtain his crown for him immediately his mother had acted like a shrew to his young queen, who in her knowledge of the law knew that she had no power to give it. But he died bravely when his time came to do so. As for his little wife, it took the sight of his headless body in the death-cart to shake her sweet serenity. Submissively she had heard herself sentenced three months before to be beheaded or burnt alive according to the Queen's pleasure. Now she recovered herself quickly and in her black cloth gown and black velvet hood—"like a French coif"—her eyes bent upon her prayer-book, followed the scarlet figure of the gigantic executioner through the grey chill of the February morning.

Since she was of the blood royal, it was her privilege to die within the Tower walls. Before the scaffold, especially favoured among the small assembly chosen to witness the execution, were ranged the jury of forty matrons, whose affirmation that she was not pregnant had deprived her of a

LADY MARY, MOTHER OF SIR PHILIP SIDNEY

from the painting at Penshurst, by courtesy of Lord De L'Isle and Dudley

reprieve that might have saved her life. She made a brief speech to the people, admitting the guilt of the act for which she was to suffer, but denying that her intent had been guilty. She asked them to pray for her, but only—strict Protestant that she was—"so long as she should be alive." The Queen had sent Abbot Fakenham to her in the hope of converting her to Catholicism. Failing in that, he had remained to perform his priestly functions on lines more broadly Christian. She turned to him now. "Shall I say the *Miserere* psalm?" she asked.

Down at Broadgate, her birthplace, in Leicestershire the woodsmen pollarded the oaks in sign of mourning for her. It was whispered about that for several hours after her execution her body lay upon the scaffold half-naked and neglected; and it was not long before men believed that they saw her ghost dash up to the door of the beautiful Tudor house in a phantom coach in search of a grave to rest in.

Only seven months had passed since Lady Mary Sidney had conducted her to Sion House to receive the formal notification of the fatal greatness which had fallen upon her small shoulders. The sixteen-year-old Queen and her eighteen-year-old chaperon had travelled by river; and the memory of that journey between the quiet banks of the Thames in the loveliness of the summer Sunday morning must have added a sharper pang to Lady Mary's grief.

Two days before Lady Jane's execution death had struck again among those close and dear to Lady Mary. On February 10th her father-in-law had died at the age of seventy-two. Sir William Sidney's life ran back into a departed time. In his youth great feudal nobles still had power of their own, and men still went crusading. The Spanish kingdom had just been made by the union of Castile and Aragon: Martin Luther had not been heard of. Sir William had shared the glorious early days of King Henry, before the bitterness of the Reformation had poisoned the brimming wine-cup of the Renaissance. He had remained at least so much in sympathy with Queen Mary's way of thought that the Protestant mob from Tunbridge had plundered his beautiful Penshurst on their way to join Wyatt. What with his experience, his wisdom and his knowledge of kings and courts, it must have seemed to his stricken daughter-in-law that she and her husband had lost by his death the one great guide and prop which had not been swept away by her father's ambitious folly.

Nor were her family sorrows all that she had to bear. The Princess Elizabeth, friend of her childhood, was accused of a guilty knowledge of Wyatt's plot. "Lofty, scornful and magnificent," she was brought to London a prisoner and led into the Tower through that ill-omened portal, the Traitor's Gate. And soon after, Lady Mary was left with only her widowed mother to share her griefs and fears. For her husband had so far established himself in the Queen's favour as to be made a member of the embassy that went to fetch from Spain the royal bridegroom. So it is not to be wondered at, if there was a strain of thoughtful melancholy in the famous son whom she was to bring to birth eight months later —whatever may be the current medical opinion on prenatal influences.

Before very long, however, the clouds about her fortune began to lift. The case against the Princess Elizabeth broke down of its own flimsiness. Sir William Howard, who ruled the fleet, was her stout champion; and she was placed in less rigorous confinement at Woodstock in May. Sir Henry's appointment to the marriage embassy proved to be an earnest of increasing favour at court, although, as he wrote many years later, "neither liked nor liking" there as in the old days. Another July rolled round with its burden of dreadful anniversaries. But it brought the Prince of Spain as well, and with him not only Mary Sidney's beloved husband but the famous Don Diego de Mendoza. A friend of the Dudleys since the days of his embassy to England in King Henry's time, he had been godfather to the ill-starred Guilford, and was now a potent advocate at court for the surviving members of their ruined house.

The nuptial airs were laden with mercy and forgiveness. Down came the weather-beaten corpses which had made London horrible since February. The gibbets gave place to festive decorations for the royal entry. The influence of the Duchess of Alba was exerted in the Dudleys' cause; and by autumn Lady Mary's mother had the manor of Chelsea back again together with much of the furniture and her wardrobe, which—down to her "cast kirtles"—had been seized by the officers of the crown. Her four sons were released from the Tower. John, the eldest, survived his imprisonment by only three days; but at least his sister Mary had the satisfaction of caring for him under her own roof in his last hours.

The Queen ratified all letters patent granted to Sir Henry Sidney and his father by her predecessors. In November she gave him another sign of her royal approval, though it was one which he would doubtless have cheerfully gone without at just that time. He was sent to join the retinue with which Lord Cobham was escorting Cardinal Pole, the Papal Legate, from Rochester to Westminster. So while his wife lay at Penshurst in daily expectation of the birth of her first child, he followed with such equanimity as he could achieve in the train of the splendid silver cross that graced the prow of the Legate's barge as the tide swept it up from Greenwich to Whitehall Palace stairs.

De Quadra, the Spanish Ambassador, once wrote to his master that Sir Henry Sidney was singularly ill-informed in matters of religion. In fact, although he was a man sincerely religious at heart, Sir Henry never succeeded in interesting himself in the doctrinal points of the conflict between the rival systems of salvation of his day; and he must have listened with a covert smile as the Italians in the Cardinal's suite, having never seen a tidal river before, exclaimed in delight at what they took to be a miracle, when the current bore them inland.

But he was a man with a fine perception of the pitiful things in human life; so his courtly countenance was doubtless lighted with sympathetic understanding at the palace a few hours later. The Legate greeted the Queen in Latin with the salutation of the Angel of the Annunciation: "Hail Mary, filled with grace. God be with thee, thou blessed among women." And she, poor self-deluded wife of forty, so bore herself as to display the evidence of her supposed pregnancy more conspicuously.

His duty done at last and leave of absence granted, Sir Henry sped down to Penshurst. Evidently he arrived in time. There still exists in the library of Trinity College, Cambridge, the volume bound in oak boards with leather back, brass corners and richly illuminated pages, which was the family Psalter of the Sidneys. In it they kept much the same kind of record as one finds in the family Bibles of later years. There in Sir Henry's hand appears the entry:

"Philippe, on Friday, the last of November, being Saint Andrew's Day, a quarter before five in the morning."

The proud father was only twenty-five, a fact which it seems well to emphasize, considering the difficulty we have in imagining these remote personages, in their ruffs and strange beards, as of any age at all, except perhaps a stodgy middle one. The young mother, now "femme heuruse" indeed, was not yet twenty.

CHAPTER III

"A VERY PARFIT GENTIL KNIGHT"

THE CHOICE OF THE OTHER TWO GOD-PARENTS AT THAT splendid christening which King Philip never forgot was characteristic of Sir Henry Sidney and his lovely lady. The life of the court was their career by birth and family tradition, but theirs also was a sturdy independence, which manifested itself thus early and lasted them, to the detriment of their fortunes, till their death. Among their contemporaries were many of wealth and influence who might have been able to help their son when the time came for him to make his way in the world. But they preferred to have his own grandmother and the old Earl of Bedford, though the one was the attainted widow of an arch-traitor to the Queen and aged before her time, and the other could not have long to live.

He died, indeed, in the following March. The Duchess had already been a month in her grave by that time. But with death at her elbow she drew up with her own hand a will that shows the stern strength of principle which the little Philip inherited from her as well as from his father's side. She left him two hundred marks, and a like amount to his mother, who also received a gown of "black bard velvet" furred with sables, a gown with "a high back," of fair wrought velvet, the Duchess's own nag and his saddle of black wrought velvet. To Sir Henry she gave the hangings of the gallery at Chelsea, "that is gold and green," with her lord's arms and hers emblazoned upon them; to the Duchess of Alba her green parrot—having, she wrote equivocally, no more fitting remembrance for her; and to "the Lord Dondagoe Demondesay"—in which bewildering conjunction of letters one must recognize the name of Don Diego de Mendoza—her "little book clock that hath the sun and moon in it."

"With great weakness hath this my last testament been written," she added in excuse for possible mistakes. One imagines it was a considerable admission from a woman of her indomitable character. She appointed Sir Henry Sidney her chief executor, and impressed upon him and his associates her preference for full payment of all her creditors to any funeral pomp. Let her children and servants be considered, she wrote, rather than her body "that is but the meate of worms." She died before her little grandson was quite two months old.

In the following April the mourning of the young Sidneys was brightened by the wedding of Sir Henry's youngest sister, Frances, the only one that still remained unmarried, to Thomas Ratcliffe, Lord Fitzwalter, son of the Earl of Sussex. The royal favour now shone brightly upon the family. Not only did the new Spanish king honour these nuptials with his presence, but Sir Henry was placed under orders to be ready at any moment to ride post-haste to the King of the Romans with certain glad tidings of great joy. For the Queen was now expecting her confinement from one day to the next. He must, indeed, have spent the whole month of May with one foot in the stirrup, unless he shared a rather general doubt that the Queen could have a child at all.

A false report of the event amused the sceptical. On April 30th a messenger had galloped up to London from Hampton Court, whither the Queen had retired for her lying-in, with the news that the birth pains had begun. The church-bells rang; bonfires were heaped; *Te Deum* was chanted in St. Paul's. At Antwerp, where the news arrived as that of the actual birth, the great bell of the cathedral pealed the general joy. But the pains had ceased, though the Queen protested that she could feel the movement of the child; and up and down the city, in the spring sunshine and by torchlight through the spring nights, went the intercessory processions behind the Holy Sacrament: men and women from the almshouses telling their beads, schoolboys, priests and bishops, the Mayor, the Aldermen, and the officers of the Guilds. The city rang with chanting, re-echoed with prayers. But no child came in answer to them.

The Emperor's negotiations for peace with France were seriously hampered by this check to his dynastic prospects. The Flanders bankers grew reluctant to increase their war loans to him. He was already paying interest at sixteen per cent. If he were not to be grandfather to the future King of England, he was not so much the man for their money as they had supposed. By July even Queen Mary had to admit that he was not to be, at least this time. And whether there would be another time seemed more than doubtful, especially when in August the King Consort quitted England for the Netherlands. The Emperor had begun to fail in health. Worn out by a life of incessant labour at government and war, he desired to lay a part of his burden on the shoulders of his son; and the appearance of a certain comet in the heavens made this an auspicious time to do so.

The wretched Queen was left with her disappointed hopes to offer up her burnt offerings for her husband's safe return, and to outface as best she could the unpopularity which the persecution soon began to arouse against her among Catholics and Protestants alike. To sharpen the general discontent the crops had failed for the second year in succession. Crime was so prevalent that criminals were being hanged in batches of sixty. Rebellious English gentlemen, turned pirate, infested the Scilly Islands and preyed upon the commerce of the subjects of their foreign king. Treason was rife. In the taverns men hummed, "Good man, priest, now beware your pallet," rhyming it with "fire and faggot" and "helm and sallet." Sir Henry Dudley—not Lady Mary Sidney's brother Henry, but only a distant cousin, she could thank God—fled to France early in the new year. But the Towei rack was horribly busy all that spring and summer of 1556 with the limbs of other conspiratorial young gentlemen, whose daring was greater than his, or their discretion less.

It was not a time when any young man would choose to go on foreign service, leaving a beautiful young wife and a little son behind him. But in February Henry Ratcliffe, the old Earl of Sussex, had died at Sir Henry Sidney's house "in Chanon Roo," whereby little Philip's aunt became a countess; her husband, the new Earl, was appointed Lord Deputy of Ireland; and in April Sir Henry Sidney, as his vice-treasurer, departed in his train for that ever-troubled and ever-troublesome island.

In going he had at least the consolation that he left his dear ones in an almost perfect retreat. Penshurst, on the western border of Kent, within a day's ride of either London or Canterbury, lifted its sturdy, square, embattled towers in the midst of a park which Henry VIII, some time its owner, had increased to a twelve-mile circuit. It was even then famous for its gardens; and it is a striking example of the compactness of English literary history that where one of the most aristocratic of English writers grew from babyhood into a rather delicate child of five the grandfather of Mr. H. G. Wells was head gardener some three centuries later.

There the little boy must have drawn in something of the history of his country with every breath. As Penchester the place appears in *Doomsday Book.* The effigy of Sir Stephen Penchester in chain armour, who died in 1299, lies in the parish church near by. In the time of Edward III Sir John Pulteney received the royal permission to "embattle" the house. Sir John Devereux was allowed to fortify and enlarge it in 1393. John, the Duke of Bedford who sent Joan of Arc to the stake, added a wing to it; and his brother,

Duke Humphrey of Gloucester, who made the Emperor Sigismund renounce all intention of infringing the King's authority before he would allow him to land in England, wrote himself down its owner in one of the books which he gave to the University of Oxford. It had passed to Philip's grandfather from Sir Ralph Fane, who lost it along with his head at Somerset's fall, and who had rallied the English cavalry and led them to victory over the Scots at Pinkie only seven years before Philip's birth.

Over the great hall, which measures fifty-four feet by thirty-seven, the steep oak roof rises to a height of sixty feet above the floor. Ten corbels, carved into the likeness of grotesque human figures, support the spars of this roof. Tall Gothic windows of remarkable, decorated tracery pierce the walls on which at night long years ago pine torches flamed in iron brackets while on the stone-edged, octagonal hearth in the centre of the room great logs on iron firedogs three and a half feet high sent up their smoke to find its way out of a hole in the roof. There is a minstrels' gallery above a screen of panelled oak and beneath an unusually beautiful window filled with ancient glass. From his seat on the dais the baron could survey the feasting of his retainers and his guests of lower degree. On his either hand small doors gave access, the one to the cellar, the other to his lady's bower where a narrow slit in the wall afforded the means to spy upon those in the hall below.

Two long tables nearly six centuries old remain from the days of baronial hospitality which was already beginning to go out of fashion in Philip Sidney's time. Ways of living were changing, gentlefolk demanding more privacy in their daily lives than their forebears had been able to enjoy. But the spirit of the life was still feudal. For the wealth which they owed to their sovereign great men must still be ready to pour out their blood and their treasure in their sovereign's service. Their tenants and labourers served them in war as well as in peace, and they gave in return counsel and help, leadership and protection. At least this was so at Penshurst. Years later Ben Jonson was to write of it:

> . . . all come in, the farmer and the clown,
> And no one empty-handed, to salute
> Thy lord and lady, though they have no suit . . .

and that none that dwelt about its stately walls wished for their ruin. In the gardens, which still run down to the Medway, he saw "the blushing apricot and woolly peach" hanging within the reach of every child. The hospitality of the place was given in like profusion. Here was none of those noblemen's tables at which a poor poet might sit through the meal and then be fain to go out and try to find something to eat elsewhere.

Philip Sidney himself, when he wished to put a charming house into his *Arcadia*, described this home of his childhood. "The house itself," he wrote, "was built of fine and strong stone, not affecting so much an extraordinary kind of fineness as an honourable representing of a fine stateliness . . . handsome without curiosity, and homely without loathesomeness: not so dainty as not to be trod on, nor yet slubbered up with good fellowship."

To Lady Sidney in this abode of ancient peace the news of London and the court came down by letters and by occasional guests. The lonely Queen was riding in her chariot from St. James's in the fields through the park to Whitehall, there to take her barge to Lambeth of a summer afternoon. Her favourite progress was to visit Cardinal Pole at Croydon. She was troubled. Pope Julius III had sent her the Golden Rose three years before; but the new Pope, Paul IV, was siding with France in the war with Spain and the Empire. He had declared the Queen's husband deprived of the Kingdom of Naples, and he detested the Cardinal Legate of England; and Pole, like his royal mistress, had begun to feel the tension of a divided loyalty.

In November the Princess Elizabeth rode in to Somerset

Place with a great company in velvet coats and gold chains clattering up Fleet Street behind her, and was off to Hatfield again five days later in the same state. January 1557 came in with a muster of the gentlemen pensioners before the Queen and the Cardinal at the palace at Greenwich—two hundred men in all on their great horses, with green coats guarded with white over their armour, lances striped white and green, and at their head a standard of red and yellow with a white hart on one side and on the other a black eagle with golden legs. The Duke of Muscovy arrived in London in February, wearing a garment of tissue broidered with pearls, his men in cloth of gold down to the calf of the leg.

A month later something happened which many people had believed never would happen. The King returned, now a king in his own right. For the Emperor Charles had retired to the Spanish monastery of St. Just, and King Philip had succeeded to the sovereignty of Flanders and the crown of Spain.

Lady Mary's beloved brother Robert brought the news of his coming, a mission which was all to the good as a sign of the royal favour. But the great event for her that spring of 1557 was her husband's return from Ireland, where he had mixed his administrative duties with the particularly dirty kind of hit-and-run fighting which went on continually in his brother-in-law's viceregal domain. Men had noted with admiration there that, rich and highly-connected though he was, Sir Henry had served "like any other private captain"; and he had slain in single combat "James Mack O'Niel," a redoubtable champion of the Scottish invaders of Ulster. He had demonstrated, as any son of his father must have longed to do, that he was not merely *eques auratus*, though it had been for diplomatic services that he received his knighthood. He came home in April and remained until July. The government of Ireland was in need of funds—the twenty-five thousand pounds which he had taken with him as vice-treasurer the year before was exhausted—and his mission was to get more.

But the Queen, what with her efforts to buy back for the Church the lands of which her father and brother had despoiled it and a sudden need to prepare her country for war, had no money to spare for Ireland. King Philip had not returned to the kingdom which he so thoroughly disliked out of any consideration for his doting wife. He needed help in the long-drawn-out struggle with France and, like everything else which it was in her power to give him, he got it. They rode through London together, to the accompaniment of trumpets and guns, attended by the Lord Mayor, the Sheriffs and Aldermen, with the waits playing dutifully on the leads of St. Peter's in Chepe. There was a stage play of the Passion of Christ at the Grey Friars, while at Smithfield and elsewhere appeared many a fiery example of the seeming futility of that Passion when men of the ecclesiastical type of mind are in ascendance over government. The London contingent of the expeditionary force, five hundred men in blue cassocks, marched down to their transports; and on July 5th King Philip sailed from Dover to put himself at the head of his army.

Henry and Robert Dudley went with him; Sir Henry Sidney returned to his post in Ireland. So in the one month Lady Mary had to bid farewell to husband and brothers setting forth, all three of them, on dangerous service. Two months had not gone by before she must weep for one of them. For in August there were *Te Deums* in London for the victory of Saint-Quentin, priests marching in procession about the cross at Paul's, singing *Salva festa dies,* and the City dignitaries out in their scarlet robes. But Henry Dudley had gone down in the thick of the battle, fighting with the recklessness of a gentleman who was resolved to wipe the stain of treason from his family's 'scutcheon.

Even the public rejoicing was short-lived, however. Scotland, true to her old alliance with France, began to lay waste the border and, thanks to King Philip's limitations as a general, the French were at the gates of Calais in overwhelming numbers by the end of December. On the 8th of January the news ran through London streets that England had lost the last vestige of her mediæval empire on the continent of Europe. Shame, anger at the bungling of the government, and fear as well, spread through the country. With that Channel bridge-head of hers in the hands of the enemy England must arm in bitter earnest. Every nobleman and gentleman with an income above a thousand pounds a year was called upon to furnish sixteen horses equipped with steel harness, forty corselets, steel caps, long bows and the like in proportion. Married women whose husbands were serving in France in 1917-18, and who remember their struggles with the family finances in order to meet the constant rise in prices, will surely sympathize with Lady Mary wrestling, as she must have had to do, with the preparation and dispatch of sheaves of arrows, black bills, morions and haquebuts. In April died a little daughter, Margaret, a baby not yet two years old; and in her double sorrow it must have seemed a hollow compensation when she and the other surviving members of her family were "restored in blood" by act of Parliament in recognition of her brothers' services on the battle-field.

Nor was there any cheering news from the great world beyond the lovely confines of her retreat. For the Queen the lengthening days of 1558 had grown briefly bright with the renewed belief that she was with child. But with its disappointment her persecution of heretics increased in severity. "Here was nothing," wrote Sir Thomas Smith of those times, "but heading, hanging, quartering and burning, taxing and levying. . . . A few priests in white rochets ruled all." So bold became the popular demonstration of sympathy with those burnt at Smithfield late in June that Bishop Bonner lost his nerve and had the rest of that group burned secretly by night at Brentford. Watching from his refuge at

Geneva, John Knox, who had endured the horrors of the French galleys for his faith, deemed the time ripe at last and, to his endless regret, published his *First Blast against the Monstrous Regiment of Women.* Unhappy wight! How was he to know that before the year was out a woman, whom that book made his obdurate enemy, was to mount the English throne and thereby to become the brightest hope of Protestantism?

Queen Mary took to flitting restlessly from room to room of her palace at night as well as by day, or sat upon the floor with her knees drawn up against her face in the pain of the slow disease which had deluded her into such glorious hopes. In September she caught the fever which was prevalent that year, and soon the news got about that she was dying. Her husband sent the Duke of Feria to her bedside—to make sure that she did nothing to prevent the succession of her sister, whom she hated.

"*Agnus Dei, qui tollis peccata mundi,*" intoned the priest in her chamber on November 16th.

"*Miserere nobis, miserere nobis. Dona nobis pacem,*" responded clearly the desolate woman from her death-bed. Jane Dormer put her arms around her.

A few hours later London was aflame with bonfires; there was feasting in the streets; the church-bells rang a universal joy. For those fiery sacrifices of the poor and humble—there had been pitifully few of higher rank among the victims—had made her generally detested. Queen Elizabeth came back through streets new-gravelled riding to the Tower, which she had last entered five years before by the Traitor's Gate and under the shadow of a traitor's death. She was not forgetful of her altered fortune.

"As thou didst with thy servant Daniel the prophet, whom thou deliveredst from the den, from the cruelty of the raging lions," were the words on her lips as she left those frowning walls for Westminster and her coronation.

Of those about her there was at least one who must have

breathed amen to that thanksgiving. This was Lord Robert Dudley, who rode in her triumphal procession, her master of horse. He and his brother Ambrose had shared her prison and knew better than she did the dry foretaste of death. She had summoned both men and their sister Mary to her court at once and appointed Lady Mary one of her ladies-in-waiting.

Honours fell thick upon the Dudleys and their connections in the next few years. In the following April Robert was made a Knight of the Garter and Privy Councillor. Ambrose became Master of the Ordnance the year after, Baron de L'Isle and Earl of Warwick in 1561. A few days after the coronation lovely Jane Dormer was married to King Philip's ambassador, the Duke of Feria, though her uncles, the Earl of Sussex and Sir Henry Sidney, were reluctant to give their consent to the match.

De Feria was a foreigner, for one thing, and he had stayed away from the coronation because some of the more Catholic rites were omitted from the ceremony. He was, moreover, the bearer of King Philip's proposal of marriage to the new Queen and was doing everything in his power to frighten her into putting herself in every way under his master's thumb. When he left for Flanders in May he took with him a great number of monks and nuns. For it was already apparent that England would no longer offer them a home. But Dudleys, Sidneys and Ratcliffes owed a good deal to Spanish influence. So, late in July, Sir Henry, who was home from Ireland again by that time, joined Sussex in riding down to Dover, whence Jane departed to rejoin her husband.

Sir Henry, too, had been greatly honoured by his sovereign. He was now Lord President of the Council of the Marches of Wales. He did not take up his new duties for some months, however; and this interlude at court and in the country must have been most welcome, for owing to the frequent absences of his chief from Ireland he had been four times acting Lord Deputy there and had put in two winters of campaigning against the wily rebel, Shane O'Neil, who kept a large part of that kingdom in terror of his name.

There was plenty to engage Sir Henry's interest both at home and abroad during his holiday. King Philip, driven by the necessity of keeping England's friendship, had patched up a peace between Elizabeth and the King of France. There was bull- and bear-baiting at Paris Garden to entertain the French ambassadors. The Queen went down to Woolwich in brilliant state to christen a new warship and again commemorated her deliverance—this time with a different Old Testament character—by calling the vessel *Elizabeth Jonas*. At a tournament at Greenwich they had a banqueting house built of fir poles, decked with birch, roses, lavender and marigolds, and strewn with sweet-smelling herbs.

But events in France did not promise a lasting peace between the two countries. King Philip, whose proposal Elizabeth had finally rejected, took another Elizabeth, the daughter of King Henri II, to his twice-widowed side that July. In the jousting in honour of the nuptials King Henri was accidentally killed; and his successor, whose fascinating young wife was Mary, Queen of Scots, had the audacity to proclaim himself and her the sovereigns not only of France and Scotland but of England as well. French troops began to concentrate about Calais and the other French ports on the Channel. They garrisoned the forts along the Tweed.

To the mind of every loyal Englishman the best answer to these threats would be a husband for their queen. She ought to marry, and marry quickly, a husband who could give her powerful assistance. But who should he be? Lady Mary Sidney, not forgetful of her old debt of gratitude to his master, gave Bishop de Quadra, the new Spanish Ambassador, the confidential, backstairs information that her mistress would be willing at least to inspect the Austrian Archduke Charles, who was King Philip's candidate for her hand. Elizabeth, however, had a better answer in the shiploads of weapons and munitions that Sir Thomas Gresham purchased for her in the Low Countries. She put on her armour in February of the new year and was out every day on a Neapolitan courser with the train bands in St. James's Park. And luck, as it was seldom to fail to be, was on her side.

While the Council was urging the Austrian marriage upon her, the Huguenots at Amboise made their unsuccessful attempt to kidnap their king and thereby demonstrated to the Guises that they dare not commit France to a foreign war. In Scotland the Protestant Lords of the Congregation rose against their queen's mother and regent, Mary of Guise. An English army crossed the Tweed to assist them late in March. An English fleet blockaded Leith; and a month later Lord Grey, Elizabeth's general, wrote of the beleaguered city with that touch of the dramatic of which English gentlemen had not yet learned to be ashamed, "Yet it burns—yet—yet." Early in July the Treaty of Edinburgh was signed; the French troops evacuated Scotland; and Queen Elizabeth was free to consider the question of her marriage without the perturbation of having an enemy at her back door.

Meanwhile Sir Henry Sidney had ridden away to his new government in June with seven score horsemen behind him. His family followed him soon, leaving one charming and romantic home only to enter another, or perhaps two others, which must have been as interesting and as stimulating as Penshurst to the little Philip, who was to live in them from his sixth to his tenth year. For while Sir Henry established his family at Tickenhill House at Bewdley, he had his headquarters at Ludlow Castle some twenty miles to the westward. John Milton was to make that place memorable three-quarters of a century later by the performance of his *Comus* there. Samuel Butler was to write much of his *Hudibras* within its walls. But its memories in Philip's childhood were chiefly martial. It had been the centre of the power of Edmund Mortimer, Earl of March, and Shakespeare had yet to train that starling "to speak nothing but Mortimer" and thereby call instantly to mind the names of Harry Hotspur and Prince Hal, Glendower and Falstaff and Bardolf and Poins.

Built by Robert of Montgomery, with a keep like that of Rochester, inner and outer courts, and two moats, it was one of the chain of castles that kept the Welsh border more or less in subjection during the Middle Ages. The state apartments and the great hall dated from the fourteenth century. The manor house of Tickenhill at Bewdley had been made into a palace for Prince Arthur, Henry VIII's elder brother. There Arthur had married by proxy Katherine of Aragon and thus furnished King Henry with the case of conscience which was later to prove so convenient for his second matrimonial venture. Between the two places little Philip's English history may be said to have been brought down to his own time. For after Prince Arthur the Princess Mary had lived there as titular vicereine in 1529.

In the following decade Rowland Lee, Bishop of Lichfield and Coventry, hanged five thousand Welshmen in the six years of his term as Lord President. "Thieves I found them, and thieves I shall leave them," he wrote; they had hanged him in imagination, but he trusted to be even with them shortly. They were stubbornly Catholic, sympathized with Katherine of Aragon and the Princess Mary in King Henry's Reformation days; and Sir Henry Sidney's indifference to the technicalities of religious belief probably made the governing of them easier for him than it would otherwise have been. It was at the rooting out of the pirates, for which the coast was infamous, that he went sternly to work.

That and the suppression of trade in piratical plunder in the Welsh and Cornish ports, the violence and armed disorder, and the abuses in government and in the administration of justice, which he found on his arrival in the country, kept him busy. But he was equally active in the repair of castles and bridges, the collection and preservation of Welsh records and antiquities, and in all else that made for order and prosperity, while his "gallant behaviour and comeliness of person," his good humour, fairness and honesty soon made him generally beloved.

He reciprocated the affection of his subjects. "A better people to govern than the Welsh," he wrote, "Europe holdeth not." And near the end of his life—for throughout many other employments he continued to be Lord President—he wrote in touchingly humble appreciation of his position among them:

"Great it is that in some sort I govern the third part of this realm under her most excellent majesty; high it is, for by that I have precedence of great personages and by far my betters; happy it is for the goodness of the people whom I govern; and most happy it is for the commodity I have, by the authority of that place, to do good every day."

To the little Philip of these years the able and honest gentleman must have been simply his father, a tall, broad, bearded presence that came and went merrily, radiating an affectionate good humour. Unlike many of the gentlemen's houses of the day, the Sidneys' was a happy home for their children. They suffered there none of those "nips, pinches and bobs" which made the childhood of Lady Jane Grey a minor martyrdom. Music abounded, as indeed it did everywhere in England before the blight of Puritanism fell upon the land. There were books in plenty. Sir Henry shared with Elizabeth's new archbishop, Matthew Parker, the pleasure of collecting rare volumes old and new. There were excellent tutors. Lady Mary could stimulate her children's study of French, Italian and Latin with her own knowledge of those tongues, and learning was made a delight.

But before the child could read he must have been enchanted by the stories that would be told him of the exploits of his forebears. Through the female line his mother's ancestry went back to those Talbots, father and son, who fell at Chastilion; to the barons de L'Isle, who fought honourably in France and Scotland under Edward III; and to their elders, sturdy rebels under de Montfort and against the

Spencers of Edward II; until one came to that Robert de L'Isle who was among the barons in arms against King John.

The Sidney line was far less illustrious. Sir Henry's accounts show an expenditure of six pounds "for making my lord's pedigrew," on the strength of which item it has been assumed that Sir Henry was bolstering up a claim to ancient lineage which he knew to be false. But "making" is a large, loose word, and may easily have meant no more than the certification and recording of an authentic traditional descent. It is true that the King-of-Arms who drew the document had a bad reputation for falsifying pedigrees; but the reputation of the brother officer who fastened it upon him was no better. Six pounds was no trifle in those days; and it seems unlikely that a shrewd buyer like Sir Henry would have been content with an ancestor no more distinguished than a chamberlain of Henry II, if he was throwing in his integrity as well as that sum in payment for him. It should be remembered, too, that Sir Henry Sidney was generally unwilling to press his claims even for the things to which he was justly entitled. His son Philip, with whom he grew to be on terms of the closest intimacy, seems never to have doubted the genuineness of the record.

But for a boy nothing in the family history can have been more fascinating than the tales of Sir William, his Sidney grandfather: how under Lord Darcy he had gone to Spain with five hundred English archers to fight the Moors in Africa and, when there proved to be no war in which to earn it, had refused knighthood at the hands of the great King Ferdinand himself; how he had commanded "The Great Bark" in the naval operations before Brest and been knighted for valour at "the burning of Conquest"; and how he had led the right wing of the English army at Flodden with such skill and courage that his pennon was transformed into a banneret. Going to the coronation of King Henry's sister Mary as Queen of France, he had landed at Calais with Charles Brandon and his ducal retinue, "all in green coats and hoods with intent not to discover themselves" till their arrival at Paris, where at the jousts in honour of the occasion three hundred and five cavaliers ran five courses with sharpened lances. He had followed King Henry to the Field of the Cloth of Gold and seen Bayard there, the knight "sans peur et sans reproche," the brightest star in the chivalry of Europe, who had come in the train of King François. Sir William's resemblance to Chaucer's Knight must have struck his grandson as forcibly as it strikes the modern reader:

> And evermore he hadde a sovereyn price,
> And though that he was worthy he was wyse
>
> . . . . .
>
> He was a very parfit gentil knight.

By the time Philip was seven he had two small sisters: Elizabeth, born in 1560, who was to die seven years later, and Mary, born in 1561, whose fame as Countess of Pembroke his *Arcadia* was to make as lasting as his own. In 1563 came into the world his brother Robert, so much his inferior in most things but possessed of what in him was most lacking, a certain willingness to take the world as he found it, which makes for success as by the world success is counted. Between-whiles their mother was long and often absent from home at her duties about the Queen; their father was frequently called away from his work in Wales to give his advice at court or to go on special military or diplomatic missions. But both evidently understood the incommunicable art of entering into the lives of their children and admitting their children into theirs, for no family can have had a more sympathetic understanding of one another or faced the world in the years to come with a more united front.

Shane O'Neil, Sir Henry's old antagonist in Ireland, came to England about this time. He had not ceased to give trouble. He had made a Countess of Argyle his mistress, and kept her chained to one of his horse-boys when he was away from home. When he was drunk and wished to be sober, he had himself buried in earth up to the chin. Elizabeth summoned him to her court to answer for his numerous crimes, but allowed him to come with all the state of a prince. "The wild Irishman," as Machyn the diarist called him, had a bodyguard of bareheaded axemen, with curled hair hanging down, who wore "surplices" dyed yellow with saffron "or man's stale," short coats and hairy mantles. His regal airs amused the whole court, and perhaps it was Sir Henry Sidney who suggested the "style" which the courtiers invented for him and which he accepted with the humourlessness characteristic of his compatriots when their own greatness or that of their country is involved. "O'Neil," they hailed him, "great cousin of St. Patrick, friend of the Queen of England, and enemy to all the world beside."

But the chief interest at court, not only to the Sidneys but to the whole kingdom and much of Europe as well, was the project of the marriage of the Queen with Lord Robert Dudley, Lady Mary's brother. As early as January 1560 the Spanish Ambassador wrote to King Philip of "my lord Robert in whom it is easy to recognize the king that is to be." The intimacy between him and Elizabeth formed the gossip of their friends, the scandal of their enemies. In September Lady Dudley, the Amy Robsart of romance, died her mysterious death, and all England was upset by the rumour that the marriage was now imminent.

"If her Majesty do so foully forget herself . . ." wrote her ambassador from Paris. But Sir Henry Sidney, of whom de Quadra wrote as "a high spirited, noble sort of person and one of the best men the Queen has about the court," called on the Spanish Ambassador in January of '61 to enlist King Philip's favour for the match. "The Queen and Lord Robert were lovers," he explained, "but . . . nothing wrong had taken place between them that could not be set right" with the help of the King. Sir Henry added that he had investigated and found Dudley guiltless in the matter of the death of his wife.

De Quadra's favour toward the project was based on the belief that the marriage would cause such an uprising in England that King Philip could invade the country and place a sound Catholic on the throne; but whether Sir Henry understood this and was only leading the wily Spaniard on, or really hoped to see his brother-in-law made his king, is not clear. Sir William Cecil, the Queen's secretary of state, understood it perfectly, at all events, and with the ulterior purpose of defeating them was soon apparently doing everything in his power to bring the negotiations to a successful issue.

In France, meanwhile, poor, spindling François II had been gathered to his fathers. The Queen of Scots was left, a fascinating widow of twenty, and rather in the way of her mother-in-law, Catherine de Medici, who was now setting out on her course of ruling by division. From Scotland Elizabeth's ambassador wrote that "it would be a mad world" if Mary Stuart returned to her kingdom, as she had decided to do; and Elizabeth refused her permission to pass through England on her way thither. But when Mary boarded a galley at Calais, she was allowed to reach Leith four days later without let or hindrance from the English fleet. Soon she was asking permission to visit England in order that she and her royal cousin might meet. Elizabeth went so far as to make an appointment with her for September 1562. But by midsummer the news of this had stirred up such angry opposition among the Protestants, and among the Catholics such wild hopes that their queen was about to recognize the Queen of Scots as next in succession to the English throne, that the engagement had to be cancelled.

Sir Henry Sidney was selected as bearer of the unwelcome news. Doubtless the fact that he was the uncle of the beautiful Duchess of Feria, who on her way to Spain two years before had paused long enough at the French court to become the friend of the Queen of Scots, must have helped to make him *persona grata* at Holyrood. He brought with him, too, a present of fine English arrows for the sport-loving Queen. But when Mary understood the character of the message which he was to deliver to her, she kept him waiting for a whole day while she sulked in bed; and when she received him, "the demonstration of her grief," he wrote to Cecil, "appeared in words, countenance and watery eyes."

This passionate, impulsive girl of twenty-one, matching her beauty and charm, her inexhaustible energy and shifty brain, against her lawless barons and dour reformers, must have made a strange contrast in the young Ambassador's mind—he was now only thirty-three—with another queen to whom he had lately borne his sovereign's messages. Earlier in the year he had been to the Queen Mother of France with Elizabeth's offer of help in keeping the peace between the Catholics and Huguenots who had flown to arms in consequence of the massacre of Vassy. Catherine de Medici, fat, white, cold, "worm out of the tomb of Italy," who had attempted to have vitriol thrown in the face of a rival in her younger days, now relied upon her maids of honour, the notorious "escadron volant," to supply the seductiveness for which the Queen of Scots relied upon herself, but she might have known better how to deal with John Knox, who called Mary "Honeypot" and treated her accordingly. Knox Sir Henry met during his two weeks' stay in Edinburgh, and with his faculty for enjoying the best in everybody cultivated an acquaintance with him which he kept up by correspondence until the old man's death.

Another special mission, one quite different from the last, took Sir Henry from his beloved family and his duties in Wales soon after his return. The troubles in France had broken out in open warfare; the summer's fighting had ended in such reverses for the Huguenots that the Prince of Condé, their leader, had offered Elizabeth Le Havre and Dieppe, if she would send troops to his assistance; and the Flemish bankers forwarded a report that as soon as the Guises had completed the ruin of the Protestant cause at home they intended to invade England with a mixed force of Catholic French, Spanish and Papal troops.

Since it appeared that she was soon to have a war on her hands, whether she would or not, it seemed surely the part of wisdom to wage it abroad and against an enemy who was still disunited. The Queen, moreover, had never ceased to regret the loss of Calais, and here was a perfect opportunity to make it up with interest. So, early in October, an English army of three thousand men occupied Le Havre. Philip's uncle Ambrose of Warwick commanded it, and Sir Henry Sidney accompanied the expedition to give his brother-in-law the benefit of the experience in the quartermaster's department which he had acquired in Ireland. Sir Henry remained in France only a month, but while he was absent there befell his wife one of the cruelest misfortunes that can happen to a young and beautiful woman.

Smallpox was abroad in England. The Queen herself was one of its victims. She became so ill that she thought she was dying and confessed her love for Robert Dudley, though even then she protested that "nothing unseemly" had passed between them. Lady Mary Sidney, nursing her with devoted self-forgetfulness, caught the dreadful disease, and Sir Henry returned to find her whom he had left "a full fair lady . . . to me at least the fairest . . . as foul a lady as the small-pox could make her."

Her son Robert's birth the next year, together with the births of other children later, may be regarded as a token of her husband's continuing love for her. But her proud spirit never ceased to suffer from her disfigurement. She continued to perform her duties at court, but she wore a velvet mask there and elsewhere in public. At other times she avoided society, "dwelling," as Sir Henry said, "solitary, *sicut nycticorax in domicilio suo*"—like the night-heron in his habitation. Upon her children the influence of the ruin of her beauty can only be imagined. It must have been very great, however, for there is no love of beauty more ardent than that which children feel for the beauty of a mother whom they adore.

CHAPTER IV

"WITH HIS SATCHEL AND SHINING MORNING FACE"

IN THE AUTUMN OF 1564 LITTLE PHILIP SIDNEY, NOT YET quite ten years old, was sent out from the sheltered and loving home life of Tickenhill House to make a place for himself in a school of which the headmaster had no more than two ushers to assist him in teaching and supervising about four hundred boys. This was the Free Grammar School of King Edward VI at Shrewsbury. The destruction of the religious foundations by Henry VIII and the ministers of his son had reduced education in England to a wretched state; and so far as housing and equipment were concerned the school at Shrewsbury was no exception to the general rule. The boys paid little or no tuition at this time: the tithes of the dissolved collegiate churches of St. Mary and St. Chad were supposed to meet all expenses. A timber structure near the castle gate and some adjoining rented houses were the only school buildings. In these the boys studied and classes were held. But even for such meagre quarters the financial support was so inadequate that not many years after Philip's time they were reported to be "inclining to ruin."

If there was neither chapel nor library, however, dormitories also were lacking. So a sensitive child of ten was spared those horrors not uncommon in the English public schools in that day and for three centuries after. The boys were lodged and boarded—"tabled" was the local word for it—among the householders of the town, who were called "hosts" and were held responsible for the behaviour and well-being of their charges. Since Shrewsbury lay within the jurisdiction of the Council of Wales, the Lord President's son was sure to be well looked after by his guardians. He had, moreover, a small establishment of his own. A *famulus,* a boy of his own age, half-servant and half-companion, shared his lessons and his games; and Thomas Marshall, a confidential upper servant of his father's, kept his accounts, took care of his clothes, and watched over his health.

He was by no means a sturdy boy, and the life he had to lead at so tender an age certainly justified these arrangements. There was a special warning against any "slogardie a-night," which seems superfluous since he bought "wax sises to burn in school a-mornings before day." From the beginning of February until the end of November the school bell began its fifteen-minutes clangor at a quarter before six in the morning. Prayers were said and sung at six, and during the rest of the year the hour was seven.

It was, to be sure, not so many years since great nobles had been in the habit of rising at four and breakfasting at five. But the school hours were long by any standard. Dinner came at eleven, and lessons, recommencing at a quarter before one, lasted until five in summer and until half past four in winter if the daylight held out so late. On Sunday monitors kept track of the boys' attendance at the various parish churches. On Thursday, the weekly holiday, the first form had to give an act of a Latin comedy before they were free to enjoy themselves. Running, wrestling, leaping, chess and archery were the authorized recreations. No betting was allowed, but apparently one might hazard a stake, though it must not be greater than a penny on a game or four pence on a match.

The Statute of Winchester, re-enacted in the reign of Henry VIII, had outlawed bowls, tennis and other games as distractions from the practice of the longbow, that weapon which had once been the means of England's pre-eminence on the battle-field. Roger Ascham's first book, *Toxophilus,* had been written about the merits of it and the pleasure to be had from shooting with it. Its use was greatly favoured at Shrewsbury school. But the development of various types of hand guns was pushing it aside. Bowmen were not what they had been; and in 1577 the Reverend William Harrison was to lament that the Frenchmen in open skirmish would "turn up their tails and cry, 'Shoot, English!' " when, if some of the bowmen of King Edward III had been present, "the breech of such a varlet should have been nailed to his bum with one arrow, and another feathered in his bowels before he should have turned about to see who shot the first." The day was gone when the heavy war arrow of England was effective at two hundred and twenty yards. When Philip went off for his second Christmas holidays, he took cross-bow bolts with him rather than arrows for bird shooting.

The curriculum at Shrewsbury was made up chiefly of the Latin classics, as it was elsewhere at the time. The boys read Cæsar's *Commentaries,* Cicero, Sallust, Livy, Vergil, Horace, Ovid and Terence. The future author of *Astrophel and Stella* struggled with a textbook on prosody by Tigurinus. The Greek hardly went beyond the New Testament and Xenophon. French grammar was taught. There were "example books" for practising "the secretary's hand" and for writing in Latin and French; and Philip wrote to his father from school in both of these languages.

Calvin's *Catechism* was the basis of the religious training. But Calvinism was almost as far as Romanism from the faith of Philip's later life. Like his father, he could have worshipped as devoutly in St. Peter's at Rome as in Geneva, and he was a Protestant largely because Philip of Spain and the Pope were Catholics. No music was taught apparently. It may be that the need of it in school was not felt in a country where every christening, wedding and funeral went to the strains of flutes and trumpets and the sound of drums and singing; where May Day games and the feast of St. Nicholas resounded with music, and travellers reported everywhere the beautiful playing of violas and pandoras and

SIR PHILIP SIDNEY AND HIS BROTHER ROBERT
from the painting at Penshurst, by courtesy of Lord De L'Isle and Dudley

that "even in small villages the musicians wait on you for a small fee." Years later Philip in a letter to his brother lamented his "want of music" to solace his melancholy hours, which seems strange, since the other members of his family evidently sang and played well on various instruments. Perhaps he meant only that he did not excel in it as he did in other things. He was always an ardent lover of it.

The school vacations were as brief as the hours of recreation in term-time: eighteen days at Christmas, twelve at Easter, and nine at Whitsuntide. But these may have been limited by an expectation of those plagues and pestilences which were almost annually coming to the relief of the pupils and causing even the universities to close for months at a time. All in all it does not sound like a very attractive school life to modern ears. Thomas Ashton, the headmaster, however, was a friend of Ascham's and like him a believer in making study interesting and inspiring to his pupils. It was he who placed such emphasis on dramatic performances that the school became famous for them; and the later records of the boys who studied under him make it clear that their minds were not dulled by too much work.

Philip Sidney must have found the school very much to his liking, for Fulke Greville, his lifelong friend and biographer, who entered Shrewsbury at the same time that he did, wrote of him:

> Though I lived with him and knew him from a child, yet I never knew him other than a man: with such staidness of mind, lovely and familiar gravity as carried grace and reverence above greater years. His talk ever of knowledge, and his very play tending to enrich his mind.

And after he had been at school for more than a year his father thought it wise to write, reminding him that the prescribed study hours were "both sufficient for your learning, yea and safe for your health."

But in these days apparently, quite as much as in later

years, his tact, honesty and sweetness of character prevented him from being regarded as a hypocrite or a prig by those about him, who did not aspire to the lofty standards of conduct and achievement for which he strove. There was a thick sprinkling of noblemen's and gentlemen's sons among the middle-class boys who were by far the most numerous in the school; and even in that age, when rank and position were given so much outward respect, the Lord President's son would have gained little liking had he assumed the airs of superiority.

Shrewsbury town was a clearing-house for Welsh products. The Council of the Marches often met there, and Sir Henry's visits were marked by both the civic and the scholastic authorities with the pomp and ceremony proper to the reception of the personal representative of a Tudor sovereign. One St. George's Day a solemn service was sung "to the glorifying of God and the great honour of the said Sir Henry," who bowed to the Queen's chair in the chancel, as he passed it in the procession; and afterwards three hundred and sixty of the boys in battle order in the meadows by the Severn took an oath before him to be ever ready to give their lives for Queen and Country. Perhaps it was with the effect of such displays in mind that he wrote to Philip to advise him to be courteous and affable to all, since nothing else "winneth so much at so little cost."

This was in the same letter in which he warned the pale, over-eager child against too much study; and he went on at some length with other matters of life and conduct. Let Philip both pray and wash with regularity. The latter, he told him, "shall make you grateful in each company and otherwise loathesome." He should learn to obey in order to know how to make others obey him. He should eat moderately; drink seldom, yet often enough to know what he is about when he must drink in company. There was much more in the same Polonius strain, which has been so discredited since Robert Louis Stevenson led the attack upon it fifty years ago, and of which the obsolescence has left open the way to so many a young headache and heartache. But the anxious father was no mere dull platitudinist.

"Give yourself to be merry," he wrote before he ended, "for you degenerate from your father if you find not yourself most able in wit and body to do anything when you are most merry."

Sir Henry was famous for his "quick drole." In his unceasing efforts to keep the courts of his presidency clear of the bickerings of the litigious Welsh he settled many a dispute with a devastating flash of his trenchant humour, and would then demand, "Is this not better than going to London or to Ludlow?"

"Take her home," he advised, when a gentleman, who had had his wife stolen from him, consulted the Lord President as the local Fountain of Honour with regard to the propriety of taking her back together with a large sum of money from the ravisher in compensation for the injury. "By my troth, take her back, and take the money. Then, whereas other cuckolds wear their horns plain, you may wear yours gilt."

He had a smile for himself as well as for his serious little boy at the end of that letter of advice: "Well, my little Philip, this is enough for me, and too much, I fear, for you." But he signs himself gravely enough, "Your loving father, so long as you live in the fear of God."

There was a loyal unanimity between the child's parents, which is rare among married couples who, like them, are much involved in affairs outside their own homes. His mother wrote to him to emphasize the importance of his father's advice, recommending that he read it over every four or five days. Sir Henry counselled him never to forget that he was a Dudley, for he suffered from no sense of inferiority but rather was proud of the fact that his wife's family was more distinguished than his own. But later he had the wisdom to point out that "if his children meant to live in order, they should ever be thoughtful whose sons they were, and seldom think whose nephews they were." In his comparatively modest circumstances he could foresee the danger of their growing up to become mere hangers-on at the skirts of their richer and more powerful relatives.

In May of 1563 Philip's uncle Ambrose, though still absent from England, commanding the army at Le Havre, was given the Garter; and Sir Henry, as his proxy, marched in the procession of the Order, with the Earl's hood and collar of the Garter on his arm. Sir Henry had been busy all that spring with the dispatch of reinforcements to his brother-in-law, who now found himself in a tight corner. The Prince of Condé, the leader of Elizabeth's allies in France, had been captured at the battle of Dreux; a peace had been signed at Amboise between Huguenots and Catholics, that left England out in the cold; and an army of reunited Frenchmen, with a German mercenary force to help them, slaughtered the English garrison of Rouen and attacked Le Havre itself.

The plague broke out in the beleaguered town, taking men faster—the death-rate rose to sixty a day—than replacements could be shipped from England, though the prisons of Newgate and the Fleet were emptied of tall fellows fit for cannon fodder. The bombardment grew murderous. Toward the last of July the Earl was wounded by a poisoned bullet. He was mustering the few survivors of his garrison for a last, desperate stand against a general assault, when life and honour alike were saved by a boat that slipped into the blockaded harbour, bearing the Queen's permission to surrender.

Early the following year the Treaty of Troyes brought peace between the two countries and with it a Garter for Sir Henry himself in recognition of the skill with which he had furthered the negotiations. Then it was Uncle Robert's turn to become a centre of public interest again. The finding of a husband for the Queen of Scots was almost as important as the finding of one for the Queen of England. But Mary did not share her royal cousin's reluctance toward the married state and was by no means averse from taking a man of her own choosing.

With what seems to have been enormous self-abnegation—only one never knows whether the woman meant what she said or would actually do what she seemed to mean —Elizabeth offered her the hand of her darling Robert Dudley. Thus for a second time an air-drawn crown glimmered before the calculating eyes of "the handsomest man in Europe." To give him rank appropriate to this high destiny she made him Earl of Leicester. It was done on Michaelmas Day at Westminster with great splendour. But, "You like better yon long lad," said Elizabeth, indicating to the Scottish envoy the handsome nineteen-year-old Lord Darnley, who stood near by and who, as great-grandson of King Henry VII, had some pretensions to the English throne. The envoy did; and so did Mary of Scotland; and so for a second time the gleam of a crown matrimonial faded for Robert Dudley.

In the summer of 1565, when Philip had been a year at school, his father was dickering with his queen about becoming Lord Deputy of Ireland. It was a ticklish business. For accepting employment under Elizabeth was rather like supping with the devil. One needed a long spoon or, rather, a long pen for drawing the contract, as most of her servants found out to their cost—at least those whose integrity, like Sir Henry's, she could rely upon without continually sweetening it with honours and riches. Few knew better than he that Ireland was in a dreadful state of disorder; that his little Philip's uncle Thomas of Sussex had been a total failure there; and that the Queen, who amid the distractions of the French war had given the outrageous Shane O'Neil a free hand, had thereby made her Irish government a laughingstock to its subjects.

Now her double-dealing in Scottish affairs had made matters in Ireland still worse. Queen Mary had married her young Darnley against Elizabeth's will and against the will of her own Lords of the Congregation, and the latter had taken up arms against her on receiving a promise of help from the Queen of England. But when Mary rode out at the head of her troops in steel bonnet and corselet, with a great horse pistol in her dainty hand and her boy husband shining in gilded armour at her side, Elizabeth had refused to move a single soldier to support the rebels. In retaliation the Duke of Argyle, who had been holding O'Neil in some sort of restraint, turned him loose. O'Neil had rebelled openly, was giving himself the airs of an independent prince, and had his agents at Paris, at Edinburgh, and at Rome itself.

Ireland was quite as much the grave of reputations in Elizabeth's time as South Africa was in Queen Victoria's. It was commonly regarded as "the general dirt heap for the outcasting of England's vileness." But Henry Sidney could seldom resist the challenge of a difficult task; and improved relations with Spain offered some promise of success. De Quadra, that over-zealous churchman, whom Elizabeth had so baited with protestations of her longing to become a nun that he had declared her to be possessed of a devil, was dead. His successor was a friend of Sir Henry's, Don Diego Guzman de Silva, a gentleman by nature as well as by birth.

The Queen took to him at once, and her entertainment of him at the palace at Richmond was the beginning of a friendly intimacy that lasted throughout his residence at her court. During supper she made the band play "The Battle of Pavia," which celebrated the ruin of François I by Spain and the Empire thirty-nine years before, and said she liked it the best of any music in the world. All this suited King Philip's plans exactly. He would risk no war with England while the factions of France were at peace with one another. His Netherlands, moreover, were beginning to rumble with disaffection, and at Malta the Knights of St. John of Jerusalem were fighting in the last ditch to hold their fortress against the Turk. It was no time for him to listen to the appeals of rebellious Irish chieftains.

So, early in December of 1565, his young godson Philip Sidney got extra holidays to ride to Chester to bid farewell to his father and mother, who were on their way to take shipping for Dublin and the responsibilities of viceroyalty. That was the beginning of a stirring twelvemonth for a boy of eleven. At Christmas he visited at Sir Henry Newport's near Wroxeter. A son of the house was about Philip's age, and it was for this occasion that those crossbow bolts were purchased. At Whitsuntide the boys of the school gave *Julian the Apostate* as their annual play in "the Quarrel" near the Severn. These performances were the direct descendants of the old miracle and morality plays of the district. People came in from miles around to see them; and the town corporation and the Drapers Company contributed funds to embellish the production of them. In June came the Plague.

In London, two years before, people had died of it at the rate of two thousand a month. The bishops said it was a judgment of God on the prevalence of theatre-going. Sandalwood and musk, fires of rosemary and bay, failed to check it until the winter rains washed the streets clean of the accumulated filth of summer. The soldiers of Warwick's disbanded army spread it through the country. Thomas Ashton closed his school, and Philip spent three weeks, partly with the Newports again, and partly at the home of Sir Andrew Corbet, a member of the Council of Wales, of whose eldest son, Robert, Philip was to write from Venice eight years later as "my very greatest friend."

But the epidemic at Shrewsbury cannot have been very serious, for Philip was back there again early in July and began what seems to have been an important side line in the life of every prominent man of his age by standing godfather to the son of Mr. George Leigh, at whose house he was tabled. Thomas Marshall, his confidential servant, who had entered in his accounts the shoeing of "the little nags" at Chester the previous December, provided him with a green cloth coat with a sarcenet collar and trimmings of fourteen yards of lace and eight pennyworth of buttons for the occasion. But within two weeks the faithful retainer was confronted with a much more important sartorial problem.

With his school-books in a bag of "linen alum" and no less a person than his headmaster at the head of a party of twelve, which included Marshall and Philip's *famulus*, the son of the Lord Deputy of Ireland rode off for his uncle Robert's castle of Kenilworth, and thence to visit Oxford at the time of the Queen's coming thither in September. He had a fine new horse and a new saddle, presents from Lord Ferrers, who was to become Earl of Essex a few years later, the father of the ill-starred favourite of Elizabeth's old age. But he had no proper clothes for courtly society; money was never plentiful among the gentry of the time, whose capital was almost entirely invested in land; and Sir Henry, already painfully aware of the hard bargain which his queen had driven with him, had evidently made no provision for this journey. Marshall had to borrow the money for travelling expenses, and do the best he could for his young master's appearance with "a pair of overstocks that I made him of his old black velvet gown" and a white leather jerkin, "whereof the skin came from my fellow Knight." It must have been as great a relief to him as it was a delight to Philip, when the Earl of Leicester, whom they found at Coventry, sent off an order to Whittel, his London tailor, for an outfit worthy of the nephew of the Queen's favourite and best-dressed courtier.

The record of the Earl's generosity includes "a short damask gown guarded with velvet and laid on with lace" and "a double taffeta coat guarded throughout with the same and covered with lace." There were five doublets, of crimson satin, green taffeta, and canvas "streaked" with blue and with red and silver; hose of carnation colour, crimson, green leather and blue leather; jerkins red and black; shoes of white, black and blue; and silk shirts of black, and of black and silver.

Philip had been ill shortly before the Chester journey in the winter. Now he was troubled with "merry galls" and "breaking forth with heats." Marshall provided linen hose and a box of ointment for the boy's chafed thighs, but the two days' ride from Kenilworth to Oxford brought on the "merry galls" again. He had, however, seen the splendours of his uncle Robert's castle. That of his uncle Ambrose at Warwick was close by, and Dudley Castle not far off. At Oxford, lodged at Lincoln College, he was at the University where within a year and a half he would be an undergraduate like his father before him. And in a week the Queen was coming.

She came. It was Saturday, the last day of August, bright and glorious and, it is to be hoped, cool. For she wore a headdress of woven gold and pearls and a triumphal purple robe lined with ermine over a scarlet silk gown woven with gold. Before her open chariot the sword borne by Philip's uncle, the Earl of Sussex, flashed with gold and jewels. The huge maces of the royal lictors were all about her. Two hundred of the royal guard, armed with great bows and iron clubs, followed her. Three esquire bedells on horseback, with golden staves, led the van, followed by the Earl of Leicester, who was Chancellor of the University, and by the Mayor of the city, while behind them, marshalled by Clarenceux King-of-Arms in heraldic splendour, rode the Marquis of Northampton, the Earls of Warwick, Ormonde, Rutland, Oxford and Huntingdon, and other important nobles.

For the occasion Philip had been provided with a retinue of his own from his father's men at Ludlow or Penshurst. With four uncles among the highest of the celebrities present he was sure of a good place in the procession. His father's friend, de Silva, who, like other ambassadors, generally accompanied a royal progress, was sure to notice him in a friendly way. Cecil and the Queen herself were bound to be interested in the thoughtful-looking boy with his pale face and finely-cut features and bright, auburn hair, who was the son of so able a father and might well inherit Leicester's greatness.

Elizabeth was in high good humour. She thoroughly enjoyed herself in these visits to the universities. She liked to retort upon their pedantic welcomers in the same learned tongues in which they addressed her. "*Non est veritas,*" she had replied to their praises of her at Cambridge, and shouted, "*Loquimini altius,*" at a mumbling don. Here, when the undergraduates shouted "*Vivat Regina!*" she called back, "*Gratias ago,*" and answered a Greek oration in Greek. She adored youth, and the youth of England adored her as their liberator from the grim and dreary Catholicism of her sister's rule and as their champion against the dour and ugly fanaticism of the Reformers. Had not the new Pope, Pius V, lately united Charles IX of France, Philip of Spain, and the Queen of Scots in a Catholic League which was aimed at her? Had not the Sacred College promised remission of sins and other rewards to anyone who would make way with her? On the other hand, had she not placed a cross and candles on her private altar, revived the Carnival with tournament and masque on Shrove Tuesday, and at the same time laughed at de Silva, who refused to eat the supper which was served after midnight, because Lent had begun?

Her high spirits carried her through a week of lectures, disputations, plays in English and in Latin, and "a very comfortable and eloquent oration in Latin" which she delivered in St. Mary's Church to resounding plaudits. The whole University in all the rich splendour of academic regalia saw her on her way as far as Shotover on the Friday. "Farewell, the worthy University of Oxford," said she at parting: "farewell, my good subjects there; farewell, my dear Scholars, and pray God prosper your studies; farewell—farewell." It was not in her character to remember at such a moment how, only a few years before, Bishop Jewell had found Oxford so "malignant" that he dared not exercise his powers as a sort of ecclesiastical policeman there. These were her people; by every sign they loved her as she loved them; and she craved affection. It was not two months since she had got news from Edinburgh at a gay party at Greenwich and had cried out in sudden bitterness of spirit: "The Queen of Scots is lighter of a fair son, and I am but a barren stock."

Philip went back to school by way of Bewdley, where he was the guest of Sir Charles and Lady Blount. It was necessary to borrow a horse and purchase a trunk and a pack-saddle, all complete and emblazoned with the Leicester "Ragged Staff," to transport his new wardrobe. He was evidently still dominated by memories of the grandeur in which he had lately participated, for at an inn where they stopped for the night he ordered the doubtless reluctant Marshall to reward a blind harper with twelvepence—a sum whose purchasing power was about equal to that of thirteen shillings at the present day.

The next summer he spent with his parents in Ireland. Nearly thirteen now, he was considered old enough to wear a rapier and dagger, which cost one pound, nine shillings. But he was not such a paragon of discretion as not to break two gold chains, which he was allowed to wear, and lose the greater part of one of them; and he lost three shillings and fourpence at tennis.

He found his father busy with the fortification of Carrickfergus and Athenry, the garrisoning of Belfast and other places, and with the construction and defences of a stone bridge over the Shannon at Athlone, by which the western part of the island would at all times be readily accessible to the English forces of pacification. The preservation and housing of public documents and records also occupied his attention, as it had done in Wales. They were being used to rub the heels of horses when he arrived. His working hours were from six in the morning until nine at night, although they were more and more frequently broken into by attacks of the fierce pain of gall-stones, from which he had been suffering for more than a year. Philip's mother, also, was in poor health. But the pickled head of the arch-rebel Shane O'Neil grinned on a pole above Dublin Castle, and the Irish realm enjoyed such peace as it had not known for many years.

The hardships and dangers, the feats of courage and endurance, by which these results had been accomplished, and the small appreciation with which they were rewarded, must have made a stirring story for the boy who had not seen his parents for a year and a half. And it seems likely that he heard the greater part of them, for Sir Henry was not the man to bring up his children in a fool's paradise. After parting with him at Chester his father and mother had lain for some weeks, weather-bound, at Holyhead. Then a gale had overtaken them at sea, and one of their ships, which carried Sir Henry's wines, his wife's whole wardrobe and a part of her jewels, was lost. From Ireland, upon his arrival, Sir Henry wrote that he found the people living in "such misery as in troth hardly any Christian with dry eyes could behold." In Ulster tyrannized O'Neil, "the prince of pride . . . the dangerousest man and most like to bring the whole estate of this land to subversion and subjugation either to him or to some foreign prince"; and the best way to deal with him which the Earl of Sussex had been able to think of had been to try to poison him.

Munster, which Sir Henry had known when it was, he said, "as well inhabited as many counties in England," had been laid utterly waste in the wars between the great feudal lords of Ormonde and Desmond, who were heads of the clans of Butler and Fitzgerald. "A man might ride thirty miles and find no houses standing." The usages of religion had disappeared; and where a little prosperity remained, "coin and livery," by which the nobles' retainers lived at free quarters upon the defenceless people, were fast eating it up. Within the English Pale, the district surrounding Dublin, conditions were not much better: gentry and people alike impoverished; crime unchecked; the garrison unpaid, licentious, insolent, and ripe for mutiny.

Worse still, the new viceroy soon discovered that the support from home, which had been promised him, was not forthcoming. Back in the Earl of Sussex's term of office, Cecil had written that at court there was no one who did not wish either so well to Shane O'Neil or so ill to the Earl as rather to welcome the news of O'Neil's success than regret an English loss. The same spirit was still alive there. Sussex was jealous lest his brother-in-law should succeed where he had failed; and, though Sir Henry had written home that Sussex deserved the Garter for his Irish services, the Earl did not scruple to hint to the Queen that Sidney was O'Neil's secret friend. The Catholics among the courtiers would have been glad to see the tyrant of Ulster victorious as a step toward the recovery of England for the Papacy. The Earl of Ormonde, who was the Queen's cousin, and who saw that the new Lord Deputy's plans for reform would weaken his feudal authority in the island, accused him of favouring the Desmonds, his great rivals there.

The Desmonds had to be treated fairly, however, or they would join forces with O'Neil; and Sir Henry, tried beyond endurance by the Queen's demands on this point, his letters unanswered and his promised supplies intolerably delayed throughout the winter of 1566, wrote bitterly to Cecil in April, asking to be relieved from his "peregrination in this Purgatory." In June the Duke of Argyle and the Scots of the Isles threatened to combine with O'Neil, and the neglected viceroy sent warning that, if men and money were not forthcoming to strengthen him, Ireland would become another Calais.

For this he was snubbed sharply. Sir Francis Knollys was sent over to control his expenditures. Copies of a letter from the Queen were circulated in Dublin and spread a general fear of the revival of "coin and livery" before the original reached the Lord Deputy, to whom it was addressed. Sir Henry wrote to Leicester, begging him to get him recalled. For it was generally believed in Ireland, he said, that the Queen had no confidence in him. "Here," he wrote to Cecil, "I do good neither to the Queen, the country or myself," and he hoped for his "revocation from this miserable and accursed island by the next east wind." He would go to Hungary rather than stay where he was.

East winds were rare that summer. A succession of westerly gales stopped all communication from England for weeks at a time. Sir Francis Knollys's appointment proved to be a boomerang for Sir Henry's enemies, however. He wrote to the Queen, heartily approving both the Lord Deputy's expenditures in the past and his plans for the future. Elizabeth, always short of money and never ceasing from her efforts to pay her debts to the Flemish bankers, railed against the required outlay like a hen-headed housewife over a coal bill, but she finally gave her approval. Reinforcements and the sinews of war arrived at last, and on the 17th of September—the day after Thomas Marshall sent home from Shrewsbury the borrowed pack-horse which had carried Master Philip's new clothes from Oxford—Sir Henry took the field at the head of two thousand men.

That "Cannibal," as he called O'Neil, promptly countered with a thrust at Drogheda in hopes of carrying off Lady Sidney. By a tyrant notorious for his lechery the threat was not a light one. But the garrison of Dublin came to Lady Mary's rescue, and her husband, leaving his artillery behind as too cumbersome for the rough country which he meant to traverse, marched for a month through O'Neil's domains, taking twenty castles, burning the houses, slaughtering the cattle and laying the lands of his supporters, "as fruitful a country as was in England or Ireland, all utterly waste." Patience and conciliation made up the policy which Sir Henry loved to follow, but few could be more ruthless than he when he believed that the situation demanded stern measures. He restored the loyal old O'Donnel to his estates in Donegal. Then by Ballyshannon and Sligo, and on over the bogs and mountains of Mayo and Roscommon, he swept in a triumphant circle and returned to the Pale by swimming the Shannon at Athlone, where Philip found him building the bridge the next year.

Enthusiastic Irish supporters compared his march to "Alexander's journey into Bactria." Not once had O'Neil dared to face him in the field. That rascal's luck had turned. Desmond had resisted all his blandishments. Argyle, persuaded by Murray to sacrifice his vengeance against Elizabeth, had dropped him. In November his army was surprised and routed by a force from the English military colony lately planted where the city of Londonderry now stands. The Scots of the Isles fell upon him in December. Sidney raided his territories again and again. He lasted but six months longer. While the Lord Deputy with a force of light horse was driving off his cattle, he was defeated by his former victims, the O'Donnels, and, desperate, sought a doubtful refuge among the M'Connels in remotest Antrim. There he fell in a drunken brawl, gashed by fifty dirks; and in due course the Lord Deputy "flowered the top of the Castle of Dublin with the arch-rebel's head."

But all this formed only a part of the task which he was called upon to accomplish. In January at the Queen's orders he had been compelled to march into Munster, where Ormonde's and Desmond's followers were waging such a struggle that, he said, he had never seen such desolation even in war-torn countries. At one place he had come upon the scene of a massacre so recent that unborn children were felt and seen to stir in the bodies of their slaughtered mothers. Yet the Earl of Desmond had feasted in the house of the author of this outrage, who was one of his servants. The people, Sir Henry reported, "with open mouth and held up hands to Heaven cried out for justice."

He was out for eleven weeks on this mission, hearing causes and sifting the complaints of either party against the other for fifteen hours a day. On his return in April he wrote to the Queen a report which runs to thirteen large printed pages, and in which he spared her neither the shortcomings of her favourite Ormonde nor a plenitude of ghastly detail. Edward Butler, the Earl of Ormonde's brother, was, he admitted, "the White Knight" among the depredators, but the Queen must resume the government of the district or the Earl must appoint better officers. Desmond, "blowing out words of evil digestion," Sir Henry brought back to Dublin a prisoner, and gave him to understand "in rough and rigorous terms" that "if any outrage were offered, he should be the first that should die for it."

The Queen demanded that her lord deputy should proceed to give judgment against Desmond and in favour of Ormonde in their quarrel. This without the advice of English lawyers he refused to do. She did indeed write him one appreciative letter after the extermination of O'Neil. As far back as April of 1566 he had promised her the accomplishment of that by the midsummer of the following year; he had kept well within his time; and she began her letter with "Harry" and ended it with "your loving mistress Elizabeth."

But soon Dublin was once more agog over copies of her letters to him, which were filled with discontent, and he was once more begging Cecil for his recall, since "the people here know what the Queen thinks of me and I can do no good." Years later, recalling these times in a letter to Sir Francis Walsingham, he wrote of "many a bitter letter" which he had from her this year and how they "so perplexed my most dear wife as she fell most grievously sick upon the same, and in that sickness remained once in a trance above fifty-two hours." So Philip's Irish holiday that summer cannot have been one of unalloyed happiness.

He returned to school; and his mother, whose health

had been wretched since the beginning of her residence in Ireland, grew so ill that she, too, went back to England, leaving her other children behind her. In October her husband followed her. His suffering from "the stone" had become almost unbearable. At Chester indeed he had to pause and undergo a species of operation before he could proceed upon his journey to court.

What with prisoners and hostages, whom he had thought it well to bring with him, and the other Irish chieftains and their attendants who rode in his train, his arrival at Hampton Court made such a stir that the Queen, observing it from her window, asked who had come. When they told her, "It is well enough," she said, "for he has two of the best offices in the Kingdom." But it was by no means well enough for Sir Henry. By way of welcome he was told "that it was no war that I had made nor worthy to be called a war, for that Shan O'Neil was but a beggar, an outlaw and one of no force, and that the Scots stumbled on him by chance. . . . And within few days after I was charged for not redressing the damages done to Ormonde and his followers by Sir John of Desmond."

How much Philip was allowed to hear of this is unknown, but it was doubtless enough to give him a good idea of what it meant to serve a queen who was the most temperamental of her sex. It may have been as well that he became acquainted with his father's Irish troubles thus early, for within a few years they were to be a part of his own.

CHAPTER V

"BRAVE OXFORD, WONDROUS WELL BELOVED"

WITH THE END OF 1567 PHILIP'S SCHOOL-DAYS ENDED. He presented his headmaster with a gratuity of ten pounds and joined his father and mother for a short visit before going up to Oxford at the beginning of the new year to become an undergraduate at Christ Church. They must have made a sorrowful trio, his parents in wretched health and bruised in spirit by their queen's ingratitude, and all three of them saddened by bitter news from Ireland. The other children, Elizabeth, Mary, Robert and Ambrosia, had been left at Kilmainham, the viceregal residence at Dublin; and there, not long after Sir Henry's departure, the seven-year-old Elizabeth had died without either father or mother to care for her or comfort her in her last hours.

At supper with his friend de Silva, Sir Henry said frankly that he was much dissatisfied with the way in which the Queen had treated him. He seems to have put it moderately. The beggar, the outlaw, the one of no force, as the court now chose to consider O'Neil, had been received by Elizabeth almost as an independent prince and had for years defied the efforts of Sussex to reduce him to subjection or to destroy him. Sir Henry had accomplished this task in less than eighteen months. He had spent three thousand pounds of his own money in his Irish service. It had cost him the ruin of his wife's health and of his own, and—what must have been dearest of all to a man of his strong paternal affection—the life of his little daughter. He found himself ignored in the conduct of affairs which were of vital importance to his government. Before he could protest against such drastic action the Earl of Desmond, whom he had brought over with him for the purpose of settling the dispute with Ormonde, was clapped into the Tower. Thereupon Sir Henry tendered his resignation as Lord Deputy and took care that it was accepted.

Thanks to the conditions upon which he had accepted the post, he still had the Presidency of Wales to occupy him. He could retire to Penshurst for a period of rest and recuperation; and when things began going badly in Ireland, as they immediately did—the Scots pouring into Antrim and the people "gaping for the Lord Deputy's return"—the report of his physicians gave him ample excuse for not complying with the Queen's request that he take up his duties there once more. "The State of Sir H. Sidney's Body" set it forth that after a year and a half in Ireland he had "avoided two stones" and, eighteen months later, at Chester another stone, of the size of a nutmeg, which the surgeons had to break before it could be voided.

"The stone in my lord is *morbus hereditarius,*" the report explained, but added that its development was owing to the hard and active life which he had been leading, and that he could not be cured unless this were given up. A dry climate, a dry house and gentle exercise were essential for his recovery. The list of things which he must not do included almost everything necessary to the successful prosecution of a lord deputy's duties in Ireland, such as the riding of "a sturring horse" and "galloping the felde, clad in hevie armeur." Sleeping "uppon or neigh the grounde in the feild greatly hurteth." He "maie not feede much of such females, the males whereof be of themselves to moist." Otherwise "joint aches and gowtes" are but too likely to follow. By the help of this lugubrious document Sir Henry managed to postpone his return to Ireland until the following September. But by the middle of February he had agreed to go, after much persuasion, and he wrote to de Feria in Spain in April of his intention of doing so.

As for Philip in the meanwhile, sorrow cannot for long entirely possess a boy of thirteen, who has college just before him and all around him the sights of London. For him there were the rich shops and the new Royal Exchange with its wax lights and Sir Thomas Gresham's grasshopper crest on the towers. There was the square tower of St. Paul's, whence the glorious spire had crashed down in flames upon the organ-loft a few years before. There were the aisles of the cathedral, filled with bargaining hucksters and strutting loungers. The streets were thronged with grave merchants, apprentices dodging on their errands, groups of idle servingmen badged with blue and gold, whose swords and bucklers might clash at any moment in some bloody outbreak of their noble masters' rivalry at court. Gallants swaggered through the press, so extravagant in the width of their ruffs and the length of their swords and daggers that a law had to be passed to regulate them; and the wives of merchants sailed along, as proud as galleons, bearing "the cost of princes" on their "unworthy shoulders."

There was the stirring danger of cutpurses at night. There were stage plays; and even a sensitive boy had been so toughened by the brutal sights common at the time that he could look on at a bull-baiting or a bear-baiting with as much enjoyment as one of the present day gets out of a boxing match. Criminals were strung up publicly and as nearly as might be on the scene of their wrong-doing. Dead pirates clanked their chains on the gallows on the river-bank. With a little luck one might see at Tyburn the ghastly business of a traitor's disembowelment alive. The heads and quarters of such, all shiny-black with the tar that preserved them from the weather, decorated the spikes above London Bridge and Temple Bar.

Then there was the river. Below the bridge it was filled with ships: the ships of the Hanseatic merchants at the Steelyard; English ships that had been to Spain and to the eastern Mediterranean and on the African voyage; and here and

FULKE GREVILLE, LORD BROOKE

from a print in the British Museum

there, perhaps, one from Muscovy or the Indies. To visit them one might shoot the arches of the bridge on a roaring ebb tide. Above the bridge and on up as far as the Queen's palace of Whitehall the gardens of the great noblemen's town houses ran down to their stairs and landings, and the broad surface of the stream was streaked by the swift wherries of the watermen, whose independence and inconsiderateness were such that Walter Raleigh, even after he had become a seasoned navigator, preferred the long way round by London Bridge to crossing over to Lambeth with one of them. It must have been with a head full of such delightful and exciting memories that Philip went up to his university in January.

Thirteen was not a conspicuously early age at which to enter Oxford in those days. A year or two before Philip's arrival there Richard Carew, afterwards poet and antiquary, had become a gentleman commoner at Christ Church when he was eleven. Early in the century Erasmus had praised the order and discipline kept at the English universities; and what with proctors, taskers, masters of the streets, and the like, the boys, who had "lodgings and chambers after a sumptuous sort" in "divers goodly houses four square of hard free stone or brick," were probably well looked after according to the standards of the time.

In the halls, such as Broadgates, where Philip's schoolmate Fulke Greville now took up his quarters, there was more freedom than in the colleges. Harrison entered in his book a few years later the complaint that the rich gentlemen's sons, who had ousted from the colleges the poor boys for whom they were originally intended, wasted their time over romances, backgammon and dice, and would "ruffle and roist it, exceeding in apparel and banting riotous company," coolly excusing themselves on the ground that they were gentlemen. But anyone acquainted with any university of the present day will recognize this set and realize that it was not necessarily typical of the undergraduate life at Oxford in Philip's time.

Certainly it can have had small attraction for him, while all around him were spirits kindred to his own and, many of them, possessed of the best young brains in Europe. At Oriel Walter Raleigh was airing the rich Devonshire accent which a lifetime of court, camp, fleet and field never quite smoothed away. Richard Hooker was at Corpus Christi, cultivating the learning which was to flower in the *Ecclesiastical Polity*. Henry Savile, studying for his M.A. at Merton, was on the road to becoming the most learned Englishman of his time. At Broadgates was George Carew, afterwards an able lieutenant of Sir Henry Sidney's in Ireland and later Earl of Totnes. At Christ Church was Richard Hakluyt, who was to be the indefatigable chronicler of voyages and Philip's lifelong friend. Thomas Thornton, Philip's tutor, later Vice-Chancellor of the University and "a common refuge for poor young scholars of great hopes and parts," discovered poor young William Camden at Broadgates, brought him to Christ Church, where he became a friend of Philip's, and lodged and kept him there at his own expense until the future historian could fend for himself. John Lyly, whose *Euphues* was to bracket his name for centuries with that of the author of the *Arcadia*, was indulging his aversion to "the crabbed studies of logic and philosophy" at Magdalen.

A junior proctor at St. John's was Edmund Campion. As a boy at St. Paul's school he had welcomed Queen Mary in Latin upon her state entry into London. When Queen Elizabeth came to Oxford in 1566, he had done the like and debated before her on the effect of the moon upon the tides. Now, at twenty-eight years of age, he was trying to eat his cake and have it too, in an attempt to reconcile the God of his pope with the Mammon of his queen. Both Philip's father and his uncle Robert were Campion's friends; and Philip's life and his were to cross their threads several times after this—most often pleasantly, but tragically at the last, when the gentle Jesuit missionary to the English was already in the toils of his martyrdom.

In August of that summer of 1568 Philip's father came to Oxford to receive an honorary degree of Master of Arts. He stayed at Christ Church, the guest of the Dean, and when he departed took Philip to Wales with him for a few weeks with his reunited family before he set out for Ireland again.

Sir Henry seems to have enjoyed himself thoroughly during these months that followed his reinstatement in his sovereign's confidence. While he was still in London he had a pleasant evening with his old friend and fellow bibliophile, Archbishop Parker. He had heard that Philip was not well, and he had called upon the Archbishop to ask for a dispensation which would permit the boy to eat meat in Lent. For, though the papal injunction as to fasting no longer held good in England, the encouragement of the national fisheries made reasonable the enforcement of the rule. But what with old books, and old wine from the Lambeth cellars, his errand was forgotten, and he had to send over a note about it the next morning.

On their journey to Ludlow father and son stopped for a few days at Kenilworth. Leicester was not at home. But there were other guests; and Sir Henry, the state of whose health prevented him from hunting, amused himself with fishing: "a hundred good breames at a draught." With his insatiable love of building he delighted in the additions and improvements which his brother-in-law was making in the castle. "I was never more in love with an old house," he wrote to him, when he had gone on to Shrewsbury, and promised that, if the Earl would get him home again by the next spring, he would build the new chapel at his own cost.

His mind was already running zestfully upon his work, however. Although he signed himself "In Haste and Paine" after three days of "my disease," he promised that the Scots "shall not winter between the sea, Loughefoil, Strangford and the English Pale, if I be able to keep the field." To Cecil the same day he sent a letter by a certain Douglas, a secret agent, whom he described as "true of his report (though a Scot) and diligent." The Queen, he said in it, must stiffen her forces in Munster and Connaught, for he would have to meet a Scottish combination in Ulster with ships which were already prepared.

Cecil wrote more than one friendly letter in return, promising Sir Henry his good offices, wishing health to Lady Sidney and "all goodness to your son, my darling Master Philip," who "is worthy to be loved and so I do love him as if he were my own." Perhaps the fact that Leicester had ceased to fish in Catholic waters accounted for the Secretary's cordiality toward the brother-in-law of the Earl, to whom he was almost always opposed on questions of policy. For Sir Henry had carried his pride in his wife's family to the point of placing their "Ragged Staff" on the pennon which was borne before him in Ireland. Or it may be that Cecil had by this time taken a more accurate measure of the Lord Deputy and knew him for one whom family feeling would never deflect from his duty to his queen. At all events he continued to send cordial notes; a humorous scolding for taking "your son and my scholar from Oxford, not only from his book but from the commodity to have been seen by my lords his uncles . . . and to have pleasured both me and my wife"; and, out of several, one in November, stating that he had received no answer to "sundry letters" but "if I may once hear that you do well I will take that only for a full satisfaction. . . . My lady, your wife, shall, I trust, be here on Monday, and so I end."

A lesser man than Sir Henry would have counted as well spent any time he took from his duties to cultivate the friendship of the powerful minister. But Butler was now fighting Butler in the Ormonde country, and he was handicapped in restoring order by continual rumours from England that he had no authority there. Moreover it was his "own ill hap to use physic at this instant," he reported. The Earl of Clancarre—"this new Earl made of an old rebel," who had ports, galleys and mercenary soldiers of his own, was holding intercourse with the rebels in Kilkenny, Tipperary and the North; and Spanish ships had lately supplied him with abundance of sword-blades, "hargabuserie" and other war material. Sir Henry recommended that William Winter and his ships should attend to this, for he himself could spare none from Ulster; and it was "needful that the Spanish ambassador of Spain [sic] be talked with" about it. Only in a letter which evidently crossed the one in which Cecil told him of Lady Sidney's approaching visit did he strike a more personal note: "I most heartily thank you for your courteous visit to my wife. I pray you sometime harken of our boy, and be working to get home the Father." And he sent affectionate greetings to "my sweet juell your daughter." This was poor little Anne Cecil, of whom there will be more to tell later on.

Cecil's interest in "our boy" was such that Philip spent that Christmas with him and his family at Hampton Court. The Secretary, although he was now a man of forty-eight, whose brown beard was beginning to whiten, and whose elder son was proving to be a disappointment to him, combined a fondness for books with his knowledge of statesmanship and practical politics in a way that must have delighted Sir Henry Sidney's son. Evidently he made a point of talking with his young guest; and there were plenty of exciting things to talk about: Alba's subjugation of the Netherlands; the fortunes of the Duke of Condé and the Huguenots in France—Cecil was a thorough-going Protestant; the ignominious dismissal of the English Ambassador at the court of Spain; and King Philip's substitution of the bigoted and unscrupulous Don Guerau de Espes for the urbane and reasonable de Silva at the English court.

One other subject, and the one which was exciting the

most furious public interest at the time, the Secretary may have avoided as too ticklish for discussion with anyone in whose experience and discretion he could not have the most absolute confidence. This was that silver casket filled with "horrible and long letters" and "fond ballads of filthy love, abhorring her husband that was murdered," which her enemies insisted that the Queen of Scots had written to her lover Bothwell.

The short four years since her marriage to Lord Darnley had been stormy ones for Queen Mary. She had come to loathe her handsome, young husband, and not without good cause. But his death by powder-blast and strangling had so ugly a look, when she followed it with marriage with the Earl of Bothwell, who was notorious for his "insatiableness towards women," that her infant son had been crowned in her stead. Since then Bothwell had been driven to seek the perilous shelter of the court of Denmark; and she, after escaping from Lochleven Castle and losing the battle of Langside, had been glad to throw herself upon the hospitality of her royal cousin of England.

To her who had heard the mob of Edinburgh rave round her with cries of "Burn the whore! Burn the murderess of her husband!" the enthusiasm with which she was received by the Catholic population of Northumberland was intoxicating. But it was dangerous too, for it left Elizabeth with no alternative but to turn her guest into a prisoner, unless she wished to have a rebellion on her hands. A divorce would soon open the way to fresh matrimonial ventures by Queen Mary; and already the Queen of England was called upon to decide whether she should allow a sister sovereign to be tried for murder and adultery or consent to a scheme for her marriage with the Duke of Norfolk, one of the leaders of those English Catholics whose loyalty was, to say the best of it, divided between their ruler and the Pope of Rome.

Characteristically she refused to make the decision. But the whole affair worked out to some advantage for the Sidney family. For Philip's uncle of Sussex was sent to preside over the Council of the North, which had the captive Queen in its territorial jurisdiction; and since this gave him a standing in the government equal to that of Sir Henry, his jealous maleficence was for the time suspended.

When Philip returned to college at the end of his Christmas holidays, Cecil did not forget him, but kept up with him during the next few months a correspondence, which Philip neglected like any modern undergraduate and to which he contributed—judging from the two Latin letters which have come down to us—nothing of any interest, unless it be the fact that in writing to a friend of his father's he could be as dull and correct as any other well-bred boy of his age in like circumstances. But late in February of the new year a bit of academic chicanery threatened to keep his tutor out of a vacant canonry, the promise of which young Philip and others had obtained for him from Leicester and Cecil; and the ardent lad tore off a letter in the vulgar tongue, in which his indignation at such double-dealing sputtered and stammered and snarled up most abominably the intricate epistolary style of the day.

Meanwhile he continued to read Latin authors, not only for what were known in the curriculum as grammar and rhetoric, of which the latter included the literary and historical study of those classics, but also for logic, since Greek had fallen to so low an estate that Aristotle himself was read in a Latin translation. The mathematics included music; and there were philisophy, moral and natural, and metaphysics, which delighted him.

With the retrospective glance of one who was ten years out of college Philip recommended to his brother Robert the study of Livy, Tacitus and Plutarch, but damned what he called the Ciceronianism of Oxford, which would place style before subject-matter. He would doubtless have added—had Robert needed the reminder—that if one intended to use one's Latin as the universal language which was spoken by the learned of the Continent, one must learn to pronounce it all over again in the Continental manner. But Robert seems to have been a thoroughly practical person, which may have been the reason why Philip the poet said nothing to him about the Latin poets and passed on to recommend the study of laws and commerce, arithmetic, geography, topography and fortification, and enough geometry and astronomy to serve one's need in such matters.

Philip took part in the college disputations this year, with his uncles, Leicester and Warwick, in the audience, and "divers other great personages" with them. "Upon a wrong conceived opinion touching my sufficiency," says modest Richard Carew of this occasion, "I was there called to dispute extempore (*impar congressus Achilli*) with the matchless Sir Philip Sidney." But Carew's biographer states in Latin hexameters that Richard did not get the worst of the debate—a fact worth noting in the almost unbroken record of excellencies which Philip's contemporaries have chosen to set down about his youth.

But news from the world outside must have frequently caused the pursuits of undergraduate life to be forgotten by Philip and his companions. Oxford, unlike retired Shrewsbury, was a centre of thought and life. What men wrote and said there counted throughout England and on the Continent; and what happened in England and abroad altered directly and swiftly the lives of students and faculty alike. Philip saw it work among his friends and acquaintances. Campion, driven into a political and theological corner at last, left for Ireland, where the liberal Lord Deputy would gladly have made him head of the university which Sir Henry hoped to establish at Dublin. He gave the unhappy young man shelter while he was writing his *History of Ireland* and, when the royal pursuivants became too hot upon his trail, winked at his escape from the country in the livery of a footman.

Walter Raleigh, too, left Oxford in the late winter of

1569. English volunteers were marching off to aid the Huguenots, for the forces of the Prince of Condé, who had been ruling like a second king at La Rochelle, had been driven back from the Loire. "*Doux le péril pour Christ et le pays*" ran the motto on Condé's pennon. Raleigh's cousin commanded a company, and the seventeen-year-old boy went with him. But they arrived only in time to see the Prince pay with his life for his impetuosity on the fatal field of Jarnac.

That spring an important event occurred in the Sidney family: the birth of a third son. In token of the improved relations between them and Sir Henry, the Earl of Sussex and Cecil were chosen as the child's godfathers. He was named Thomas after his reconciled uncle, but this was rather to his father's disappointment. Sir Henry wrote to Cecil that he had intended to have his son bear the Secretary's name of William. Indeed the friendship between the two men had increased to the point that the betrothal of Philip to Cecil's daughter Anne, who was about Philip's age, was being discussed between them.

At first Cecil had replied quite frankly to Sir Henry's proposal that he looked for his daughter to make a more advantageous match: "Thus," he excused himself gracefully, "you see a father's fondness, which to a father I dare discover." But upon Sir Henry's protesting that he regarded Anne's "virtue above every other *dot*"—which must have eased her father's mind on the subject of the amount of the settlement which was expected to go with her—and upon Sir Henry's adding that he did not know of more than a hundred pounds of his which he had not assured to Philip, Cecil gave a rather hesitating consent. The Earl of Leicester had interested himself in the project; and after all, Philip was still his uncle Robert's heir, and the Earl seemed to be committed to celibacy by his continuing devotion to the Queen.

Even Sir Henry, however, proved to be unequal to the

task of putting down an Irish rebellion and conducting the negotiations for the marriage of his son at the same time. In the hurly-burly of the Munster insurrection that summer the tentative settlements, which had been sent over for his approval, were lost. In vain he wrote that if he might have "the greatest Prince's daughter in Christendom" for his son, he would not have the match broken off. The project languished and finally, as Sir Henry's favour with the Queen declined and Cecil rose to be Lord Burghley, it died.

What Philip thought of it we do not know: probably at his age, and with his temperament, not much. What Anne thought of it, as the years went by, it is possible to guess. In December of 1571 her father, dazzled by the prospect of so brilliant a marriage for his daughter, offered her up to the rapaciousness of the rich, young Earl of Oxford. That bad young man, while he was still a ward of Cecil's, had killed a servant in one of his fits of rage; but the Queen approved of the match. Neglected by her husband, who kept her in seclusion in the country, Anne did not live many years, but she must often have indulged a fond regret for what her life might have been with the handsome, gentle lad who had needed but a little more wealth to meet all her father's requirements for a perfect husband for her. But then, "marry thy daughters in time, lest they marry themselves," was a maxim of the great Lord Burghley.

Philip went to Ireland again for the summers of 1569 and 1570—a stirring scene and one of absorbing interest for a boy whose taste for public affairs was as strong as his liking for study and literature. His father had begun the first of these years by opening the Irish Parliament with great pomp, seated under a "cloth of estate" and dressed in viceregal robes of crimson velvet lined with ermine. In his House of Commons, however, a contemporary comments that it was soon a case of "the more words the more choler, and the more speeches the greater broils." From Cork in February had come a report of "a lewd enterprise" by "the popest traitour in Ireland" and some others in the Southwest who sought the aid of the King of Spain; and in March "the only news of this wretched country," Sir Henry wrote home, was of Captain Piers's prolonged skirmish at Knockfergus, in which two hundred and twenty-five of the Irish were slain, and many English wounded by Scottish arrows.

Worse was to come. The imprisonment of the Earl of Desmond and the forfeiture of his lands had aroused his clan, under the leadership of his brother Fitzmaurice, to fury. In carrying out a plan for colonizing Ireland by English settlers a number of gentlemen from the west of England had set the population around Cork by the ears. Sir Peter Carew, who was pressing ancient claims to lands which were held by the Butlers, attacked a castle of Edward Butler, the Earl of Ormonde's brother, and slew all he found within its walls, including a little boy three years old. And that nothing might be lacking to drive the Irish to desperation, this year was chosen to stamp out the Roman Catholic religion and substitute for it the Anglican organization and doctrine, which they regarded as the means of damnation and the watchword of Antichrist.

Following the lead of the Desmonds, the country flamed into revolt. Ormonde's brothers took up arms, although they refused to join the general movement to expel the English from the island with the help and under the sovereignty of the King of Spain. The colonists had treated like wild beasts the Irish who had resented the expropriation of their lands, and like savage beasts the Irish now retaliated. Lady St. Leger and Lady Grenville found refuge within the walls of Cork in the nick of time to escape an unspeakable death. Many others were not so fortunate. The English Pale itself was filled with terror. The troops were few and unreliable; the inhabitants, worn out with the exactions of the unpaid soldiery, hardly loyal. And always in the back of the viceroy's mind lurked the threat of a Spanish invasion.

For gone were the good old days of a year ago, when the

Spanish Ambassador could celebrate Alba's victory over the Protestants in the Netherlands with a bonfire in a London street, hogsheads of beer and good claret set out for all comers, and loyal Englishmen drinking thereof with nothing to fear but the comments of strait-laced neighbours that "we were partakers of their fornication because we drank their wine." Since then the news that the fleet of Sir John Hawkins and Francis Drake had been treacherously attacked and all but destroyed by the Spaniards at San Juan de Ulloa had set England boiling. There had been reprisals, and counter-reprisals in which France had joined with Spain. In London the house of a Spanish merchant had been searched by the police. The crucifixes and images of his chapel had been mocked and insulted and burned by the mob in Cheapside with shouts of "These are the gods of Spain!"

The sight of his father in these desperate times must have moved young Philip to admiration. Sir Henry had been striving to get through his Parliament measures for the establishment of grammar schools and the restoration of Dublin University. His indefatigable hearing of "causes" had been making the Irish "more willing to leave their Obrian law, and to embrace the course of the English laws" before these troubles came on. But he was quick to see that he had but one line of action left open to him by the circumstances, and he took it with his customary promptness and energy. He marched at once against the rebels. Then, gathering his demoralized soldiers around a tun of wine, he made them a speech that put such heart into them that "every man thought himself good enough for five rebels"; and thereafter no Irish force dared to make a serious stand against them. In September he led them by Waterford, Cork, Limerick, Galway and Roscommon, in one of those swift marches of his that drove Fitzmaurice into the Kerry mountains and left a trail of burned villages, ruined castles and swinging corpses behind him. As he had written of the severity of one of his lieutenants the year before, "the doing was evil but the deed was good."

But this was the man whose doctors had enjoined him to avoid "pensiveness and cares, as anger, which do most cause the stone." Edward Tremayne, whom the Queen had sent over in July to bring her a report of the Irish situation, wrote back that the Lord Deputy would die if he were not soon relieved. The strain was indeed telling on him heavily. "If there remained any rejoicing humours in me . . ." he wrote to Cecil. As in his previous term as Lord Deputy, he had just cause to complain of scanty support from home. "I have such a Familiar of Penury," he said, "as I think never none endured as a Prince Deputy." Everybody hated him, he added: the nobles because he had destroyed their tyranny; the merchants, who were bankrupt through giving credit to the soldiers; the gentlemen, whose tenants, with soldiers quartered on them, could pay no rent; the tenants, eaten up by the soldiers; and the soldiers because they had no pay even to shoe their horses or themselves. "And to knit up this sack of sorrows" there was his failing health.

Nor was his father the only figure fit to stir Philip's admiring emulation in these Irish summers. The gentlemen from the west of England, who led the colonists, had been trained in the French wars, in the rougher school of the African voyages, and in that sea service which was counted privateering if it proved successful, but which carried the grim penalties of piracy if it failed. But there were men of intellect and high purpose among them. Old Sir Peter Carew himself, whom his father had vainly coupled with a hound "to frame this young Peter to smell of a book," had about him the polish of one who had seen the court of the great King Francis from the widely different viewpoints of a page and a stable-boy, who had changed sides after the battle of Pavia and been page to Bourbon at the storming of Rome, and who, disguised as a merchant in the alum trade, had barely escaped with his life from Constantinople. He had taken part in the siege of Buda with that emperor who had sent home the Sultan's ambassadors without ears or noses; and between-whiles he had blended his pleasant voice with that of King Henry VIII in such songs as "By the Bank as I Lay" and "As I Walked by the Wood So Wild." He promised to see that the King of Spain should "be as well barked at as ever man was." When he came to die a few years later, they appropriately filled the church at his funeral with the smoke of five farewell volleys of musketry.

In Ireland in these days, too, were Sir Richard Grenville and Sir Warham St. Leger, whose father had been viceroy there under three sovereigns. And there was Humphrey Gilbert, half-brother to Philip's college friend Raleigh. Educated at Eton and Oxford, a man of cultivation and an eager student of the sciences, Gilbert was already dreaming of a voyage that should discover the Northwest Passage "to Cataia." He had been a captain in Ireland since the beginning of Sir Henry's first coming there as Lord Deputy. That steadfast and unquestioning faith, with which fourteen years later he met his death in an Atlantic gale, made him a perfect pacificator of the wild, papistical Irish, whom he, like most of his associates, regarded as mere cumberers of the earth. Sir Henry made him Governor of Munster in October of 1569 and knighted him for his services the following New Year's Day.

Campion Philip would naturally see again on these Irish holidays, and John Hooker, a Corpus Christi man, uncle to Richard, Philip's friend at Christ Church. John Hooker was a leader of the English party in the Parliament at Dublin; he was Sir Peter Carew's man of business for his Irish claims; and if his biography of his patron can be taken to indicate his personal quality, Philip must have found his acquaintance delightful.

In Dublin Castle, a prisoner by order of the Queen, who was weary of hearing complaints against him, lay Thomas Stukeley, that spectacular ne'er-do-well of whom the best to be said is that Sir Henry Sidney seems to have found some good in him, and not the worst that he had been a bosom friend of Shane O'Neil. For Stukeley's piracies the English Ambassador at Madrid had "hung down his head for shame." When Sir Henry, after trying vainly to get him pardoned, accepted his parole and packed him off to England to answer the charges against him, he fled to Spain and got a knighthood and the title to an Irish dukedom out of King Philip in exchange for his plan for conquering Ireland and making it a Spanish possession.

In underhand ways Spain was now very busy in plots against England and England's queen. Let the Duke of Norfolk marry the Queen of Scots, or let the great nobles of the North carry her off to become the bride of Don John of Austria, and his king, the Spanish Ambassador promised, would give prompt support to the rebellion that was to follow. Norfolk lost his courage, and from York the Earl of Sussex—wrong as usual—reported that the stables of Northumberland and the other disaffected nobles were too empty to horse a rising in the autumn of 1569. But in November Oxford thrilled to the news that the Northern lords were in the field for Queen Mary Stuart and Holy Church. The old banner of the Five Wounds of Christ, piously preserved from the days of the Pilgrimage of Grace, was flying in their van. In Durham Cathedral the communion table, the Bible and the prayer-books were overthrown, torn and desecrated, and mass was celebrated in the edifice thus purified. The rebels swept down past York; and Uncle Thomas, irresolute as ever, could see nothing for it but that the Queen must make any possible composition with them: Alba had a flotilla ready in Flanders to ferry an army across to assist them the moment they had set the Queen of Scots at liberty.

But the Earl of Huntingdon, husband of Philip's aunt Katherine Dudley, hurried his royal prisoner farther from their reach; Mary's reputation and influence in England had never recovered from the blight which Darnley's murder had cast upon them; and there was no rising of the Catholics of the South, as Northumberland and his companions had been led to expect that there would be. While his arms were being solemnly "spurned" down the steps of St. George's Chapel as a sign of his degradation from the Order of the Garter, his army was beginning to break up from lack of support. Three days later—it was Philip's fifteenth birthday—his other two uncles, Warwick and Leicester, were driving its fragments toward the Scottish border; and by the end of the year Northumberland's little daughters looked out from their nursery window upon the dangling corpses of their father's servants, who had paid the penalty for his treason, while he and his duchess rode for their lives across the snowy moors to the doubtful refuge of Scotland.

The sequel was one of hangings and headings. For almost the only time in her life Elizabeth gave herself to wholesale cruelty.

> She turned her grace then once about
> and like a royall Queene she sware
> sayes, "I will ordeine them such a breake-fast
> as was not in the North this thousand yeere."

On parish greens and in the market-places of the towns the gibbets creaked with bodies which, it was ordered, should remain "till they fell to pieces where they hung." These were the misguided poor, who were hanged out of hand. The wealthy and all others who had property worth confiscating were formally tried for treason; and for this purpose, such was the rapacity of the royal prosecutors,

> Lads with money were counted men . . .

or so says a popular ballad of the day.

In the following April Sussex led an army into Scotland against the fugitive rebels and their supporters beyond the border. But England still simmered with privy conspiracy and rebellion. One morning, nailed to the door of the Bishop of London's palace, appeared a papal bull excommunicating Elizabeth as "the servant of iniquity," absolving her subjects of allegiance to her and threatening them with a similar penalty if they any longer obeyed her. The Queen might give "one of her odd, unearthly laughs"—the bull had been suppressed by royal command in France and even in Spain—but its publication in London was the work of the Bishop of Ross, Queen Mary's agent there. Elizabeth's envoy in Scotland sent her a gold brooch that represented the Scottish lion crushing the skull of the English leopard; and straws show which way the wind is blowing. The Catholics of the South of England were now bitterly sorry that they had not come to the support of the Northern rebels. They sent message after urgent message to the King of Spain, who had assembled a great fleet in Flanders ostensibly to convoy the Archduchess Anne of Austria, his fourth matrimonial venture, to his royal couch. But France was now enjoying another of her brief interludes of internal peace, and King Philip would not risk attacking England with a united France upon his flank.

Elizabeth, however, had been, for once, thoroughly frightened—frightened enough at all events to be willing to think of marriage once more. Back at the height of the Queen of Scots' popularity she had consented to consider "the archduke with the large head" again; and Sussex had spent some months at Vienna, eating choice fruits from the gardens of Schönbrunn, while the negotiations were dragged out until Queen Mary's marital troubles made them no longer necessary. Now, with her genius for consenting to do the thing desired of her, but only if she were allowed to do it in the most unsatisfactory way, Elizabeth proposed to marry Henri, Duke of Anjou, the French King's brother. She could hardly have made a more unpopular selection. Her Protestant subjects hated the idea of it. Not only was the Duke a Catholic; he had commanded the armies which had half-ruined the Huguenot cause at Jarnac and Moncontour. The

Catholics abhorred it, for it meant the end of their hopes for the Queen of Scots as their sovereign and for the preponderance of Spanish influence in England. Norfolk sent word to the Pope and the King of Spain that the feeling against it was such that he could assemble twenty thousand foot and three thousand horse to dethrone the Queen and begged them for three thousand harquebus-men, harquebuses, corselets, cannon and horses to support and equip them. Sir Henry Sidney, coming home from Ireland in the March of 1571, found the country in a turmoil.

At his embarkation at "the key of Divelin . . . the Estates and Worshipful of Ireland" had given him an enthusiastically affectionate farewell. "Stately without disdain," wrote Campion of him in the conclusion of his *History*, "familiar without contempt, very continent and chaste of body, no more than enough liberal . . . of wit fresh and lively, in consultations very temperate, in utterance happy, which his experience and wisdom have made artificial, a preferrer of many, a father to his servants, both in war and in peace of commendable courage." He left peace behind him, the only peace obtainable, though it was but the peace of the sword. He had striven hard to give it a more substantial foundation. A form of "submission" had been got out of the Earls of Ormonde and Desmond. In Munster a president and council, which he had long and earnestly recommended, had been created and sworn into office: "so help you God and the Contents of this Booke."

He returned again the poorer in his private fortune by three thousand pounds. Indeed so crippled had been his finances by Elizabeth's niggardly response to the requirements of his government that his wife had not known where to turn for money to satisfy her creditors during his absence. Her health had continued to be miserable since the birth of the baby Thomas, but she had been much of the time on duty about the Queen, though she received small appreciation for her services. The friendship of Cecil had been her great refuge in these difficulties, and to him she had appealed more than once, even after the betrothal negotiations between the two families had begun to languish and during the brief interval when the strength of the Queen of Scots' party in the Council seemed to threaten his very existence at court. She was too ill to plead her cause with the Queen in person, she had written to him in the June of 1570, nor would she "have the face" to do it well; but if he would do it for her, she did not see how the Queen could "stick at so small a trifle as poor £22 a year for twelve years service."

Sir Henry's own health was so broken that in August of the year of his return he went to take the waters at Spa in Luxemburg. But before and after that he had duties to attend to in the Parliament that met in April. There were affairs to be straightened out in Wales after his long absence, and the Council needed his advice as to the best way to deal in Ireland. His sole reward for all his service and self-sacrifice was the offer of a barony with nothing to support it on. The prospect of so calamitous an honour sent Lady Mary, "a poor perplexed woman," running to Cecil again to help her to devise some means of staving it off without incurring the Queen's displeasure.

But now the family could at least be together again, at Penshurst or at Ludlow. Sir Henry had sent home before him the children whom he had kept with him in Ireland, and Philip was free to join them. For the Plague broke out at Oxford that spring so fiercely that almost a year went by before the University was functioning regularly once more. It is possible that he went to Cambridge at this time, and that he met Edmund Spenser there. But this seems unlikely.

In any case his college days were nearly over. Penshurst, Ludlow, Kenilworth and London, with a glimpse or two of the court, filled in the time until the spring of 1572. Then came the preparations for the grand tour on the Continent, which was to complete his education—three horses, four servants, a letter of credit from Acerbo Velutelli, the Italian banker in Lombard Street, and on May 25th the Queen's permission to her well-beloved Philip Sidney, Esquire, to go into parts beyond the seas "for his attaining the knowledge of foreign languages." He lacked just five days of being seventeen years and six months old.

CHAPTER VI

LEADING-STRINGS

"HE IS YOUNG AND RAW AND NO DOUBT SHALL FIND THOSE countries and the demeanours of the people somewhat strange unto him."

So wrote the Earl of Leicester in introducing his nephew to Mr. Francis Walsingham, Elizabeth's lately appointed ambassador resident at the French court. But that Philip was no gawky greenhorn even at seventeen is made clear by the impression which he evidently left in the minds of all who met him. His small personal retinue included Griffin Maddox, his father's Welsh steward, and Lodovic Bryskett, "a natural Italian" but born in England, the son of an Italian merchant living in London. Bryskett was some fifteen years Philip's senior and had been a pensioner at Trinity College, Cambridge. He had gone to Italy on business for Sir Henry three years before this journey and had been for a time Clerk of the Council in Ireland. Nevertheless the little party was not allowed to set out alone. Edward Fiennes de Clinton, Lord High Admiral of England, and lately created Earl of Lincoln, was bound for Paris as the Queen's special ambassador to King Charles IX, and Philip rode in his train.

Lincoln's countess, born Elizabeth Fitzgerald, had been, at twelve years of age, the Fair Geraldine of the Earl of Surrey's Petrarchian sonnets a generation earlier. But even the genuine love affairs of one's elders seem pretty musty stuff when one is seventeen. It is safe to assume that Lincoln, who was about sixty, was more interesting to Philip as his uncles' companion-in-arms from Saint-Quentin days down to the recent suppression of the Rising in the North, and most interesting to the young student of contemporary international affairs in his diplomatic capacity. He was to ratify a treaty of offensive and defensive alliance between France and England—so much fruit had the Queen's French marriage project produced—and he was to discuss the marriage itself. But Henri of Anjou was no longer the prospective bridegroom, that honour having devolved upon his younger and even less attractive brother, François, Duke of Alençon; and Elizabeth had begun to show a certain reluctance towards the match, though the change in candidates could hardly be held to account for the alteration in her attitude.

During the previous year the revelations and events which had followed Northumberland's insurrection had not been such as to cause her to draw back when she found that she could not have the particular French prince whom she had chosen. A clever counterplot by Sir John Hawkins had discovered the readiness of the King of Spain to invade England with his Flanders army whenever the time should be ripe for such a venture; and the Spanish Ambassador had been given four days in which to leave the country. Nor could she any longer regard the problem presented by the presence of the Queen of Scots in England with the scornful confidence with which she had written of her not so long ago:

> The daughter of debate,
> That discord still doth sow,
> Shall reap no gain where former rule
> Hath taught still peace to grow.
> No foreign banished wight
> Shall anchor in this port:
> Our realm it brooks no stranger's force;
> Let them elsewhere resort.

The Duke of Florence had obligingly forwarded the details of a conspiracy, organized by a busy young man named Ridolfi, which proved that the Queen of Scots was up to her neck in a plot to kill her royal cousin and seize the English crown, and that the Duke of Norfolk was deeply implicated in the affair. Lenox, the Protestant Regent in Scotland, had been murdered by Queen Mary's partisans. Burghley had escaped assassination by mere good luck. Norfolk had been tried in Westminster Hall, where the pine torches had flared and sputtered in the January twilight, and been convicted of high treason. The House of Commons, Sir Henry Sidney being a member of the special committee on the matter, had resolved upon the attainder of the Queen of Scots.

In France at the same time Catherine de Medici, who was determined that she alone should rule through her feeble son, had found the Guises neither to hold nor to guide. Allied with England she could check them, as Elizabeth with her aid could countercheck the machinations of their niece in England and Scotland—while England and France together, with the advantage of holding the interior lines between the Pyrenees and the North Sea, could present against Spain an impregnable defence. A treaty was drawn up, and Walsingham and Sir Thomas Smith signed it for England. In it the Queen of Scots, who had for so long been a precious piece in the French diplomatic game, was not so much as mentioned. King Charles remarked unfeelingly that she would never rest until she lost her head.

A French army seized Mons. The Dutch fleet captured Brill from its Spanish masters, and Flushing and other Flemish towns rose in revolt. Elizabeth began to draw back. She had accomplished what she desired by involving France in hostilities with Spain; the Duke of Alençon, who had taken Anjou's place as her suitor, was small, pock-marked, vicious, and young enough to have been her son; and she did not like to see rebels become too successful—not even rebels against a sovereign who was her secret enemy. She ordered off her coast the Dutch vessels which had been preying thence upon the Spanish commerce. She patched up a treaty with Alba, which reopened the ports of Flanders to English trade. As to the Queen of Scots she still hesitated, though her clergy in convocation reminded her that Saul was punished by God for sparing Agag because he was a king. Burghley, sick with anxiety, had himself carried into her presence in a litter to protest against her procrastination.

To Catherine de Medici, whose mind was quite as vigorous, subtle and feminine as hers—and even more unscrupulous, it became clear that the chains of holy wedlock would be none too strong to bind her to the new alliance. So Lincoln and his attendant lords and gentlemen were welcomed with distinguished cordiality. They were lodged in the Louvre, which was stuck just then between being the stout little Gothic castle of its mediæval past and the spacious Italianate palace which the kings of the Renaissance had intended to make of it. In the courtyard, like a sign of the times, yawned the hole left by the destruction of the ancient keep, that "fine, large tower and good for shutting up great men." But one corner was filled with the light grace of the new architecture of the South, which must have afforded pleasant quarters for the visitors.

The embassy was entertained by the King at his "château of Madrill," where the King, his brothers of Anjou and Alençon, the Earl of Lincoln, Walsingham, and Sir Thomas Smith dined alone together. There were comedies, concerts and splendid banquets without number. Another marriage, that of Margot, the King's sister, with the young King of Navarre, was to take place in August; and at court they were already celebrating this symbolical union of the Catholic and Huguenot factions which had been disrupting the nation for a decade. Lincoln took his departure, loaded with presents and carrying in his memory the expression of the King's hope that his sister's marriage would soon be not the only one which they could rejoice over.

Philip, meanwhile, had been established at Walsingham's house for a prolonged stay. The King and the court retired to the country for the hot weather, and he was free to devote

AN ENGLISH ARMY ON THE MARCH

from John Derricke's "The Image of Irelande," 1586

THE MASSACRE OF ST. BARTHOLOMEW

from a painting by F. du Bois (d. 1584), *who was probably an eye-witness*

by courtesy of the Museum Urland, Lausanne

himself to the sights of the city, whose quarter of a million inhabitants made it by far the largest he had ever seen. It was still, like London, a city of the Middle Ages, with tall, timbered houses thrusting out their successive stories over the narrow, winding streets and the stone turrets of the nobles' great hôtels blocking the small slits of sky at the end of tortuous alleys. The jumble of steep roofs and pointed gables bristled with church spires; and at night the watchman marked the hours with the exhortation:

> Réveillez vous, gens qui dormez;
> Priez Dieu pour trépassés.

Even beyond the walls to the westward, where the Queen Mother's palace of the Tuileries lifted its low walls and spread its gardens between the river and the tile and pottery works which gave it its name, the suburb of Saint-Honoré was crowded with the buildings of the religious orders and the houses of the nobles. Within the city the Salle du Légat and the Hôtel de Ville with its one completed pavilion and its central hall under a temporary roof were almost alone in their promise of the airy spaciousness which was to be full three centuries in realization.

It was August before the court returned. Then all Paris hummed with preparations for the wedding. Nobles and great men, diplomatists and scholars and poets, Huguenots and Catholics, came crowding in. Walsingham took his young guest to court, where "the graver sort," it is recorded, were delighted by the wit of the handsome English boy and by the fluent colloquial French in which he expressed it. It would be among the graver sort, the Huguenots and the more liberal and thoughtful Catholics, that he would be introduced by the English Ambassador who had chosen a Continental exile for himself during the entire reign of Catholic Mary Tudor. But there was nothing of the sour puritan about Francis Walsingham; and one did not have to be a narrow-minded kill-joy to be ranked with the serious-minded at the court of the Valois kings of France.

Philip became acquainted with Coligny, the great Huguenot leader, with Teligny, his son-in-law, with Ramus, the critic of Aristotle, and with many another whose life was to be stabbed and hacked out of him before the month was gone. There he met Coligny's beautiful seventeen-year-old daughter, Louise de Teligny, of whom he was to be the trusted friend years later, when she had become the widow of William the Silent. He learned the worth of Michel de L'Hôpital, the grandly tolerant former Chancellor. Young Condé, less than three years his senior, was his friend, and so was the young King of Navarre, who had come into the world not quite a year before him, and of whose feeling for him it was written that "he found out this master-spirit among us and used him like an equal in nature." So says Fulke Greville in his biography of his friend, evidently thinking of a later time. For one must wonder what those two made of each other at this meeting: the studious English lad, fastidious and gentle, and the lusty, peasant-trained youth from the Pyrenees with his bawdy jokes about the preference of his prospective bride for another suitor.

That other was young Henri, Duke of Guise, head of the Catholic party. "Of his family it was said that its members made other princes look plebeian, and of him that France was mad about him." He had a difficult rôle to play in these days. Not only must he watch the Princess whom he loved, and who loved him, married to a rather boorish heretic, but he must extend the hand of friendship—which he did—to Coligny, whom he believed to be responsible for the assassination of his father. He bided his time, however, and to good purpose, at least so far as his political projects were concerned. For, as Coligny's influence over King Charles grew stronger with every passing day, the Queen Mother had less and less reason to be satisfied with this Huguenot scheme which she had devised to keep her power from the clutching hands of the house of Guise. There was talk of sending Coligny against the Spaniards in the Netherlands at the head of an army of united Frenchmen; and Catherine de Medici was not the person to accept such a state of affairs without a struggle.

Now past fifty, stout, and red-faced, with dull eyes, flabby cheeks, a white neck and beautiful hands, her presence must have been a sinister one, especially when she chose to be ingratiating. Philip must have heard about her in his father's account of his embassy to the French court in 1562; and her ten years' struggle for power since then, a hated foreigner and the widowed mother of many helpless children, cannot have made her more pleasing. Seven years later he wrote of her as "the Jezebel of our age." But this was doubtless owing more to the murderous wholesale treachery, which at this time she can hardly have begun to meditate, than to his observation of her, for which he now had ample opportunity.

He was much at court. The King had taken a fancy to him and made him a baron and "gentilhomme ordinaire de notre chambre . . . considerans combien est grande la maison de Sydenay en Angleterre." The Earl of Leicester's nephew had, in other words, been made a pawn in the game of Anglo-French rapprochement. The appointment assured him a good place on the scaffold which was built in front of Notre-Dame and hung with cloth of gold for the royal wedding, since the bridegroom's religion prevented it from being solemnized within the walls of the cathedral. The bride, who was so beautiful that no less a conqueror than Don John of Austria said that the conquest of her would be worth more than the conquest of a kingdom, wore a dress of royal ermine. Three princesses bore the blue velvet of her five-yard train. But the story went about that her only acknowledgment of the nuptial vows was made when the King, her brother, pushed down her head in a nod of assent; and an atmosphere of distrust and dangerous expectation hung over the banquets, the tournaments and masques that followed the ceremony.

People began to whisper once more of the death of Queen Jeanne d'Albret, the bridegroom's mother, who had come to Paris to do her shopping for the wedding in the early summer and had died with suspicious suddenness. Nor were the Huguenot consciences so clear of past offences that they needed to fear nothing by way of reprisal. There was the matter of the assassination of François of Guise for one thing and, for another, Coligny's march across the South of France two years before, when murder, rape, and unnamable outrage had equalled any of the abominations with which they could charge their adversaries.

Four days after the wedding the tension snapped with the roar of an arquebus in the Rue des Fossés; and Coligny, who was returning from a meeting of the Council, reeled into the arms of a friend. The bullet had torn off one of his fingers and shattered one of his arms. The assassin escaped, but the shot had been fired from the house of a supporter of the Duke of Guise and the weapon, which was found in the house, was identified as one of those issued to the Duke of Anjou's own guards. The King, boiling with righteous wrath and promising punishment for the perpetrator of the outrage, whoever he might be, took his mother to visit the victim of it. Queen Catherine was full of solicitude for him. She was glad, she told him, that the surgeons had been able to extract the bullet because—she added in her fine Italian way—they had said that they could have saved the late Duke of Guise if they had been able to do the like in his case.

Loud with suspicions and accusations, the Huguenots demanded justice upon Guise. With the bad manners which, curiously enough, the extreme evangelical is always so apt to borrow from the Old Testament Hebrews they thronged the court, demanding an investigation—which Catherine dared not face—in terms which drove the frightened woman to counsels of desperation. Dead was her hope of reconciliation by means of the marriage with Navarre. She held secret, hasty meetings with Guise and her son Anjou. She persuaded the King of the existence of a gigantic Huguenot conspiracy against his life, and that his only salvation lay in striking first.

The Prévôt des Marchands was sent for from Paris and given orders about closing gates, running chains across the streets and the river, and calling out the municipal troops at the appointed signal. As the twilight fell on St. Bartholomew's Eve, a little more than thirty-six hours after the attempted assassination, her arrangements were complete. Her secret was perfectly kept. Of the Huguenots a few, suffering from the sense of impending danger, left the city that Saturday; a few more sent off their dear ones, mothers, wives and children, whom most of them were never to see again; but to almost all it was incredible that they were not safe under their king's sworn safe-conduct.

Down at Walsingham's house in the suburb of Saint-Germain, on the left bank, they hardly heard the tumult that burst forth in the city soon after midnight: the alarm-bells clanging from every steeple, the shots, the clash of steel, screams, shouts, groans, the frantic pad of barefoot fugitives hunted from their beds with the thudding of booted assassins behind them. Only with the full opening of Sunday morning came the clear knowledge that the incredible had occurred. Refugees brought it: English merchants and their wives and children, English students, young English nobles and gentlemen, the Protestant pastors of the English colony, all bearing tales of miraculous escapes from the blood-spattered bands with white brassards and white crosses in their hats, that ranged the streets like packs of wolves.

The Ambassador's house became crowded, and yet it seemed but a doubtful refuge. The Paris mob was loose in its thousands, armed with pikes, muskets, swords and knives. They were hanging up women by the hair, tossing babies on their spear-points, filling the air with "strange noises and whistlings" as a lucky bullet brought some fugitive rolling down a roof or sent another bubbling to the bottom of the Seine, into which he had plunged to escape. A detachment of the royal guard clattered up to protect the English embassy. But Coligny had had a similar guard around his house, and in the city the soldiers were killing, shoulder to shoulder with the scum of the slums. The corpses piled up in the streets faster than the dripping carts could haul them to the river.

In the corridors of the Louvre the royal bride of less than a week had her nightdress spattered with the blood of a Huguenot gentleman who was cut down before her eyes. In the courtyard the morning sun glittered on pools of the blood of those who had trusted themselves to their king's hospitality. Blood ran in the gutters, gleamed between the cobblestones, oozed into the river, where it writhed and eddied around the piers of the bridges and in the shadow of the quays. Brave young Condé and gallant Navarre—princes of the blood though they were—only saved their lives by denying their religion at the point of the sword. And when at last the grisly work was done, the King, his mother and the court rode out to view the shameful spectacle of the mutilated body of Coligny, Admiral of France, hanging by its feet, naked, on the common gibbet of Montfaucon, while with a belated attention to what the opinion of the world might be they took steps to prevent his pickled head from being sent to the Pope as a souvenir of the blessed occasion.

The Pope had *Te Deums* sung and a medal struck to commemorate the event. When King Philip of Spain heard of it, he laughed—for the only time in his life, it is said—and well he might, for not only had so many accursed heretics been sent to their account, but a less astute politician than he was could see that now it would be many a long year before a united France would trouble him again. In England Elizabeth put her court into mourning, and the

French Ambassador passed between lines of silent gentlemen of whom not one returned his salutations or gave him a civil look.

It was one thing to hang rebels after an armed revolt, quite another to murder them in cold blood after swearing forgiveness and amity with them and guaranteeing their safety with one's royal oath. The Ambassador was handicapped in his explanations, moreover, by the presence of Huguenots who had escaped from Paris and from Rouen and other of the principal cities of France, where massacres by royal order had followed that of St. Bartholomew's Day. At the French court Walsingham coldly told the Queen Mother and the King that, if indeed they had believed the Huguenots guilty of plotting against them, they should have had them tried, not punished "with the bloody sword of murderers."

Thanks to the protection of the embassy, only two or three English subjects had been killed. But in England the anxiety of those who had friends or relatives in France was naturally intense. Burghley and Leicester signed an order of the Privy Council for Philip to come home at once; and his foreign travels would have ended then and there, if Walsingham, who had sent his wife and four-year-old daughter to England as soon as it was safe for them to make the journey, had not packed him off to Lorraine before the order reached Paris. Fortunately the Very Reverend John Watson, the Dean of Winchester, was travelling that way; and Walsingham wrote those at home that the clergyman would be a check upon one of Philip's servants of whom he did not approve. The Dean was doubtless a good companion in the circumstances, for he was so well versed in the ways of the world that with every change in the royal theology he had risen in rank in the church.

Philip spent that autumn and winter at Strassburg and Heidelberg in the soothing atmosphere of the upper Rhine country and the valley of the Neckar. He said afterwards that he wasted his time there. Certainly, if he made any serious attempt to master the German language in these months he did not succeed in doing so. Strassburg had a university which had been recently founded; even in the Germany of that day the University of Heidelberg was the oldest after those of Prague and Vienna. But it can be understood, if he found himself in no mood for study and seized upon the time to readjust himself after such a terrible experience. Its influence upon him lasted his lifetime. Combined with the revelations of the Ridolfi plot, those breathless narratives of the refugees who crowded into the English embassy through that long August Sunday imbued him with a lasting distrust and antipathy toward the Papal policy and a hatred of Spain as the prime mover behind it. Of those brave, new French friends of his nearly all were dead, murdered in cold blood upon the broken oath of the King from whom he had accepted distinction as an honour.

And the surroundings in which he now found himself were not such as to soften his judgments. Strassburg, a Free City of the Empire, had been holding Protestant services in its marvellous minster for fifty years, while Jacob Sturm von Sturmeck guided it unscathed through the perils of the religious wars. There Johann Sturm, the scholar, who was a correspondent of Burghley's, had Philip in his care. Heidelberg was the capital of the Count Palatine of the Rhine, an active and powerful champion of Protestantism. Melanchthon, Luther's great co-worker, had made its university the headquarters of German humanistic learning under the reformed religion. There had been published the famous *Catechism* which was so attractive to all men whose religion was a spiritual experience and not merely a philosophical system or a political expedient.

In March Philip moved on to Frankfort which, since the coronation of the Emperor Maximilian II there ten years before, had become the successful rival of Aix-la-Chapelle as the place where the German emperors should receive their crowns. It was the centre of the German book trade; and Philip lodged at the house of Andreas Wechel, the great printer, celebrated for his Greek and Hebrew texts, who had himself barely escaped with his life during those dreadful August days at Paris. Bound for Vienna in June, the young English student traveller stopped at Basle. Erasmus, who had made the University there the fountain-head of humanism in his day, and who lay buried in the cathedral, had frankly confessed that he was not of the stuff that martyrs are made of; and Montaigne a few years after Philip's visit found that different ways of administering the sacrament formed the principal topic of conversation. But at Constance, not so many miles farther on up the Rhine, was the scene of John Huss's martyrdom, where the temporal head of Christendom itself had broken his pledged word to a heretic.

In all these travels and sojourns Philip can have found few, if any, willing to defend or even palliate the enormity of St. Bartholomew's Day: not Count Louis of Nassau surely, a younger brother of the Prince of Orange, with whom he spent a day while he was at Frankfort; nor Henri Estienne of the great Geneva printing house, who was the author of the Greek *Thesaurus,* and whose honest scholarship had got him into trouble with Protestant and Catholic theologians alike; nor Hubert Languet, the diplomatic agent of the Duke of Saxony, who was Philip's fellow guest at Wechel's. It was Languet who had saved Wechel's life on St. Bartholomew's Day, and he had himself escaped death by grace of the protection of the Bishop of Orléans.

Born a Burgundian, Languet had studied at the Universities of Poitiers, Bologna and Padua. At Wittenberg Melanchthon himself had converted him to Protestantism. His travels had ranged from Spain to Lapland. Gustavus I of Sweden had offered him diplomatic employment. For the past fourteen years he had been the representative of the Duke of Saxony, organizing the forces of the Protestants, and pleading their cause with such energy at the court of

France that he had been especially marked down for destruction in the great massacre. Walsingham was his friend; so Philip might easily have met him at the English embassy. This summer of 1573, at Vienna, whither the Elector's business took him also, he cultivated eagerly the friendship of the attractive and intelligent young Englishman.

Fifty-five years old, childless, unmarried, he seems to have seen in Philip what many a man at his time of life has thought that he saw either in his own son or in some other promising boy, the opportunity to make out of him the man that he himself might have become had he known in youth what more than thirty years in the life of the world had taught him. He began to devote himself with anxious diligence to the development of those brilliant possibilities through the application of his seasoned knowledge and wide experience. He became Philip's constant companion and soon began to regard him as a kind of spiritual or intellectual son. He made sure that he missed nothing of importance at the Emperor's court, and directed his reading, his study and even his travels: vainly dissuading him from going to Italy but successful in exacting a promise that he would not visit Rome.

Between the two there grew up as intimate a friendship as can exist between a man in his fifties and a boy of eighteen. Their tastes were similar. Languet combined with his practical knowledge of affairs a love of learning, and his protégé was soon made acquainted with all the learned men of Vienna. Vulcobius, Abondius, Crato, who had been one of Martin Luther's intimates: their lasting friendship bears witness to Philip's promise and his charm. Estienne had given him a book of Greek maxims which he had written out in his own hand. Years afterwards Banosius, the biographer of Ramus, told him that the first sight of him in his travels had reminded the scholar of Gregory's famous "*Non Angli sed angeli*" at sight of some British captives.

It will hardly suffice to explain all this on the ground

that the friendship of an agreeable and studious youth, who was closely related to the most influential men in England, was worth the cultivation of these scholars of international reputation. There were always plenty of young Englishmen travelling on the Continent, many of them rich in their own right, whose patronage and influence were far greater than those of the son of the Lord President of Wales, nephew and heir to the Earl of Leicester though he might be. It was Philip Sidney whom they remembered, whose portraits they cherished, and to whom more than one of them wrote frequently and dedicated their books from this time until his death. If they ever saw that "toyful book"—as he himself called it—which he wrote a few years later, it must have drawn from them, at most, an indulgent smile. With their vast stores of laborious learning it can hardly have occurred to them that they would be rarely remembered three hundred years after their deaths but for their interest in its author.

"Nothing is impossible to your abilities," Languet was to write to him, when almost a year of acquaintance and correspondence had confirmed his judgment of his young friend. But even Philip's docility under instruction rebelled at last against this continual cultivation and supervision. In September he slipped away from Vienna on the pretext of a three days' trip to Pressburg and spent three glorious weeks on his own in a somewhat dangerous excursion along the Turko-Hungarian frontier, visiting the border fortresses and listening to the songs at wild, Hungarian feasts.

Perhaps nobody but a boy who has endured reiterated warnings against temptations which have no attraction for him and indiscretions which it would never have occurred to him to commit can quite appreciate the impulses behind this truancy. There was never the slightest danger that Philip would become "a spending sot, meet only to keep a tennis-court," which had been Cecil's fear for his son Thomas. But after so many weeks of intensive paternalism he had the need to call his soul his own.

Nothing in his life shows the wisdom and sweetness of his character more clearly than his sympathetic and even grateful tolerance of Languet's everlasting fussing over him. While he was in Italy the following winter; after his return to England; and even when he had been his queen's ambassador and was taking a man's place in the world in every way, the old man kept it up. Philip must not be too grave and serious; he must be careful as to what he ate; if he would go to one less dance a week, he would be able to write as often as Languet wished to hear from him. Had he intended that Languet should not hear of his going to Ireland? It looked like it. A necessarily imperfect knowledge of events that happened at a distance was never a bar to well-meant criticism. No situation was so complicated or so partially understood as to stay the flow of advice, admonition and gentle censure.

But never did Philip reply save with appreciation and patient explanation. Never does it appear that he forgot the affection which prompted this solicitude, or that it was a small price to pay for all the treasure of practical knowledge and tested wisdom which he gained by it. "I have derived more advantage from my acquaintance with you," he wrote to Languet in the following April, "than from all the time I have spent in my travels." Never does he show that he has been bored or irritated by it. It is quite as much to his credit as to Languet's that after his father and, perhaps, Walsingham the somewhat infatuated old bachelor diplomatist exercised the greatest influence on the development of his mind and character. Of him he wrote in some verses, when many years had mellowed their friendship:

> Languet, the shepherd best swift Ister knew,
> For clerkly read, and hating what is nought,
> For faithful heart, clean hands, and mouth as true:
> With his sweet skill my skilless youth he drew,
>
> . . . .

> He liked me, but pitied lustful youth:
> His good strong staff my slipp'ry years upbore:
> He still hoped well because I loved the truth . . .

Philip's "skilless youth" appears in the record chiefly in a row he had with his travelling companion, young Thomas Coningsby, who was afterwards to marry Philip's cousin Philippa, daughter of Sir William Fitzwilliam and Philip's paternal aunt Anne: a row which, like that between Horace Walpole and Thomas Grey on their grand tour, has been more important to biographers seeking to enliven their story than it seems to have been to the participants. A rascally innkeeper at Vienna appears to have asserted that he had not been paid, although Philip had given Coningsby the money to settle the bill. Coningsby had already departed; so Philip paid it again and rode after him in a state of mind that showed that he did not have all that red in his hair for nothing. According to one account the word "thief" passed at their meeting. If so, the misunderstanding was easily explained. When Languet heard of it, he suggested writing to the man. But Philip had worldly wisdom enough to reply that a fellow who was knave enough to perpetrate such a trick would surely have the effrontery to deny having done so. It was thus that they set out for Italy, Venice being their destination.

It is not always easy to remember that land travel in those days did not, as in these, consist of being swiftly borne from place to place without the smallest contact with the intervening territory. After centuries of neglect the magnificent Roman roads had subsided into the mud. Nearly all the bridges had disappeared. Wherever they would serve, the rivers were made use of for transportation. Rhine, Main and Danube formed a highway across the Empire, the boats being towed up-stream by men or horses. Otherwise every foot of the ground had to be covered by sheer physical effort, on foot, in the saddle, or by what can have been hardly less fatiguing, the jolting, springless stage-wagons that maintained a slow and halting communication between some of the most important towns over roads as bad as those in England before the advent of the automobile.

We forget all that this implies: the innumerable incidents of such journeys, the difficulties of finding the way, the exposure to the vagaries of the weather, the rivers to be crossed by ford or ferry, the danger from robbers and villainous innkeepers, from government spies and prying ecclesiastics. Travellers were cautioned to examine any large pictures in their bedrooms, lest these should hide a secret door or window which might give access to a thief; to place their swords beside their pillows on going to bed; and to avoid discussion of politics and religion with strangers. And one was advised to have one's doublet lined with taffeta, which was proof against vermin.

Every journey partook of the nature of an expedition in its adventures and hardships. But there were compensations, as everyone knows who has travelled on horseback in a thinly settled country: those thrills and delights of discovery and unpredictable episode, which can be attained in no other way. When Bryskett was growing old and Philip had become for him only a dear and treasured memory, that "natural Italian" recalled this journey with melancholy pleasure: how they rode,

> Through pleasant woods and many an unknown way,
> Along the banks of many silver streams,

scaling "the craggie rocks of th' Alps" and "still with the Muses sporting." The month was October. The lower hills must have been gorgeous; and they descended from the mountains into the warm splendours of a North-Italian autumn.

Philip seems not to have been greatly taken with either Venice or its inhabitants at first sight: Montaigne had been disappointed in it. But Philip was not well, and perhaps the weather was bad, when he wrote to Languet early in December that he expected shortly to return to Vienna. At all events he stayed on, selling his horses as not worth keeping, and began to study "the sphere and a little music," although Languet invited him to go with him to Cracow, where the Duke of Anjou, recently elected King of Poland, was soon to be crowned with tremendous pomp. Languet had arranged for Philip to be the guest of a promising young nobleman in the Polish diplomatic service. Italy, he added, was no use to a rising young statesman: it was so soon to be overrun by the Turks.

But, though Philip wrote back rather contemptuously of "all the magnificent magnificences of these magnificoes" and that, from the tapster up, the Italians were all discoursers, the Venice of that day cannot have failed to be intensely interesting to him. The substance of her glory was rapidly departing, but the semblance of it remained. In the war which she had just been waging with the Turks she had lost Cyprus. The skin of its defender, Bragadino, had been torn from his living body, stuffed with straw and flaunted from the mast of the Turkish flagship. But Tintoretto was this very winter painting his picture of the victory of Lepanto, for which the Venetian fleet deserved the most of the credit, and the arsenal of Venice was still the military wonder of the world.

The city was a neutral ground, where men of all nations, races, and creeds could meet and mingle, for there it was said, "no man marketh another's doings or meddleth with another man's living." Englishmen gathered there in such numbers that the Pope protested against the city's toleration of the presence of so many heretics. Flagellants and Turks, Jews and infidels, diversified the throngs beneath the marble balconies of palaces in streets so clean that one could walk them in silk stockings and satin slippers. Soloman the Jew, the Sultan's physician, was there, negotiating a treaty of peace, and the Sultana Safiye, a Venetian lady of the house of Baffo, was assisting in the negotiations. Titian, ninety-six years old this year, who was a boy in his teens before there was any New World and in his forties before the Reformation, was still painting, with three years more to wait for the Plague which killed him. Palladio, Tintoretto and Paulo Veronese were flourishing.

"Let not thy sons pass the Alps," wrote Lord Burghley. Ascham said that he saw more liberty to sin in Venice in nine days than he ever heard tell of in London in nine years. For some reason the moral atmosphere of Italy seemed to be especially deadly to Englishmen. The Italians had a proverb about it, which Philip himself translated into:

> An Englishman that is Italianate
> Doth lightly prove a devil incarnate.

And the comedies of Shakespeare are strewn with allusions to the fopperies and affectations, and the vices natural and unnatural, which were brought back to England by those who had "swam in a gondola."

But when Languet wrote to protest against Philip's staying on, saying that one could not sit in the dirt and keep clean, it was the fear that his young friend might be converted to the Church of Rome that was troubling him. He knew quite well that there were other things that were of far more interest to Philip than the golden-haired, deep-breasted courtesans, whose numbers, beauty and wealth reflected a kind of sinister glory upon the city, whose wiles so terrified the traveller Coryat, and whose wickedness makes so interesting an episode in Thomas Nashe's *Unfortunate Traveller.*

By the Council of Ten Philip was given permission to bear arms within the dominions of the Republic. Some of the splendid palaces of the Venetian merchant-princes opened their doors to him. The French Ambassador, Arnaud du Ferrier, was naturally civil to a gentleman of his King's bedchamber. Du Ferrier was sixty-five years old. He was a liberal where religion was concerned. As the representative of Charles IX, he had departed in anger from the Council of Trent, when he had been compelled to yield precedence to the envoy of the King of Spain. So there were at least two points of sympathetic contact between him and Philip. He wrote to Languet of the young Englishman, praising him highly.

But there was Sir Richard Shelley too, the last Grand Prior of the Knights of St. John of Jerusalem in England. Languet may have seen a dangerous influence on Philip's Protestantism in one who had been a member of that great company of exiles for conscience' sake which the Duke of Feria had conveyed out of the country at the beginning of Elizabeth's reign. Shelley's must have been an interesting and attractive personality to any intelligent young man. He had travelled overland to Constantinople with the Venetian Ambassador in his youth: the first Englishman to visit the city, he maintained, since its capture by the Turks. He had been in Spain and at Vienna in the service of Philip II, and at Malta soon after the knights of his order had stemmed the Ottoman tide by their famous defence in 1565. Now he lived at Venice, but he longed for England, refrained from assuming his title of Grand Prior, which had been abolished by English law, lest it should prejudice Elizabeth against him, and furnished her with secret intelligence of the Jesuit intrigues against her throne in the hope of being allowed to return and privately practise his religion there. Philip called him cousin and saw a good deal of the pathetic old man, who died at last without returning to the home where all his old friends were persecuted recusants.

Early in January (1574) Philip moved on to Padua, where he took a house and became a student at the University. He wrote to Languet on the thirteenth of the month, marvelling at the speed of Languet's letter, which had already reached him, although it had been written only on the first! Languet warned him against geometry as "likely to wear out the powers of the intellect," an opinion held by many a younger and less learned student before and since that day, and advised him to spend his time on German rather than Greek. The English ought to learn German: the German nation was already the most powerful in Europe and was still growing. As for Italian, were the English afraid that the Italians would not take their money unless they spoke their language?

He thought that Philip's Latin style was improving—they wrote to each other in Latin—but warned him against neglecting to cultivate the Continental pronunciation of that language. Let him pay his teacher a small fine for every slip. But above all let him guard against his tendency to a seriousness which was excessive for one of his age and occupation. He must really strive to cultivate enlivening companions. Meanwhile Languet was missing him terribly, had again seen a certain portrait of him at Abondius's house and had been moved to write verses on it—he who had never written verses in his life before!

To all of which Philip replied good-humouredly from time to time. He wished to get only enough Greek to be able to understand Aristotle, he said, and would no more than "peep through the bars" of geometry for so much of it as he might need in war. German he absolutely despaired of: its harshness repelled him. But he would practise speaking it each day at dinner. He promised to have his portrait painted for Languet, but could not in modesty consent to having his friend's verses inscribed on the canvas. Meanwhile Languet might have the sketch of him which Abondius had made. The promised portrait was begun late in February by "one Paul of Verona," and Languet received it in May. He considered it too thoughtful and sad, also that it made Philip look younger than he was, more as he must have looked as a boy.

But life at Padua can hardly have been depressing. Tilting and combats at the barriers divided with the courses of the University the attention of the young gentlemen students; and Philip, to whom the knightly exercises were always a delight, considered the Italians pre-eminent in horsemanship, vaulting, and the use of weapons. There was, moreover, a daily boat service by which the foreign students could escape from the university atmosphere to the gay distractions of Venice whenever they felt disposed to do so, for the authorities left it entirely to them as to getting their money's worth for the tuition which they paid. As companions of his own age Philip had Coningsby, Robert Corbet, the older brother of his schoolmate Vincent, and for part of the time Philip Louis, Count of Hanau, who had already attracted some attention as a supporter of the cause of the Reformed Religion.

When the Count rode away on a tour of Central Italy, as he did late in the winter, Philip regretted the promise not to go to Rome, which Languet had extracted from him, but he kept it. Instead, he made a trip to Genoa and back, visiting Florence and Milan on his way. Bryskett had connections at Florence, which must have helped his sight-seeing there, and Genoa must have been absorbing from a military point of view, though Languet wrote sourly that, since England was helping the rebel Hollanders, it would be safer for him to keep out of places dominated by Spain, and that all he would get at Genoa would be the sight of ships fitting out against his Protestant friends and "the music of the fetters that bind the poor rowers" in the galleys.

Back at Padua once more Philip planned to meet the "Bishop of Acqs," the French Ambassador at Constantinople, who had just arrived at Venice. He expected the Count of Hanau to return soon and hoped that they could leave together for Vienna immediately after that. But Hanau, when he came, towards the end of May, postponed his departure for three weeks. Languet began to worry about the effect of the heat of the Italian summer on Philip's "spare frame" and saw an added danger for him in his fondness for fruit and the drinking of large quantities of water. Let him beware of fever and dysentery; it was hot even in Vienna; and Philip had better follow the storks.

Five weeks later, with an honesty that would make any mentor lovable, he confessed in another letter that he himself was suffering the consequences of "yesterday's excesses." The arrival of the new King of France, who had entered Vienna riding in the same carriage with the Emperor, had set the diplomatic corps all agog and, "hurrying about . . . in all this heat, we sometimes drink more than is altogether good for our health."

The new King of France was Henri, the former Duke of Anjou. "Our King of Posts," as Languet had called him in mild derision, had reached Poland in February and been solemnly crowned. But since then a wax figure of his brother Charles IX, transfixed by a needle, had come to light at the French court, and Charles had died soon after, leaving his throne to his brother at Cracow. The reluctance of the Poles to lose a sovereign whom they had so lately acquired had caused the departure of King Henri III from among them to be characterized by the haste and dangers of a flight. But now that he was safely out of their reach he determined to visit Venice before returning to France.

Immediately Languet grew busy, enlisting for Philip the friendship of various members of the royal suite, and wrote, urging him to make use of all his friends at Venice to get himself presented to the King. Du Ferrier's friendship should greatly further the business. Philip must overcome his natural bashfulness. For the presentation would be of the greatest value, if he should be sent to France on a diplomatic mission at some future time.

Venice put forth all her gorgeousness for the King's reception. Palladio designed the triumphal arches; Titian supervised the decorations; the Doge went out to meet the King in the *Bucentaur*, "the golden galley" of state; there was a galley specially built to convey the royal guest; and barge-loads of golden-haired, white-shouldered Venetian beauties graced the scene. But Philip had fallen ill, as Languet feared that he would. He had narrowly escaped pleurisy and was still feeling wretched. To do as Languet urged, moreover, involved his principles and his prejudices. It is true that to his mind, as to the mind of any other gentleman of his time, a king was a king, what though he had been a bloody-minded cutthroat before the sacred oils had made him into the Lord's Anointed, the Source of Justice, and the Fountain of Honour. But there was no such miraculous metamorphosis to charm away the guilt of those about him, the supple courtiers who had been drabbled by the blood of St. Bartholomew's Day, and to whom Philip must be facile and pleasant if he should do as Languet wished.

Of these the Seigneur de Pibrac, lately the King's chancellor in Poland, stuck hardest in his throat. The Poles had chased their sovereign and his suite all the way from Cracow to the frontier with a troop of Tartar mounted archers, and the unfortunate Pibrac had been compelled to hide all day, up to his neck in a swamp, and had narrowly escaped having his nose cut off by the barbarous peasantry. His hands were guiltless of the blood of any Huguenot. But he had written a defence of the St. Bartholomew massacre; and for that Philip loathed his name.

Languet wrote a gentle admonition against going off half-cocked in judging a man. Pibrac, he reminded Philip, had actually sheltered certain Huguenots in his house. He had spoken against the massacre at great personal risk. He had, indeed, written in defence of it, but only because it would have cost him his life not to do so. And Languet added that, for his own part, unless a man was utterly depraved, he selected his good qualities and thought of his errors and weaknesses as little as possible. It was good advice for the young man whose intentions were always so righteous and benevolent that it seldom occurred to him that they might be mistaken or misdirected.

He went through with the business. King Henri III confirmed him in all the honours and dignities which had been conferred upon him by King Charles. But "the Baron de Seydenay the younger" never wrote himself other than plain Philip Sidney until the touch of his queen's sword upon his shoulder permitted him to add the title of knighthood. He had bowed down in the house of Rimmon, since by so doing he would be able to do Jehovah better service, but he had no wish to remind himself of the compromise.

CHAPTER VII

"*A BOW TOO LONG BENT*"

THIS ITALIAN YEAR OF PHILIP'S WAS RICH IN INTELLECTUAL experiences. At Venice he crossed the old trail of Jacques Amyot, who had worked with the Greek manuscripts there in translating Plutarch for King François I. During the months of Philip's sojourn at Padua, Paolo Sarpi was often in the city. So, too, was Torquato Tasso. The latter was engaged in finishing his *Jerusalem Delivered*, and the former had still to launch his attack upon the heaped-up abuses of a thousand years, which sheltered the Sacred College. But already both men had sufficient reputation to excite the interest of a young Englishman who loved poetry and who, like many other cultivated and tolerant men of the day, did not consider the cleavage of the Reformation to be necessarily a permanent one. It had been chiefly owing to King Philip of Spain that the Council of Trent had refused to make concessions with regard to the marriage of the clergy and the giving of the sacramental cup to the laity; Queen Elizabeth had not altogether ceased to play with the possibility of reconciliation with Rome; and, politics apart, many of the theological differences involved did not appear to be of great importance to many of her leading statesmen and supporters.

Philip himself had come to understand that the Pope was human and, in his personal life, "what is called a good fellow." So much has been written, however, about the young man's thoughtfulness and seriousness at this time that it is easy to get a one-sided impression of him. He was no pedant, and the constant interchange of small jokes that passed between him and Languet in their letters shows that he was not lacking in humour even at the generally humourless age to which he had now attained. One episode of the winter amused him greatly. An Italian brought out a book called *The French King's Stratagem,* which was written with true Italian admiration of the duplicity used at the massacre of St. Bartholomew's Day. But the guilty consciences of the French caused them to see in it an ironical attack, and they were so successful in persuading the Pope to suppress it that Philip had trouble in getting a couple of copies of it for his friend.

The study of heraldry and pageantry lightened his application to mathematics, Greek, Latin, biography and history. He would have sympathized with Tranio's advice to Lucentio in that same Padua, as Shakespeare related it in *The Taming of the Shrew:* not to let Aristotle make Ovid an outcast quite abjured, but to balk logic with acquaintance, practise rhetoric in his common talk, and quicken himself with music, while he fell to mathematics and metaphysics as his stomach served. Delighting in learning as he did, he could safely adopt the principle that "No profit grows where is no pleasure ta'en."

International politics were his constant preoccupation, however: and in these Languet kept him informed of the latest developments. Soon after Philip's arrival at Venice the old diplomatist had written him that "Satan is beginning to gnash his teeth because he sees his kingdom tottering." Things were not turning out well for the Powers of Darkness in France and Belgium, Languet believed. England was profiting by the disorders in those countries; Alba had been relieved of duty in the Netherlands, and Requesens, his successor, was promising immunity to all who "shall give themselves up to be tortured." Holland and Zeeland remained loyal to the Prince of Orange. The Emperor was planning to expel the Italian monks from his dominions.

But things did not go on so cheerfully as the new year advanced. In April Languet took to writing of the wickedness of the Pope, whom he held responsible for all of Europe's troubles from the execution of Egmont and Horn in Brussels in 1568, through Alba's policy in the Netherlands, to the St. Bartholomew massacre and the present disruption of affairs, which laid open not only Italy but its neighbour states to conquest by the Turk. The situation was not, indeed, a promising one from the Protestant point of view. John Knox, that Hammer of the Lord, had died in November 1572. Although the "Beggars" in the Low Countries had made the Spaniards feel the strength of their sea-power, a Spanish fleet of sixty sail was fitting out in the Bay of Biscay. In France Catholic and Huguenot were again ready to fly at each other's throats; young Condé was a fugitive, Navarre still a prisoner at the French court, where they wore armour under their silks and satins: so deadly was their fear of assassination.

An English army had marched to Edinburgh, breached the castle wall with a battery in Princes Street, and hanged the commander, who held the place for the Queen of Scots, at the cross in the High Street. But in England the Scottish Queen was now treated less like a prisoner than a guest; and Elizabeth, who had soon so forgotten the horrors of St. Bartholomew's Day as to stand godmother by proxy at a French royal christening, had ordered the return of Sir Humphrey Gilbert and the rest of the English volunteers who had entered the Dutch service. English depredations in the West Indies had been balanced against the Ridolfi plot. The doctrine that an English ship was English soil had been so far accepted that the crews of English vessels were now safe from the Inquisition in the ports of Spain. Philip II was thus left free to fall upon the Protestants of the Continent. The Turks alone might hamper him in doing so, but only if they succeeded in making peace with Persia. And if they should succeed in that, all Southern Europe might well expect to be overrun by them.

In reply Philip admitted that the age was like a bow too long bent, which would break if it were not unstrung.

The state of Europe, he said, was such that a man who was not moved by it must be classed with the gods or the brutes; but the wisest men, Socrates and Sir Thomas More, had jested in their hour of death. So let us be merry, he proposed, and went on to tell how the Spanish garrison which Don John of Austria had left in Tunis "were shivering in spite of all the heat" at the prospect of an attack by the Turks. He rallied the old man gently upon his forebodings, advising him to consult his own good judgment as an antidote for them. The Huguenots were doing well in Aquitaine. As for the horrors in Belgium, it was better that Saguntum should burn than that false Hannibal should seize it without a struggle. Finally, should the Turk capture Italy, an infected and infectious member would thereby be amputated from the body of Christendom; the warring princes would be forced to unite against the common danger; and "this baneful Italy would so contaminate the very Turks . . . that they would soon fall down of themselves from their high place."

But early in May this gay mood was wiped out by the news of the Protestant defeat at Mook in the Netherlands, which Philip got "from no obscure persons, but even from the Council of Ten." On the very day when he was writing to Languet so cheerfully, the Spanish general d'Avila had destroyed the army led by Count Louis of Nassau, with whom Philip had spent that day at Frankfort but little more than a year ago. The details of the affair were not such as to make his grief less bitter. Seeing his army routed, the brother of the Prince of Orange had gathered a handful of the most resolute about him, at their head had hurled himself against the victorious enemy, and had never to any certain knowledge been seen again. There was a rumour that he had crawled from beneath a heap of the slain on the following day and had been murdered for his gold chain by ghoulish peasants while he was washing his wounds on the bank of the Meuse. But his body was never found.

Philip took what weak vengeance he could by writing

to the Earl of Leicester of the results which the Spaniards at Venice promised themselves from this victory. To Languet he wrote, "Believe me, my dear Hubert, I have never seen a silly woman exulting at some unexpected piece of news more than some of these Spaniards are doing at this." They moved him to add later that the Spaniards had always been slaves, with Romans, Vandals, Goths, Saracens and Moors for their masters; that it had taken a Belgian, Charles V, to raise them from the state of servitude; and that now they had sunk into it again. "God grant they may laugh with a wry face," prayed Philip, as he watched them forget in their exultation "the character of great moderation" to which they pretended.

At the end of July he had still not completely recovered from his illness, and his temper suffered accordingly. He showed so much annoyance when certain friends of his left Venice without calling to bid him farewell that Languet was moved to write him that he would always be angry with somebody, if he expected all men to be as courteous as he was. In August, however, he was able to join Languet at Vienna, though it was some weeks later still before he felt fit for that trip to Poland which Languet had been looking forward to making with him with so much eagerness. Years afterwards it was said that he took part in the Polish wars at this time, but he did not mention doing so in the letter about his Polish journey, which he wrote to Leicester. He felt that he might have travelled elsewhere with more pleasure and profit, he told the Earl.

When he returned to Vienna, he settled down for the winter, acting as a sort of under-secretary at the English embassy. Sir Thomas Challoner said of his four years as Ambassador at Vienna that in winter he lived in a furnace and in summer in a barn. But something must be allowed for the Englishman's traditional dislike of the climatic shortcomings of any country but his own. Philip, at all events, appears to have enjoyed himself thoroughly during the next few months. He was twenty years old this November. For companion he had Edward Wotton, the secretary of the embassy, who was only six years older. Wotton had spent several years in Italy and had been called "a creature of Walsingham" by the Spaniard Mendoza, who had tried in vain to discover his religious views. The Emperor's court was open to the two young men for pleasure and instruction.

Together they worked faithfully to perfect their knowledge of horsemanship under John Peter Pugliano, head of the Imperial stables, who held that soldiers were the noblest estate of mankind, and horsemen the noblest of soldiers. Philip later wrote a humorous description of him in the *Defence of Poesie*. No earthly thing, Pugliano maintained, bred such wonder to a prince as to be a good horseman. Skill in government was but a *pedanteria* in comparison. As for the horse itself, he described it as a peerless beast, "the only serviceable courtier without flattery, the beast of most beauty, faithfulness, courage, and such more, that if I had not been a piece of a logician before I came to him," wrote Philip, "I think he would have persuaded me to have wished myself a horse."

Under his instruction Philip became one of the best and most thoroughly grounded horsemen of his day and one who delighted in everything pertaining to the art. His *Arcadia* is filled with steeds whose curveting gives "such a glittering grace as when the sun in a clear day shines upon a waving water"; with milk-white withers freckled with red stains, "as when a few strawberries are scattered into a dish of cream"; and he describes the rider, centaur-like, who seemed "as he borrowed the horse's body so he lent him his mind," while "one might perceive the bridle-hand something gently stir; but, indeed, so gently as it did rather distil virtue than use violence," the spurs and wand mere "marks of sovereignty," and hand and leg "rather remembering than chastising."

And his knowledge did not by any means begin and

end in the saddle. Writing to his brother Robert, who was completing his education on the Continent six years later, he advised him as to horsemanship to give special attention to the fitting of bit and saddle and to the curing of horses, and promised him that, if he would read the book on equitation by Crison Claudio and one called *La Gloria de l' Cavallo*, he would profit more in a month than others in a year.

Vienna was an excellent place for information about political developments in the nearer East. Between Vienna and Venice letters were carried with such regularity that Philip had been able to count on receiving one from Languet on every Friday. A courier could come through from Constantinople to Vienna in twelve days. So Philip was in a position to give his "singular good Lorde and unkle" Leicester news that was quite fresh, if he could find anybody who happened to be going to England to carry his letter. The Turks were expected to advance in the Mediterranean rather than up the Danube the following summer, he wrote. The Papal dominions would be their objective. Since it would be Jubilee Year at Rome, their conscience, Philip suggested, might be moving them to "seek the benefit of Jubilee."

At the end of February in 1575 the Emperor made a long-delayed journey to Prague in the hope of getting his son crowned King of Bohemia. Languet and Philip followed the court. The Diet met; the air was thick with dickering; but while the Emperor hesitated, pulled this way and that by the Utraquists and the Papal Nuncio, Philip was summoned home. Some of those Venetian friendships of his, notably with Shelley and Don Cæsar Caraffa, who was a relative of Pope Paul IV, had started the story that he was in danger of being converted to Rome, and his family and friends in England had become alarmed. Languet wrote at once to Walsingham that these fears were groundless. To Philip, however, who was already on his way by the fifth of March, he sent a letter advising him to cultivate the acquaintance of the French ministers in the towns through which he passed, to invite them to visit him and to listen to their sermons, so that his position might be made quite clear.

Philip travelled by way of Dresden, and then retraced his steps of two years before, stopping again at Strassburg, Heidelberg and Frankfort, and renewing his friendship with Estienne and Wechel. At Frankfort Languet overtook him, and the two had a few more days together. Between Frankfort and Antwerp Philip fell ill again. But he still had his faithful Welshman Griffin Maddox to take care of him, and Edward Wotton, who was travelling with him, to keep him company; and "on the last day of May," as he wrote to his friend the Count of Hanau, "a fair wind wafted me to this our island nest." He sounds as if he was glad to be home again.

For us who read of the plots, conspiracies, attempted assassinations, rebellions, mutilations, headings and hangings and even burnings at the stake in England during those years, it is hard to realize that in comparison with almost any country of Continental Europe at that time Elizabeth's boast of the "still peace" that grew there was no idle one. There were no massacres perpetrated under cover of sworn faith; no killings without those forms of law which, hypocritical as they seem to us, at least prevented the setting up of a precedent for executions at the tyrant's whim; no civil wars in which the antagonists vied with each other in horrors of unmentionable abomination.

The pillory, the Tower rack, Tyburn with all its ghastly accompaniments of drawing and quartering, even the fiery stake itself, must have seemed short and sweet to one who had heard the delirious jibbering of culprits broken on the wheel and left upon it to die of thirst and pain and the mortification of their wounds in German market-places, or who had stopped his ears to the shrieks of men hung up alive in chains with two starved mastiffs tethered underneath them to feed upon their living flesh on German roadsides.

While Philip was in Venice the roistering sons of two noble families paid the penalty for a brutal and blasphemous debauch by having their tongues torn out and their right hands lopped off before they were decapitated in St. Mark's Square. The Englishmen of the time, discontented with many things as probably the majority of them were, had sense enough to know that they were better off under Elizabeth than they were likely to be after a civil war—with its inevitable participation of foreign soldiery, Spanish tercios, German "black ritters," or French Leaguers—had got through with them.

"She is to us a Meleager's brand," Philip wrote in his letter to Hanau; "when it perishes, farewell to all our quietness." To his twenty-year-old eyes this woman of forty-two was, "though somewhat advanced in years, yet hitherto vigorous in her health, which, as it is God's will that our safety should hang on so frail a thread, is with good reason earnestly commended to the care of Almighty God in the prayers of our people."

Philip told the Count that he found his family well. But his little sister Ambrosia had died in February at the age of ten. The Queen, in one of her few manifestations of kindness toward the Sidneys of which there remains a record, had written warmly to express her sympathy. She suggested that in order to remove young Mary, their sole remaining daughter, from the danger of "those parts of unpleasant air" at Bewdley and Ludlow she be sent to court to be under Elizabeth's own protection. So Philip found her, not yet quite fourteen years old, with her pretty, sharp oval face and reddish-golden hair set off by the white and silver dress of a maid of honour, already beginning to earn a court poet's opinion that:

> Though young in years, yet old in wit, a gest due to your race.
> If you hold on as you begin, who is't you'll not deface?

Philip's mother had not been well. The previous September she had written her husband's secretary what for her would once have been a timorous letter, asking news of Sir Henry's possible employment abroad or "contentful abode at home." Her "unrecovered unhealthful carcas," she told him, made her suffer in the inconvenient and uncomfortable lodging assigned to her when she was on duty at court. "Three or four linen peices of hangings" would have been a welcome protection against the cold. From the indifference of the Lord Chamberlain, her still not too friendly brother-in-law, the Earl of Sussex, who now held that office, she had appealed once more to Burghley's "great courtesies and noble dealings"; and she had been reduced to writing to her "servant" John Cokram for ten pounds.

Like the wife and mother in all times and in most families, gentle and simple, Lady Sidney seems to have borne the greatest stress of any financial stringency. Not that she ever lived in a style unbefitting the daughter of her father and the wife of her husband. She kept her coach and her house, "Colharbert" at Greenwich, "Carlillhouse" at Lambeth, or the one in "Chanon Row" at Westminster, when her duties did not require her to live in the palace. It was a question of ready money, not of solvency, for Sir Henry with a wise mistrust of debts diminished his patrimony more than once by the sale of land rather than follow the example of his brother-in-law Leicester and mortgage it.

The Sidneys seem to have been all much alike in their attitude toward money: it meant little to them except for what it would buy. To live splendidly and graciously in beautiful houses, surrounded by beautiful things, and to be generous in all their dealings, whether with servants, tradesmen or their sovereign, meant far more to them than the possession of large balances with the goldsmiths or the Italian bankers in Lombard Street. Philip on a travel allowance of two hundred pounds a year spent almost seventeen hundred in his three years' absence from home, giving his bond to Languet for enough money for his return journey. A few months later he paid his London tailor's bill for forty-two pounds by borrowing the money, and sent a boot bill of four pounds, ten shillings and fourpence to his father's steward. But we hear of none of the recriminations customary in such circumstances. In July father, mother, daughter and son set out together along with the rest of the court to accompany Elizabeth on her famous progress to Kenilworth.

They were like the movement of a small army, those royal progresses. Back in Edward VI's reign steps had to be taken to limit the number of persons participating in them. But it remained very great. For not only did it include the court attendants and their servants, the gentlemen pensioners and other troops of the royal household, but the government departments moved with the sovereign, that there might be no intermission in their business; the foreign ambassadors followed along, attended as their dignities required; and the great nobles with their swarms of gentlemen hangers-on and serving-men swelled the train to proportions which made it doubtful at times whether the visitation were the blessing it was supposed to be or a local calamity.

The sudden demand for oxen, calves, sheep, poultry, corn and other provisions was, of course, enormous. The supplying of carts for the transport of baggage and the furnishing of horses for courier service were most burdensome. The benefits of increased business in the districts visited were offset by the endless red-tape that enmeshed the payment of the requisitions of the royal pursuivants. Indeed, such were the irregularities of some of the latter that they answered for them before the Court of the Star Chamber until Elizabeth, jealous of the prerogatives of the royal household, put a stop to the proceedings. But even she had one of them hanged for forcibly taking provisions without paying for them.

For Philip the brilliant company riding through those hot, sunshiny days was as full of friends and relatives in high places as it had been when he made his first official appearance at Leicester's side during the Queen's visit to

Oxford ten years before. Elizabeth herself had welcomed him kindly on his return. Uncle Robert had promised him his powerful assistance. Walsingham, who had become his warm friend at Paris, was now sharing the office of Secretary of State with Sir Thomas Smith. The beautiful boy of the state entry into Oxford had grown to be a handsome young man of the world whose experience of Continental capitals made him quite at home in these splendid surroundings. He may have been a bit conspicuous in "his black Venetian velvet," but he was not, like the Earl of Oxford a few years later, so stupid as to make himself disliked by the affectation of foreign airs and a travelled superiority. "Most of us travellers," he told his brother Robert, when the latter was setting out for his Continental studies, were such that they would soon be made sport of in the comedies: "Marry! my heresy is that the English behaviour is best in England and the Italian's in Italy."

Neither Paris, Venice nor Vienna, however, had showed him anything more magnificent than the entertainments which his uncle had prepared in honour of his queen. The lake before the castle was spanned by a bridge, on which the attributes of all the virtues, the gifts of the Olympian gods and the compliments of the spirits of ancient Britain were showered upon her in living allegories. The days were gay with hunting, hilarious with the horse-play of a country wedding, thrillingly bloody with the baiting of thirteen bears by a pack of savage ban dogs. Every night was filled with feasting and the performance of comedies and ended with the glare and thunderings of fire-works.

The Lady of the Lake rose from the waters to do homage to her suzerain. "Certain good hearted men of Coventry," under the leadership of Sir Henry Sidney's versatile old friend Captain Cox, who was a master mason, a collector of plays and songs, "very cunning in fens," and the best "ale cunner" in the parish, gave their historical play about the overthrow of the Danes. There was an Hombre

Salvagio dressed in moss and ivy, who made his submission to the Queen by breaking his oak-plant of a staff with such vehemence as to frighten her horse. But:

" 'No hurt,' quoth her Highness." She was in grand good humour; and when the "harrowing" hounds drove a hunted hart into the pool, where it "was taken quick," she gave it "pardon of life," only commanding that its ears should be cut off for ransom. Up in London the next week they burned a couple of Anabaptists at the stake "in great horrour, crying and roaring"; but not even that brings out so clearly the tough fibre of the age as this light-hearted and wanton mutilation of a noble animal rendered helpless by its exhaustion.

In the apartments of Lady Sidney and of the other ladies-in-waiting, when they were not on duty, the evenings closed with small, cosy parties at which there were dancing and singing to the strains of the gittern or the virginals. The Council held its meetings: Burghley, whose son Thomas had served as a private gentleman at the siege of Edinburgh, had the satisfaction of seeing that rather unsatisfactory young man knighted, along with several others, by the Queen: and when the court moved on to Lichfield after almost three weeks of festivity, Sir Henry Sidney was made a member of the Privy Council and, three days later, Lord Deputy of Ireland once again.

While Philip was away his father had been leading the life he loved, correcting the abuses in his Welsh dominions, which had grown up in his absence in Ireland, repairing and enlarging the royal castles, improving water supplies, and collecting and preserving the antiquities of the country. But Elizabeth had soon found out once more that, if things had not run perfectly in Ireland under his government, they ran very badly indeed under that of his faithful but not so capable brother-in-law, Sir William Fitzwilliam, whose wife, Sir Henry's sister Anne, was said to be the real ruler of the country. Ireland had fallen into such a state that English vagabonds preferred hanging to service in the "winter war" that was being waged there. The Queen's parsimony had ruined a chivalrous plan of Walter Devereux, the Earl of Essex, for the colonization of Ulster; and he had written with bitter truth that no Irishman would ever trust Elizabeth again.

Very loath to go, and determined that this time he should be hampered by neither lack of authority nor want of funds, Sir Henry bargained sharply; and Elizabeth, who never treated her servants so well as when they stood up to her, finally agreed to his having a free hand and twenty thousand pounds a year for his administration. In August, while the court was making its leisurely way from Lichfield to Worcester, he set out. Philip went with him as far as Wales to see him off. At Shrewsbury the Corporation gave a banquet to the Lord Deputy and the young but already distinguished alumnus of its school, to whom they presented the small cash balance remaining in the entertainment fund after the festivities had been paid for. Philip witnessed his father's will on the twentieth of the month; and on September 8th Sir Henry landed in Ireland, where mutinous soldiery vied with insolent Irishry and proud Scots in such a "biene venum" to welcome him to the country that he could hardly find a safe place, he said, "to put my Heade in."

To make matters more difficult the Plague was abroad in the land, and "many dead of it in Dublin itself in the last two days." Soon it was the old story again, the worse for being a twice-told tale. There was no money left for Fitzwilliam, who had to borrow the wherewithal to get home. Within three weeks Sir Henry was once more dipping into his own pocket to meet government charges. Walsingham, who wrote him sympathetically of "the cursed destiny of that island," warned him to let his ears "be cooled against tale-bearers," for that nation, he learned, was cunning in that profession. But within three months the Secretary had to admit that there might be some truth in the Irish rumour of the Queen's backing out of her agreement with the Lord Deputy.

Sir Henry, meanwhile, had taken the field with his old-time energy, however, though the fact that he rode among the ruins of his former works would have made his task disheartening to a lesser man. In Knockfergus there were "no ploughs going, where before were many," and "the miserable state and servile fear" of the inhabitants were pitiable. The English grantees had become absentees, doing nothing for their land; so the Queen could expect no rent from them. Frequent "night stealths and some Daylight Bodraggs" harassed the borders of the county of Dublin. The county of Kilkenny was "the sink and receptacle of many cattle and goods stolen."

Sir Henry patched up a peace with the Scots, who under the rebel Sorley Boy had killed some English officers and men in September; another rebel, Rorie Oge, who had been wasting where he would, made solemn submission to the Lord Deputy in the Cathedral Church of Kilkenny; and Waterford received Sir Henry "with pompe as well upon the water as the land." At Cork, where he held court sessions from Twelfth Night until the end of January, people "were persuaded to leave their barbarity and wilful misery." Many Irish nobles and gentry came in to pay their court to him, as did also "the ruined relics of the ancient English inhabitants," Arundels, Barrets and others, as well as "many noble wives and widows, all keeping Christmas in plentious houses."

But it was late April of 1576, more than half a year after his departure, before he was back in Dublin; and he wrote of his journey as "pleasureless travell and toyle" in "this unhappy and cursed Estate." Munster he had found full of papists "of the malitioust degree and *novarum rerum cupidi.*" In Thomond there had been plenty of murder, rape, burning and sacrilege, which he had punished with appropriate executions. He did not cumber his letters to the Council, he explained, "with the name of each particular varlet" who had been executed or killed in the fighting since his arrival, but, he told them, "the number is great, and some of the best, and the rest tremble." "Hasten my money . . . the string to my bow," he begged; and he hoped for the return of Essex, whom the Irish held "both in honourable and dreadful terms." Essex and William Drurie would be "as two good wheels, holding up the South and West ends of this realms axeltree."

Essex had dreadfully earned his Irish reputation. One winter of the subtle barbarity of the natives had ruined his fortune and cured him of the idealistic enthusiasm with which he had undertaken his venture. Going on as Elizabeth's governor, he had crushed the O'Neils by massacre and treachery as foul as any of which the Irish themselves were guilty. While Elizabeth was feasting at Kenilworth, he had caused six hundred refugees on Rathlin Island, the women and children of the Scots who were in arms against him, to be put to the sword. Two of the brightest names in Elizabethan annals divide with his the shame of this atrocity. Francis Drake commanded the ships employed in it; and John Norris, a grandson of the Sir Henry Norris executed for adultery with Anne Boleyn, who was later to make so great a reputation in the Netherlands, received through Essex the Queen's praises as "the executioner of his well-designed enterprise." So at the name of Essex the Irish might well tremble. Sir Henry wrote to Philip to do all he could to expedite the Earl's return to the country.

After bidding farewell to his father at Holyhead, Philip had rejoined the court. With his family connections, his education, experience of foreign courts, acquaintance with foreign statesmen and languages, and his knowledge of Continental and, especially, Eastern European politics, a brilliant career seemed to be open to him. His mother now made her home at a house of hers at Paul's Wharf, but he lived chiefly this winter at Leicester House, which stood on the Strand, west of the Temple, in gardens of its own that ran down to the river. His father's transfer to him of the office of Chief Cup-bearer gave him a regular standing at court. His income from this and from one or two church livings, which he held as lay rector, was small, but his prospects as the probable heir of his uncles, Warwick and Leicester, were magnificent. He was in request at smart social functions like the christening of Lady Russell's baby, where he appeared as godfather, "with a towel on his left shoulder"; and it was at this time that Languet blamed the dances when he got no letter from his young friend for six months. There were also the distractions of the tilt-yard and the tennis-court, but Philip was not well and may have deserved Languet's warning against too much violent exercise.

Don Cæsar Caraffa wrote to him from Venice; Abondius and Clusius from Vienna. The latter, who was the botanist Charles de l'Ecluse, told him that they had drunk his health in a good wine and would drink it in a better when he came again. Languet's letters brought the latest information about European politics. But these things gave less than satisfaction to the earnest and ambitious young man, conscious of unusual powers, who had returned home eager to take a hand in that conflict which, either openly in arms or secretly by diplomacy and intrigue, was going on all around him.

Nowhere could he find an opening, however. His queen refused to be lured into the struggle, even by the offer of the sovereignty of the Netherlands, which was made to her that winter. Alençon, who had become Duke of Anjou when his brother ascended the throne, and who had come out for the Protestant cause in France, offered him service; but while Philip was considering this, Huguenot and Catholic joined in another of those evanescent treaties of theirs.

In the Earl of Essex, who was living at Durham House on the Thames just below Charing Cross, while he was attempting to restore his fortunes and strike out some new line of endeavour, Philip discovered a nature in many ways like his own. To both men great deeds were more attractive for the doing than for any of the material rewards to be won by them. Essex, who was the Lord Ferrers who had given Philip that fine new horse on which he had ridden to see the Queen at Oxford, was only thirty-six. His wife, the avid and impetuous Lettice Knollys, was cousin to the Queen on the Boleyn side and was regarded by her with more than cousinly dislike.

In her husband's absence the Countess had entertained Elizabeth at Chartley Castle in the previous summer, soon after the court left Kenilworth; and there Philip had met the little family over whom had not yet begun to brood those clouds of scandal and tragedy which were to darken their lives for a quarter of a century to come. The future Earl, who was to force his doting queen to send him to the block, was not yet eight years old at this time; his sister Penelope, the notorious divorcee of the court of James I, was only a forward minx in her teens; and their mother was still to entangle herself in the web of dubious circumstance surrounding the death of her husband and her secret marriage with the Earl of Leicester.

In Philip, Essex believed that he saw an excellent husband for his daughter. By the end of the winter he was calling him his son by adoption. The girl with her golden hair and bold black eyes that could dream or sparkle as she chose possessed a heady beauty which, a few years later, was to make Philip careless of all else in his desire to possess her. But he seems to have given no more than a languid acquiescence to this proposal of her father's. Perhaps he felt unwilling to complicate his life with marriage so early in his career. "What you write in jest about a wife I take seriously," Languet warned him. "Be not too confident of your firmness; more cautious men than yourself have been caught. For my part," the lonely old bachelor wrote affectionately, "I should be glad that you were caught, that so you might give to your country sons like yourself." As for Penelope, precocious, pas-

HUBERT LANGUET

from the painting at Penshurst

by courtesy of Lord De L'Isle and Dudley

sionate and enterprising, perhaps she was already too deep in her boy-and-girl affair with young Charles Blount to be interested in attracting the handsome, but serious and correct, young paragon whom her father recommended to her.

Meanwhile the Earl persevered in his determination to carve out a new fortune for himself in Ireland; and for once Elizabeth was sympathetic towards one whose services had been as misdirected as they were well-intentioned. After all, her supporters among the old nobility were not so numerous that she could afford to let one of them go down to ruin in her cause. She wrote to him appreciatively at a time when, as she said, she found "the most of men, as it were, a prey to delicacy." But Leicester had got the idea that Sir Henry Sidney did not really want Essex back again; Walsingham wrote to the Lord Deputy of the proposed arrangement that "the suddenness of both your judgements" made him fearful of it; Sir Henry, viceroy though he was, considered his own native rank too low to entitle him to offer employment to an earl of such ancient and exalted lineage as Walter Devereux's; and Devereux hesitated lest he seem to presume upon his rank in offering his services to Sir Henry. Such were the meshes of policy and high delicacy of feeling which Philip had succeeded in untangling when, on the 9th of May in 1576, the Earl's patent as Earl Marshal of Ireland was signed. Essex landed in Ireland in July, and Philip went with him to round out his education with a course in actual war.

For Ireland was to England in those days what the Indian Northwest Frontier has been to Great Britain in the past hundred years, with little wars continually simmering and sputtering within its coasts. Small reputation was to be gained there, except for failure. There were no pitched battles: one must go to the Continent to learn how to draw up a great army in formal array. But at a time when, in England, as Walsingham phrased it, "we ground our quietness on other men's harms" and "martial men bear no price," the young man who aspired to a military career could find a thorough training in the rudiments of warfare in Ireland. There he learned to scout and to collect information from the frightened and treacherous inhabitants of a hostile countryside, to deal with doubtful allies and to be sure that his sentinels, with matches burning and arquebuses in rest, were well-placed and alert. Or, if he did not, he got his throat cut the first time he was placed upon his own responsibility. Unpaid, half-mutinous soldiers taught him that tact is as important as sternness in maintaining discipline; and under Sir Henry Sidney it was made plain to him that consideration towards a beaten enemy will yield more lasting results than extreme severity.

Shortly before Philip's arrival the sons of no less a personage than the Earl of Clanricarde had gone on the warpath. Stealing away over the Shannon, they had cast off their English clothes and, donning their native saffron shirts and long mantles, had called out their friends and sacked Athenry with savage fury, burning the new gates and fighting among themselves for the privilege of smashing the arms of England, which were carved upon the stones. With his customary swiftness Sir Henry drove "the traitorous boys with their loose Rascal and Kerne . . . away to the mountains" and frightened Clanricarde himself into surrendering his strong castle. Within twelve days of leaving Dublin he was able to report that "instead of two beggarly boys" he had their father, an earl, and all his castles. He added that he hoped soon to have "these misbegotten brats . . . either quick in prison or dead in the field, or banished the whole land."

But Walsingham warned him of nine score galleys filled with Scots who were likely to join the rebels; and the Secretary recommended the use of severity, doing first and reporting afterwards, since at court, as Sir Henry had been suspecting, "our ears (underhand) are over much open unto Irish advertisements tending to the countenance of the disorderly government of that country." A few days later two thousand Scots had landed and joined Clanricarde's sons. Sir Henry was on the march against them, when Philip, with his war-horses Pied Pepper and Grey Synott, joined him towards the end of August.

It was indeed, as Sir Henry wrote modestly from Galway in September, "a kind of an actual war," and was complicated by "the hollowe Hartes" of the inhabitants, who had once been loud in their complaints against Clanricarde's boys, but would now give no information that might help him against them. The Scots had fled and hidden at his approach, however; and although he was "not a little wearied in tracing and searching the rebels from place to place," he hoped soon to be able to return to Dublin.

Philip missed the close of this brilliant little campaign. For news reached the Lord Deputy's headquarters in the field on September 20th that the Earl of Essex was dying at Dublin. Philip left the expedition and set out at once in the hope of seeing him before the end, but arrived too late. The Earl died on the twenty-first, lamenting on his daughter's account "the time, which is so vain and ungodly . . . considering the frailness of women, lest they should learn of the vile world." To Philip his last message was to "tell him that I send him nothing, but I wish him well, and so well, that if God do move both their hearts, I wish that he might match with my daughter. I call him son, he is so wise, so virtuous, and so godly; and if he go on in the course he hath begun, he will be as famous and worthy a gentleman as ever England bred."

It was three weeks since he had fallen ill. At first he had not taken his condition seriously. When the "grief in his belly" began, he remarked that he never had hearty grief of mind but a flux must accompany it; "the Irish looseness" was a malady painfully familiar to all who served Elizabeth on the farther side of St. George's Channel. He neglected to take proper care of himself, eating as usual, riding far and rapidly and making overnight visits to the Archbishop of Dublin and Viscount Baltinglass.

Soon his sufferings became dreadful to behold, though he struggled manfully to conquer them. "Courage!" he would cry out from time to time, "courage! I have fought the good fight." To the Queen he wrote: "God forgive me for Jesus Christ's sake. For three years I have lived very negligently, and have not served God, but have lived soldier-like. Although a soldier should fear God and serve him." The night before he died he called upon his musician to play upon the virginals.

" 'Play,' said he, 'my song, Will Hewes, and I will sing it myself.' So he did it most joyfully, not as the howling swan which waileth for her end."

It was a hymn asking for God's mercy, which he had composed in the intervals of his torments. At last, when he could no longer speak and his chaplain, praying aloud, came to the name of Jesus, "he held up both his hands, and with that fell asleep in Christ as meekly as a lamb." Sir Henry Sidney said that he had "never heard of a man die in such perfectness"; and when, ten years later, Philip lay upon his deathbed at Arnhem, the way in which he endured his sufferings and met his end makes one believe that he remembered then what had been told him of these sad days.

Chancellor Gerrard wrote to Walsingham that the Earl's disease "was thought by the three physicians it had been the flux; but in truth," the learned man continued, "it is the abundance of adust choler turned to a very melancholy humour, which, apostumated in some parts, turneth to his stomach." A severe attack of dysentery is probably what it would be called today, although the Earl's curiously modern precaution of drinking only boiled water with his wine makes this diagnosis less certain. But immediately the story ran about that he had been poisoned and that Leicester was the poisoner. The very timely demise of Amy Robsart had never been forgotten. The Queen's liking for Essex, Essex's ability and high-mindedness, his gallantry and pleasing manners, all seemed to supply a sufficient motive in the judgment of the myriad enemies of the jealous and not too scrupulous favourite, even before the revelation of his speedy union with Essex's widow increased the apparent probability of his guilt. But Sir Henry Sidney, after a careful investigation, reported that not only had Essex been dosed sundry times with "Unicorn's Horne," that sovereign remedy against poison, but the post-mortem showed no trace of poison. In the following February he wrote to Leicester himself concerning "the fals and malycyus Bruite of the Earl of Essex poisoning" that death was caused by "a meere flux, a disease appropriated to the country."

Philip returned to England not long after Essex's death. Probably he attended the Earl's funeral at Carmarthen in November. His keenest interest must now have lain in defending his father and mother against the mean intrigues of those who have been well described as "the eunuch race courtiers." There was need for him to do so. His father was in the field again, taking castles and driving "the beggarly Scots." He held Clanricarde a prisoner in Dublin Castle and hoped to prove him a bastard so that he could have him tried "by a Jewrye of common Persons." "Down they go in every corner and down they shall go," the doughty Lord Deputy had written early in the year. But "busy headed" lawyers were stirring up trouble for him at home; the return thither of Ormonde, though the Earl had dealt fairly with him in Ireland during the summer's troubles, did not help his standing with the Queen; and he was accused, among many other things, of encouraging disorders by granting too many pardons.

His letters went unanswered, or foul weather in the Irish Sea delayed the replies to them. His recommendations for the cheap and easy way of securing loyalty by the distribution of knighthoods and other honours seemed to be ignored. His lieutenants, forgetful of the conciliatory part of his policy, slew, burned and exterminated at every opportunity with appalling zest. In February, as if he had at last found his burden more than he could bear, "Good my lord," he entreated Leicester, "send Philip to me; there was never father had more need of his son than I have of him. Once again, good my lord, let me have him."

But by that time Philip had been given other work to do, and work better suited to his talents and his taste—much as he would have loved to help his father—than bushwhacking against the Irish rebels. The Emperor Maximilian II had died the previous October, and Philip was chosen to carry to the Emperor Rudolph II, his successor, the Queen's condolences and her congratulations on his accession.

CHAPTER VIII

FALSE DAWN

The Most Illustrious and Most Noble Gentleman,
Philip Sidney of England,
Son of the Viceroy of Ireland,
Nephew of the Earls of Warwick and Leicester,
Most Serene Ambassador of
The Queen of England to the Emperor.

SO, IN LATIN, BENEATH HIS COAT OF ARMS, READ THE TABlet which Philip, aged twenty-two years and a few months over, set up in front of his lodgings in the late winter of 1577, as he journeyed through the Low Countries and up the Rhine on his mission to the Imperial court at Prague. In its time it carried none of the air of ostentation which it bears to the modern eye. When Montaigne visited the baths in Lorraine as a mere private gentleman, his landlady asked for his escutcheon to put up in her house. Sixteen years earlier the Earl of Bedford had three dozen escutcheons prepared for a similar purpose, when he went on an embassy to France; and almost a generation later Sir Henry Wotton set up a tablet of the same kind wherever he lodged on the Continent.

Such things served as a courteous notice to the inhabitants and to other travellers of the presence of the personal representative of a reigning sovereign and of the consequent necessity of comporting themselves with appropriate circumspection. The mention of distinguished relatives reflected quite as much glory upon his queen as it did upon Philip: it showed that her envoy was a man of race and breeding, and not merely some distinguished lawyer or clever politician who had risen from the mercantile class or even lower station.

It was an age in which outward show and ceremony were regarded as essential to the proprieties; they even had a good deal to do with the comfort and safety of travellers. When the Duke of Feria took his young wife and infant son on the long journey overland to his Spanish home in 1560, he borrowed fifty thousand ducats for his expenses. He moved with two complete retinues of servants and a double equipment of furniture so that his lodgings were not disturbed until after each day's departure and at the end of each day's travel new lodgings were ready and waiting. But even this embassy of Philip's, composed though it was only of gentlemen, and gentlemen who were by no means unaccustomed to the fatigues of the road, cost his father eight hundred and forty pounds.

Fulke Greville, his old schoolmate, went with him. The others in his suite were older and more experienced. Edward Dyer, who had proved himself a staunch friend of Lady Sidney's, and who was soon to become a great intimate of his own, was one of them. Dyer had studied at Oxford, travelled abroad, and had been a considerable figure at court in the past ten years. Another member of the party, Sir Henry Lee, a nephew of Sir Thomas Wyatt, was still Queen's Champion at the age of forty-seven. Another was Jerome Bowes, who had served in the expedition to avenge the loss of Calais in 1558 and who, six years after this mission of Philip's, was to begin that sensational career as Ambassador at the court of Moscow which caused Samuel Pepys to hear about him from Russian visitors to England three-quarters of a century later.

Doctor Thomas Wilson, Elizabeth's envoy to the Netherlands, who had seen the inside of the dungeons of the Inquisition at Rome, rode with the young Ambassador from Brussels to Louvain. There Philip paid his respects to Don John of Austria, whom Greville regarded as "that brave and high-minded Prince" and Languet called an "illegitimate libertine." The haughty victor of Lepanto began by condescending to "this hopeful young gentleman," but he was not long in finding out that he was no mere good-looking pet moppet of the English Queen, sent forth in leading-strings, and ended by treating him with honour and respect.

Philip's ostensible mission was, indeed, a purely formal one. But he had made a condition of accepting it that he should be allowed to visit on his way the various Protestant princes of Germany and discuss with them measures for the protection of the Reformed Religion and of their own liberties against the encroachments of Spain and the Papacy. The formation of a Protestant League, a *Fœdus Evangelicum*, was what he had in mind, a project which he never ceased to scheme and work for.

At Heidelberg, however, where he arrived late in March, and where he might once have planned to lay the cornerstone of his edifice, he found things sadly changed from what they were when last he stopped there two years before. The wise and liberal Elector Frederick III had died a month before the Emperor, and his son Louis, a Lutheran, was more interested in rooting out of his domains the Calvinism favoured by his father than awake to danger from Rome and Spain. He was not at Heidelberg at this time; but when Philip on his way back to England saw him at Neustadt on the 1st of May, he could do little more than urge him to deal gently with his father's Calvinist clergy, and he wrote home that his hopes of a Protestant League grew daily less and less.

Meanwhile he cultivated John Casimir, the new Elector's Calvinist brother, who told him of a rumour that Don John was to marry the Queen of Scots as part of a Spanish project to conquer England. Philip had been instructed to try to collect a considerable loan which Elizabeth had made to the late Elector. He pointed out that prompt payment would be the best means of obtaining further financial assistance from his queen. But it appeared that the King of France had never paid a sum of eleven million francs, which he owed to the Elector Frederick for past services, and the best that John Casimir could tell Philip about the matter was that the French King's jewels, the collateral for that sum, had been put up as security for the overdue pay of his troops and could be bought at a bargain. Casimir himself, at odds with his brother on religious grounds, was about to lead his mercenary reiters to the French wars. He was determined, he told Philip, who evidently got upon terms of some intimacy with him, that he would perish in the conflict or leave behind him "a miserable France . . . of the papishe side."

Philip arrived at Prague on Maundy Thursday, just in time for the lugubrious pageantry of Good Friday and the splendid pomps of Easter. And again he had reason to be greatly disappointed by what he found there. For to a zealous believer that the success of the Roman Church meant the Spanish domination of Europe the changes which had taken place at the Bohemian capital since he left it were disheartening. Then the cautious and liberal Maximilian, who had refused the Catholic sacraments on his death-bed, had been bidding for the crown of Bohemia for his son with guaranties of religious freedom. Now that same son, stiffened by a Spanish education and dominated in such matters by a bigoted mother, was suppressing the Protestants wherever he felt that he could safely do so.

Only two years Philip's senior, a great collector of works of art, and himself something of a scholar and an artist in his own right, Rudolph II, who was to become the patron of Kepler and Tycho Brahe, might have won Philip's liking and admiration but for the political gulf that yawned between them. But after his formal audience on Easter Monday Philip wrote of him as sullen, secret, resolute, given to wars, lacking entirely his father's winning manner and, both him and his brother, "extremely Spaniolated."

Certain of Philip's biographers in the tradition of Puritan boorishness have saddled his reputation with the story that at this interview he delivered himself of a moving oration against the iniquities of Spain, to which the Emperor and his court are represented as listening open-mouthed. But surely in dealing with such a prince as Philip described, a young diplomatist far less acute than he would have had more tact than to commit such a blunder; and a prince far less hidebound than Rudolph II would hardly have rewarded the perpetrator of such an outburst, as the Emperor actually did reward the young Ambassador, with the gift of a very handsome and valuable gold chain.

He showed equal discretion in delivering his queen's condolences to the Empress Dowager and to her daughter, who was the widow of King Charles IX of France. Philip must have known the latter in those short, gay weeks at Paris when he was a gentleman of her husband's bedchamber; and it may have been the memories which the sight of him recalled that so moved her as to cause him to be brief in his address, lest the emotion of the Imperial and royal ladies should overcome their composure.

He found an old friend at Prague, his father's former protégé, Edmund Campion. After his escape from Ireland Campion had lingered in England long enough to see in the execution of the unlovely Doctor Story the punishment prepared for malignant recusants. Apparently strengthened by that atrocious spectacle, he had sought the seminary at Douai, acknowledged himself to be a Catholic, made his way to Rome on foot and become a member of those shock troops of the Counter-reformation, the Jesuits.

He was professor of rhetoric at the Jesuit college in Prague at this time, and he seized eagerly upon the opportunity to do the work of his order, which he thought he saw in renewing his friendship with the distinguished and highly-connected young Englishman. Perhaps he was misled by his hopes. Perhaps, like many another man of subtle force, he mistook Philip's gentle courtesy for a wavering of conviction. He wrote off to Doctor Nicholas Sanders, the leader of the English Catholic exiles on the Continent, expatiating on the value to their cause of such a potential convert and urging that arrangements be made in England "for the watering of this plant." The repercussions of his disappointment are to be read in the statement of his biographer that Philip promised at this time to help him, if he should come to England, but declined to do so when Campion found martyrdom there four years later.

Still another old friend whom Philip saw again on this journey was Hubert Languet. The old man joined him in his return from Prague and travelled with him as far as Cologne. In him Philip doubtless found a wise comforter of his disappointment at the lukewarm reception of his proposals by the Protestant princes whom he called upon. At Nuremberg he had a holiday from politics in the company of some scholarly acquaintances whom he entertained with "a very memorable discourse," as one of them described it, on the extermination in England of the wolves, which were still a dangerous nuisance in the rest of Europe, and another on St. Patrick's Hole in Ireland, which had been the goal of pilgrimages in mediæval times.

Philip had been eager to visit the Prince of Orange on his way home, but had reluctantly made up his mind that this would be exceeding even the spirit of his instructions. Now, however, he received the Queen's orders to do so. Perhaps Elizabeth, who had been treating the Prince as scurvily as she well knew how to treat a friend, felt a special sympathy for his new wife, whose marriage, like Anne Boleyn's, based its validity upon her husband's doubtful divorce from a former wife, the dipsomaniac and lunatic Anne of Saxony.

The beautiful and high-spirited Princess Charlotte of Bourbon-Montpensier, whom William the Silent had married two years before, had been shut up by her father in a convent at the age of thirteen. She had been forced to take the vows of the Order and had been made Abbess, but had run away shortly after to the protection of the Elector Frederick and remained at his court until her marriage. The Imperial Diet was scandalized by the match. The father of the mad Anne was naturally furious. Philip of Spain, not unnaturally, accused William of living in adultery with an infidel nun. But Queen Elizabeth to emphasize her approval sent her young ambassador to be her special representative at the christening of the child lately born of this union. Philip was one of the godfathers of the little princeling; the Princess added "a fair jewel" to his collection of honourable trinkets; and the Prince began to form the opinion, which he expressed to Fulke Greville some years later, that in Sidney Elizabeth had one of the ripest and greatest counsellors of state that lived in Europe.

This was all to the good for a certain project for the furtherance of the Protestant cause, of which Philip and Languet had talked long and earnestly as they walked up and down together beside the mouth of the Main a few weeks before. Philip had hardly been home a month before Languet began to make guarded references to it in his letters. Neither of them ventured to write about it except in terms too obscure to be easily understood by others. But soon it became one of those red herrings with which Elizabeth loved to confuse the scent of her foreign policy. By the following spring the new Spanish Ambassador, Mendoza, had got wind of it and forwarded to his master the report that Philip Sidney was to marry the sister of the Prince of Orange and to be made the Lord of Holland and Zeeland.

For Philip was still heart-whole and fancy-free. Back in the November of 1576 Edward Waterhouse, who was settling up the affairs of the Earl of Essex, had written to Sir Henry Sidney that, if the marriage between Philip and Penelope, which the Earl had hoped for, should be allowed to fall through, it would be a greater dishonour than any other match could repair. But so it was allowed to do, although Philip's Huntingdon uncle was Penelope's guardian and his Leicester uncle was courting her mother. Perhaps Sir Henry was too busy just then to engage in negotiations for the marriage of his son. But surely the chief reason is to be found in the indifference of the young man who, with the single-minded devotion characteristic of his years and temperament, seems to have been quite willing at this time to choose his wife for the good of his country.

Hymen had, however, been busy in his family during his absence. In February his father had written to thank the Earl of Leicester for the influence of his noble house in arranging a marriage between Mary Sidney and the Earl of Pembroke. With his "own mean lineage and kin," he gratefully admitted, he could never have managed so splendid a match. He would give his daughter a cup worth five hundred pounds for a wedding present, and a marriage portion of three thousand pounds, though he would have to borrow to do it. Her trousseau, too, must have been difficult for him, for two pair of silk hose for the bride cost six pounds, which was equal to many times that sum in modern money.

The wedding of the brilliant and piquantly lovely girl of fifteen took place on the 21st of April. The bridegroom, Henry Herbert, had been twice married already and was nearly thrice her age. His father, "Black Will Herbert," says Aubrey, the collector of stable gossip, could not read or write, had to flee the country for killing a man at Bristol, changed his religion whenever his sovereign did so and, after letting the nuns come back to Wilton Abbey under Queen Mary, had driven them out at Elizabeth's accession with cries of "Out, ye whores; to work, to work, ye whores; goe spinne."

Mary's husband was of another sort and allowed her to indulge her taste for literary men and scholars to the point that Wilton became, it was said, "like a college": she kept the house so full of them. But when Lady Sidney saw her tender child standing at the altar beside this man who was her own contemporary, one wonders if she was not troubled by the memory of the ill-starred bridal twenty-four years earlier, when Henry Herbert was married to Lady Jane

Grey's sister. It was the same day on which Lady Jane became the bride of Guilford Dudley.

Philip, on his return from his embassy, reached Greenwich, where the Queen had her court, early in June. Waterhouse wrote to Sir Henry of the excellent reputation which the young Ambassador had brought back with him, of the Queen's approval of him and that of the Lords of the Council, of the Emperor's gold chain and the Princess' jewel. Francis Walsingham reported as promptly: "There hath not been any gentleman, I am sure, these many years that hath gone through so honourable a charge with so great commendation as he." Philip's success, he added, was "no less a refreshinge unto me in these my troublesome business, then the Soile is to a chafed Stagge."

This friendly approval of his son must have been equally refreshing to the Lord Deputy, for Irish affairs were not less difficult than they had been, and his standing at court was on such slippery ground that Philip, who had at first thought of joining him, decided to stay at home to defend him from his detractors there. In vain had Sir Henry written to Elizabeth, "the onely Sovereign Salve Gever," of the state of religion in his domain: the churches roofless, the clergy "very simple sorry curates" or Irish priests or Irish rogues; and how more and more the young nobles and gentry were going over to Louvain, Douai and Rome for their education. Repeatedly had he deplored the delay in sending over lawyers for his legal establishment. Elizabeth took little interest in his efforts to base the government of the country on the institutions of religion, education and the law. He was kept, as always, so short of money that he made to Leicester an offer to discount each quarterly payment of his allowance by a thousand pounds if it were only sent promptly.

In March rumours that Fitzmaurice was coming from France with four thousand musketeers and the Pope's blessing had incited Rorie Oge to rebellion and the burning of Naas, his men running through the town "like Haggs and

Furies of Hell, with Flakes of Fier on Pooles Ends and so fiered the lowe thatched howsies," while the inhabitants, only "manlike in appearance," lay asleep, having "filled themselves and serfieted upon their Patron Day." By the middle of May Sir Henry was asking for a "Mass of Munition," additional troops, and that a fleet be prepared to oppose the foreign descent upon the west coast of Ireland, which he expected before the next harvest.

But worse than all this were the steady and stealthy efforts at court to undermine his credit with the Queen and the Council. To various charges against his troops he made answer that, although soldiers were no angels—"not amongst them the harmlessest of creatures"—yet there was not a garrison in Christendom that did less harm to good subjects than his soldiers in Ireland. He had been striving to collect the taxes—the cess, as it was called—on the basis of a more just apportionment than had existed in the past, and thereby raised a storm of protest from those who had been enjoying an undeserved immunity from this burden. He wrote to the Queen to tell her how these gentry, who wailed of their poverty, had raised a thousand pounds to send her a delegation, of whom the "least unhonest" thirsted to see the English government a failure; and he sent over Edward Waterhouse, who was now in his service, to make matters clearer than his letters could do.

Waterhouse arrived at Greenwich in time to welcome Philip. He found the court gay with embassies from the Emperor, the King of France and Don John of Austria, the last composed of one hundred and twenty persons, of whom fifty wore chains of gold. The Queen, he reported, was angry at first, saying that "Henry Sidney did always seek to put her to charge"; but Leicester talked her into allowing the munitions and treasure asked for. Waterhouse felt safe in advising that "in this ticle time" the Lord Deputy "might laie as many by the Healis" as he thought were inclined to rebellion, and it would be "allowed him for wisdom." The deputation from the protesting cess-payers was in fact laid by the heels in the Fleet prison; and Waterhouse flattered himself that he had straightened things out between the Earl of Ormonde and Sir Henry, for the Earl assured him that he had never given the members of the deputation so much encouragement as they pretended to have had from him.

The differences between the two men, however, were probably too deep-rooted to be reconciled, though both of them had brought the best of goodwill to such a purpose, which is by no means certain. It was hardly possible for a zealous servant of his queen like Henry Sidney to do his duty as he saw it without offending the great noble who was also the Queen's kinsman and favourite. The towns of Dublin and Drogheda appealed to him against certain of the Earl's prerogatives; and the Earl, who was emphatic in his assertions that he wished no jurisdiction but the Lord Deputy's, insisted that he could not get justice against the Lord of Upperosserie, who had seized a castle of his, and whose men had stolen his ploughs and millstones and even threatened to shoot him.

Walsingham wrote to remind Sir Henry that Ormonde was wise and valiant and that he stood very high at court. But Sir Henry replied that he could not like a person merely because he was commanded to do so. "There be secret instincts in those cases," he added significantly. And, sure enough, the Queen wrote him "somewhat offensively" in July, and in August she ordered that Ormonde's lands should be exempt from the payment of cess. Other objectors began to receive encouragement from England. Finally Sir Henry was moved to write to Leicester in dignified protest, "My Lord, I am the Queen's principal officer here . . . and ought to be credited as soon as another."

Waterhouse wrote to his distracted master that, as soon as he returned to court, he trusted to be able "to untwine all that they [Sir Henry's enemies] have twisted." He had been in the west of England, arranging for the transportation of reinforcements to Ireland and, with a colloquialism curiously familiar to modern ears, made the comment on his instructions that, if the expedition were not finally sent, "the whole provision must light upon my neck, for the Queen would be no loser."

The repercussions of his father's troubles fell heavily upon Philip. He went down to Wilton for a short holiday with his sister and his brother Robert, who was now a boy of fourteen; and when Waterhouse on his way back to London stopped to pay his respects to the young, new Countess, Philip told him that he could not advise him as to what he had best do at court, things changed so rapidly there. Upon his arrival at Greenwich, however, the zealous secretary found that his master could rely upon the support of Leicester and Walsingham; and he had the pleasure of deflating the Earl of Thomond by asking him how, when that plausible Irishman was telling the whole presence chamber that he could save the Queen four hundred pounds out of every thousand she was spending in Ireland.

Thomond was now trying to get the same exemptions that had been granted to Ormonde. Philip rejoined the court at Oatlands, and before long the machinations of his father's enemies became so intolerable to him that he declined to acknowledge Ormonde's salutation. The affront was deadly —or he meant it to be—for he gave it before a large assembly. But the Earl received it philosophically. At his age and with his rank, his blood and courtly standing, he lost nothing of prestige—possibly even gained a bit—by refusing the quarrel of this young cockerel of two-and-twenty. He said that Philip was bound by nature to support his father, and followed this with a thick application of blarney about the many virtues with which Philip was furnished. The angry young man, who was soon to be reputed one of the best swordsmen in Europe, was left nowhere, for he had nothing definite on which to base a challenge.

His sword thus rendered useless, he turned to ink and

paper and drew up such a defence of his father's administration that Waterhouse wrote of it to the Lord Deputy: "Let no man compare with Mr. Philip's pen." The next spring, however, Sir Henry was recalled. A "nobilitation" or some other reward to sugar this bitter pill was promised but never granted. But it may have been owing to this *Discourse on Irish Affairs* of Philip's that his father was allowed to save his face by remaining in Ireland until the expiration of his third term of office in the following autumn.

Meanwhile Ormonde's people supported the rebels, juries in Ormonde's country refusing to indict them even on their own confessions. The Queen's unwillingness to bring the Earl of Clanricarde to trial made the inhabitants too fearful of his vengeance to withdraw their support from his rebellious sons; and the favour shown at court to Irishmen hostile to the Lord Deputy's rule encouraged the recalcitrant cess-payers, who in turn supported Rorie Oge in his career of barbarity. Sir Henry, riding in pursuit of this bandit, straining every nerve to make preparations against a threatened invasion by Fitzmaurice from France and another by Stukeley under the banner of the Pope, and at the same time suffering so severely from his old malady of "the stone" that he believed he must return to England for "physic," was accused of delaying his return purposely—so Walsingham warned him—in order to "prolong the benefit of your entertainment."

For this entertainment he was again the poorer by three thousand pounds out of his own pocket—a sum, by the way, which he was still owing Pembroke for his daughter's dowry. But the Queen was very angry about his exceeding his allowance. She refused to understand that the alarms of the previous year and the trouble about the cess accounted for it, and eagerly credited the plan of "some about her" by which everything needful in Ireland could be done for one-half of the present charge. Walsingham stood his staunch friend, recommending that he conciliate the hostile elements before his departure. This and some other matters which he was asked to settle Philip advised him to seize upon as a pretext for delaying his return until Michaelmas so that his "enemies cannot glory it is their procuring."

Philip thought it well to add that his father had better write him of his intentions with his own hand, since nothing was written to him, or for him by his secretaries, but his enemies learned of it. The Earl of Thomond had even had the effrontery to deliver to the Lord Deputy letters from the Queen and Council with their seals broken. At the end of May in 1578 the anger of the sorely tried young courtier at this open espionage flamed into unjust fury in a letter to his father's secretary, which gives a not unpleasing variety to so much that has been written about his wisdom and prudence.

> Mr. Mollineux [he wrote]. Few words are best. My letters to my father have come to the eyes of some. Neither can I condemn any but you for it. If it be so, you have played the very knave with me; and so I will make you know. For that is to come, I assure you before God, that if ever I know you do so much as read any letter I write to my father, without his commandment, or my consent, I will thrust my dagger into you. And trust to it, for I speak it in earnest. In the mean time farewell. From court this last of May. By me. Phillipe Sidney.

The secretary's reply is so perfect an example of how to answer an angry letter that it deserves more frequent quotation than it has received. Apparently he took ten days to think it over. Then:

> Sir [he began], I have received a letter from you, which, as it is the first, so the same is the sharpest that I ever received from any; and therefore it amazeth me the more to receive such a one from you, since I have (the world can be judge) deserved better somewhere, how so ever it pleaseth you to condemn me now. But since it is (I protest to God) without cause, or yet just ground of suspicion you use me thus: I bear the injury more patiently for the time, and my innocencie, I hope in the end, shall

try mine honesty; and then I trust you will confess you have done me wrong. And since your pleasure is so expressed, that I shall not henceforth read any of your letters; altho I must confess, I have hitherto taken both delight and profit in reading some of them: yet upon so hard a condition as you seem to offer I will not hereafter adventure so great a peril, but obey you herein. Howbeit if it had pleased you, you might have commanded me in a far greater matter, with a far less penalty. From the Castle of Dublin, the first of July 1578. Yours, when it shall please you better to conceive of me, humbly to command, E. Mollineux.

Sir Henry came home in the early autumn, humming from the Latin version of the Psalms as he embarked, "When Israel departed out of Egypt, and the house of Jacob from amongst a barbarous people." When he reached Ludlow, he set up at the end of the dining-chamber in the castle "a pretty device how the hedgehog [his crest] brake the chayne, and came from Ireland to Ludlow." All in all he had sound reason for satisfaction. He had contrived to leave matters in very fair condition behind him. The Desmonds were quiet. The Lord of Upperosserie, to whom Ormonde had accused him of showing favouritism, had killed the marauding Rorie Oge for him. He brought the Earl of Clanricarde and one of "that arch traitor's" sons with him to answer to the Queen for the misdeeds of their family. Thomas Stukeley, viscount, earl and marquis in his own estimation, and "General of Our Most Holy Father, Gregory XIII, Pont. Max.," had gone charging down to death in the wild Moroccan Battle of the Three Kings. And it was no fault of Sir Henry's that he left his successor to face the threat of an invasion by Fitzmaurice.

But he was so ill that again he had to rest a few days at Chester before going on to face the music which the Queen and his enemies had prepared for him at court. How unpleasant this was may be gathered from the attitude of the court officials—those perfect barometers of the royal favour—toward Lady Sidney's efforts to obtain a room in the palace, where Sir Henry could receive the crowd of Welsh and Irish who were sure to wish to wait upon him. Of all Sir Henry's friends, Philip had written to him, "none proceeds either so thoroughly or so wisely as my lady, my Mother. For myne own Parte I have had onely Lighte from her." Now she observed shrewdly that Hampton Court seemed, mysteriously, to have less room in it than when three times as many people were lodging there.

Her own quarters "being very little and myself continually sick," she explained to Molyneux, had, moreover, to be ready to receive the Queen at any moment until sunset. After that her "dear good Lord shall be as best becomes him, Lord of his own." For the rest of the day it appeared that he was to be left without a place in which he could perform his necessary duties. "When the worst is known," she added with the not unnatural bitterness of a woman who had lost her beauty, her health, and years of a beloved husband's companionship in the service of a neglectful sovereign, "old Lord Harry and his old Moll will do as well as they can in parting like good friends the small portion allotted to our long service in court, which, as little as it is, seems something too much" (i.e., seems so to those who grant it).

It is to be wondered at, if Philip did not ask himself whether a part in such backstairs bickerings was worth the boyhood and youth which he had given to earnest study and observant travel. He seemed to have gained little else by them. For the past three years he had done his best to follow Languet's advice: to cultivate Walsingham's friendship and Burghley's, to curb the fiery temper that glowed beneath his gentleness, and to check his touchiness at manners less courteous than those with which he described himself as being "burdened." But at court, as Fulke Greville wrote of him, "he found greatness of worth and place counterpoised there by the arts of power and favour. The stirring spirits sent abroad as fuel to keep the flame far off: the effeminate made judges of danger which they fear, and honour which

QUEEN ELIZABETH AT A PICNIC

from George Turbervile's "The Noble Arte of Venerie," 1575

they understand not." Those who are young and high-spirited can understand how Philip must have suffered under Elizabeth's foreign policy of watchful waiting.

The flame which Greville wrote of was again no farther off than the Netherlands and was blazing fiercely. The Treaty of Ghent had been broken, and Don John of Austria had smashed the army of the States at Gembloux. Philip's friend John Casimir and the Austrian Archduke Matthias were both in the field on the side of the patriots. Six thousand English and Scottish volunteers, with John Norris as their general and the eldest son of Lord Shrewsbury as one of their colonels, were in the Dutch service. At Rymenant, fighting in their shirts in the burning heat of August, they had defeated Don John and killed a thousand of his men. To Mendoza, the first Spanish ambassador to be sent to England in six years, Elizabeth had exclaimed, "By God, I will have the treaty of Ghent allowed!"

In the June of that year Mendoza had heard that Philip Sidney was going vice-admiral of a fleet which was to be commanded by Lord Howard, and thought the story likely enough to report it to his master. July had found Philip all ready to join John Casimir as a volunteer. But the Queen had charged him with messages so discouraging to the Count-Palatine that Leicester supported him in his refusal to go if he must carry them.

Philip's disappointment was naturally keen, but Languet heard of it with satisfaction. It was the folly of the age, he wrote, that men of high birth thought a soldier's work more honourable than a leader's and preferred a reputation for boldness to one for judgment. The result was that there was hardly a veteran commander to be found in Europe, he pointed out, except among the Spaniards; and their successes proved their wisdom in this respect. Instead of sharing in this madness for a reputation founded on bloodshed let Philip use that particle of the Divine mind (as he had so beautifully expressed it), which he possessed, for the preservation and not the destruction of men.

Better still, urged the old man, let him marry a wife suited to his character. He would do more for his country by begetting children like himself than by cutting the throats of a thousand Spaniards or Frenchmen. And this is not to recommend a life of idleness, he added humorously. Let Philip believe the poet who advises any man who wishes plenty of trouble to get him a wife. How one "reared in the lap of the Graces," as Philip had been, should stay so long unmarried, Languet could not understand. For cold comfort he added that, if Philip had gone to the Netherlands, he would have found himself among incompetent leaders and a mutinous soldiery, who made the want of pay an excuse for cowardice and laziness.

Deep in his sense of frustration, Philip had been thinking of "some Indian project." Such ventures were in the air all about him. Drake had sailed for the other side of the world in the December of 1577. Philip's uncle of Warwick had backed Frobisher's voyage the year before, and Philip had got home from his embassy to the Emperor almost in time to see the Queen wave her farewell from a window of the palace at Greenwich as Frobisher set out on his second voyage to the coast which she had been graciously pleased to honour with the name of *Meta Incognita.* Nearly a quarter of a century earlier Sir Henry Sidney had invested money in "the new viage to the newfoundelande." Leicester and Sussex had interested themselves financially in Frobisher's ventures. Elizabeth speculated to the extent of five hundred pounds. The young Countess of Pembroke subscribed twenty-five. Philip had managed to scrape up a like sum for the first voyage, fifty for the second, and sixty-seven pounds and ten shillings for the third, though he was frequently forced to borrow to meet his expenses in these years.

When Frobisher brought home black earth that seemed to be rich in gold, the Cathay Company was organized with privileges like those of the Muscovy Company, and a colony was planned for the gold island, "where the currents roared like the ebbing tide through the arches of London Bridge." In the intervals of his squabbling with Ormonde in his father's behalf Philip was writing to Languet for his opinion of the best way to combat the Danish and Spanish rivalry for these rich possessions and to obtain a copy of the laws governing the silver-mining town of Guttenburg. These rich islands should be of great assistance to the true religion, he exulted.

He got another douse of cold water in return. The old Carthaginians, Languet replied, used to kill such discoverers as Frobisher, lest their population rush off in pursuit of easy wealth. These new riches were likely to complete for England the ruin which the enclosure of the commons had begun. Philip had better follow the example of the Talbots and the Chandoses than the lure of gold. Languet so far unbent, however, as to admit that Frobisher ought to be honoured, and to point out that the Portuguese, who had been at Goa since 1510, had demonstrated that a town was better than a fort for such enterprises. As for books to be read for the undertaking of mining, he recommended Georgius Agricola's *De Re Metallica*, which was destined to enjoy a revived celebrity three and a half centuries later for its part in the education and the romance of a president of the United States of America.

When the "gold ore" which Frobisher brought back "after great charges proved worse than good stone," Philip strove to comfort himself with the importance of the discovery that the ocean could be crossed at the fifty-second parallel. But his mind, he told Languet, was relaxing through "indolent ease" in an age which he called corrupt. He could exchange long letters with the Prince of Orange, could even —so he wrote—be of more assistance to him than the Prince was aware of, but it brought him no nearer to marriage with the Prince's sister and the lordship of Holland and Zeeland. Even if Leicester had been willing to give him the necessary financial help, the Queen would never have consented to a subject's greatness of which she was not the source.

It was all very fine at his age to be courted by the envoys of the Protestant leaders on the Continent: Doctor Peter Butrech from John Casimir, whom Philip described as "the best doctor among reiters and the best reiter among doctors"; and Du Plessis-Mornay, the devout and able representative of Henri of Navarre, who brought over with him a blank sheet of paper with his king's signature at the bottom and instructions to let Elizabeth write above it any terms she might choose to name as the price of her assistance. Philip, like many another lofty idealist, was a realist in judging his own accomplishment and could not blink the fact that in spite of his help these people went home disappointed. It was all not much like his dream of the *Fœdus Evangelicum* which should thwart the whole power of Spain. Discouraged, disillusioned by the Queen's treatment of his father, and bored by his trivial employments, he wrote to Languet that he was disgusted with court life and wished to retire to the country. The old Huguenot wrote back a dry reminder that he must stick to his duty in the state of life into which God had called him.

Philip entertained his brother-in-law the Earl of Pembroke and some others at a bachelor house-party at Penshurst in the April of 1578. He was godfather to Du Plessis-Mornay's daughter, who was born in England. He sent a present of English dogs to his friends the Count and Countess of Hanau. He answered Languet's patient and painstaking letters and his packets of books and the like, which informed him of the happenings in Persia, Turkey, Poland and Germany, down to the details of the fortification of the Hungarian frontier. He found solace one Christmas with his sister at Wilton, and the next he joined with his mother in presenting to the Queen a smock, two cambric pillowcases, and a white sarcenet bodice quilted with gold, silver and silk of divers colours and trimmed with gold and silver lace. They received in return gold plate weighing thirty and twenty ounces respectively, while Sir Henry, whose present was a gold Diana set with diamonds, rubies and pearls, was rewarded with gold plate weighing one hundred and thirty eight ounces.

The year 1579 brought Philip the pleasure of welcoming Hubert Languet to England. Of Count John Casimir of the Palatine the historian Motley says, "Robbery and pillage were his achievements; to make chaos more confounded was his destiny." But it suited Elizabeth's weathervane policy at this time to forgive the ineptitude of his operations in the Low Countries in the previous summer and to receive him in England with the highest honours at her disposal. And Languet accompanied him as a member of his suite.

Philip and his father were chosen to receive the distinguished guest. He landed at the Tower Wharf in the early January twilight by the glare and blaze of cressets and torches, to the sound of trumpets, fifes and drums. For three weeks there were banquets, with the Lord Mayor, with the Duchess of Suffolk at her house called the Barbican "by Redcross Street," and at the Steelyard. There was valiant jousting, and fighting on horseback with swords at the barriers in his honour, hunting at Hampton Court, and a grand climax when the Queen made him a Knight of the Garter "by delivering to him the collar, and putting the garter on his leg at Whitehall."

But Languet found time for a visit with his friend at Penshurst. He became acquainted with Sir Henry Sidney. The two men took to each other as both of them must have hoped that they would do. The friendship of Edward Dyer, whom Languet had met as a member of Philip's embassy, became "like a precious gem" in the old man's store. Sir Henry's finances were not in such a state that he could not show his gratitude for Languet's kindness to his son by the gift of a gold chain of great value; and Languet, though he was aging and not well, promised to oversee the education of young Robert Sidney, when he returned to Germany. For Robert, who had started on his travels some months before, did not appear to have been very successful in following in his brother's footsteps so far.

When the two friends parted, says Fulke Greville, who accompanied Casimir's party to the Netherlands from the Foreland of Kent, "they made many mutual tears ominous prophesiers of their never meeting again"—which, alas, was true: Languet died some eighteen months later. But actually in the confusion of a hurried departure they missed saying farewell to each other. Languet wrote from Flushing to express his regret for this: "I should have given great offence if I alone had behaved with commonsense instead of being mad with the rest"; and he added with the Frenchman's incorrigible misuse of the English title of knighthood that he would have been left behind, if "Sir Hales" (Sir James Hales) had not loaned him a horse.

Aside from this visit Philip's most congenial employment had been a brief mission to the French court the previous December to delay the coming of a still more important visitor. This was Monsieur Simier, a gentleman of the household of the Duke of Anjou, whose arrival early in 1579 set England buzzing once more with rumours of a marriage between the Queen and the wretched little Prince who, as Duke of Alençon, had been a candidate for her hand seven years before.

The French King approved the match; the Duke had been in arms the past year, if to little purpose, in the cause of the Protestant Dutch; and a sudden death in Africa had opened the way to such an enormous increase in the power of Spain that, unless something could be thrown into the French side of the balances of which England was the knife-edge, the equilibrium which was essential to England's safety would be destroyed. The King of Portugal had fallen in that battle in Morocco, which had ended Stukeley's crazy career.

King Henry, his successor, was an old man and a cardinal into the bargain; and Philip of Spain was the next heir to the Portuguese throne, unless one counted the late King's cousin, who was known as Antonio the Bastard.

But the marriage of England's queen with the heir presumptive to the throne of France would be an awkward thing to get out again, if the balances should incline the other way at some future time; and Anjou had changed sides so often that he seemed a dubious makeweight. In May the Council rejected the conditions with which the Duke accompanied his proposal. The Queen was furious. But when the conditions were moderated, she began to hesitate about signing a passport to cover even a visit from her suitor. Then Monsieur Simier grew very busy and soon could lay before her proof that her precious Leicester, her girlhood idol, her reputed lover and constant adorer, had married Essex's widow, Lettice Knollys, the cousin whom she especially hated—had, indeed, married her so many months ago that the nearness of the date of the wedding to that of Essex's death made a scandal of the affair.

In her rage Elizabeth ordered Leicester to prison, though she was afterwards content with his confining himself to his own house; and Anjou came over incognito and remained for several days. To hide the depth of her chagrin she, who loved above all things to have handsome men about her, swore that she had never seen a man that she would sooner have for a husband than this ugly, stunted debauchee. With his croaking voice he well deserved the name of "Frog," which she called him by—her "Frog Prince." And so, accommodatingly, he signed his love letters to her, her "Grenouille," for months to come.

Philip's close connection with Leicester made the situation a difficult one for him. He could not deny that he had long been in the secret of his uncle's marriage. His ardent sympathy with the Protestant cause in France was well known. His memories of St. Bartholomew's Day made the idea of his sovereign's marriage with a member of the house of Valois hateful to him. And neither his nature nor his position would permit him to embrace any cause without becoming a leader in it. The marriage project was so generally unpopular throughout the country that Mendoza believed that there would be a revolution if it were persisted in; but there was at court a strong party that favoured it, and among the leaders of that party was Burghley's son-in-law, husband of poor Anne Cecil, Edward de Vere, the Earl of Oxford.

After his marriage he had gone off to Italy, spending enormous sums and living at Florence in greater state, it was said, than the Duke of Tuscany himself. He had returned completely Italianate, with a present of perfumed gloves for the Queen and "a little apish hat couched fast to the pate like an oyster." He was Great Chamberlain of England by hereditary right, was still, though "a great embeciller of his estate," enormously rich, and through his appeal to that streak of coarseness in Elizabeth, which undoubtedly contributed to her strength of character, stood high in the royal favour. So it was quite natural that one day, when he found no one but Master Philip Sidney and a few friends of his on the tennis-court he wished to play on, he should roughly order them off. Philip refused to budge. He and his friends, he told the Earl, might have yielded the court to him, if he had asked for it politely, but they most certainly would not do so at his command. The noise of the altercation quickly filled the gallery with onlookers—among them the French commissioners for the marriage—as Oxford perhaps intended that it should; and at once the squabble of two hot-headed young men became an issue of high politics.

Having started well up the scale of Touchstone's seven causes of a quarrel, the affair passed swiftly from the "countercheck quarrelsome" to the "lie direct." The Earl called Philip a puppy, and Philip retorted that puppies were gotten by dogs, children by men. Then, with the significant suggestion that a quieter place would be better suited to a continuance of the discussion, he led the way out of the court.

Oxford did not follow. Perhaps he was not eager to take on an opponent who, if he lived up to his advice to his brother, practised his swordsmanship for two hours every day, and that not with the foils but with real swords and padded caps so that blows might be given with no stint of force. When the lapse of two days did not bring a challenge from him, Philip sent him the taunting message that his French friends could tell him the next step which he ought to take. Oxford then sent a challenge. Walter Raleigh carried it, and his friendship for both of the young men may account for the fact that no meeting took place before the Privy Council heard of the matter and interfered.

They forbade the duel and strove to bring about a reconciliation. But Philip's blood was up. He had been grossly insulted; he had retorted by giving the Earl the lie; and he refused to withdraw it. He wrote to Sir Christopher Hatton, a member of the Council, that if he could have forgiven Oxford, he could not have forgiven himself for swallowing such an affront, and he added that he thought "tying up makes some things fiercer than they would be." The truth was that Ormonde, with his patronizing urbanity, had made him look silly not so very long before. This affair should not end in a mere squalid wrangle, if he could help it. It should be dignified by bloodshed, or Oxford should carry the stain of an unavenged insult upon his escutcheon to his dying day. He utterly refused the good offices of the Council.

He was sent for by the Queen.

CHAPTER IX

AN INCOMPARABLE PEN

PHILIP PRESENTED HIMSELF BEFORE HIS SOVEREIGN WITH a respectful firmness. If the Sidneys asked little of their queen and got even less than they asked for, they enjoyed the corresponding advantage of having little to lose by her disfavour. By their retirement from her service she, on her part, stood to lose a disinterested devotion which all her lavishness could not purchase from her favourite courtiers; and if she had not been shrewd enough to know this without being told, their manner of dealing with her would have made it clear. Like another honest servant of hers they could have said, "Better she be angry with me than herself feel the smart hereafter." The unwelcome but wholesome truths which Sir Henry wrote to her from Ireland he couched in a minimum of the courtly locutions which custom required in an age of the most fulsome adulation of monarchs. Philip wrote of her to Hanau as "somewhat advanced in years"—a statement fairly treasonable in her eyes, and a reckless indiscretion, considering how little the sacredness of private correspondence was respected at her court. One cannot imagine young Francis Bacon taking such a risk.

Father and son alike, they saw her as she was, with her painted cheeks and enamelled bosom, her false hair and pencilled eyebrows, her ruffs and hoops and flounces. They heard her loud, unearthly laughs and round oaths: "Jesus!" she exclaimed, breaking in upon a conference between her Council and a number of her bishops. They watched her delight in the bloody spectacle of dogs disembowelled by bears and bears torn to pieces by dogs; her "jars," when the day was hot and the only ale to be had proved to be spoiled; her tears and tantrums, and her blasting fury at the news that Leicester was false to his lifelong vows of passionate devotion. They saw the turns and twists, the lies and broken promises which were of the very fabric of her statecraft. Often they suffered from them.

But they saw also the long years of peace with which that statecraft had blessed the country. Beneath all the faults and tarnish they saw a queen who counted no cost of labour or of danger in living up to the ideal of duty which she had set for herself. They saw a sovereign who in twenty years had lifted her kingdom from bankruptcy to such prosperity that she could borrow at five per cent where Philip of Spain could not borrow at all. They saw a sovereign who never harboured a personal grudge to the detriment of the service of the state, and who enforced the loyalty of a doubtful subject by the very completeness of the confidence which she thrust upon him.

They saw one who for nineteen years, true to her belief in the sacredness of royalty, had protected Mary of Scotland from the vengeance of her subjects, though the trail of that "bosom serpent" was discovered in every one of the continual plots against her throne and life. They saw her walking constantly, publicly and knowingly, through an unending labyrinth of intrigue, of which the primary object was to expose her to the assassin's pistol or the bravo's dagger. They saw her do this gaily, as if the knowledge of her danger made her heart beat high. And they adored her the more as their sovereign because they could admire her as a woman and like her for the human frailties that made so perfect a foil for the greatness of her spirit.

If any fear of man, God or devil abode for long in that dauntless heart of hers, it was perhaps a fear of such clear-sighted and honest spirits as those of Philip Sidney and his father. She had once told her Parliament that she thanked God he had dowered her with such qualities that she could have taken care of herself in any station of life in which it might have pleased him to place her, and she must have felt that these Sidneys could have told her as much of themselves had their sense of what was fitting permitted them to do so. They owed her little or nothing that they would not have been materially better off without; they knew that she knew this; and she was quite clever enough to understand that in the queen who commanded their devotion they saw the flighty, moody, fickle and unreasonable woman whose bounty alone could buy the doubtful service of lesser men.

In a little masque which Philip wrote for her entertainment he made one of his characters tell her, "Your face hurts oft, but still it doth delight"; and very soon he was to write with quiet irony of a queen of his imagining, "She was a queen and therefore beautiful." She, whom Anjou addressed as his "perfect Goddess," may well have sensed the tongue in the cheek when Philip and his father grudged her the extravagant compliments which were the small change of courtly intercourse with her. The nicknames she delighted in showed the different value she placed upon those two. Simier was her "Monkey," Anjou her "Frog," Hatton her "Mutton," Lady Norris her "own Crow." Leicester was "Robin," even Burghley and dark Walsingham her "Spirit" and her "Moor." But Henry Sidney was "Harry," at least when he had pleased her, and Philip "my Philip" to distinguish him from the King of Spain. She was never at her ease with them as she was with those who were not only content but ever eager to be in everything merely her creatures, but she respected them greatly and trusted them as fully as it is in any woman of large affairs and responsibilities to trust her agents when they are beyond her immediate supervision.

So Philip could obey her summons in the matter of his quarrel with the Earl of Oxford with far less misgiving than that which might have been felt by some young courtier who owed her less or desired more for his services than he had ever done. She began by ordering him to apologize to Oxford because he was a mere gentleman while the other was a lord. He refused to do so: Oxford was no lord over him, he reminded her. She pointed out that the gentry's disrespect for the nobility taught the peasants to insult them both. The manners of the common people of England were notorious for "a stubborn stoutness and an unmannerly, disordered boldness" at the time. He answered that high place had never been intended to give its possessor the privilege of doing wrong. Then, assailing her where she was most open to argument,—for she adored her father's memory,—he recalled to her how King Henry VIII had given the gentlemen the right to appeal to him against the oppression of the nobles. "This constant tenor of truth he took upon him," says Fulke Greville, "protected this gentleman (though he obeyed not) from the displeasure of his sovereign"; and there, between those two, the affair seems to have rested.

But the quarrel made a stir which seems to indicate that duels were by no means so common in those times as a reader of historical novels might have supposed them to be. Languet was greatly upset by the news of it, and took to reading up the law on the subject. He admitted that "the habit inveterate in all Christendom" was to inflict disgrace for failure to resent such an insult as Philip had received, but, he wrote, "You can derive no true honour from it"; and he warned Philip to be on his guard, lest the Earl come upon him suddenly with a crowd of fiery-natured Frenchmen.

Two years later Lord Henry Howard said that Oxford had planned to murder Philip in his bed, with a boat on the river, in which to escape after the crime. If that bad young man was as Italianate in his nature as in his clothes, his proposal to Philip that they let the matter drop, since they were not allowed to fight it out, may have been a part of such a Machiavellian plot. But Oxford in his cups was prone to rip out wild sayings even against the Queen's Majesty, and some such drunken vapourings may have been the basis of Howard's statement. Philip and the Earl were soon performing in the tilt-yard together; and there exist two poems which they have been supposed to have written to each other.

Altogether Philip came out of the affair so much better than second best that he was regarded at court as a champion of the anti-marriage party. This was a strong one. Of the powerful nobles Sussex alone stood against them. Burghley, scared by the fact that the life of an aged churchman was all that kept Philip of Spain from the crown of Portugal, hesitated. Pembroke held a meeting of those opposed to the marriage at his London house, Baynard's Castle, on the night of the day on which Leicester was permitted to return to court after his disgrace. Among others Sir Henry Sidney was present there, and not improbably Walsingham and Hatton as well. The Parliament would have something to say about the matter, some of them remarked afterwards; and Sir Henry Sidney came out roundly in the Council that the marriage could not be made good by all the counsel between England and Rome. "A mass may not be suffered in the court," he said.

That incomparable pen of "Mr. Philip's" was now called into the service of his party. So it would appear that it had accomplished something by its defence of Sir Henry's Irish policy. It speaks highly, moreover, for Philip's standing with the Queen that his father should have permitted him to undertake the ticklish task, which was no less than the placing before her on paper of all the objections that could be urged against this marriage which she seemed to have set her heart upon. He proceeded to do this without fear or hope of favour.

As he had not minced matters with regard to Ormonde in treating of the Irish situation, so now he spared her nothing but Anjou's physical shortcomings in the recapitulation of her suitor's unsuitabilities. Anjou's "race" was "unhealthful," he told her; his mother was the Jezebel of the age; "his brothers had made oblacion of their owne sisters mariadge, the easier to make massacres of all sexes." Anjou himself, breaking his promise to the Huguenots, to whom he owed his liberty and estate, had sacked La Charité and spoiled Issoire. He had continually plotted against his own brother, had thrust himself into the Netherlands, and had sought now the Queen's hand, now that of the daughter of the King of Spain, showing every way that he loved greatness, however come by, with Alexander's image in his head, no doubt, "but perchance evil painted." And his followers were like him or worse.

Once married to the Queen, Philip went on, neither a common fear nor the desire of a common end would bind him to her. As a papist he would be only human in wishing to make all others papists. The Protestants, the majority of her people, hated the idea of the marriage. The Catholics, rich because they took no share in the burden of the service of the state, united and very discontented,—"*quibus opus est bello civili,*" as Cæsar said,—would find in him the head which was all they lacked to make them dangerous.

And what did she expect to gain by the marriage, he asked. The bliss of children? Any other marriage was as likely to give her that. The easing of her cares? That would mean only the easing of her being a queen sovereign in this case. She must expect no other advantage. Even if Anjou should become King of France, he would be like Ajax's shield, which weighed down rather than defended those who bore it. As for the contempt of "certain hellish minded people," of which she had told him, neither Christ's holiness nor Cæsar's might had protected them from that. Let her remember Charles V, who "to one that told him: *Les Hollandois parlent mal; mais ils payent bien,* answered he."

In "so rare a government [as hers], where our neighbours' fire giveth us light to see our quietness," she might be well content to do as she was doing: so should she be as she was, the example of princesses, the ornament of her age, the comfort of the afflicted, the delight of her people, the most excellent fruit of all her progenitors and the perfect mirror of her posterity. Only so much did Philip's forthright earnestness vouchsafe in belated courtesy to his queen.

As to how she received this ruggedly honest exposition accounts differ. For long it was said and generally believed that in one of her towering rages she forbade him the court, and that her smouldering anger denied him her countenance for many months. But she had already frequently permitted him to discuss the marriage with her; and Fulke Greville, who was in a position to know all about it, wrote, "Yet, I say, that princely heart of hers was a sanctuary unto him." According to Greville, he "kept his access of Her Majesty as before" and continued to be "reverenced" for himself by the worthiest of the Frenchmen. So the story of the Queen's furious displeasure may belong with the tale of Philip's anti-Spanish harangue before the Emperor and the legend, which gained credence many years after his death, that at some time in his short life the crown of Poland was offered to him.

The marriage treaty, nevertheless, was signed late in November, and Languet was so stirred up by some report of his young friend's difficulties that he wrote from Antwerp of the Count Palatine's promise to support Philip's cause at the English court. On his recent visit that court had struck Languet as so unmanly and affected that he had feared Philip's character might suffer from his associations there, and he now advised him to seek service in the Netherlands, if he could be spared from watching over his father's affairs. He would try to obtain for him the command of a wing or a squadron of horse to start with. This would provide places for the poorer friends whom he might bring with him. It would be an excellent opportunity for him to learn the whole art of war, for he would have the best of teachers. The veteran François de La Noue, who was the only general able to command the mixture of English, Scottish, Belgian, Dutch and French captains and colonels serving in Flanders, and who bore the name of Bras-de-fer because of an iron hook which replaced the bridle-arm he had lost in the Huguenot wars, had saved the Protestant army after Condé's capture and death. And John Norris, seasoned by service under Coligny and in Ireland, was always by his side.

In January 1580, and again in March, Languet repeated this advice. There was nothing, he said, which the Prince of Orange would not do for Philip, if he would enter the Dutch service. At the same time the worldly-wise old diplomatist reminded him that nothing was to be gained by keeping at outs with a man of Anjou's rank. He had better patch things up in that quarter. Anjou's party was gaining strength in the Netherlands. If Philip went on too long in his opposition to him, he might find himself alone in it. Only La Noue's capture and the refusal of Alexander Farnese, who was now the Spanish commander in the Netherlands, to exchange him for Egmont and de Selles—"to give one lion for two sheep" —put an end to Languet's urging.

But Philip was in no such desperate situation as his old friend's affectionate anxiety caused him to imagine. Against humble folk who meddled in matters above their station Elizabeth proceeded with a savagery like her father's. John Stubbs, who had written *The Discovery of the Gaping Gulf in Which England Is Like to Be Swallowed by Another French Marriage*, and Page, who sold the pamphlet, had their right hands struck off "with a cleever driven through the wrist with a beetle" by the hangman on a scaffold before the palace at Westminster. But Philip's subsequent eclipse seems to have been due to financial troubles rather than to the Queen's displeasure.

For, although Languet as late as October in 1580 wrote to congratulate him on emerging from "a certain cloud," Philip had written to Leicester in the previous August that only the want of money and a hard cold were keeping him away from court: since his "only service is speeche and that is stopped" by the loss of his voice. The Queen, who he felt sure would ask for him, knew of his straitened circumstances, he said, but so long as she saw a silk doublet upon him she would think him "in good cace." His best course, he believed, was either to be in constant attendance or "constantly to holde the course of my poverty, for comming and going neither breedes deserte, nor wittnesseth necessity."

This letter was written from Wilton. After a short stay at Leicester's London house in January, Philip had gone down to visit his sister, who was expecting her first child, and there he remained for the greater part of that year. His mother had retired from court, still in miserable health and glad perhaps to seize the excuse for doing so which was afforded her by her brother's brief disgrace, when his marriage with the hated Lettice was brought to light. It is possible, too, that Elizabeth was glad to be relieved of the sight of that velvet mask with which Lady Sidney covered her ruined beauty, for there are sacrifices so great that the continual reminder of them becomes a burden hardly tolerable. Sir Henry, out of favour on account of his opposition to the French marriage, had gone to his post in Wales.

There he busied himself with his antiquities and heraldic manuscripts, with building the great portal of Ludlow Castle and the stone bridge, with raising troops for service in Ireland against the rebellious Desmonds, and with giving Lord Grey de Wilton, the new Lord Deputy, the benefit of his experience there: although he said with his usual courtesy and humour that in offering advice to a veteran of Saint-Quentin and Leith he might well be likened to the "Puttock that taught the Faulcon to fly," or, "in martial designs," to the scholar who offered to read the *De Re Militare* to Hannibal. But he had by no means recovered his health: his hand shook, he said, so that he could hardly read his own letters. He was annoyed to find that the Welsh administration had again been run into debt during his absence; and he was not left to quiet enjoyment of his duties.

The papist plots of the past four years had done much in sweeping away his easy latitudinarianism, but he was more interested in building a bridge at Cardiff than in prosecuting the recusants in his jurisdiction; and his enemies at court were so successful in basing an attack upon him on his neglect of this duty that the Queen, Walsingham warned him, was only too ready "to give ear to any that shall ill you." When the birth of his first grandchild tempted him to make frequent visits to the young mother at Wilton, the Secretary was constrained by the Queen's command to order him peremptorily to remain at his post constantly in those parlous times when there might be sudden calls upon him. If Philip wrote his poem "In Dispraise of Courtly Life" about this time, the experiences of his parents may well have accounted for his doing so.

That his father could give him little if any help financially seems obvious, for Sir Henry's purse seems always to have been open to him so long as there was anything in it. But the money troubles of the Elizabethans in high places present a puzzle to the modern mind, at least to one trained in the principles of middle-class New England economy. If Sir Henry was poor this year, he had chiefly his own extravagance to blame for it. Philip had spent part of the previous summer down at Penshurst, overseeing the construction of the gatehouse and the beautiful north and west façades which his father was giving to the house; and Sir Henry's liberality to his builders moved his steward to continual remonstrances. On the other hand, he had sent Robert abroad on a travel allowance so much smaller than Philip's had been that Languet had to write more than once about the young man's need of money.

Sir Henry's parsimoniousness in this respect, however, may have been owing less to his wish to economize than to what he felt was best for his son. To be the younger brother of one who had always been counted such a paragon as Philip had been cannot have been easy, and Robert had found some difficulty in adjusting himself to the rôle. His father worried about him as he had never worried about Philip. He had absented himself all too frequently from Oxford,

Before his departure for the Continent, Sir Henry had extracted some sort of promise from him and later wrote insisting on being told "whether you keep it or no, and if you break it in some dark manner, how."

As for money, his father told him that he must either manage better or come home. Regarding a sum of thirty pounds, which Robert called his "arrearages," Sir Henry replied, "Term it as you will, it is all I owe you till Easter." He advised him to follow his brother's rule, "who won love and could ply ceremony with ceremony," and who was "a rare ornament of this age." "Perge, my Robyn," urged the troubled father. "Perge, in the filial fear of God and the lovynge direction of your most lovynge brother." But he offset this in some measure by thanking him for a gift of marten skins, "which is more than ever your elder brother sent me." As a reward for good accomplishment he promised him such a suit of apparel as should beseem his father's son to wear in any court in Germany; and he ended with the hope that God would bless his "sweet child in this world and forever, as I in this world find myself happy in my children."

Languet seems to have been rather appalled by the charge which he found that he had taken on in this youth who differed so much from his precious Philip. He thought that Philip had neglected Robert's education and that the boy, though he showed great readiness of understanding, had enjoyed so much liberty that it would not be every tutor that could handle him. He found him a tutor and established him at Strassburg at the house of no less a person than Sturmius. But Robert let the tutor go; Robert's servant, Henry White, avoided German society; Robert spoke English in his own quarters and was soon scaring the old man by talking of joining an expedition of the Count Palatine's into France.

But, if he lacked Philip's sweet tractability and love of learning, Robert showed no want of common sense in the letter which he wrote to his father from Prague eight months later. While there he intended to learn to ride, if he might

—by which he must have meant the higher degrees of horsemanship, for boys of his time and class were all but weaned in the saddle. Philip had suggested to him that "if there are any good wars," he should go to them, but the thought of the expense of horse, armour and maintenance in the field had given him prudently to pause. Between France and Italy for the next summer he inclined to the latter as nearer, and to take France afterwards, with his father's permission. He had come to Prague by way of Nuremberg, Ingolstadt, Augsburg, Munich and Regensburg, and after Christmas planned to see Vienna, as much of Hungary as possible, and Cracow, if the King of Poland should come thither.

That sensible letter must have delighted Philip's heart no less than his father's. For never did elder brother hold a lighter or more skilful rein over a younger than he held over Robert. No touch of priggishness, moral or intellectual, no hint of superiority or patronage, tinged the frank comradery of his letters to him. About his mental attitude at the time of his own highly creditable travels, he wrote, "a great number of us never thought to ourselves why we went, but only of a certain tickling humour to do as another man hath done." He suggested, however, that there was not much use in travelling just to travel, or to be able to say that you had travelled; and there was more to be learned in foreign lands than "how to put on one's cap with a new found grace." The purpose of travel for a "Gentleman borne" was to acquire such knowledge as may be serviceable to his country: "hard sure it is to know England without you know it by comparing it with others." What was to be learned in and about other countries followed naturally after such a beginning. To prepare the boy's mind for some excellent advice on the proper method of studying history, he took him into his confidence about Sir Henry's anger, giving his opinion frankly that "they are but passions in my father, which wee must beare with reverence."

Philip, who had so greatly exceeded his own travel allowance, could remember what it was like to be short of money in a foreign land. Poor as he was, he sent what he could to increase Robert's limited supply and told him that, "Nothing that I spend so pleaseth me as that which is for you"; and those "odd 30li. shall come with the hundred or else my father and I will jarle." After that Robert could hardly take it amiss when he added, "I would by the way that your worship would learn a better hand; you write worse than I and I write evil enough." He went on to urge him to have a care of his diet and consequently of his complexion, for "*Gratior est veniens in pulchro corpore Virtus.*"

One might justifiably be a little bored with hearing the praise of an elder brother's excellencies, but it must have been impossible for Robert not to feel complimented by the confidences of one considered "the very Formular that all well disposed young gentlemen of our court do form also their manners and life by"; to hear from him "how idlie wee looke on our Naighbours fyres"; to be told by him that "Portugall wee say is lost," that all he knew of Drake's return was that "about the world he hath bene, and rich he is returned," and that, for his own part, this *lumen familiæ suæ,* as his father called him, had "given over the delight in the world."

For Robert the best of this last was that, if Philip said it, one could be sure that he meant it. In his own eyes he was indeed a failure at this time, however admirable he might appear to others. To sharpen the smart of his disappointment came a letter from Languet, written at the suggestion of some of Philip's friends in the Netherlands, who thought that his long retirement was hurting his reputation. They had expected him to do so much for England with his high position and excellent qualities. He had carried away the admiration of all men, when he returned from the Continent, Languet assured him. Count Casimir had heard the Queen eulogize him. So he ought not to feel discouraged because she rejected his advice.

Actually circumstances were now driving Philip, as they have driven many another, if few better men, to that work which was only secondary in his wishes, but which, along with his heroic death, is all that has made him generally memorable. He liked the process as little as others have liked it and was as little aware of its significance as they. Down at Wilton in the winter of 1580, while Countess Mary was awaiting the birth of her baby, he began to write, solely for his sister's amusement in her enforced seclusion, his famous romance—or rather, as he called it, hers—*The Countess of Pembroke's Arcadia,* which was to become the most successful book of the Elizabethan age and still stands as one of the great landmarks of English literature. Pacing the leafless alleys of Wilton's wintry gardens in meditation on it, or pulling up his horse after a gallop on Salisbury Plain to jot down upon his tablets a happy phrase for it, he found distraction from his disappointments and frustrations.

It was not the first time he had turned to his pen for an outlet for his feelings. He had indeed already won a considerable reputation as both critic and writer of verses. It had been he, and other returning travellers like him, who had brought back from France the challenge of the *Pléiade,* which claimed as the field of poetry the whole universe, material, intellectual and spiritual. In England the morning splendour of the Renaissance had been obscured by civil wars and religious controversies. Although it had long been said that at the universities the young men were more interested in the modern than in the ancient tongues, the prestige of Chaucer as the sure guide for English poetry had remained undiminished. What was new in Wyatt and Surrey had been of little effect. But at his first going abroad Philip had found the court of France ringing with a poetry that was new.

Du Bellay and Ronsard had brought out their *Deffense et illustration de la langue françoyse* there in 1549. It was a stirring appeal for the cultivation of their native tongue and a defence of poetry, especially poetry written in that tongue. French, they maintained, rather than Latin, was the language for French poets and could be so widened and developed that anything could be expressed in it. As for poets, they would admit none to their company who were not consecrated to their art at birth and dedicated to its mystery. François I and his successors, the Queen of Scots and the Princess Marguerite, were among their patrons; Henri III founded his Académie du Palais for them. Their achievements in diplomacy and arms, and those of their disciples, marked poetry as a proper avocation of men of brains and action.

President de Thou said that France gained in Ronsard all that she lost at the battle of Pavia, which was fought on the day on which he was born. Queen Elizabeth sent him a diamond; and Chastelard went to the block reciting his "Hymne de la Mort." Du Bellay served at Rome as secretary to his kinsman the Cardinal. The Sieur du Bartas, whose *Semaines* rivalled Ronsard's *Œuvres* in popularity, was the emissary of the King of Navarre to England, Scotland and Denmark. D'Aubigné, the Huguenot soldier, wrote his *Tragiques* in the saddle or in the trenches, "la botte en jambe."

Beyond the Alps Philip had found the Italy of Tasso. Petrarch's influence had turned the cavaliers of Spain to imitations of his manner and matter half a century before. Garcilaso de la Vega had served at Pavia, fought the Turks at Vienna and Tunis, received his mortal wound, when he was thirty-three, in the great retreat of the Emperor Charles from Marseilles, and left his pastorals and sonnets to the admiration of his countrymen. Alonso de Ercilla, who had been at the wedding of his king with Mary of England the year that Philip was born, had begun his *Araucana* in the bivouacs of a campaign in Chile. So Philip had good cause when he wrote, "Poetry is the companion of camps." The thing was being done by just the sort of man he hoped to become.

He knew not, he said, by what mischance in these his "not old years and idlest times" he had "slipped into the title of a poet" and before he "durst aspire unto the dignity was "admitted into the company of paper-blurrers." The truth was that, "onely over-mastered by some thoughts," he had "yeelded an inckie tribute to them." He had been doing that now for several years, notably in an elegy on the death of his friend Essex and in some verses which he had found time to send off to the fair Penelope when he was crossing Flanders on his embassy to the Emperor.

In the late spring of 1578 at Wanstead he wrote for the Queen's entertainment the masque in which he reminded her of her face-ache, and showed in it that originality which great talent brings to the performance of the most trivial tasks. As she entered the grove with her train, "one apparelled like an honest man's wife of the country" besought her judgment in a squabble between certain foresters and shepherds over "the Lady of May," who could not decide between two suitors, one from either occupation. The rustic arguments of both sides, the shrewd thrusts at the knavishness of foresters and the dulness of shepherds, the tags of misapplied dog-Latin and scholastic knowledge with which Rombus, a schoolmaster, strove to "indoctrinate their plumbrous cerebrosities" with "learned wisdom," which got him "many unlearned blows," must have delighted Elizabeth with their freshness after the long-winded allegorical flatteries with which she was accustomed to be bored by giants and nymphs and the like on such occasions. With its foreshadowings of Dogberry and Verges, Touchstone and Audrey, the little play more than once surprises even the modern reader into a smile. But this was the summer when Philip was fighting to keep his father from being brought home from Ireland in disgrace, and one may wonder whether the staging of this performance, the stresses and strains which have ever been inseparable from the production of theatricals, was not responsible for his writing that furious letter to Molyneux.

In July of that same year he met a greater poet than his

own brief life was to allow him to become, and one who never ceased to be grateful for the encouragement he received from the young man who was so far above him in station and, at that time, in reputation as a poet. The Queen was the guest of Sir Thomas Smith at Audley End. In the entertainment offered to her, the near-by University of Cambridge was conspicuously represented by Gabriel Harvey, Fellow of Pembroke Hall, who saw a chance to accelerate his brilliant academic career by winning the favourable notice of his sovereign. He came "ruffling it out hufty tufty in his suit of velvet," according to one that hated him, pushing in among the nobles, though he was only a rope-maker's son, and took the wall of no less a person than Mr. Philip Sidney. But the Queen liked him well enough to give him her hand to kiss. He was a protégé of Leicester's. Philip became his friend and, through him, the friend and patron of his friend Edmund Spenser.

To the Earl of Oxford, Sir Christopher Hatton and Philip, Harvey dedicated the fourth book of his *Gratulationes Valdensis,* calling him "*nobilissimum humanissimumque juvenem mihi multis nominibus charissimum.*" "*Χαῖρε alliis dixi,*" wrote the courtly scholar: "*tibi dico χαῖρε, Valeque.*" For Philip was reporting to the Queen at this time with his armour and field equipment packed, ready to join the Count Palatine in the Low Countries when her change of mind stopped him. And it was through this disappointment that he had the opportunity of cultivating Spenser's friendship during the following winter. The next year Spenser dedicated to him his *Shepheardes Calendar.*

Philip had filled many an idle hour with verse-making that winter, and when Stephen Gosson brought out his *School of Abuse,* as he did in 1579, Philip answered it as a poet speaking for poets. *The School of Abuse* contained, so its author said on the title page, "a pleasant invective against Poets, Pipers, Plaiers, Jesters and such like Caterpillers of the Commonwealth." He called them "peevish cattle" and, with the stupidity characteristic of his type of reformer, dedicated the book to Philip.

Only a few months older than Philip, he had entered Oxford the year that Philip had started on his Continental travels, and four years later had quickly made a reputation for himself in London as a playwright and a writer of pastorals. Now, when he was twenty-five, success had turned to dust and ashes in his mouth. He had turned sour moralist and, having spoiled all pleasures for himself by his abuse of them, wished to deny them to everyone else. Plays like *Catiline's Conspiracies,* which he claimed as a "Pig of mine own Sowe," might, he admitted, be defensible because of the moral lesson which they taught. But he held that the popular melodrama and low comedy were debauching society. Going further, he condemned the cultivation of imaginative beauty in all its forms with the childish bigotry of the most benighted Puritan.

Philip's moral sense was often even inconveniently strong, but he felt, he said, that Nature had endowed him with an inner sense by which he reasoned from the beauty before his eyes "to the light and eminence of a more excellent spiritual beauty which is light, majesty and divinity." He was too intelligent to believe that man could be made to be good by laws or other mechanical means; and "What!" he demanded. "Shall the abuse of a thing make the right use of it odious?" He liked *Gorboduc* and thought that the tragedies of Buchanan did "justly bring forth a divine admiration."

His uncle of Leicester had induced the Queen to grant to James Burbage and others the first royal patent for players on record in England. Philip supported these "Earl of Leicester's men" when they got leave to build the Blackfriars Theatre to compete with The Theatre and The Curtain in Shoreditch, and he did not scorn to be godfather to the child of Tarleton the actor, of whom Fuller wrote that when

Elizabeth was "serious (I dare not say sullen)" he could "undumpish her at his pleasure." He couched his trusty pen as a champion of all that Gosson attacked. But when he was not baited beyond endurance it was not in him to have recourse to violent measures. So his *Defence of Poesie* was no scorching counterblast, but one of the most charming personal essays ever written.

He began with those days when he and "the right virtuous E. W." were learning horsemanship together at the Emperor's court and playfully excused his defence of his profession as a poet by the example of old Pugliano's championship of the horse and its rider. But it was very seriously that he put forth his claim for poetry as "the first light giver to ignorance" in the noblest nations and languages, telling how to the Romans the poet was a prophet, to the Greeks "a maker." The poet, he held, was indeed the only true maker. For under his hand Pylades, Orlando and Cyrus became speaking pictures that taught and delighted in tales that "held children from their play and olde men from the chimney corner." Compared with Ulysses praising beggarly Ithaca amid the delights of Calypso's island, the eloquence of Cicero left the reader cold. And who could read of Æneas carrying old Anchises on his back and not wish for the opportunity to do something as fine? He recalled how his heart was moved "more than with a trumpet" by the rude old song of Percy and Douglas that day when, as a little boy, he had shocked Thomas Marshall by the gift of a whole shilling to the blind crowder on his way back from seeing the Queen at Oxford. And there were those Hungarian feasts which he had attended, with their songs of ancestral valour, "which that right soldierlike nation think one of the chiefest kindlers of brave courage."

As for the charges against poetry: there could be no other knowledge more worthy than this, which taught goodness. The poet never lied, because he never had to affirm, as astronomers, physicians and historians were often compelled to do on doubtful evidence. Were Æsop and Nathan the Prophet liars, he asked. What child at a play, "seeing Thebes written in great letters upon an old doore," believed that it was actually Thebes? Nor could Plato's exclusion of poets from his Commonwealth, over which the enemies of poetry "cry out with open mouth as if they had overshot Robinhood," have been on account of fear lest their love lyrics and comedies infect a society in which every man "might have what woman he listeth." It was poets that spread wrong notions of the gods that Plato aimed at. Aristotle himself wrote of the Arte of Poesie and why, if poetry ought not to be written?

But the poets themselves were to blame, Philip stated, if England in these days regarded poets not quite so highly as mountebanks were held in Venice. It was because the poets in England were depending on Artificiall Rules and imitative patterns. And he found it strange that, when Chaucer did so excellently "in that misty time" of his, "we in this cleare age goe so stumblingly after him." The way of writing which was in fashion turned out "the hony-flowing Matrone Eloquence apparrelled, or disguised in a Courtisanlike painted affectation," using art to show art instead of hiding it as it should. The poets of the day spent their time in "coursing a letter" and in rifling up the Herberists and the stories of beasts, fowls and fishes. And he called himself "sicke among the rest."

In dealing with the absurdities of the contemporary drama he was so far the product of the Oxford of his time that he based his criticism on Aristotle's unities. He deprecated "the olde rusticke language" of Spenser's *Shepheard's Calendar,* since he could find no precedent for it in Greek, Latin or Italian. He thought that the "gorgeous eloquence" of Pindar would have improved "The Ballad of Chevy Chase," which an uncivil age had apparelled in "dust and cobwebs." But when it came to the excellencies of the English language, the members of the *Pléiade* were not more uncompromising in their championship of their native tongue. If it was "a mingled language," he maintained that "it took the best of both the other." If it "wanteth grammar . . . it needs it not, being so easie in it self."

English indeed, like French, was growing so swiftly, broadening and refining itself by borrowing and experiment, that Jane Dormer, Duchess of Feria, down in Spain, took pride in her successful efforts to keep pace with its development. Already Philip could write of it that "for the uttering sweetly and properly the conceit of the minde, which is the end of speech, it hath it equally with any other tongue in the world." While for versifying he held it "before any Vulgare language . . . fit for both sorts": by which he meant the ancient, based on quantity, and the modern, based on accent and rhyme, and he proceeded to prove this by instances.

He ended as lightly and gracefully as he had begun, with a playful burlesque of the current form of dedications, leaving to such earth-creeping minds as could not look up to the sky of poetry only "thus much curse . . . that while you live you live in love, and never get favour, for lacking skill of a Sonet, and when you die, your memory die from the earth for want of an Epitaphe."

So much for his profession of his artistic faith. It was in no such mood of lofty criticism that he set about the killing of time for himself and his sister down at Wilton a few months later. The *Arcadia,* as he wrote in the dedication of it, was owing to "a young head, not so well stayed as I would it were, and shall be when God will, having many, many fancies begotten in it, that if it had not been some way delivered, would have grown a monster." The tale's "chief safety," he added, "shall be the not walking abroad." But this first version of it shows everywhere the work of the keen observer, the skilful writer and the original artist in words. A brook runs over the "pible stones" with a "sweet purling noise"; a shepherd boy pipes "as though he should never be old"; the lamplight falls upon the beauty of his sleeping heroine "as the moone doth when it shines into a thinne wood"; and one can guess at the memory of some Irish skirmish in the grotesque attitude of the corpse of a man decapitated in his flight, that lay "as though the fellow had had great haste to gather up his head again."

When he rewrote the book some years later, he began like his beloved and admired Chaucer in the *Canterbury Tales,* with Earth putting on her new apparel and "the sun running a most even course . . . an indifferent arbiter between the night and the day." But in this original version it is as if he could not lead his sister out of the scene of their dulness and vexations quickly enough.

"Arcadia," he began, "amonge all the Provinces of Grece was ever had in singular reputation, partly for the sweetnes of ye Aire and other naturall benefittes: But, principally, for the moderate & well tempered myndes of the people . . ."

To Arcadia's reigning duke, Basilius, however, the Oracle at Delphos spoke as follows:

> Thy elder care shall from thy careful face
> By princely mean be stolen, and yet not lost;
> Thy younger shall with nature's bliss embrace
> An uncouth love, which nature hateth most.
> Thou with thy wife adultery shalt commit,
> And in thy throne a foreign state shall sit,
> All this on thee this fatal year shall hit.

Properly frightened and determined, if possible, to escape such direful events, Basilius sought safety with his wife and his two young and lovely daughters in rural retirement, "where he was daily delighted with the Eglogues and pastymes of Shepeheardes."

But the young novelist's public, limited as it was to one eighteen-year-old girl who was for the first time about to become a mother, had already had quite all that she desired of rural retirement; and for his own part, although he might disturb Languet by writing of his wish to withdraw from public life, and might believe that he meant it when he wrote it, his story betrayed his real feelings. For it turned on the fact that Basilius's retirement was a mistake and that by running away he brought upon himself all the evils which the Oracle foretold. As the young Countess was longing for the gaiety of courts and balls, tournaments and pageants and the cheerful junketing of royal progresses, Philip was longing to be using his talents in diplomacy, in council or the field of arms. So for all its background of forest and desert and rustic lodges, its shepherds and shepherdesses, flocks and herds, its bear and its lion, the Countess Mary's *Arcadia* was no true pastoral.

The Spaniard Montemayor had showed the way with his *Diana,* which had been devoured in every country of Europe as fast as it could be translated into their various languages. Already John Lyly had set the cultivated world of England not only talking about but talking like his *Euphues,* which had appeared in 1579. Into the *Arcadia* went the things which the sister and brother in the great, lonely house wished to be doing and seeing, and people such as they knew, princes and lords and ladies, knights and gentle dames, whose society they sorely missed in the rural chill of the late winter and early spring.

The wooing and winning of the two young princesses by their knight-errant lovers, the guilty passion of their mother for one of these young gentlemen, the senile infatuation of old Basilius for the same young man, whose Amazonian disguise he failed to penetrate, made up the story. The shepherds and shepherdesses, clowns and other members of the lower orders, were brought in according to the ancient

SIR FRANCIS WALSINGHAM

from the painting, dated 1587, at King's College, Cambridge

by courtesy of the Provost and Fellows

tradition of high romance, merely to supply the comic relief, to do the dirty work, and in their brutish rebellion to furnish material upon which the two young heroes might display their prowess.

The Countess Mary's baby, who was to grow up to be Shakespeare's patron, and whom it is pleasant to identify as Mr. W. H., "the onlie begetter" of his sonnets, was born early in April. At his christening the Countess of Warwick stood proxy for the Queen, who was his godmother. The godfathers were his two great-uncles, the Earl of Warwick, and Leicester, whom Philip represented at the ceremony. But the writing of the *Arcadia* was not given up with little William Herbert's arrival. His mother stayed on in the country that summer, ill and in much pain, and Philip remained with his "most dear, and most worthy to be most dear, Lady,"—as he called her in the Epistle Dedicatory of the book—writing his "idle work . . . in loose sheets of paper" mostly in her presence. The rest was sent to her after his return to court, "by sheets . . . as fast as they were done"; and one senses something like "fashion notes" in the elaborate descriptions of beautiful dresses, which Philip put into his pages. But, in spite of all these touches of actuality, the *Arcadia* dealt with a day-dream world, a world in which all the women were as good as they were beautiful, and all the men were handsome, gallant and noble. Even Gynecia, guilty in intention though she is, is never so well aware of the beauty of virtue as when she is determined to sacrifice it to her adulterous passion.

Such was the tale of which Philip wrote to Robert from Leicester House in London on October 18, 1580, "My toyful book I will end with God's help in February." By the end of the year his old travelling companion, the Reverend Doctor Watson, had reached in the bishopric of Winchester the summit of his skilful climb. Through Leicester's influence Philip's financial troubles were lightened by his appointment as steward of the bishopric. But his summer cold had left him ill and depressed. It was in the same letter in which he wrote of his book that he announced his renunciation of the delights of this world. How far he was from actually doing so became very soon apparent.

CHAPTER X

ORLANDO INNAMORATO

PHILIP WAS ONLY JUST TURNING TWENTY-SIX WHEN IN the autumn of 1580 he came back to the court: still, that is to say, in those years, which are so drearily long in every young man's life, that stretch between his entrance into the world of manhood and his adjustment to his place there. Philip's place, as his father's son and the nephew of his distinguished uncles, was by no means a poor one. But some of the ablest men of his time had encouraged him to believe that he was possessed of exceptional powers of character and intellect; he had represented his sovereign at the court of the Emperor at the age of twenty-two and been permitted to attempt to put into effect his own pet theory of his country's foreign policy; and he did not find it easy to be content as a mere ornamental hanger-on and handy-man about the court. He wrote of it as it seemed to him:

To my birth I owe
Nobler desires, lest else that friendly foe,
Great expectation, wear a train of shame;
For since mad March great promise made of me,
If now the May of my years much decline,
What can be hoped my harvest-time will be?

All round him, however, was pulsing the full life of the Renaissance. Early in the century in his *Il Cortegiano* the Italian Castiglione had told how it should be lived. Sir Thomas Hoby, whose wife was a warm friend of Philip's mother, had translated this book into English as *The Courtyer of Count Baldessar Castilio.* Two hundred years later Doctor

Johnson was to call it "the best book that ever was written on good breeding." It was one of the two indispensable guides to success in public life in Philip's time, Machiavelli's *Prince* being the other. And when Philip died, he was said to have been the most perfect living exemplar of its teachings.

So, while the nineteen-year-old Francis Bacon was bending over his law-books at Gray's Inn with that viper eye of his fixed upon the main chance, Philip was striking out in half a dozen directions, resolved like Cyrano de Bergerac upon that simplification of life which was merely to make himself "in all things admirable." Since Castiglione's paragon must be, first of all, proficient in arms and perfect in horsemanship for the peace-time exercises of the barriers and the lists, Philip had made himself the prize-winner at more than one great tournament, and books on horsemanship bore his name in their dedications. Since the Courtier should excel in games, Philip became a leading tennis-player of his day. Graceful dancing, merriment and wit were requisite; and Spenser wrote of him as

Merrily masking both in bower and hall.

Learning should be joined with arms and the social graces; so he made translations into English from Aristotle and the Psalms. The Courtier must be able to speak and to write clearly and easily in his native tongue, and Fulke Greville, viewing his friend's achievement by the magic light of other days, described him as bringing the affection and true use of letters into court and camp. But above all else, these excellencies, though they were acquired by painful study, must be performed with the appearance of negligent ease, while this appearance itself must not be allowed to look like an affectation. Thus, in his *Defence of Poesie*, do we find Philip praising the art which conceals art.

But, impeccable courtier though he trained himself to be, it was not at court that he found happiness. His companions there, he wrote, were so "puffed in mind" that they were, like "Juno's birds of pride," scarcely able to abide each other; and friends were as rare as black swans. In Edward Dyer and Fulke Greville, however, he had two that were as congenial as they were trusty, and he celebrated their meetings in the poem which makes a companion piece for his "Dispraise of Courtly Life" with all the frank warmth of feeling which must have been his greatest charm.

> Join mates in mirth with me,
> Grant pleasure to our meeting;
> Let Pan, our good god, see
> How grateful is our greeting.
> Join hearts and hands, so let it be,
> Make but one mind in bodies three.

They were in effect a small poetry society, these three young men, whether or not the name of *Areopagus*, which was bestowed upon it, is to be understood as indicating the existence of a formal organization. They entered earnestly into the hot debate upon the relative excellence of quantity and accent, blank verse and rhyme, in English poetry. They experimented endlessly with classical metres and Italian verse forms. Gabriel Harvey, the prancing scholar of Audley End, took a hand in these discussions and parodied their hendecasyllables—"all composed in the metre of Catullus"—so perfectly that readers of a later day took his ridicule for serious effort. Edmund Spenser congratulated himself upon receiving their patronage; and it was Philip's encouragement at one time that kept him going on his *Faerie Queene*. In the universities abroad as well as at home, says Fulke Greville, Philip was considered a general Mæcenas of learning. Apart from poetry, he adds, logic, philosophy and history were his true vocations. His interests, however, included painting, music, the drama, and science.

His writings, of course—especially his creative work—were not done for publication. By a polite fiction of the day such things were supposed to be merely the genteel exercises proper to a gentleman of liberal culture. That attitude towards his poetry which brought down such a storm upon the head of the youthful Byron more than two centuries later was very much like the one which convention required of the well-born Elizabethan versifier. If his literary efforts were copied and copied again and widely circulated in manuscript, as those of Philip and his friends, of Oxford and many others, constantly were, it was assumed that this was done without his approval. Such things were held to be but a part, and a quite unimportant part, of all that went to make up the accomplished gentleman. The skilful and gracious service of his prince was considered the serious business of his life. It was not to Philip as a fellow craftsman but as "the President of noblenesse and chevalree" that Spenser dedicated his *Shephearde's Calendar.*

The earlier months of 1581 gave Philip many opportunities for the gratification of his taste and the exercise of his talents for chivalrous display and knightly feats of arms. The Queen was dragging out the negotiations for her French marriage as few knew better how to do than she: and the court was gay with the entertainment of fresh embassies. For their refection a great banqueting hall was built of canvas, painted outside like stone and within with vines and fruits, and its ceiling like the firmament. Its perimeter measured three hundred and thirty-two feet; its windows contained two hundred and ninety-two lights of glass; and it cost upwards of seventeen hundred pounds to build. There were pageants and tournaments. For the Queen loved such things. Such was her delight in jousting that in her eagerness to watch the sport she had been known to lean out of her chamber window above the tilt-yard at Whitehall, presenting such a spectacle of Majesty in undress that Gilbert Talbot got "a great fillip on the forehead" through staring at her instead of keeping his eyes on his antagonist.

In May Philip joined the Earl of Arundel, Lord Windsor and Fulke Greville in honouring her with a pageant and tournament which lasted through the Monday and Tuesday of Whitsun week; and when one has read the contemporary account of their magnificence on this occasion, it is easy to understand why he was again in financial difficulty before the end of the year. Calling themselves the Foster-Children of Desire they demanded the surrender of the Fortress of Perfect Beauty, which was naturally the Queen's gallery, in ringing verses that were no disgrace to either of the poets among their number. They advanced against it behind a rolling trench equipped with "divers kinde of most excellent musicke" and armed with "two fayre fielde pieces of ordinances" made of wood, from which two gunners in crimson sarcenet shot very odoriferous and pleasant charges of sweet powder and sweet water, while footmen planted pretty scaling ladders and threw "flowers and such fancies" against the walls.

Six trumpeters with the motto "*Sic nos, non nobis*" on silver scrolls worn scarfwise sounded before the Earl, who led the challengers in. Four spare horses, richly caparisoned and ridden by gorgeous pages, followed each of them. They had splendid trains of gentlemen and yeomen, Arundel's in crimson velvet and yellow satin, Windsor's in scarlet and orange tawny with velvet caps. The Earl was "all in tylt and engraven armour"; Greville's armour was gilt; Philip's "very sumptuous," part blue, the rest gilt and engraven. Nine defendants—if we count Sir Henry Leigh, who came later "as unknown," broke six staves and departed—ran six courses against the Foster-Children. And so the first day ended.

On the second day the challengers, looking "forewearied and halfe overcome," entered the tilt-yard in a fine chariot, a beautiful lady with them to represent Desire, the horses caparisoned in white and carnation silk, Desire's colours, and musicians inside the vehicle playing dolefully. The defendants followed them in. All did nobly throughout the day. At the barriers "they lashed it out lustily . . . as the shivering of the swords might verie well testifie." But at the end a boy dressed in the ash colour of humble submission presented to the Queen the apologies of the challengers. They owned that they had been wrong to make Violence the companion of Desire and admitted that Virtue was too strong for Desire to overcome it.

Meanwhile, since the beginning of the year, Philip had not been neglectful of the reminder which Languet had sent him about the time of his return from Wilton to the effect that good citizens ought to pardon their country every wrong and ought not for any such reason desist from working for her preservation. He had taken a seat in Elizabeth's Fourth Parliament, which had reassembled in January, and had been busy on several committees, of which one dealt with matters of the first importance. The prevention of the false packing of hops and the suppression of certain heretics known as the Family of Love may have seemed small beer to one who had hoped for high employment, but the drafting of measures for dealing more severely than heretofore with recusant Roman Catholics was a matter of such delicacy and involved so many potential dangers to the country that it must have excited his deepest interest and challenged his most earnest thought.

The aspect of affairs throughout Europe was such that the members of the House of Commons came together with a feeling that the machinations of the Catholics within her borders had become a threat to England's safety which could no longer be endured. In Scotland the English party was in eclipse, the Earl of Morton a prisoner, and the Catholic faction under the leadership of Esme Stuart, Count d'Aubigny and Earl of Lennox, paramount. In the Netherlands William of Orange had been proscribed by a royal edict which offered twenty-five thousand crowns and a patent of nobility for his assassination or capture; and at Rheims the assassination of Elizabeth had been preached to the English Catholic exiles. In Ireland, although the Papal expedition under Fitzmaurice had been annihilated by Lord Grey de Wilton in a massacre of prisoners that made *Graia Fides* a byword in Europe, a general pardon had been granted, excepting only the Earl of Desmond and his brother John. Upon this Languet wrote to Philip that the general opinion on the Continent was that England was managing the Irish war more as if she wished to keep it alive than to suppress it.

The armies of Spain were for the time being, to be sure, occupied with making good their master's claim to the crown of Portugal; and in revenge for affronts which would have moved him to vigorous action in other circumstances Philip II had done no more than allow Fitzmaurice to base his expedition on the Spanish coast. But he could only be waiting until his hands were free. In expectation of his reprisals marine insurance rates had been soaring in London ever since the first news of Drake's exploits had filtered through from Chile.

Drake had sailed into Plymouth harbour with the hold of the *Golden Hind* bursting with the loot of Spanish towns and Spanish ships which he had plundered all the way from Valparaiso to Lower California; and Elizabeth, after seeming for a while to hesitate between hanging him for a pirate or honouring him as a hero, had allowed him to pay off his backers at the rate of one hundred per cent on their venture and richly to feather his own nest, and had kept the remainder of his takings for herself. She travelled down to Deptford to knight him and feast upon his vessel's deck. The French Ambassador went with her. She lost her garter; the Ambassador picked it up; and they exchanged some lusty Elizabethan jests about his right to put it on for her as the price of restoring it.

Whether her subjects liked the idea of the French marriage or not, the prospect of the addition of Portugal to the King of Spain's dominions was forcing England and France to draw together for their common safety. On her return from Deptford the Queen refused even to receive Mendoza with his complaints. Walsingham and the rest of the war party at court, of which Philip Sidney was an ardent member, were delighted. Now was the time, they felt, to strike at Spain. Burghley and all others who strove for peace were correspondingly depressed. King Philip might be embarrassed for the time being, they admitted, but his troops were meeting with little resistance in Portugal. Soon he would be firmly seated on his new throne, free to turn with redoubled strength to the subjugation of the Netherlands; and England's turn would follow shortly, if she had provoked his anger against her. Once more, however, Elizabeth's love of half-measures prevailed, and the nominal peace was preserved.

Meanwhile the danger from within had steadily increased. The kingdom—the court itself—was honeycombed with papist intrigue. With the spring of 1580 devoted members of the Society of Jesus had begun slipping into England in disguise, travelling from Catholic country-house to country-house, lying hidden in secret chambers while the local Dogberrys sniffed perfunctorily about the wainscots, saying mass in secret and spreading the doctrine that one who served God could more easily serve Mammon than a heretic and excommunicate queen. London streets were mysteriously strewn with handbills setting forth the right and reason of the Papal claims. In December arrests began to be made; the Tower rack was put to work; a royal proclamation made it known that those caught harbouring Jesuits would be treated as rebels. But even Protestants ran this risk rather than deliver these courageous and ingratiating young Englishmen to the hangman's noose and quartering knife. The number of converts, especially among those in high position, became alarming. In the Parliament in which Philip took his seat for the first time the attendance in the House of Lords was significantly sparse.

Among the Commons, however, the spirit was blatantly Protestant. They were the same who had been returned back in the angry days of the Ridolfi plot, for there had been no dissolution since then. They began by arranging for a daily sermon at seven in the morning and ordained a fast. The Queen was annoyed. She was no Protestant in that sense of the word; she was not forgetful of what the Scottish Protestants had done to their queen; her quarrel with the Pope was a political one. Let her Commons be mindful of that. And when she prorogued them in March, she excluded from her thanks such of them as had "dealt more rashly in some things than was fit for them to do."

But the Catholics were in despair at what had been done against them. Converts to the See of Rome had been declared to be guilty of high treason. A fine of five hundred marks and a year's imprisonment had been made the penalty for the celebrating of mass in private houses, a thing which had been winked at ever since Elizabeth's accession. Those who absented themselves from the services of the Church of England must now pay a fine of twenty pounds a month, a ruinous sum in the money of the time. Jesuits who were arrested were stretched upon the rack till they were a foot longer than God ever made them, the rack-master boasted. Some of them endured the torment to the end, but others spoke, fully and disastrously for their co-religionists.

Philip, whose opposition to the Church of Rome was, like his sovereign's, based chiefly on political considerations, must have suffered more than a little as the stern penalties, which were the work of his committee, descended upon loyal Englishmen whose only fault was their honest refusal to attend a service in which they could not believe. Made as he was, he must have sympathized heartily with their dissatisfaction with the Established Church of his day. The worldliness and lethargy of its clergy were notorious; and among the recusants were many of his friends. Only a week after the close of the session he wrote to Lady Kitson about the troubles of Sir Thomas Cornwallis, comforting her—and himself, too, no doubt—with the assurance that "there is meant a speedy easing of your burden."

What he felt when Edmund Campion, his father's one-time protégé and his own old friend, was arrested and led to the Tower through the roaring London mob, a placard on his breast and his legs tied beneath his horse's belly, can be easily imagined. For more than a year the gentle, dauntless Jesuit had been going to and fro in England, preaching and saying mass in the kind of open secrecy which was made safe for him and others of his order by the easy-going tolerance of public opinion and a certain amount of protection from persons in high places at court. At Oxford the pews of St. Mary's Church were strewn on one occasion with copies of his *Ten Reasons for Being a Catholic*. In London, where he walked up and down unchallenged for many weeks, he was wont to touch his hat to Tyburn gallows with grim humour.

Nothing but his own insensate imprudence was responsible for his capture. The greatest efforts were made to treat him with leniency. Perhaps Philip did what he could for him in arranging interviews for him with Leicester and with the Queen. At all events he had them. Elizabeth had not forgotten his speech of welcome to her at Oxford so many years before. She offered him the means of saving his life—the only means it was in her power to offer—and added the promise of a rich reward besides. But they were means which he could not use. Protestant feeling was running high. In Scotland Morton had just been executed. The Catholic English exiles were loud in their jubilations over the rapid success of the Jesuit mission in England. The law took its course.

Poor, sensitive, aspiring creature, they racked him on two successive days, and he revealed enough to save himself from further torture at the time. But he endured a third application of it without yielding and stood up with broken joints to receive the ghastly sentence for high treason. November had come round again by that time. The Duke of Anjou was back in England in disguise at that grotesque courting of his once more. On the tennis-court a French abbé begged him to intercede for Campion's life. But Anjou had by that time accepted the sovereignty of the Netherlands: he had the feelings of his Protestant Dutchmen to consider. Sharply he turned away from the suppliant and called, "Play."

On the bitter, windy morning of December 1st a vast crowd saw the end of the courageous missionary at that same Tyburn which he had so often saluted.

> Good subjects of England, rejoice and be glad;
> Give glory to God—with humble knees down—
> That Campion, the traitor, his hire hath now had. . . .

So ran the popular ballad. Some mercy was shown him at the last, however: he was allowed to hang until dead, instead of being revived and disembowelled alive as the sentence required.

Philip went down to Wilton for Christmas and did not appear for the tournament in Anjou's honour on New Year's Day. It hardly seems too much to suppose that he was in no mood for gaiety. Certainly he was short of money again, and by keeping away he avoided the obligation of giving a present to the Queen, which he had discharged two years before with a crystal cup and the year after that with a piece of jewellery in the form of a golden whip. The presidency of nobleness and chivalry was an expensive position to keep up. His income from his small court offices, from the church livings in Wales, of which he was lay rector, and from his stewardship of the bishopric of Winchester, even though these were augmented by an allowance from his father, was altogether inadequate.

In November he wrote to Hatton to get him the Queen's help out of his "cumber of debts." Apparently she owed him something for expenses incurred in her service; and he needed the money so badly that if Hatton could not get it for him, he was prepared to go to her for it himself, for "neede obayes no lawe, and forgets blushinge." In December he was constrained to ask Walsingham to reward the messenger who brought a letter from Robert on the Continent. The servant of the "yonger brother of so yongeli a fortuned famili as the Sidneis," he added in an attempt to turn his poverty into a jest, was probably "more stored with discowrces than monei." And he wrote the Vice-Chamberlain "something largeli" about his "discomfortes."

As a consequence of the prodigality of his expenditure earlier in the year Philip was now contending with something which to one with his scrupulous ideal of conduct must have seemed like a temptation of the devil. The Queen was using the fines collected from recalcitrant recusants to reward her favourite courtiers. He had only to have his name placed on the list of such beneficiaries to be rid at least of his more pressing obligations. In October he had so far yielded as to tell Burghley that, if he could not have some office that would pay him well, he would like a grant of a hundred pounds per annum from the impropriations from the Catholics. But, two months later, he asked Hatton to advise him on the propriety of taking such money: "It goeth against my harte, to prevent a Princes mercie," he wrote. And the fact that he had been a member of the committee that devised these penalties must have made his case the more repugnant to his own eyes. Three days before the end of the year he had evidently made up his mind that, if he sold his soul to the devil, it should not be for less than enough to pay his debts in full. He wrote Leicester that he would have three thousand pounds or nothing from the papists' forfeitures. But still he added wistfully that it seemed very hard his reward should be built on other men's punishments.

It was a dilemma in which he must have sorely missed that good, strong staff which had upborne the slippery years of his lustful youth. For old Languet, who had poured forth such wise and noble counsel in his every need, had died at Antwerp on the last day of the previous September. Which way Philip's unaided judgment guided him in the matter is not quite certain. It is stated that his name does not appear in the lists of those who were thus benefited. But another careful and equally friendly biographer seems to think that there is little doubt that he was among their number; and there exists a note of monies leviable upon recusants, in which Philip is named along with Sir Thomas Cecil and the Earl of Leicester as a participant in the division of the spoils. If this is taken at its face value, at least he must be judged by the standards of his time. Other courtiers were making a tidy profit out of the traffic in reprieves; and there were few about him who would have been troubled by such scruples as his, though they had not been driven by his necessities. He was back at court again, after only a few weeks' absence, early in 1582.

His life, in spite of its many difficulties and disappointments, must have brought him much happiness during the year just ended and at least the greater part of the one that followed: for he filled it with a variety of activities in which his pleasure was keen, and he had the artist's temperament, which even suffers adversity with a certain zest. Of his various interests, his delight in his pursuit of them, and what he thought about them in failure and success, he left an excellent record in his sonnets and other verse. Statecraft and its two handmaidens, diplomacy and war, he undoubtedly regarded as his true vocation. Poetry probably stood next highest in his liking, even above the warlike exercises of the tilt-yard, great though his enjoyment was in these.

What has already been told of his association with Dyer and Greville, Spenser and Harvey, has made it clear that his versifying was no mere compliance with what was expected of any cultivated young gentleman. He was both the conscious and conscientious artist through and through, and said what he thought of the conventional and the perfunctory with more plainness than politeness. Having himself discovered the futility of "turning others' leaves," he mocked at "Pindar's apes . . . enam'ling with pied flowers their thoughts of gold." Their "strange similes . . . of herbs or beasts which Ind or Afric hold," and "Jove's strange tales . . . border'd with bulls and swans, powder'd with golden rain," moved him to ridicule. To him who sang "poor Petrarch's long deceasèd woes" he gave warning that stolen goods were sure to come to light at last, and he turned with merciless laughter from those

> Who think themselves well blest, if they renew
> Some good old dump that Chaucer's mistress knew.

For himself, he said rather arrogantly and somewhat less truthfully than he may have realized—for he owed a good deal to Du Bellay, Ronsard and others of the new French poets—he had no need "of others' children changelings use to make." Although he did not know what others meant when they talked of the poet's fury, he was "no pickpurse of another's wit"—he swore to that "by blackest brook of hell"—and yet his verse, he made bold to say, "best wits doth please." His artistic creed he put into what is probably his most famous line—his only line, perhaps, of which there is any general knowledge at this day:

> Fool, said my Muse to me, look in thy heart and write.

And few poets have stuck closer to their profession of artistic faith than he did.

At the beginning of his poetical career, however, he had so far yielded to convention as to follow Castiglione's model and select a lady to the glorification of whose excellencies his effusions should be addressed. Such a course was strongly recommended in *The Courtier*. The ideal of the relations between this divinity and her adorer was that they should be based entirely on make-believe, and that all which passed between them should be understood in a merely Platonic sense. He had chosen Penelope Devereux and made her the "Stella" of his sonnets.

At that time she must have seemed admirably suited to the rôle. She was still hardly more than a child and had known him since the time when he can have been little more in her thoughts than one of her father's younger friends. It is possible that Philip was in the secret of her attachment to young Charles Blount. It is certain that her father's earnest desire for a marriage between her and Philip can have done nothing to throw the light of romance over their relations. As time went on, she may well have seemed almost like a member of his family, or at least a near cousin. After her mother's scandalous marriage to Leicester, Penelope lived with Philip's maternal aunt, the Countess of Huntingdon; and Philip, who made his quarters at Leicester House whenever it suited his convenience to do so, had unlimited opportunities of seeing her.

So, when he looked in his heart for literary material in these earlier years of his versifying, he saw many things more vividly than his heart's titular queen. Everything was grist that came to his mill. Tournaments, horsemanship, war and politics furnished not only his similes but his subject-matter. His mouth is too tender for the hard bit of virtue. Stella's heart is a citadel fortified with wit and stored with disdain. In allowing herself to be used as the means of Love's attacks, from which she herself goes free, she is like "some weak lords neighboured by mighty kings," who yield their coasts as bases for attacks on others as the price of immunity for themselves. The Turkish hardened heart has caused Love to flee his native Greece.

When people found Philip dull and moody, they put it down, he says in one of his sonnets, to verse-making, to pondering the problems of statecraft in which the Queen was then employing him, or "harder judges" laid it to "ambition's rage." And after all they may have been nearer right than he was when he attributed it to "only Stella's eyes and Stella's heart." Certainly it was less the mooning lover than the keen young statesman that wrote the following:

> Whether the Turkish new moon minded be
> To fill her horns this year on Christian coast?
> How Poles' right king means without leave of host
> To warm with ill-made fire cold Muscovy?
> If French can yet three parts in one agree?
> What now the Dutch in their full diets boast?
> How Holland hearts, now so good towns be lost,
> Trust in the shade of pleasant Orange-tree?
> How Ulster likes of that same golden bit
> Wherewith my father once made it half tame?
> If in the Scotch court be no welt'ring yet?
> These questions busy wits to me do frame:
> I, cumbered with good manners, answer do,
> But know not how; for still I think of you.

The same relegation of his mistress to the very end, so that she comes in more like an afterthought than a climax, is particularly notable in his famous tournament sonnet, which cannot be quoted too often:

> Having this day my horse, my hand, my lance
> Guided so well that I obtain'd the prize,
> Both by the judgment of the English eyes
> And of some sent from that sweet enemy France;
> Horsemen my skill in horsemanship advance,
> Town-folks my strength; a daintier judge applies
> His praise to slight which from good use doth rise;
> Some lucky wits impute it but to chance;
> Others, because from both sides I do take
> My blood from them that did excel in this,
> Think Nature me a man-at-arms did make.
> How far they shot awry! the true cause is,
> Stella look'd on, and from her heav'nly face
> Sent forth the beams which made so fair my race.

In the other, and less well known, sonnet of the tilt-yard, there is the same gusto for the sport, but Stella is allowed a greater part:

> In martial sports I had my cunning tried,
> And yet to break more staves did me address,
> While, with the peoples shouts, I must confess,
> Youth, luck and praise even fill'd my veins with pride;
> When Cupid, having me, his slave, descried
> In Mars's livery prancing in the press:
> What now, Sir Fool! said he—I would no less:
> Look here, I say! I look'd, and Stella spied,
> Who, hard by, made a window send forth light.
> My heart then quak'd, then dazzled were mine eyes,
> One hand forgot to rule, th' other to fight,
> Nor trumpet's sound I heard, nor friendly cries:
> My foe came on, and beat the air for me,
> Till that her blush taught me my shame to see.

Philip was writing excellent poetry, stirring and beautiful. But it was not excellent love poetry. It was almost every other kind of poetry but love poetry, in fact, except by pretence. The time was at hand, however, when he would take these sonnets and incorporate them in a sequence so charged with tenderness and longing, with passion and regret and struggling renunciation, that his *Astrophel and Stella* would stand forever among the greatest poems of human love in the language he did so much to make.

Sometime in the summer of 1581, or during that autumn, Penelope was married; and a very good marriage it was for a girl who, beautiful though she was, had only a hundred pounds a year and no more than two thousand for dowry. Her husband was considered rather a boor, but he was somewhere near her own age, and so great were his possessions that he was known as the rich Lord Rich. Many years later, when Charles Blount had become Earl of Devonshire and Penelope had been his mistress for so long that the liaison was accepted as a matter of course, she divorced Rich, and Devonshire championed this action and her subsequent marriage to himself by stating, among other things, that she had protested against her first marriage "at the very solemnity." But, if this was true, it seems strange that Philip, who gave his opinion of Rich with vigour and venom in the sonnets, did not put in something about it, when the marriage became an abomination in his sight, as soon it did.

At the time any protest which he might have made would have been purely altruistic. His uncle Huntingdon, his sincere well-wisher Walsingham, and Burghley, who was generally his friend when he felt that he could afford to be, were the girl's guardians. Had he chosen, it seems quite evident that he could have stood in the bridegroom's shoes. As he wrote, when it was too late, "I might—unhappy word—O me, I might." Worldly considerations also seem to have made him draw back, for he lamented that:

> . . . too much wit, forsooth, so troubled me,
> That I respects for both our sakes must show;
> And yet could not, by rising morn foresee
> How fair a day was near: O punish'd eyes,
> That I had been more foolish, or more wise!

From the practical point of view he was even farther from being in a position to marry than he had been some years before. Not only had his debts grown to be enormous as measured against his resources, but his brightest prospects had gone glimmering. The enterprising Lettice had not long been Countess of Leicester before she presented her new lord with a legitimate son of his own; and Philip had been compelled to put a gay front on his disappointment by sporting the single word "*Speravi*" "dashed through" as his motto in the lists. No girl who was not a considerable heiress could now be regarded as a suitable match for him. The load of debt which can even add a certain glamour to an attractive young bachelor makes a top-heavy cargo for the matrimonial bark whose mistress brings no ballast to its launching.

How long it took Philip to come to a realizing sense of what he had lost is not certain. With his brother-in-law of Pembroke and his uncle of Leicester he went to Oxford that summer and saw William Gager's tragedy *Meleager* performed in the hall of Christ Church College. In September he was down at Dover in attendance on Don Antonio, the Portuguese Pretender. In December in the letter from Wilton, in which he begged a reward for Robert's messenger, he asked Walsingham to give his humble salutations to his "ecceeding like to be good frend" the Secretary's daughter Frances: which sounds as if he were already engaged in those negotiations which resulted in his marriage with her nearly two years later.

If so, his infatuation with Penelope must have begun after the end of 1581, for the internal evidence of the sonnets shows that it cannot have flared up and died away in the brief interval between her wedding and this visit to Wilton; and on the other hand, after making every allowance for the Elizabethan's utilitarian attitude towards marriage, it is impossible to imagine a man of Philip's make-up planning a marriage with a young girl, who was moreover the daughter of one of his closest friends, at the same time that he was making passionate love to another man's wife. The affair with Penelope caused him to suffer enough in conscience without that.

Gentle, fastidious, idealistic and intellectual, the son of a father whose life was notably chaste, and of a well-educated, wise and humorous mother, and the affectionate companion of a sister whose brains were as good as his own, he lacked the robust health and the strong tide of animal spirits which might have led him into amorous adventuring in spite of the moral background of his childhood and youth. "Apt to like," as he said he was, when he saw beauties "of many carats fine," he had often fancied himself in love: had "thus with this young lion played." And it is not probable that he found any dearth of young court beauties to join in the game with a young man so handsome, pleasant and distinguished as he. Of the risks he ran in doing this Dyer had once seen fit to warn him in a sonnet about a satyr who burnt his mouth by kissing Prometheus's fire. Philip had answered with a sonnet about another satyr who ran away from the sound of a horn that he himself blew, and rhymed about "the pursuit of my desired prey" with quite the air of the courtly libertine.

But he had in fact reached his later twenties without becoming romantically interested in any woman and had acquired a reputation at court for invulnerability to feminine attractions, of which he himself was well aware:

> Because I breathe not love to every one,
> Nor do not use set colours for to wear,
> Nor nourish special locks of vowèd hair,
> Nor give each speech a full point of a groan,
> The courtly nymphs, acquainted with the moan
> Of them which in their lips love's standard bear:
> What, he! (say they of me): now I dare swear
> He cannot love: no, no, let him alone.

Until now he had found romance in politics. His choice of Penelope Devereux as the sovereign lady of his verses may well have been due to the fact that she seemed so safe.

Thus it was quite natural that, when he did fall in love, he should fall with passionate intensity, and that, rooted in dishonour as the affair necessarily was, the torments of an outraged conscience should be added to the pangs of unrequited affection. Back in the days when he was merely amusing himself and pleasantly flattering Penelope with his verses, he could scorn the "rubarb words" of the gross moralist who insisted that Desire must plunge his soul into a slough of sinful thoughts, and retort confidently that:

> If that be sin, which in fixed hearts doth breed
> A loathing of all loose unchastity,
> Then love is sin, and let me sinful be.

But with Penelope the wife of another man there was no disguising from himself the antagonism between Virtue and his longings. His love, he believed, was pure, but Desire so clung to it that he could hardly tell the one from the other. An æsthetic delight in her beauty: her golden head and swelling lips; the "beamy black" of her eyes and her fair skin, which were "like morning sun on snow," never ceased to make up a large measure of his feeling for her. He loved her the more because in her Venus had learned Chastity, Love was chasteness, and no man could enter her heart. After enumerating some of the charms by which he "might be fully blest"—his "maiden Muse doth blush to tell the rest"—he calls upon Virtue to awake, with the reminder that "beauty but beauty is." But the moment that Stella appears:

> O me, that eye
> Doth make my heart give to my tongue the lie.

The virtue lodged in Stella's beauty bends his love to good;

> But, ah, Desire still cries, give me some food . . .

and how to banish it he cannot tell.

Writing in an age which has become proverbial for the volcanic utterance of sensual passion, he wrote little of his love that could offend even a Victorian taste. Burned and dazzled by Stella's beauty, he prays indeed that it "may go down with meeker beams to bed." In the strife between Virtue and Love,

> While each pretends that Stella must be his,

Love claiming her "fair outside," Virtue insisting that Stella's true self is her "virtuous soul," he even proposes a shameful compromise:

> Well, Love, since this demur our suit doth stay,
> Let Virtue have that Stella's self; yet thus,
> That Virtue but that body grant to us.

But this was only a brief truce in those "civil wars," which he described as raging within him.

It becomes obvious that he was not of the material of which great lovers are made. Like Ronsard, he loved women too well to be even a successful lover. With him, as he said, Desire went upon "stilts of fear"—fear of his lady's displeasure at some over-boldness, still greater fear lest his love should bring her to harm. When he is tempted to steal a kiss while she is asleep, he reminds himself of the danger of "her just and high disdain." It is only in the intoxication of the moment after he has overcome this dread that he can play the hardy transgressor, when

> . . . she makes her wrath appear
> In Beauty's throne; see now who dares come near
> Those scarlet Judges, threatening bloody pain.
> O heav'nly fool, thy most kiss-worthy face
> Anger invests with such a lovely grace,
> That anger's self I needs must kiss again.

When he has harmed her, not from carelessness, "but wit, confus'd with too much care," he cannot forgive himself:

> Only with pains my pains thus eased be,
> That all thy hurts in my heart's wreck I read;
> I cry thy sighs, my dear, thy tears I bleed.

Nor, true to the precepts of his Italian mentor, did he forget to modulate the expression of his love with a lighter touch:

> Dear, why make you more of a dog than me?
> If he do love, I burn, I burn in love.

And there was "Good brother Philip," who peeped love ditties in her neck. For, like Catullus's Lesbia, Penelope had a pet sparrow, which she had named after him. He bears it, with envy, even suffers it to sleep

> In lilies nest where Love's self lies along.

But to see it "through those lips drink nectar from that tongue" is more than he can stand.

> Leave that, Sir Phip, lest off your neck be wrung!

Only when he writes of Rich, her husband, do his feelings rip through the finely-wrought fabric of chivalrous courtesy in which he keeps them draped. He propounds a riddle about a nymph rich in beauty, in reputation, in affection and "those gifts which give the eternal crown"; who indeed

> Hath no misfortune but that Rich she is.

Of all rich fools who damn "their own selves to Tantal's smart" he lays his curse on one,

> . . . who by blind fortune's lot
> The richest gem of love and life enjoys,
> And can with foul abuse such beauties blot;
> Let him, deprived of sweet but unfelt joys,
> Exil'd for aye from those high treasures which
> He knows not, grow only in folly Rich!

And winding up an eloquent description of jealousy as he evidently sees it personified in Penelope's husband, he asks savagely,

> Is it not evil that such a devil wants horns?

What was Penelope's response to his wooing remains almost as debatable as what it ought to have been. Nor is the evidence sufficiently clear to warrant the passing of judgment. The record, partial and obscure, was purposely still further confused by placing certain sonnets out of their proper order, so that one person's guess about much that happened seems to be as good as another's. Some, who like their saints in solid plaster, have been unable to get beyond the fact that, if Philip was in earnest, he was guilty of cherishing an adulterous passion. They would sacrifice his own record of his long struggle against it in order to make him the hero of a Sunday-school book. Others have gone to the opposite extreme and by giving an unnatural significance to certain quite ordinary words and ignoring the evidence of the last sonnet of the sequence would represent him as carrying the affair on into the years after his marriage. There are those who believe that they can read in the poems the record of a single yielding on Penelope's part to his impassioned pleas. And again there are some who have chosen to see in her no more than the insensate object of an idolatry which she encouraged for her selfish gratification, and—forgetting that nobody has ever succeeded in laying down a proper line of conduct for the Fanny Brawnes of this world —have left her to the tender mercies of those who can find no excuse for young ladies who do not surrender at discretion to the exigeant demands of enamoured young geniuses. According to these partisans they are flirts and minxes if they treat the ardent youth with friendliness, mere decorative lumps of clay if they extinguish him with a merciful brutality.

But, peering through the golden haze that shrouds her reflected image in her lover's verses, one can see Penelope, not too dimly, as she was: beautiful, physically hardy, with such a skin that

> The sun, which others burned, did her but kiss;

impulsive and passionate, but kind, essentially honest, intelligent, and, above all, clear-sighted in estimating the wistful idealist who had fallen in love with his own conception of her. It was not an easy situation in which the lovely bride of nineteen or twenty now found herself. Her guardians had got her well off their hands; her mother was committed to a matrimonial adventure with a man so notorious for his inconstancy and shiftiness that his new father-in-law had insisted upon a repetition of the marriage ceremony in his presence; and she was neglected by a husband who has left such a reputation behind him that Philip's bitter references to him seem to have been quite just.

If it took her some time to become convinced that the amatory fire-works with which Philip had been entertaining her for several years had now turned into the flames of a genuine conflagration, one can easily understand why. Obviously she liked him. It must have been amusing to discover that she could sweeten his pains, as he put it, by singing his plaints, and could delight him by reading aloud the piercing phrases in which he wrote the anatomy of all his woes. It must have been flattering to her, who was flouted by a loutish husband, to find that she could snub and call back at will one of the most charming and distinguished personages in Europe. It should be remembered to her eternal credit that, when at length she told him that she loved him, she added that she

> . . . loved a love not blind;
> Which would not let me, whom she loved, decline
> From nobler cause, fit for my birth and mind.

She saw clearly what he, perhaps, never understood, that a nature such as his could find nothing but misery in the sordid expedients of a backstairs intrigue.

For a time came when he caught her eyes fixed upon him, and "they fled with blush which guilty seemed of love." Soon he could exult:

> Gone is the winter of my misery!
> . . . .
> For Stella hath, with words where faith doth shine,
> Of her high heart giv'n me the monarchy.

But the gift was conditional: he was only to enjoy it while he kept a virtuous course. The phrase seems to have been liberally interpreted, however.

> Sweet kiss, thy sweets I fain would sweetly indite
> . . . .
> Nest of young loves, schoolmaster of delight,
> Teaching the mean at once to take and give;
> The friendly fray, where blows both wound and heal,
> The pretty death, while each in other live.
> Poor hope's first wealth, hostage of promised weal;
> Breakfast of love . . .

Still hers were lips "where Beauty's blush in Honour's grain is dyed"; and the sweet garden-nymph that kept the cherry-tree banished him for greediness until he promised,

> I will but kiss, I never more will bite.

All dates in this connection are purely conjectural, but it does not seem improbable that the affair reached its climax in the late spring of 1582, during a visit of Penelope's to her mother. Philip also was a guest at the house. With a heart high with hope he blessed the very road that led him thither:

> And that you know I envy you no lot
> Of highest wish, I wish you so much bliss,—
> Hundreds of years you Stella's feet may kiss.

At the sight of the house he instructs his eyes, ears, breath, arms and lips to take each its share of Stella's beauty, lest his heart, overcharged with happiness, miss all in trying to comprehend all. In the Fourth of the *Songs* which are interspersed throughout the sequence he described the meeting to which he went with such sanguine expectations.

The setting was perfect: a night of stars, a garden sweet with flowers, and just moon enough to disclose Penelope's beauty. All chance of discovery had been guarded against;

PENELOPE RICH

from the painting in Lambeth Palace

by courtesy of His Grace the Archbishop of Canterbury

Jealousy himself had been lulled to rest. The Countess Lettice had gone to bed, thinking that her daughter was writing letters. In the stately old house all lay asleep, but Philip fancied that

> Yet asleep, methinks they say,
> Young fools, take time while you may.

Only the lady remained obdurate, though he pleaded and more than pleaded.

> Sweet, alas, why strive you thus?
> Concord better fitteth us;
> Leave to Mars the force of hands,
> Your power in your beauty stands.

The resort to such force as a gentleman might properly use in the circumstances was met by a defence which to him was impregnable.

> Woe to me, and do you swear
> Me to hate, but I forbear?
> Cursed be my destinies all,
> That brought me so high to fall;
> Soon with my death I will please thee:
> "No, no, no, no, my Dear, let be."

For a time "those blest eyes," which had been his heaven, became his hell. In his chagrin and an anger that seems to have been not altogether unjustifiable he wrote a long poem, calling on his Muse for revenge.

> Sweet babes must babies have, but shrewd girls must be beaten.

He calls her a thief, and none of your gentle English thieves who rob but do not slay, but a murdering thief, a tyrant, a rebel runaway from Venus, a witch who has turned his heart to lead, a devil "clothed in angel's shining," whose words of refusal have poured hell upon him. But let her mend her ways, and his Muse shall turn all these cruel words to praises.

When they met again, as he told it in the Eighth Song,

> Him great harms had taught much care,
> Her fair neck a foul yoke bare;
> But her sight his cares did banish,
> In his sight her yoke did vanish.

All round them was the beguiling beauty of the Maytime woods, and when neither of them could speak for pent-up emotion, Love itself spoke through his lips. But all his passionate wooing went for nought. He was dearer to her than her sight, she said, dearer than her beauty; she pledged him all her love and all her faith; it was not she that denied him:

> Tyrant Honour thus doth use thee,
> Stella's self might not refuse thee.

And again she interposed to his urging the same invincible defence:

> Therefore, dear, this no more move,
> Lest, though I leave not thy love,
> Which too deep in me is framed,
> I should blush when thou art named!

For a gentleman—probably for a mere man of proper feeling—acquiescence was the only course left open to him. Again her hands had repulsed his, though with an infinite grace. It was the end, in spite of all her vows, in spite of all the rendings of passion to which she left him, although neither of them, probably, could have believed it at the time. In the subsequent separation, which she wisely enjoined, he missed her horribly, of course, and comforted himself with thoughts of a day to come,

> When I blessèd shall devour
> With my greedy lickorous senses

Beauty, music, sweetness, love:
While she doth against me prove
Her strong darts, but weak defences.

He assured her that if

Some beauty's piece, an amber coloured head,
Milk hands, rose cheeks, or lips more sweet, more red

pleased him in his exile from her, it was only because they resembled her as wooden globes resembled the glist'ring skies. The choice delights and rarest company of a lady who was Dian's peer failed to cheer him. But he had to take himself in hand when another tried to lure him from his loyalty, and he struck a note of human frailty that is rather refreshing to mortals whose moral attainments are less high than his were:

Out, traitor Absence, dar'st thou counsel me
From my dear captainesse to run away,
Because in brave array here marcheth she
That, to win me, oft shows a present pay?
. . . .
Cannot heav'n's food, once felt, keep stomachs free
From base desire on earthly cates to prey?

When she returned to London it was a delight to look from his window and see her in a boat upon the Thames, her golden hair loosened by the wind so that she blushed at her dishevelment. But she insisted upon the wisdom of their keeping apart, and it maddened him to feel himself watched, to bear the comments when he symbolized his love with stars upon his armour, to glide away from a serenade beneath her window in fear of "Argus' eyes," and to have but a glimpse of her by the flare of a dropped link as her coach dashed past in the darkness.

Curst be the page from whom the bad torch fell:
Curst be the night which did your strife resist:

16

Curst be the coachman that did drive so fast,
With no less curse than absence makes me taste.

As *Astrophel and Stella* was originally printed it ended on a note of the deepest despair. But time was working its cure actually. Philip's passion, starved of even the sight of its object, waned, as every passion—requited or unrequited—eventually must. Even the last sonnet of the original sequence gives one more of a feeling of ingenuity than of depth of sentiment if it be read in the light of the two which have more lately been added as obviously meant by their author to conclude the poem. Already he had hinted to Penelope with courtly artifice that his preoccupation with his love was distracting him from a "great cause, which needs both use and art"; and it is a bad sign for the beloved when the lover begins to complain that his devotion is interfering with his work. From this it was no long step to the feelings with which, in the penultimate sonnet, he rounded on the passion which had hag-ridden him until he could bear it no more.

Thou blind man's mark, thou fool's self-chosen snare,
Fond fancy's scum, and dregs of scattered thought:
Band of all evils; cradle of causeless care;
Thou web of will, whose end is never wrought:
Desire! Desire! I have too dearly bought,
With price of mangled mind, thy worthless ware;
. . . .
For Virtue hath this bitter lesson taught,—
Within myself to see my only hire,
Desiring nought but how to kill Desire.

For natures such as his the bonds of holy wedlock are perfect freedom compared with the rack that stretched him between his high ideal and this illicit passion. If, by this time, another spring had come around, it may be safe to understand an allusion to his intended marriage with Frances Walsingham in his mention, in the last sonnet of all, of "that sweet yoke, where lasting freedoms be." For the project of that marriage was revived early in 1583; and in that poem Philip renounced his old love with all the fervency of a man who has taken on a new one.

> Leave me, O Love, which reachest but to dust;
> And thou, my mind, aspire to higher things;
> Grow rich in that which never taketh rust;
> Whatever fades, but fading pleasures brings.
> Draw in thy beams, and humble all thy might
> To that sweet yoke, where lasting freedoms be;
> Which breaks the clouds, and opens forth the light
> That doth both shine, and give us sight to see.
> O take fast hold; let that light be thy guide
> In this small course which birth draws out to death,
> And think how evil becometh him to slide,
> Who seeketh heav'n, and comes of heav'nly breath.
> Then farewell, world; thy uttermost I see:
> Eternal Love, maintain thy life in me.

Penelope must, at least, have felt with satisfaction that she had been right all the time; and Charles Blount was not the man to make them both miserable by wanting to eat his cake and have it too.

CHAPTER XI

SETTLING DOWN

A GOOD MANY TIDES ROARED UNDER LONDON BRIDGE while Philip struggled in the meshes of his passion: that "web of will, whose end is never wrought." The Queen once more avoided marriage with the Duke of Anjou, though she still declared that she was devoted to him; and the Duke of Guise, profiting by the consequent disappointment at the court of France, made himself all-powerful there. But the success of the Spanish armies in Portugal continued to drive France and England towards a reluctant partnership. In the Netherlands the bullet of a would-be assassin tore through the neck and jaw of William of Orange; and anxiety lest he die of the wound killed his wife, Philip's friend, the beautiful Charlotte of Bourbon-Montpensier. In England the Queen of Scots went on making her prison the centre of conspiracies which aimed to place her on the English throne with the assistance of an invading army of Frenchmen and Spaniards, while Elizabeth still refused her support to the Protestant lords of Scotland, though they succeeded in kidnapping the young King James from the Catholic faction.

But the part that Philip was allowed to play in affairs was either a small one or little to his liking. He was not, however, much worse off in this respect than were most of his sort who enjoyed the Queen's favour. Dyer fared no better. Fulke Greville and Raleigh got a little of the fighting in Ireland that ended in the massacre of the Papal expedition by Lord Grey de Wilton; but Elizabeth liked to have these handsome, clever and agreeable young men about her. She was fond of them, dreaded their running into danger abroad, and punished them severely when their desire for glorious action drove them to slip away against her will. Sir Humphrey Gilbert had trouble in convincing her that his presence with the expedition which he was organizing to found a colony in North America was essential to its success.

Philip's assignment to duty as a sort of aide-de-camp to Don Antonio, the Portuguese Pretender, was by no means an unimportant one as such things were going at the time. The uneasiness caused by King Philip's seizure of the Portuguese throne was almost universal. Not only were England, France and the Dutch rebels terrified by such an enormous addition to his power, but Egypt and the Turk, Venice and the merchants of Marseilles were filled with anxiety lest the trade with India by the Red Sea route should be ruined by a commercial policy even more narrow and selfish than that of the Portuguese kings. Don Antonio's efforts to obtain the Portuguese throne were accordingly of world-wide interest.

In the May of 1581 he had written to Philip from Tunis of an expedition which he was fitting out there, of the gentlemen who were joining him, and of how he would not consider their number complete until Philip was among them. He had addressed him as "Illustrious Nephew" and signed himself "your greatest friend," which was, perhaps, not too much, considering that the agent of the Archduke Matthias had been glad when he could write home that Mr. Philip Sidney was well-disposed toward his princely master. Philip had already been in communication with Don Antonio's agent. So, when "the Strange Guest," as the Pretender was called, arrived in England that summer, a fugitive, but with jewels to pawn for English ships and fighting men, Philip was naturally enough assigned to attend him.

Here, one might have supposed, was the very opportunity he had been longing for, the opportunity of striking a shrewd blow at the power of Spain and, through Spain, at the Pope. Terceira in the Azores, where the feeling against the Spanish King was stronger than in Portugal itself, was

Don Antonio's immediate objective. Once firmly established there, he could more hopefully strike for his kingdom on the mainland. By the end of September he stayed only for a change in the wind to let his ships out of the Thames and bring them around to Dover, where he awaited them. But on the twenty-sixth of that month Philip wrote off to Hatton, begging to be relieved from so wearisome and expensive a duty. He suspected, he said, that the Queen wished him to accompany the expedition; but he could be of small service to Don Antonio, if he did so; Don Antonio himself wished to have him at court to watch over his interests there; and Philip's own affairs and those of his father required his supervision at home.

Though he may have spoken the mere truth in this, it was not like either him or his father to put their private affairs before what they regarded as an important public duty. Perhaps he did not see any signs of the natural-born leader of forlorn hopes in the green eyes of the dusky, grey-headed royal bastard who would have been his chief. Certainly he knew only too well how little real assistance Elizabeth was likely to give to the enterprise. The crown-jewels of Burgundy and of Navarre, with which those of Portugal had now gone to keep company in the Tower, bore him witness that her course in such matters was always the same. After an initial loan just large enough to make the recipient a thorn in some adversary's flesh, but too small to enable him to strike any blow that might involve her in his fortunes, the value of his collateral would suddenly shrink in her eyes; or he would be brazenly told that she could not allow an attack upon a sovereign with whom she was on friendly terms. In Don Antonio's case the co-operation of Drake and Hawkins, though repeatedly promised, was finally refused, and his own ships were detained in Plymouth harbour. The subsequent conduct of the Pretender also justified Philip's decision. For, when a fleet manned by French volunteers went down fighting in his cause in Terceira harbour the next July, Don Antonio kept to the safety of the castle on shore.

Philip's next duty, purely ornamental though it was, may have given him more satisfaction. When he returned to court at the beginning of 1582 after his poverty-stricken retirement to Wilton for the Christmas holidays, he found the Anjou marriage, though not given up, at least deferred. Ever since November, when the Duke, against the will of his brother the King, had slipped over from Dieppe in disguise, he and Elizabeth had been at their high comedy of courtship. There was the travesty of a betrothal between them before everybody in the gallery of Greenwich palace near the end of the month, in which she kissed him on the mouth and gave him a ring. But immediately after, she began to insist that she must have Calais back again as part of the marriage settlement. Out of the tangle in which she had involved herself she had to buy her way by supporting Anjou's sovereignty of the Netherlands with enormous subsidies. For the Dutch, despairing of any reliable help from her, were now ready to make peace with Spain on any terms they could get; and, with Guise back in power at the court of France, Anjou was her only means of keeping up the resistance to Spain, short of going to war herself.

So her "Frog" was packed off to his new dominions in February, his saddle-bags stuffed with sixty thousand pounds in English gold, and with promises of much more to follow. Elizabeth kept him company on his road as far as Canterbury, loud in her protestations of love and of regret and sorrow at his departure. Since he had come with few attendants, she furnished him with such a train of her own courtiers that a list of them reads like a roster of the celebrities of her time. Leicester, Hunsdon with his three brothers, Windsor and Sheffield, Raleigh, Carew, Fulke Greville, Dyer and Philip Sidney were among the three hundred or four hundred gentlemen that attended him. Lord Howard, with a fleet of fifteen ships, escorted him.

At Flushing, where he disembarked, the Prince of Orange received him with such a burst of trumpets and drums "that the aire rang with it." The Duke's guard of French and Switzers awaited him at Middelburg; and since Flushing was too small to house so great a company, he covered the few miles between the two places on foot, while cressets at ten-pace intervals flared through the twilight to illuminate his steps. At Antwerp, after endless feastings, allegories, processions and oaths to respect the ancient liberties of his subjects, the Duke was invested in the crimson velvet bonnet and ermine-trimmed mantle of the dukes of Brabant. Then his English attendants, seeing quite clearly the emptiness of the man beneath all this pomp, left him, as Leicester remarked, "stranded like a hulk upon a sandbank." Philip of Spain had an equally just measure of him. It was the throat and teeth of William of Orange, not those of François of Anjou, through which the Spaniard's bullet tore its way less than a month later. But the Duke had served Elizabeth's turn admirably for now these many years, and he was still serving it.

Returning from all this gorgeous mummery, Philip found certain family matters that required his attention. Thomas, now in his thirteenth year, was about to follow in the footsteps of his two brothers at Shrewsbury School. Robert had lately returned from his travels, a finished young gentleman of nearly twenty, and Philip began to look about for a place for him at court. He might have saved himself the trouble of doing so, for Robert had the gift for feathering his own nest, which in Philip was so conspicuously lacking. Soon the enterprising youth was asking Molyneux to write out nicely for the Queen's own eye the reasons for the creation of a certain office which he thought would suit him, and to do it quickly, as others were on the lookout for the place. It was suggested to Sir Henry that he undertake the government of Ireland once more, and he wrote to Philip about the conditions he intended to insist upon if he accepted the office.

The administration of Lord Grey de Wilton had again demonstrated that there was more to the "detestable service" of governing Ireland than putting rebels to the sword. Sir John Desmond's naked corpse swung by the feet from the tower of Cork Cathedral; his brother the Earl was a fugitive, whose skull was soon to be grinning on a pike above London Bridge. But the general pardon which the Queen had proclaimed for the rest of the rebels had been received as an evidence of weakness rather than of magnanimity; Irish affairs were rapidly falling into their old, distracted pattern; and none seemed so likely to be able to straighten them out again as the man who had twice before achieved there something that looked like success when it was compared with the performance of those who had gone before and followed after him.

Sir Henry, however, had no intention of being torn a third time between the machinations of the wily Irishmen and the utter unreasonableness of his royal mistress. Evidently feeling that he had done his full share of that disagreeable duty, he considered the resumption of it only for Philip's sake. That Philip should be his successor was his first condition for undertaking it. For himself, he was very well off in Wales. Raising troops for service in Ireland when he was called upon to do so, suppressing recusancy when he must, looking out—among other things—for the safety of two useful subjects whom he believed to be falsely accused of murdering "a very common drunkard," the building of conduits and stone fountains for the water-supply of Ludlow and Bewdley, the addition of a tennis-court to Ludlow Castle and the decoration of the castle chapel with the arms of Elizabeth and of various noblemen who had been connected with the place, kept him pleasantly occupied. His wife could visit him there as often and for as long as her continuing bad health permitted. He was not too far from his beloved daughter at Wilton and within comparatively easy reach of his sons.

The terms on which he would accept the viceroyalty of Ireland were accordingly stiff ones. First, Philip was to go with him and stay with him until he thought it wise to transfer the burden of government to Philip's shoulders. Second, the Queen must retract her reiterated statements that he was "a chargeowse and wasteful servant" when he was in Ireland before and admit that he was the best lord deputy she ever had there. Third, as a necessity for his prestige in Ireland, his former good service there must be rewarded by "nobilitation" both there and in England, "with some land or Fee Farme" to support this new dignity. And fourth, if she should decide to send him on these conditions, he would prefer the title of Lord Lieutenant to that of Lord Deputy. Considering these demands, it is hardly surprising that little or nothing more is to be heard of this proposal.

Philip went up to Wales and spent the summer with him. The broad streets of Ludlow, the fine, new houses of the members of the Council of the Marches, the warlike stateliness of the castle, were all charming. Philip made some effort to get himself appointed a member of the Council, hoping to bring in with him his cousin Coningsby. But the high gods at court saw otherwise. The same thing happened when he applied for the captaincy of the Isle of Wight. Lord Burghley, with the advancement of two sons of his own to consider, may have seen little wisdom in furthering that of one who could not help being their brilliant rival, while the Queen's feeling towards Philip from this time till his death seems to have been a feline mixture of affectionate pride, when he was at court, and a fault-finding and jealous distrust, when his holding any position in the government was involved.

For all the adulation which surrounds his name whenever it is mentioned in the writings of his contemporaries, one suspects that subtle and powerful enemies at court were responsible for many of these disappointments. Sussex was Leicester's bitter rival there and would do what he could to thwart any supporter of "the Gipsie," as he called him. Philip had given both Ormonde and Oxford good cause to dislike him, and both were favourites of the Queen. At the beginning of 1583 he made application to be associated with his uncle of Warwick in the mastership of the Queen's Ordnance, but he received only a subordinate appointment, though he had Warwick's backing in his suit. Six months later he was still writing to Burghley in an effort to get his position confirmed by letters patent. The Dutch asked to have him sent over to them at the head of a force of English cavalry, since its command would require more diplomatic than military experience. But nothing came of their request. Even the knighthood which was conferred upon him in this same January must have seemed to him a barren mockery.

It is easy to imagine how from boyhood Philip Sidney must have dreamed of the day when the sword of some great captain should strike upon his shoulder, as he knelt amid the carnage of a stricken field, and a voice hoarse with shouts of battle should bid him rise, Sir Philip. He would be *Miles:* knighted for valour, that is to say; he would be no *Eques Auratus*—which was the formal designation of one whose knighthood was the reward of merit of some other kind—if he might choose. Best of all would be to be made a banneret, like his grandfather Sir William, for valour at a splendid victory at which the royal standard was unfurled. But alas for the dreams of youth! When the Queen had presented the Garter to Prince John Casimir in 1579, there had been no time for his formal installation. This it was now arranged to perform by proxy. John Casimir chose Philip for his representative; and, since the shoulders of no mere esquire were deemed worthy to bear the splendid mantle of what for its pre-eminence was known simply as "The Order," Philip was made a knight-bachelor for no better reason than to qualify him for his place in the ceremony.

Frustrated in what was his natural course and thwarted in his love, he began to think seriously of taking an active part in the exploration and settlement of the new lands beyond the Atlantic. His interest in them had strongly survived his disappointment in Frobisher's "gold." Michall Lok dedicated his map of the New World to him in 1582, and his old college friend Hakluyt did the like with *Divers Voyages*, which had earned that avid recorder of discoveries the chaplaincy of the English embassy at Paris. As late as July in 1583, some months after the negotiations for his marriage with Frances Walsingham had been renewed, Philip wrote to Sir Edward Stafford, Elizabeth's ambassador to the French court, that he was thinking of going with Sir Humphrey Gilbert's expedition "very eagerly; whereto your Mr. Hakluyt hath served for a very good trumpet." Sir Henry Sidney and three of Philip's uncles were financially interested in the enterprise. He himself held a patent for the discovery and possession of "thirty-hundred-thousand acres"; and the scheme appealed to him especially as a possible outlet for the loyal Catholic subjects of the Queen, who yet could not conform to the requirements of the Established Church. But, when the time of departure came, the expedition sailed without him.

Thus recapitulated, his life during these years does not seem to have been an idle one. But again his want of employment drove him back to the work upon which, more than on anything else, his fame was to rest. If the young Napoleon Bonaparte had made a success of that first and only novel of his, if Abraham Lincoln had won certain of those minor elections which he lost, a writer of cheap best-sellers and a skilful backwoods politician might have been the only yield from ore that needed the fierce, slow fire of adversity to extract its pure metal. So Philip, who without it might have been only a wiser Raleigh or a gentler Gilbert, was forged into one of the great writers of his race.

In his enforced leisure he turned back to the *Arcadia*

as to a theme which he had only imperfectly developed. An heroic romance in its original conception, he determined to make it more heroical still. In addition to Montemayor's *Diana Enamorada* he knew the Greek romances and *Amadis of Gaul* and him of Greece as well; the *Aetheopica* of Heliodorus, translated by Thomas Underwood, was a popular book of the day; and he laid them all under contribution in the work of turning the straightforward tale, which he had written for his sister's amusement, into an enormous and ornate complication of characters, episodes and adventures, disguises, tournaments and feats of arms, which defy the modern reader's memory to keep them clear as thoroughly as the artificial style exhausts his patience.

Forgotten were the sensible precepts laid down in the *Defence of Poesie*. If the extravagances of *Euphues* were avoided, a new sort of decoration, which seems to the modern reader hardly less absurd than Lyly's strange beasts and fowls, fishes and plants, involves the style with long-drawn phrases of balanced sound and sense that drag each sentence down the page till the eye blurs and the brain reels in the effort to follow it. For Philip had got the idea of writing a prose poem—an idea which has meant the shipwreck of more than one young man since his day—and, like his successors, he was soon fain to sacrifice his sense to his style. Up popped the Philip who, even in the *Defence*, could think that the old song of Percy and Douglas would have been the better for the trimmings of Pindar. The Philip who condemned the use of art to show art and not hide it was gone into eclipse. The compact novel, which he had called his "toyful book," spread itself out under the evil spell of a serious critical purpose until it was longer by a quarter than the original version, and yet it was unfinished when he ceased to work upon it.

It is possible that he himself came to the regretful conclusion at length that it was labour lost, and that he had been working from false premises. On his death-bed he asked that the manuscript be burnt. The pious ministers that stood about attributed this request to an edifying repentance of having added to the number of such traps of Satan as they considered all romances to be. But Philip was not of the sort, deeply religious though he was, to be scared into Puritanism by the imminent terrors of Death and Hell. It would be artistically, not morally, that the *Arcadia* appeared in his eyes to sin against the light, if it so appeared at all.

But however he came to think of it, and however long, confused and over-elaborated it may seem in our day, it was the outstanding English novel of its time, and more than that. For almost fifty years it enjoyed a continuous popularity. King Charles I incorporated a passage from it into the prayers he used at his execution and thereby earned an extra jibe from Milton, who could never keep his politics and his literature separate. Richardson the novelist owed a debt to it. It was one of the first English books to be translated into French and was greatly admired and widely read in France; and by 1668 it is said that there were more than thirty foreign editions of it.

Its influence and reputation have placed its author in the category of writers so famous that it is no longer necessary to read their works. But long after it went so completely out of fashion as to be unreadable to the general public, it could still charm through the reflected beauty of his personality. More than two hundred years after its publication Charles Lamb, in touching upon the delicacy and restraint with which certain parts of the story had been treated, wrote of him: "In the sweetly constituted mind of Sir Philip Sidney it seems as if no ugly thought or unhandsome meditation could find a harbour."

It was November of 1582 before Philip came back from Wales. He carried letters from his father to "the Lord Hy Thresorer of England," which he hoped to deliver in person. But Lord Burghley was sorrowing for the death of his son-in-law, William Wentworth. So Philip wrote to him, enclosing the letters: "least becaws we weare deer frendes and companions together my sight might stur some greef unto yowr Lordshippe." Ambition has need to be made of sterner stuff than this, even the moderate ambition which Philip's had now become. He wrote again to Burghley in the following January, after another Christmas at Wilton and a New Year's Day at court, when his gift to the Queen was a golden flower-pot in the form of a castle, adorned on one side with small diamonds. This was his letter asking Burghley's help toward his appointment in the Ordnance Office, which, he wrote, he desired much more for the "serviseable experience" to be gained in it "than for any other commodity, which I think is but small, that can arise of it."

It was work which, even in his subordinate position, he must have found most congenial. His unwavering belief that, sooner or later, England must face and defeat the whole power of Spain made every aspect of the national defence intensely interesting to him. He had caused to be sent to him from abroad the latest edition of the maps of Ortelius, a book describing the harbours of Europe, and another, which dealt with towns and fortresses. Germany, the chief source of many important military supplies, was well known to him. The family ironworks at Robertsbridge must have given him some acquaintance with the smelting of ore and the casting of cannon. And he had been long enough a soldier in the field to bring to his new employment that fervent desire to correct the shortcomings and stupidities of the service of supply, which no fighter at the front can be long in acquiring. His uncle, who was his chief, and who had held the post through the twenty years since that poisoned bullet at Le Havre had made it impossible for him to engage in active service, was such a man that Spenser wrote of him that none envied him while he lived, and that, dead, he was "as living, counted dear." Most probably it was in his first, fresh interest in this new work that Philip wrote that sonnet, already alluded to, in which he begged Penelope:

> And on my thoughts give thy lieutenancy,

warning her lest

> . . . fools in me thy works reprove,
> And scorning say, "See what it is to love."

The power of Penelope's enchantment was indeed waning by this time. It was no later than this February that Philip's marriage with Frances Walsingham was again in the wind; and Burghley, having heard of "a comfortable purpose towards for your daughter," wrote to Walsingham: "God bless it." On the 1st of March Sir Henry wrote to his son's prospective father-in-law of his pleasure in "the joyful love and great liking between our most dear and sweet children." He gave his willing agreement to the marriage, he said, though he did feel that he might have had the Secretary's help in some small suit of his to the Queen, for he could have had a great sum for his goodwill, had Philip married in certain quarters. But then, he courteously went on, he supposed that it could have been only Philip's virtues which had caused him to be acceptable to young Frances, "who haply may have refused many richer marriages."

Thereupon the old Lord President proceeded to let himself go, as the best of men will do occasionally to a trusted friend, retailing at length those lifelong services to the Queen, for which he had received such small reward. He retold the story of the cruel years in Ireland, of his wife's tragic disfigurement, so that "now she liveth solitarily," of his waning fortune since the good old days of King Edward. He was thirty thousand pounds the poorer now, he said; five thousand pounds in debt, without enough land to pasture a mutton; old at fifty-four, toothless and shaking.

He had his three sons, he admitted: "one of excellent good proof," the second "of great good hope," and the third "not to be despaired of." Evidently, too, he had not lost his gift of humorous urbanity, which in this letter must be taken into account for his exaggeration of his ill fortune. If he was in debt, he had the magnificent additions and embellishments lately completed at Penshurst to thank for it; and his health was not too bad for him to write: "nor yet am I so old, nor my wife so healthy, but that she may die and I marry again, and get children or think I do." And he ended in a happy vein, sending "a buss to our sweet daughter" and begging Walsingham's "blessing on the young knight, Sir Philip." It is not impossible, moreover, that in this letter he was building up a basis on which to bargain in the matter of marriage settlements. If so, the letter is a masterpiece of its kind.

But the course of true love never ran smoothly for Elizabeth's young men. She personally took care that it should not. By a courtly fiction they were generally supposed to suffer from a hopeless passion for their royal mistress, and she regarded their marriages as so many faults in loyalty, forgave them only after an appropriate display of anger, and was loath to pardon the thieving girls who robbed her of their bridegrooms' romantical devotion. Philip's case was somewhat different because the innate honesty of his character forbade such nonsense between him and a woman who was more than old enough to be his mother. But he was made to suffer on another count. The Queen first heard of the marriage indirectly. Probably Walsingham had only waited to tell her of it until he should have received Sir Henry's letter of approval, for it is hard to imagine any reason for its having been kept secret from her. But after that illness confined him to his house at Barn Elms, and by the 19th of March he was fain to write to Hatton to protest against her opposition to the match.

Not unnaturally she may have felt hurt at not having been informed of a matter of such importance, which concerned two families that had been so long and so intimately in her service. And for her it was quite as natural that she should take a long time to recover her good humour towards them. Whether owing to this or not, the marriage was postponed, and for a time evidently postponed to such an indefinite date that Philip considered joining Gilbert's ill-fated expedition to America. Perhaps it was only her relenting that kept him from sharing Gilbert's death on that wild night in September, when in the little frigate Sir Humphrey led his fleet through the mighty tempest until "suddenly her lights were out."

Meanwhile the arrival of a former acquaintance from the Continent gave variety and interest to this time of waiting. "Albertus Alasco, free baron of Lasco, vaiode, or palatine of Seradia in Poland, arrived at Harwich in Essex; and on the last of April came by water to Winchester-house in Southworke, where he remained for the most part of his abode heere." He was a picturesque person even in that day of striking personalities, going about in scarlet—in purple robes for his audience with the Queen—and queer shoes which were thought to be like Chaucer's. He had an "English complection and a great, white beard which, when he was lying in bed, he delighted to spread out until it covered his shoulders." He was a good linguist, and his "unstudied answer" and "quick wittie reply" made him a social success, although it was said that "some knew him that might hardly commend him."

Philip, who had met him on the journey to Poland which Languet had forced his young protégé to take in the autumn of 1574, accompanied him on a visit to Oxford, whither he went from "the marriage of the Lord Norris his daughter to sir A. Paulet's eldest sonne at Ricot." University and town alike put forth their best for him. It was June; he was lodged at Christ Church, and "solemnelie satisfied with scholarlie exercises and courtlie fare" at All Souls. There was a pleasant comedy performed, "Rivales" by name, and "a verie statelie tragedie" of Dido, "Wherein the Queene's banket (with Eneas narration of the destruction of Troie) was livelie described in a march-paine pattern," as well as

SIR PHILIP SIDNEY

from the painting in the National Portrait Gallery

a tempest "wherein it hailed small confects, rained rose-water, and snew an artificial kind of snew, all strange, marvellous and abundant." To the usual complimentary addresses the Palatine replied in what he jovially called "*Militare Latinum*, Souldier's Latin," and took his departure in high good humour.

For the return journey the Queen lent him a royal barge complete with musicians and a cloth of estate. In such style, attended by Lord Russell, Sir Philip Sidney and other distinguished gentlemen, he came down the Thames to pay what was not his first visit to Doctor John Dee, the famous scholar, at his house at Mortlake. Philip knew the old place well, with its laboratories and workshops and, leading down to the river, its own stairs, down which the old philosopher's young children had the disturbing habit of tumbling to their considerable hurt. Its owner, though feared as little better than a wizard by the commonality, was a sound and able scientist for his day. Philip had often visited him, notably with Leicester, Dyer and others just before setting out on his embassy to the Emperor.

A graduate of St. John's at Oxford and a Master of Arts of Cambridge, John Dee had spent some time at the Dutch universities and at Louvain, had lectured at Paris and made a friend of Gerard Mercator, the great geographer. He brought to Cecil's attention the earliest elaborate treatise on shorthand, the *Steganographia* of the Abbot of Würzburg. He wrote a preface for the first English *Euclid*, interested himself in such diverse subjects as the diving-bell, the saw-mills at Prague, and optics, recommending the equipment of army officers with "perspective glasses." He invented what he called a "paradoxal compass," wrote a book on navigation, which he presented to Hatton, but of which the second volume, since it was chiefly composed of tables, proved to be too expensive for publication. Ortelius, the famous Dutch map-maker, paid him a visit.

The Gilberts, Davis, Hawkins, Frobisher and other practical navigators consulted him frequently and pored over his map of Atlantis, which was his name for America, and read the words "infinite yse" (ice), which he had written across the polar regions. The Muscovy Company got from him a chart for the North-east Passage. He published his plan for a kind of combination of coast guard, coast survey and naval training fleet under the title of *A Petty Navy Royal,* foreshadowed Trinity House with his suggestion of a "Grand Pilot General," and pointed out that most of the supplies of the foreign fish industry were taken on the English coast.

In his study was the five-foot quadrant of Richard Chancellor, who had carried the English flag into the White Sea. He had there also Mercator's globes with the path of comets marked upon the celestial one, a great piece of lodestone, a ten-foot *radius astronomicus,* which was an early form of telescope, swung in a frame, and a watch-clock that measured seconds. The Queen's heralds, the historians Camden and Stow, and the clerks of the records in the Tower spent many an evening turning over the contents of a chest of his, which was filled with seals of coats of arms, and another containing old English, Irish and Welsh deeds of lands.

In his library, besides the usual scholar's collection of classical authors, were great numbers of Persian and Arabic manuscripts. England was represented by the works of Roger Bacon and Robert Grosseteste. In the minds of the educated men of his time it was nothing against him that he had as well many books on the philosopher's stone and like matters, and that the *De Occulta Philosophia* of the famous alchemist Cornelius Agrippa used to lie open in the window of his study. There, too, stood the "gazing table" with its Sigilla Æmeth, AG AL signifying the Hebrew for "Thou art great forever, O Lord." In its crystal Edward Kelly, his assistant, foresaw the execution of the Queen of Scots, or said he did.

For what would now be called psychical research absorbed much of the learned doctor's time.

Dee had cast the horoscopes of Queen Mary Tudor and the Princess Elizabeth back in 1553 and landed in the Tower on a charge of treason in consequence. Lord Robert Dudley had consulted him as to the most auspicious day for Elizabeth's coronation. Elizabeth liked the tall, slender man, with his quiet, observant eyes, and had employed him in an attempt to discover the treasure buried and hidden by the monks at the dissolution of the monasteries by her father. When he was ill, she would send Lady Mary Sidney over to him from the near-by palace of Richmond with delicacies from the royal table; and her dwarf, Mistress Tomasin, once stayed the night at his house. Riding through Richmond Park, the Queen would pull up at his door for a learned word or two. The day of his first wife's funeral his royal patroness distracted the poor widower's thoughts from his sorrow by making him bring his famous convex mirror out into a field to demonstrate its properties. She had him frequently at court to quiet her perturbation about a "blazing star," and, as he noted, "axed me obscurely of Monsieur's [the Duke of Anjou's] state"; to which Dee replied that the Duke was *βιοθανατος* (dead alive).

She married him off the second time, though he was past fifty, to Jane Fromond, his "paynfull Jane," who was only twenty-two, clever, well-born and quick-tempered, a lady-in-waiting to Lady Howard of Effingham, whose husband was to command the English fleet against the Great Armada ten years later. Philip's friend Dyer was godfather to their son. Meanwhile the Queen had sent him to the Continent to consult famous physicians as far away as Frankfort-on-Oder about her persistent face-aches. Dee himself was learned in medicine and treated himself successfully for the stone, Sir Henry Sidney's old trouble, with "white wyne and salet oyle, and after that crabs eyes in powder with the bone in the carp's head." This he followed with "toasted cake buttered with sugar and nutmeg on it," which he accompanied with two draughts of ale, and within an hour voided much water and a stone as big as an Alexander seed.

But it was his studies in alchemy that attracted the Palatine of Siradia: "the marriage of the red man, copper and the white woman, mercury," which was bound to produce gold, if properly managed. By September the Prince had persuaded the learned doctor to accompany him to the Continent. The whole household of Dees and Kellys departed with him for Poland, travelling by night with a secrecy that indicates that the distinguished visitor had more debts than precious metal to leave behind him.

A superstitious mob sacked the Mortlake house, smashing the equipment of laboratory and workshop and scattering its treasures after its master's departure. Poor fools! Had they known it, the great *Malleus Maleficarum*, the *Hexenhammer* or "Hammer of Witches," which was first issued by the three inquisitors into sorcery in 1489, after Pope Innocent VIII's bull against witchcraft, was in that library. For Doctor Dee was all on the side of White Magic and such an enemy of the Black Art that authorities of European reputation came to consult with him about the best means of extirpating it.

Many years before, he had dedicated to the Emperor Maximilian II his *Monas Hieroglyphica*, a work composed of twenty-four theorems on variations of the symbols for the moon, the sun, the elements and fire, which were represented in the order named by the sign ☿. He soon left Alasco's service for that of Maximilian's successor, Rudolph II, and, honest seeker for truth though he was, returned to England six years later with such a magnificent train of coaches and baggage-wagons that he had to have an escort of soldiers to keep off the highwaymen as he crossed Germany.

Kelly, his assistant, who always wore a close-fitting cap to hide what the common hangman's knife had once done to his ears, and who was evidently a thoroughgoing charlatan, remained in Bohemia, where he was made a citizen and a councillor of state. By the aid of a secret powder—so at least he convinced the Emperor—he actually produced nearly an ounce of fine gold; and he succeeded in making Sir Edward Dyer his dupe also. Dyer on a mission to Prague stayed at his house and was arrested with him and the rest of his household, when the Emperor's patience at last became exhausted. But this was far in the future in the early autumn of 1583, and of no moment in Philip's life except as it indicates the intellectual atmosphere that he had to think in. For Philip had been three years dead when Doctor Dee returned home, laden with the rewards of a grateful emperor.

On September 21, 1583, the very day on which the learned man accompanied Alasco in his stealthy departure, Philip was finally married to Frances Walsingham. Hatton had used his good offices, and the Queen had withdrawn her objections. Seemingly with a view to putting his affairs in an order suitable to matrimony, Philip had sold his shares in the Gilbert project, and had done so none too soon: for twelve days before the wedding Sir Humphrey had found his grave in the Atlantic. By the terms of the marriage settlement Walsingham paid Philip's debts in the amount of fifteen hundred pounds, and it was provided—an arrangement not unusual at the time—that the young couple should have "their diet, if they will take it with him and in his house" either at Barn Elms or on Tower Hill.

The marriage has been described as one of placid affection on both sides. But so must any happy marriage appear in contrast with the affair of tempestuous passion which Philip recorded in his sonnets. From those far-off times when, as a little girl of four, she had shared with him in the terrors of St. Bartholomew's Day, Frances Walsingham had seen frequently her father's young friend and favourite, handsome, gentle, considerate and growing steadily in distinction. As a prize which she had snatched from the wiles of the reigning beauty of the court, he must have shone with added lustre in the eyes of his sixteen-year-old bride. Of her own beauty her marriage with the brilliant and erratic Earl of Essex after Philip's death, and her later marriage with the Earl of Clanricarde after Essex perished in his folly, bear witness. The forgetfulness of both herself and her unborn child, with which she rushed to Philip's side when he lay mortally wounded in the Netherlands, does as much for her love and devotion to him. Philip, for his part, had a standard for husbands as high as any of his others: his father had set it for him. He put it forth in that sonnet, which Doctor Johnson praised, and which begins,

> Who doth desire that chaste his wife should be,
> First be he true, for truth doth truth deserve.

The folly of another course and its earned penalty he described in some of the incidental verses in the *Arcadia* with as gay a touch of worldly wisdom as Boccaccio could have given to the theme.

It was not the brilliant marriage he might have been expected to make, and which, judging from his father's letter to Walsingham on the subject, he might have made, had he chosen to do so. But it seems to have been exactly the marriage he wished to make. By this time he had attained the tardy maturity which comes at last to men of his sort, and could accept with satisfaction the good things which life brought to him. He had steady and congenial work in the Ordnance. With a beautiful and affectionate bride he enjoyed a home with a mother-in-law whom he addressed with playful fondness as "my best mother," and a father-in-law whose liking and confidence were sure to place him in positions of useful and interesting employment. Already he had begun to make a close study of Scottish politics, which now loomed so threateningly on the diplomatic horizon that Walsingham had to miss his daughter's wedding to go on a special mission to King James. And by the end of the year it was evident that Elizabeth and her England must soon make the best use in their power of every loyal arm and brain at their command, if they were to escape the doom of death and ruin and conquest which their enemies had so long been plotting for them.

CHAPTER XII

MAN OF AFFAIRS

THE NEXT TWO YEARS WERE BUSY ONES FOR PHILIP AND probably as happy as any in his life. His position in the Ordnance, with his invalid uncle for his chief, was anything but an ornamental sinecure. Military weapons were changing so rapidly that in consequence, it was said, a man must learn the art of war all over again every two years, if he hoped to be successful in the practice of it. The invention of the process of casting muzzle-loading iron cannon had driven out of use the old, slow, cumbersome and always dangerous breech-loaders that had been improved but little since Roger Bacon's time. By 1582 bronze was supplanting iron for battery guns, and changes in naval architecture, fostered by Drake and other innovators in naval tactics, were all in favour of turning the traditional sea-fight by grappling and boarding the enemy into a duel of artillery.

In 1583 was appointed a Royal Commission on the Navy. The Lord Treasurer, the Lord Admiral, the Lord Chamberlain, Her Majesty's principal secretary and his sister's husband, that veteran of commissions since King Henry's time, Sir Walter Mildmay, were its imposing figureheads. The subcommissioners, who included in their number Drake, Frobisher, Carew and Raleigh, were such as to ensure a program of rapid and practical reformation. Fulke Greville was among them too; and it was not long before Philip must have been glad of the presence of this friend as well as of that of his father-in-law on the commission. For so variable and temporizing a policy as Elizabeth's was bound to aggravate the abuses inseparable from a War Office in a prolonged period of little military activity. Continual alarms continually allayed, the endemic revolt in Ireland, the underhand aids to privateers and various malcontents on the Continent—aids disavowed and often withdrawn as soon as offered—had evidently played havoc with the records of the department. Two hundred of the new bronze guns were missing and could not be accounted for.

As usual when people were hopelessly at cross-purposes, Philip was brought in to straighten matters out and smooth over misunderstandings. After he had been holding his subordinate office for more than two years he felt constrained to write to Burghley to clear himself of responsibility for the blame which the Queen was laying upon the Lord Treasurer for "the present poverty of her Majesties store." He had, he said, made it clear to her, as in conscience and duty bound, that the Earl of Warwick was not to blame; but he had not implicated anybody else, nor had the Queen mentioned Burghley in the conversation but only Sir William Pelham, who, she said, had laid the fault on Warwick's deputy. "Whereuppon," wrote Philip sturdily, "I onely answered that the money neither my lord nor anie of his had ever dealt with." The affair was destined to drag itself through a dreary sequel; and Elizabeth's stubborn wrong-headedness about it was to cost her army the services of an excellent chief-of-staff and possibly a great victory in the Netherlands within a little more than a year of the date of Philip's letter. Probably only those who have had to explain some tangle of official red-tape to an irritable and not too well-informed superior can appreciate what such interviews with the unreasonable, hot-tempered and now aging woman, who was his sovereign, cost the sensitive and high-minded Philip in nervous force. But the work was worth the sacrifice.

De Ségur, the secretary of King Henri of Navarre, came to England in the September of Philip's marriage, bringing a letter to him from Du Plessis-Mornay, and Philip entertained him down at Penshurst. But the Queen would have nothing to do with his business, which was a scheme for a Protestant alliance. Neither would she surrender the Navarre diamonds, upon which she had advanced a mere sixty thousand crowns, though payment of that sum with interest was offered to her. She insisted that the debt amounted to three hundred thousand—perhaps she counted what she had advanced to Anjou as leader of the Huguenots—and de Ségur went home bootless. Even two years later, after she had promised the King of Navarre her support and de Ségur had come over again to obtain some tangible evidence of it, she turned him off with the contemptible offer of a conditional loan of twenty-five thousand pounds. But events at home and news from abroad kept making it clearer that her policy of procrastination, double-dealing, prevarication and broken promises had all but run its course, and that the day was at hand when only swift ships and well-made guns, with well-trained English gunners and mariners to handle them, could save England from the invader.

In the November in which Philip and his bride were adjusting themselves to married life under her father's roof, a foolish and misguided young man named Somerville confessed in the Tower what he had already boasted of along the highway from Warwickshire: that he intended "to shoot the Queen with his dagg," and that he hoped "to see her head set upon a pole, for she was a serpent and a viper." The rack made it plain that he had no accomplices of any importance; but a month later the same dreadful engine dragged out of unhappy Francis Throgmorton the details of a plot that might have caused even Elizabeth's lion heart to miss a beat. Only the invariable deliberation of Philip of Spain, it appeared, had saved England from invasion and civil war any time since the past August.

Only the ships which he had agreed to furnish had been wanting. In the Netherlands Alexander Farnese had designated four thousand of his troops for the expedition. Guise was to have led them. Allen, to whom Campion had once commended young Philip Sidney as a tender plant that would repay the watering, was to have gone along as Papal Nuncio. Morecambe Bay had been selected as their landing place. A second army, the Duke of Mayenne at their head, had been quietly collected in the French Channel ports. Charles Paget had slipped across to Sussex from his Continental exile and taken soundings in the harbour of Rye as the best place for this force to disembark. Worse yet, he had made arrangements with the Earls of Arundel and Northumberland, who counted on bringing twenty thousand English Catholics into the field the moment that their liberators stood on English soil.

Such was the powder-magazine over which Elizabeth and her ministers had been living for months in blissful ignorance. To be sure, the eleventh anniversary of the massacre of St. Bartholomew's Day had been celebrated with special pomp in Paris that year, and Stafford had reported that there were rumours of a projected invasion of England. But the cry of "Wolf!" had been sounded so often and, as it turned out, so needlessly, that the revelations of the agonizing Throgmorton were doubly shocking. Northumberland and Arundel were promptly placed under arrest. So many others were suspected of having a guilty knowledge of the plot that Mendoza placed the number of prisoners at eleven thousand. Philip Sidney, with his habitual desire to believe the best of everybody, might write to the Earl of Rutland from Walsingham's house five days before Christmas that:

> Her Majestie is well, but trobled with these suspicions which aryse of some ill mynded subjectes towards her. My Lord of Northumberland I hope will discharge himself well of those doutes conceaved of him. He is yet kept in his hows, but for ought I can learn no matter of moment is laid unto him. . . .

The Embassadours of Spain and Frawnce be noted for great practisers.

It always went hard with Elizabeth when a great noble had to be punished; and even when the Armada sailed four years later, Arundel was still alive, though a prisoner in the Tower, to pray for its success. Northumberland shot himself to death there, lest a conviction for treason should deprive his children of his property.

But the less exalted in rank did not fare so easily. Suspected magistrates were sifted out all over the country. Jesuits, and ordinary priests who would not swear allegiance to the Queen, were rounded up with renewed zeal, to be hanged, banished or imprisoned. As for Mendoza, who was proved to have been up to his neck in the conspiracy, Philip suggested to Leicester and Pembroke that Alberico Gentilis, the expert on civil law, who was then at Oxford, should be consulted as to what could be done to ambassadors who so violated the hospitality of the country to which they were accredited, and thereby gave the learned Italian refugee the thesis of his first great book on international law. Gentilis gave it as his opinion that such a one might be expelled from the kingdom. Mendoza was handed his passports after a stormy interview with the Council, was refused the customary transportation, and departed, breathing threatenings and slaughter in revenge for these indignities.

The danger of invasion was still thought to be imminent. Stafford wrote to Walsingham in January of the new year that Guise and his friends were promising themselves "beau jeu" in England before long. The Nuncio and the rest of the conspirators were counting on King James of Scotland to support them, so far as it lay in his power to do so. That "old young man" was indeed writing to the Pope for assistance against the Protestant nobles who held him, he said, in tyrannous subjection. Elizabeth's persistent crookedness had left England without a friend in the world able or willing to help her. Her treatment of the King of Navarre had forced him to make such terms for his own safety that he could not come to her aid. It was a year now since Anjou, her pet "Frog," had made the kind of bloody-minded fool of himself in the Netherlands that might have been expected of him. The constitutional limitations of his sovereignty there had irked him intolerably, and in the January of 1583 he had attempted to make himself absolute by the characteristic Valois methods of treachery and massacre. His personal failure in this attempt at Antwerp had displayed his incompetence as clearly as his bad faith. Totally discredited, he had been compelled to retire to France, and the cause of the Dutch patriots had fallen so low that Elizabeth had been on the point of seizing the Dutch merchant fleet to reimburse herself for the money she had advanced for their support, when Throgmorton's confession shattered her fool's paradise.

All this meant busy days for Philip at the Ordnance, where the increased activity of the office had already outgrown its old quarters in the Tower and occupied the Minories, the former convent of the Poor Clares. It was high time that the English fleet should put to sea, and they got it out in January in three squadrons, of which one was to watch in the Downs, another off the Isle of Wight, and the third at the Scilly Islands. Military training was revived throughout the country. Harbour and coast defences were repaired and strengthened. Down at Dover the driven labourers began to sing:

> O Harrie, hold up thy hat. 'T is eleven o'clock
> And a little, little, little, little past.
> My bow is broke, I would unyoke.
> My foot is sore, I can work no more.

And Philip's advice was much sought after on account of the study which he had given to this subject in the old, bad days when military knowledge was flouted in England.

The Dutch, in despair of any reliable help from England, were making overtures to France with a view to annexation. The alternative was submission to Spain; and Farnese, whose army continued to advance, deliberate and irresistible as a rising tide, was prepared to grant attractive terms. Either a hostile Spain on the Zeeland coast or a France possessed of the whole of the Low Countries would be ruinous to England. There remained still one chance to prevent either of these catastrophes. If Elizabeth would supply thirty thousand pounds a month, the Dutch offered to furnish sixty thousand as often; the two sums would maintain an army of fifteen thousand men; and Roger Williams, the veteran Welsh soldier of fortune, assured Walsingham that with such a force Farnese could be held in check indefinitely.

Vacillating as ever, Elizabeth sent Philip's fellow Areopagite and tournament companion, Sir Edward Dyer, to the Netherlands to see what he made of the situation, and got back the report that "the cause was panting and almost dead" but not yet quite to be despaired of. So she ordered her fleet to co-operate with the Dutch fleet at once—and then sent Secretary Davison over to tell the Prince of Orange that Flushing, Brill and Enchusen must be turned over to English garrisons, lest the Dutch should leave her in the lurch as the Huguenots had done early in her reign. How ready she might be to leave them in the lurch and purchase the friendship of the King of Spain by delivering to King Philip these pledges of their faith her previous conduct made it only too easy for them to guess and the event came near proving only too well. Their answer was to send commissioners to treat with the King of France as their future sovereign. But it took the assassination of the Prince of Orange late that June to bring her to her senses.

In May disease dispatched Anjou to the next world also, though presumably to a different department thereof, and Elizabeth seized upon the pretext of offering her grief-stricken sympathy at the death of her suitor to send Sir

Philip Sidney to the French King with the Order of the Garter and "power to descend into particularities how this Spanish greatness may be prevented." She could hardly have chosen a more acceptable ambassador or one who would carry greater conviction of the sincerity of her proposals. Philip's antagonism to Spain was well known and his qualifications for diplomacy were such that Gentilis, who was just bringing out his *De Legationibus Libri Tres,* dedicated it to him as "a pattern of the perfect ambassador" in the following words:

> I am sure that this excellent pattern can be found and demonstrated in one man only, a man who has all the qualities that are needed to make this consummate ambassador of ours, and has them indeed in greater abundance and on a more generous scale than is required. That man is Philip Sidney.

But perhaps Henri III felt that he lacked the patience to listen to condolences so thick and slab as Elizabeth's were likely to be: she had written that she looked forward to being united with Anjou in heaven. Certainly neither the King nor Catherine de Medici, nor any of their advisers had any confidence left to place in the Queen of England. His Majesty, Elizabeth was informed, had gone to Lyons and in consequence would not be able to receive her special ambassador. So Philip got no farther than Gravesend before he was recalled. It must have been a great disappointment to him, for a France allied with England in a war against Spain would have fitted nicely into his new plan to prevent the Spanish domination of Europe.

As the geographical and commercial horizons of his world had widened since his fruitless attempt to form a Protestant league seven years before, so had his conception of the strategic elements of the military situation which confronted the statesmen and generals of his country. To attempt to defeat Spain in the Netherlands, where her veteran infantry gave her every advantage in the field and every city was a fortress, every village a potential redoubt, seemed to him foolish now that it had been repeatedly demonstrated that she was all but defenceless against attack by sea. Instead, he urged, let Philip II be diverted as Hannibal was "by setting fire to his own house" or, as Jason did, "by fetching away his golden fleece." In the Netherlands a force sufficient to hold Farnese in check would be enough—a mere stalemate there was all that was necessary. The victory would be won half a world away.

This policy, of which Philip deserves to be numbered among the originators, is indeed the one which England has pursued with few intermissions from that day to this. By it she won her world-wide empire; and many a conflict which has ended in Europe in what was little better for her than a drawn battle has left Britain paramount in world politics and kept her so for almost two hundred years. Gilbert, Raleigh, Frobisher, Drake, all of them understood it more or less clearly. Ralph Lane, whom Philip had recommended to be Governor of Raleigh's colony on Roanoke Island, wrote from "among savages" and "wild men of mine own nation" to tell Philip of the vulnerability of the Spanish settlements in the West Indies, which he had observed on his voyage out.

Philip had begun to dream of heading a fleet that should seize Nombre-de-Dios, and made plans for an Anglo-Dutch expedition to storm the ports of Spain and sweep her commerce from the seas. In October work was even begun on fitting out a fleet with which Drake should harry the West Indies. Preparations went on all through the winter, but were ordered stopped in the spring. Elizabeth would have no war, if she could help it. The country was prosperous; trade with Spain was flourishing; in comparison with France and the Low Countries, the peace which England enjoyed was profound; and her queen meant to keep it so, though the price should run as high as the sovereignty of France over the southern Netherlands. For in a fresh project for swinging Scottish James to her side she saw a hope of evening the balance of power that had now dipped against her.

"Our Philip" had been working on the Scottish problem. He was of the party that favoured James as Elizabeth's successor, when in the course of nature it should become necessary to find one. That he had ever seen the uncouth, shambling lad of seventeen seems unlikely, but many of the things which he heard about him, his scholarship, his love of poetry, his devotion to riding, were such as to influence him in his favour. Even James's shifty and time-serving Protestantism was better than the bigoted Catholicism of his mother, who was the only other practicable candidate: and it was, of course, only as a Protestant that James could be considered as the future King of England by men of Philip's opinions. "Your King, whom indeed I love," he wrote to a Scottish friend. James, on his part, expressed great admiration for Philip, thought nobody else wrote so "sweetly," and long regretted his untimely death. Of the Earls of Angus and Mar, exiled in England in consequence of their efforts to win Scotland for the Protestant cause, Philip had been at times so conspicuously the only friend that Walsingham felt sure his son-in-law would have to shoulder the expense of their "entertainment." Philip also cultivated the acquaintance of King James's agents in England, introducing de Ségur to Archibald Douglas and making an intimate of the Master of Gray.

Patrick Gray, handsome, fascinating, able and quite unscrupulous, had bought the friendship of his king with the secrets of his king's captive mother, which he had learned at Paris as a friend of the Duke of Guise. A professing Protestant but Catholic at heart, he went on in London with his double game, doubtless well satisfied at having the friendship of the son-in-law of Her Majesty's principal secretary as an additional cloak for his designs. From Leicester's nephew and favourite, moreover, he may have hoped to extract the inner secrets of the Protestant party.

The Earl was foully attacked in the propaganda of the Catholic party in *A Dialogue between a Scholar, a Gentleman and a Lawyer*, and Philip answered with his *Defence of the Earl of Leicester*. The *Dialogue*, which was popularly known as "Father Parsons' Green Coat" from the colour of its leaves and from Parsons, the Jesuit missionary, who was supposed to have written it, was a bitterly scurrilous screed, for which its author had raked up and strung together every scandal and rag of malicious gossip that had been circulated about the Earl since the beginning of his career. The number of these was legion and the nature of many of them such that they besmirched the name of his royal patroness almost as much as they did his own.

Philip's reply reads strangely in our days, but it must be believed that he knew his audience far better than we can imagine it. In it he began indeed by asserting what could not be denied, that for twenty years nobody had hated his country without hating Leicester, and from hating him had gone on to hate the Queen. But he devoted the greatest part of his space to refuting the charge that Leicester was not of noble blood. He enumerated the noble houses from which the Earl's father—Philip's own grandfather, be it remembered—was descended in the female line, and added that for four hundred years the Dudleys had been gentle and noble in their own right. As the great Duke of Northumberland's daughter's son, he proclaimed that his own chiefest honour was to be a Dudley. "Thou liest in thy throat," began the challenge which he hurled at his unknown antagonist by way of peroration, and offered to prove as much in arms against him within three months in any place in Europe to which a subject of the Queen might have free access.

The Master of Gray may well have smiled with subtle satisfaction over this throwback to the Middle Ages. The wily Scot did not suspect that Walsingham had his cipher and was reading all his letters before they reached his correspondents; and it may not have occurred to him that the son-in-law of the statesman who had organized the most efficient secret service in Europe formed a blind that could be worked both ways. For your unprincipled intriguer is seldom less subtle than when he is dealing with one whose high ideals of conduct and clear sense of honour he is prone to confuse with stupidity.

Of the crookedness of the game which the Master of Gray was engaged in, and of the cynical lack of principle that lay behind it, Philip can hardly have been ignorant. He was handling much of Walsingham's correspondence with Scotland; Pooley, one of Walsingham's most devious agents, was Philip's own man-servant; and Philip's old friend of Vienna days, Edward Wotton, was representing his queen at the Scottish court in 1585. Few can have known the tricks of dissimulation which were permitted in the diplomacy of the time better than Philip did. But he had well learned Languet's lesson of enjoying what he found good in a man and remaining untroubled and uncontaminated by what was evil.

Nor must it be forgotten that in his loyal and affectionate support of Leicester and in his friendship and intimate co-operation with many another of his contemporaries who seems to us even more unworthy of his respect he was dealing, not with so many sets of characteristics set forth upon a printed page, but with living men in the infinitely complicated and mutually contradictory relations of a living world, in which the possessor of the finest standard of conduct must condone many things of which he disapproves, if he would accomplish anything at all.

To wonder greatly at Philip's liking for the narrow, pedantic and unreliable James of Scotland is to forget not only the divinity that did hedge a king in those days but also to confuse our mental picture of the mature James I of England, the mean, false, timid enemy of Raleigh and friend of Spain—who was nevertheless the admiring patron of Shakespeare, too—with the harassed boy of seventeen who could hardly remember a time when his liberty and even his life had not been in danger, whose health had been undermined even before his birth, and whose morals had been perverted and confused no less, perhaps, by bitter Calvinist divines than by libertines professing the creed of Rome.

In the dazzle of Philip's reputation it is easy to make the mistake of imagining him either as some such "beautiful but ineffectual angel" as Shelley or as a kind of stupid paragon so walled in by his own excellencies as to be useless in common life or else the dupe of more practical spirits. He did, it is true, never quite cease, if not to beat his wings against the bars of circumstance, at least to gaze wistfully out from behind them. But he strove for no visionary goals. Common things such as family affection and love of country inspired his thoughts and impulses; and he worked for his ends with a knowledge of the sacrifices necessary to success in an imperfect world, that was not less clear because he did not choose to purchase his own advancement at the expense of his principles.

If this had not been so, and had not been known to be so by such keen judges of men as Elizabeth and Burghley and Walsingham, he, who had never ceased to hate the memory of St. Bartholomew's Day and all that it stood for, would never have been selected in the summer of 1584 for that embassy to the Valois court which was to have persuaded Henri III and his unprincipled mother to involve themselves in an alliance with England.

Even with the violent and atheistical Giordano Bruno he seems to have been on excellent terms. That bumptious philosopher, having made Rome and Geneva alike too hot for him, and Paris probably none too safe by his refusal of a professorship at the price of attending mass, had come to England and brought Oxford about his ears by debating there about the time of Philip's visit to his old college with the Palatine Alasco. He remained in London as the protégé of the French Ambassador for nearly a year and a half after that, openly critical of the rudeness with which the common people treated a tactless foreigner and of the dirtiness of the city which German visitors thought admirably clean.

Cultivated people received him hospitably, however. Fulke Greville had him to an Ash Wednesday supper, to which he came late and angrily because he thought that he ought to have been sent for by his host and had been hustled by the ill-mannered populace through streets foul with winter mud, after an uncomfortable experience of the independence and disobligingness of the Thames watermen. Whether or not Philip was at this party is uncertain; but he was evidently well acquainted with the truculent renegade monk, though they differed fundamentally on many important matters.

Philip so loved and admired Aristotle that he made translations from his works for his own enjoyment, while Bruno was continually attacking the great authority of the Old Learning with savage bitterness; Philip's deeply religious nature had driven him to find an outlet for it in translating the Psalms into English verse. But he had a broad tolerance of the religious views of any who did not make the Pope's excommunication of his queen an article of their faith; and, friend of Dee and Adrian Gilbert as he was, he could enjoy Bruno's disquisitions on the doctrines of Copernicus, the movement of the earth and the varying distances of the stars without feeling that he compromised his belief in Christianity by doing so. And Bruno, by the time he left England for eight years more of wandering about Europe and a fiery death at Rome after seven years in the dungeons of the Inquisition, had succumbed to the prevalent habit of authors of Philip's acquaintance and dedicated two of his books to him.

Meanwhile family matters claimed Philip's attention from time to time. His father placed a tablet on the gatehouse at Penshurst in the summer of 1584 to commemorate the gift of the house and manor to *his* father by King Edward VI. In October joy and sorrow came simultaneously. For down at Wilton the Countess Mary gave birth to a second son; and the family, gathered for the christening of the infant Philip Herbert, were saddened by the death of little Katherine, the three-year-old daughter of the house. Perhaps it was her illness that kept any of the great names like those of her elder brother's sponsors from appearing in the record of this occasion. The godfathers were the child's two uncles, Philip and Robert; and his grandmother, Lady Mary Sidney, had so far recovered her health as to be able to appear as his godmother.

In the same old family Psalter in which he had recorded Philip's birth thirty years before Sir Henry wrote down his sorrow and regret for the loss of his winsome and promising little grand-daughter. But to offset these he now had substantial proof that the family fortunes had taken a turn for the better. His "great good hope" in Robert had flowered in a spirited intrigue which ended in that enterprising young man's marriage to Barbara Gammage, the beautiful, twenty-two-year-old heiress of John Gammage of Castle Cointy in Glamorganshire. Robert, undistinguished by his brother's talents and accomplishments, with his reputation still to win, and only the prospects of a younger son whose father could not provide too well for his eldest, lacked the defects of Philip's qualities as well and was undeterred by the sordid considerations and squalid shifts of the great world's marriage market.

Of legal age and an orphan, Barbara was free to bestow her hand where she would. Suitors flocked about her, young James Crofts, grandson of the Controller of the Royal Household, at their head. She took refuge with her uncle and aunt, Sir Edward Stradling and his dame, who were fast friends of the Sidneys. Robert's brother-in-law of Pembroke and other important people rallied to his support. In vain did Walter Raleigh write down from court that his kinswoman should not be "bought and sold in Wales" or somebody should answer for it to the Queen. Walsingham sent a friendly hint that the Queen's opposition need not be taken too seriously; a royal order forbidding the marriage arrived conveniently just two hours too late; and Robert, master of the Gammage fortune two months before he was twenty-one, became Knight of the Shire for Glamorganshire a year later.

While Robert was making this brilliant match, writs went out for the first general election that England had seen for twelve years. The assassination of the Prince of Orange had made clear to all the ease with which her enemies might kill the Queen; and "those devils," according to Burghley, "were persuaded that her life was the only let why their tyranny was not planted again." The steadily growing sense of her peril had found expression early in November in the Bond of Association, by which "such noblemen and other principal gentlemen and officers as should like thereof" bound themselves to the Queen "and everyone to other, for the defence of her Majesty's person against her evil willers."

This oath was to be taken voluntarily, said Burghley. But, such was the wave of popular feeling that swept the country, the most disloyal dared not neglect to join with the rest, who flocked to sign the copies of it, which were distributed to the lords lieutenants of the counties and the mayors of the towns. When, on November 12th, Elizabeth returned to London from one of her customary progresses, she was received with a solemn demonstration of loyalty. At her manor of St. James's she was met by two hundred of the gravest citizens on horseback, dressed in velvet and gold chains, a thousand of the City Companies on foot, and a thousand men with torches, "for that the night drew on." It was in such an atmosphere of grim intensity that the new Parliament assembled at the end of the month.

Philip sat in it, probably as Knight of the Shire for Kent. Its membership included Greville, Drake, Hawkins and many other friends of his, as well as Francis Bacon, Burghley's son Thomas and Shakespeare's enemy. according to tradition, Sir Thomas Lucy. It was a busy session for Philip. He was on committees dealing with the preservation of Sussex timber, the maintenance of Rochester Bridge, the patent for Raleigh's discoveries, the regulation of carriers in London, the subsidy bill and the new law requiring all Jesuits and seminary priests to quit the country within forty days on pain of the penalties of treason. When the house adjourned for the Christmas holidays, Sir Christopher Hatton led them in a prayer for the Queen's preservation, and the four hundred members indicated the depth and ardour of the spirit that animated them by kneeling and repeating it after him, sentence by sentence.

A curious exhibition of courage by one who was neither courageous nor otherwise admirable had already moved their patriotic indignation. Doctor William Parry, the member for Queensborough, had risen to protest against the bill to eradicate the Jesuits, saying that it was "full of blood, confiscation and despair to all English subjects," and only the Queen's intervention had saved him from being severely punished. Parry had, in fact, been trying for months to screw his courage to the point of killing the Queen with his own hand. But encouragement from high ecclesiastical sources on the Continent had been counteracted by the words of conscientious priests at home, and he had let more than one golden opportunity go by. He had not ceased to cherish his abominable purpose, however, and had discussed it with the malcontent Edmund Neville, if he had not—as Neville insisted that he had done—urged Neville to join him in the deed. When Parliament reassembled early in the new year, Neville denounced him.

The discovery among his papers of a letter from the Cardinal of Como, written to reconcile his conscience to the deed, did nothing to slacken the prevalent strain. Sir Thomas Lucy urged the passage of a special law by which he could be subjected to such horrors as were perpetrated upon the assassin of the Prince of Orange. But the English temperament held true to its dislike of unusual courses. The quartering-knife of the Tyburn executioner, properly handled, was deemed to be sufficient punishment for him. He ended by summoning Elizabeth to answer for his blood before God. But, since he already owed his life to her intervention in the matter of running a man through the body before he began to plot against her life, the summons lacked something of the force requisite for such utterances.

Still she could not be persuaded to take any decisive action. She would not permit the settlement of the succession to the throne, and she quashed an attempt to prosecute the Queen of Scots for possessing a guilty knowledge of Parry's intentions, of which there was considerable evidence. She still hoped to manœuvre France into a war, single-handed, against Spain. In February she sent Lord Derby to Paris with the Garter which Philip was to have delivered the previous summer. But his mission was handicapped from the start. Although the deputies from the Netherlands were already at the French court, the ancient privileges with which they hedged about their offers of sovereignty were as unattractive to Henri III as they had been to his brother of Anjou; and Derby had to stand by and listen to a refusal of it, which threw the championship of their cause upon his mistress, unless she was willing to have them become once more the submissive subjects of Spain.

In March the Duke of Guise unfurled the banner of the Holy League. At the head of twenty thousand men and backed by subsidies from Spain, he planned to force the King to exclude Henri of Navarre from the succession and make an end of Protestantism in France forever. But by May it was being whispered about the French court that civil war was to be averted by joining Spain in an attack on England. Stafford warned Elizabeth to prepare for the worst; and the deputies from the Netherlands were welcomed in London late in June. They were lodged about Tower Street, and "their diet" was "very worshipfully appointed in the Cloth-makers Hall in Minchone Lane."

The time of their arrival was especially propitious for their mission. Philip of Spain, determined at last to teach Elizabeth a lesson in the peril of negotiation with rebel subjects of his, had suddenly seized upon the numerous English grain ships which had been attracted to Spanish harbours by the famine in Andalusia and Galicia and had sent their crews to the galleys or the dungeons of the Inquisition. The good ship *Primrose* of London, more fortunate than the rest, brought home a tale mingled of Spanish treachery and English valour that threw the country into a frenzy of warlike spirit. Boarded and placed under arrest without warning by Spanish soldiers, the plucky crew of the *Primrose* had flung their captors overboard and brought away as their prisoner no less a person than the Corregidor of Biscay, who had been so foolish as to attend to their apprehension in person.

Gone were the best of the Queen's excuses for procrastination: the trade with Spain and the general desire of her people for peace. In mid-July enthusiastic crowds flocked down to Woolwich to cheer the departure of the London ships which were to join Drake's fleet at Plymouth. For the preparations for Drake's expedition were being pressed forward again by that time. Twenty-five vessels were to take part in it. Martin Frobisher, in the *Primrose* herself, was Vice-Admiral; Christopher Carleill, Walsingham's other son-in-law, was appointed Lieutenant-General of its land forces. A grandson of Burghley, a cousin of the Queen, and a son of Winter the admiral were among the gentlemen volunteers. An itinerary of the expedition, which its daring and experienced commander left behind him, reads today like the prospectus of a modern winter cruise to the West Indies, so precise and definite is its statement of proposed arrivals at various Caribbean ports and of the time assigned to the shore excursions which were to be devoted to the capture and pillage of Spanish towns.

It was well that he could feel so confident. Walsingham wrote several months later, "Upon Drake's voyage dependeth the life and death of the cause according to man's judgment"; and he might have said the same at this time. For in the Netherlands, Dendermonde, Ghent and Brussels had already fallen before Farnese's siege-guns. Blockaded by his famous bridge, the condition of Antwerp had become so desperate that only a quick decision by Elizabeth could save her prospective allies from sustaining a mortal blow in the loss of their richest city and one of their most important fortresses. But what she saw plainest in the situation was the chance to drive a hard bargain: the huckster instinct of Henry VII was ever strong in his grand-daughter.

She began by telling the deputies that not for any consideration would she have the sovereignty of their country. If she should consent to accept even a "protectorate" of it, she must have Ostend and Sluys in addition to the towns she had already demanded. Even for becoming what she called an "aiding friend" she stuck to Flushing, Brill and Enchusen as her price. At last, in August, when it was too late, she so far yielded that a hundred ship-loads of troops were thrown across the North Sea in a tardy effort to save Antwerp that reminds one of the equally futile rush of Mr. Winston Churchill's naval reserves on a similar mission in 1914. Starving, despairing of England's aid, and too feeble to resist the expected assault of the besiegers, the city surrendered two days after the signing of the treaty that might have saved it.

How Philip Sidney's chivalrous and ardent spirit must have been bruised and mortified by the contemptible manœuvres of his royal mistress it is not difficult to imagine. With his clear insight into the military situation, her meanness, duplicity and irresolution must have driven him, as it drove Burghley and Walsingham, to the point of distraction. If she meant to allow herself to be checkmated in Flanders, Drake would strike in vain in the Caribbean, though he should strike never so shrewdly.

Philip was thirty years old this summer of 1585. His patent as joint Master of the Ordnance with survivorship had at last been granted, and he could congratulate himself upon the efficiency of his office, which had made possible the dispatch of seven thousand volunteers and regulars to the Netherlands within the week following the Queen's reluctant decision to relieve Antwerp if it should prove possible to do so. They were not well equipped, these soldiers; many essentials were lacking to them. But the wonder was that they could be sent at all.

It had been decided that no cavalry were to go at this time, which was a great disappointment to him. The arming of the nation had brought him a lieutenant-generalship of horse, and throughout July he had assuaged his longing for service in the field with plans for leading a force of five hundred mounted men overseas. His prospects for foreign service seemed to brighten, however, when the wily Dutchmen, knowing Philip's high character and Elizabeth's fondness for Leicester, sought to bind her more strongly to their cause by begging her to appoint the Earl her commander-in-chief in the Netherlands and Philip her governor at Flushing.

She consented to do this, and then, characteristically, refused to fix a date for the Earl's departure and neglected to assign Philip to the new post. As for Leicester, she was sick: she said that she was probably dying and must have him near her. To Philip's ears came a rumour that Sir Thomas Cecil was to be preferred before him for the Flushing governorship. Such treatment was more than even a Sidney's devotion could endure; and on a night early in September Philip, with the ever-faithful Fulke Greville at his side, galloped post-haste for Plymouth. Better join Drake and serve

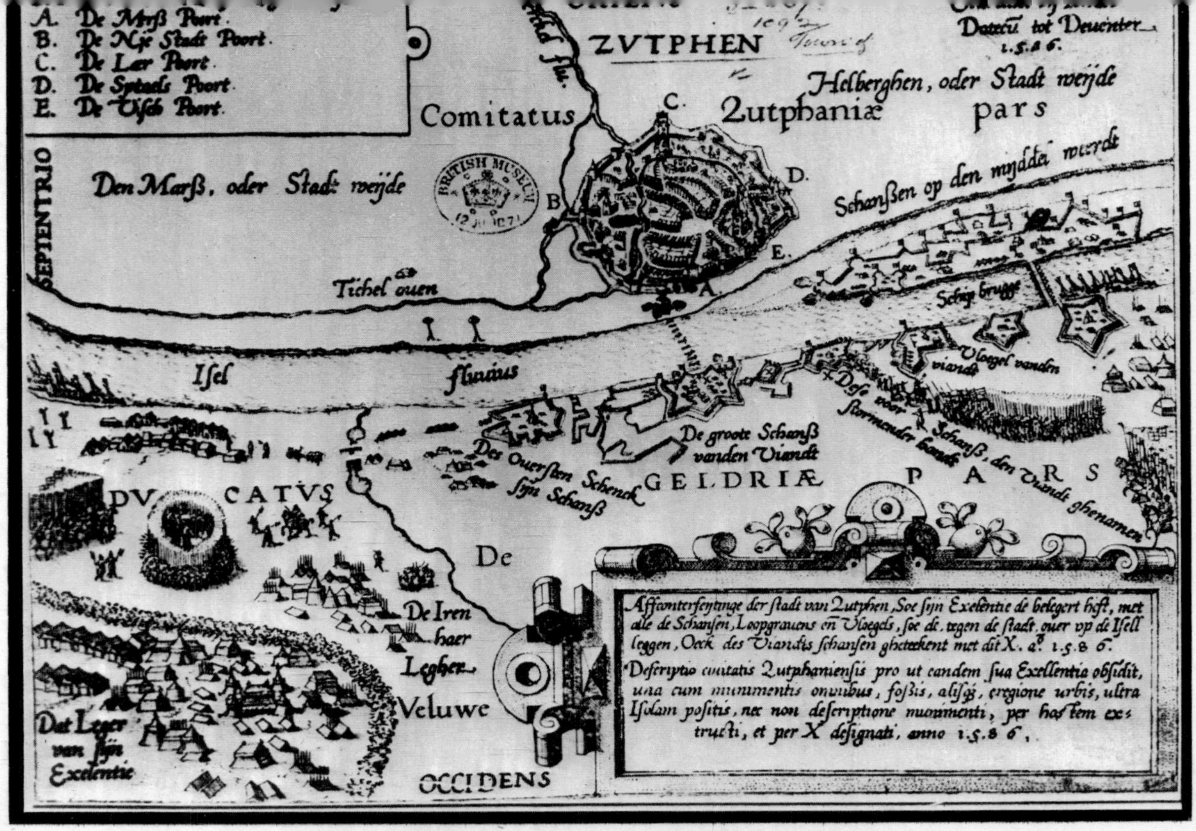

MAP OF ZUTPHEN AND THE SURROUNDING COUNTRY

from a print of 1586, in the British Museum

his queen on distant seas than put up any longer with her fickleness and ingratitude. Or so it would appear.

But what lay behind the confused and contradictory records of this episode it is impossible to ascertain. Greville, who was evidently in a position to know a great deal about it, wrote that Drake had regarded Philip as his co-partner in the expedition from the time of its inception, that the two men intended to share the command of it, and that Philip's prospective participation in it was kept a secret only because the Queen would have forbidden him to go if she had known of it. Unfortunately Greville wrote his account many years after the event; and it seems to be certain that his memory must have betrayed him.

No one can be imagined who would be more unwilling than Drake to incur the dangers of a divided command, even though it should be shared with a man of so sweetly reasonable a nature as Philip's. Philip, for his part, had been engaged during August in raising a company of Welsh infantry to serve under him in the Low Countries, and he had believed, moreover, that he was quite sure of the Flushing command. That he should ever have considered going with Drake at the price of relinquishing so honourable and important a post seems highly improbable. Nothing less than his mortification and chagrin at being superseded in that appointment, and superseded by a man whose record and attainments were in every way inferior to his, can be taken as an adequate explanation of his evasion. So keenly, indeed, did he feel his humiliation that he left his young wife either shortly before or shortly after she gave birth to her first child. The date of his daughter's birth is not quite certain, but it fell sometime in this summer. His father-in-law knew of his "hard decision" and seems not to have been unsympathetic with it. Don Antonio's expected return to England served him as an excuse for going to Plymouth at this time.

But according to Greville, "a letter" from Drake "comes post for Philip, as if the whole fleet stayed onely for him, and the wind." At Plymouth the night of his arrival Drake feasted him "with a great deale of outward Pomp and complement. Yet I," Greville goes on, "observing the countenance of this gallant mariner more exactly than Sir Philip's leisure served him to doe; after we were laid in bed, acquainted him with my observation of the discountenance, and depression which appeared in Sir Francis; as if our coming were both beyond his expectation and desire." The ships proved to be not ready to sail, after all; the work on them proceeded with incredible slowness; and Philip's observation of "some sparcks of false fire, breaking out unawares" from Drake, finally convinced him that his friend was right in believing that the commander regarded them as undesirable additions to his enterprise.

Meanwhile Drake had sent a messenger flying up to London to tell the Queen of his dilemma. A royal courier came galloping back with three letters in his bag: one to Philip, forbidding him to sail with the expedition; one to Drake, forbidding him to allow Philip to do so; and one to the Mayor of Plymouth, commanding him to see that these orders were obeyed. "Two resolute souldiers in marriners apparell," says Greville, intercepted this courier and brought the letters to Philip, who read them before he allowed them to go forward. But his plan was obviously ruined. Hard upon the messenger followed a peer of the realm "with a more Imperiall Mandate" and "carrying in the one hand grace, the other thunder": Flushing would be his, if he returned to court at once; if he did not, he knew only too well that Elizabeth was quite capable of venting her spleen upon Drake by forbidding the expedition to sail at all. He obeyed, only delaying long enough to deliver to the soldiers and sailors of the expedition a rousing speech of farewell. But Drake got such a strong hint from Burghley that he had better get him gone that he sailed with his water-casks only partly filled and indulged himself in the insolence of replenishing them on the coast of Spain.

Was the whole adventure, one wonders, an elaborate hoax, played without Greville's connivance, and with or without that of Drake, to bring the Queen to her right senses and force her to keep her promise about the Flushing appointment? "That ingenuous spirit of Sir Philip's," as Greville calls it, had been so quickened by years of training at court and in diplomacy that his failure to note those signs of embarrassment in Drake which Greville observed seems hardly possible. Even Walsingham might have been party to the plot and only keeping up the deception when he wrote as if he believed that Philip had already sailed. It was the sort of scheme that Sir Henry Sidney might have thought of and even perpetrated with a humorous enjoyment.

All that we can be sure of is that in making his peace with the Queen Philip convinced her that he had never really meant to go; though how this helped matters is not clear, for she was not a lady who would enjoy being made to understand that she had been successfully bluffed. There were, however, parts of the story that may have appealed to her sense of humour. Catching her in the right mood, Philip would have known how to make her laugh with an account of the mixture of courtesy, pretended satisfaction and ill-concealed dismay with which Drake had received the distinguished and most unwelcome volunteer. And in any event she had already promised to forgive him.

He finally got away to his Flushing charge early in November, writing her from Gravesend in the hour of his departure as confident and intimate a letter as might well pass from an honest thirty-one-year-old servant, courtier and soldier to his fifty-three-year-old queen. Let her read his heart in the course of his life, he begged, and "esteem it like a poor hows well set." A few days later she emphasized her favour towards him by travelling up from Greenwich to be godmother to his little daughter Elizabeth at St. Olave's Church in Hart Street, where, eighty years later, Samuel

Pepys was to ogle the pretty women from behind his prayer-book. Thus Philip, who had officiated conspicuously at so many christenings, had to miss this splendid occasion, in which he was so deeply interested. Already he was over head and ears in the responsibilities and troubles of his new post.

CHAPTER XIII

MY LORD GOVERNOR OF FLUSHING

A SWIFT AND PROSPEROUS VOYAGE BROUGHT PHILIP within sight of the scene of his new employment. He had for his secretary William Temple, who was to be the grandfather of the famous Sir William Temple of Stuart times. Robert Sidney had left his lovely Barbara to accompany him with a commission as captain of one of the companies in his garrison. He brought with him that great desideratum among the English expeditionary troops, money. Davison, the Queen's ambassador to the Netherlands, was on hand to greet him. But the ironic fate which so often presides over such occasions did what it could to mar his arrival. Foul weather half-spoiled the military and civil pageantry which should have honoured his reception, and which Philip never loved the less when he was a central figure in it. Prevented by a rising wind from anchoring before the town, his ships were compelled to take shelter off the Fort of Rammekins, three miles away; and he reached the town on foot "with as durty a waulk," he wrote to Leicester, "as ever poor governor entered his charge withal."

But the people seemed glad to see him; and the more he saw of the place, although it was already well-known to him from previous visits, the more it impressed him as a great and precious jewel for the English crown. To be its governor might offer small prospect of military glory, but the honour of the position was as high as the responsibility of it was enormous. For upon Flushing rested the entire structure of Anglo-Dutch co-operation. From its ramparts on the southernmost shore of the island of Walcheren its great guns commanded the mouth of the Scheldt; and its possessor controlled the commerce of the North Sea for the purposes of that war. At Dunkirk or Gravelines, the only Flemish ports upon the sea, which were held by the Spaniards, a small merchant vessel or raiding cruiser might now and then slip in or out, but neither place had a harbour adequate for any important maritime enterprise.

So long as Flushing was held for the United Netherlands, Antwerp, which Alexander Farnese had won at such a fearful cost of men and treasure, remained but an empty trophy, its merchants ruined, its population starving. Deprived of convenient access to the sea, the other subjugated cities of Flanders were in little better case, while in Holland and Zeeland trade was thriving. But let the Flushing garrison fail, let the war-weary burghers yield, and Spain would be possessed of a naval base whence she could not only interrupt the communication between her allied enemies, but send forth a fleet to strike swiftly at England herself.

Appropriately enough, it was at Flushing that Charles V and, after him, Philip II had bidden farewell to their Flemish possessions, and King Philip had hurled his insulting "No los Estados, ma vos, vos, vos!" at William the Silent. For since 1572, when the inhabitants signalized their support of the Beggars of the Sea by hanging the chief engineer officer of the Spanish army, the town had been in the forefront of rebellion. A strong, confident, bustling place, it was famous for its shipping and its skilful and valiant mariners. Its Great Church of St. Jacob looked down upon the crowded wharfs of its inner harbour, upon the handsome dwellings of its rich citizens and upon the warehouses of the merchants of Middelburg, the provincial capital, whose distant towers were visible from the northern ramparts.

In the Groot Markt lay the ruins of the Carmelite and preaching friars' monasteries. Their stones had gone to load the ships which had been sunk to block the Spanish vessels off Fort Lillo in the siege of Antwerp. Philip the Good had given the town its sturdy walls, which had been strengthened by water-gates and bastions in 1548. Its population was capable of mustering a minimum of fifteen hundred musketeers and pikemen; and its inhabitants spoke complacently of the times so lately past, when the garrison, composed of English volunteers in the Netherlands service, were paid punctually twice a month.

Since the English intervention, however, things had changed rapidly for the worse, as the new Governor discovered on his very first tour of inspection. The burghers felt that the defence of their city had now become the business of the Queen of England, and the Queen refused to lay out a penny where she could shift the expenditure of it to another purse than hers. In consequence, the auxiliary defences, stockades, barriers and the like, had already begun to fall into decay; the gun-emplacements and even the gun-carriages were in disrepair; the sentry-posts were deep in mud; the guard-house leaked in the rain; and slack discipline had allowed it to be "most beastly defiled in most loathsome manner."

As for the garrison, Philip with his customary generosity gave Captain Edward Norris, from whom he took over the command, the credit of doing all that could have been done in the circumstances; but of the thousand men that composed it two hundred were sick, and many dying of "the noysom aire of the place." "Weak, bad furnished, ill-armed and worse-trained," as Digges, the Muster-Master-General, reported of them, they were altogether inadequate for the defence of the town against any determined attack. The pay which they received at the time of Philip's arrival was the first they had seen in four months. Naturally it had been, almost all of it, spent in advance. Embittered by hardships which, they knew, were owing to nothing but the neglect and parsimony of their sovereign, they had become thoroughly unreliable. They had no barracks and, scattered through the town in billets, lay at the mercy of the truculent inhabitants whom they were supposed to dominate.

Philip wrote home wistfully that for three thousand pounds he could provide them with such quarters as would enable them to command the town in case of need. Although his father's Irish experiences ought to have deterred him, he began within ten days upon that course which was to end in his scrupulous father-in-law's financial ruin, and borrowed three hundred pounds on his own credit to relieve the worst necessities of his men in the vain belief that the Queen would reimburse him. In less than a month he was writing to Walsingham that unless he had a reinforcement of four hundred men his garrison could no more answer for the place than the Tower could answer for London, and that, if something were not done about it, he intended to lodge a formal protest with the Lords of the Council.

Corruption, as usual, was going hand in hand with incompetence. The Treasurer, he soon discovered, took "a strange course." The troops were paid—when they were paid at all—in the depreciated Zeeland currency, which meant a loss of five per cent to men who would have been hardly able to live on the full amount. Brown and Bruin, the official victuallers, corrupted the officers in what Philip called "a Gomorrah fashion" and thus forced the soldiers to pay such high prices that Philip found it cheaper to buy his supplies locally or in England. He refused to accept a shipment of twelve tuns of beer from these profiteers and spurned an intimation that the Commander-in-Chief wished him to buy from Brown. "I am better served by the one haulf by my mans provision. Now judj yow, Sir, how poor men are delt with," he wrote indignantly to Walsingham.

Nor was he left undisturbed to wrestle with the problems of organizing his command. He had hardly had time to understand them when a letter came from Errington, the Governor of Ostend, who was an old friend of his, begging him for help against the Spanish Governor of Gravelines, who was marching to attack him. Philip dispatched four of his companies to the rescue, though he must have gazed anxiously after so large a detachment of his feeble garrison as it vanished into the mists of the Scheldt with his beloved brother among its officers. The danger blew over, but Robert reported a desperate situation at Ostend: provisions and ammunition at a low ebb, not so much as an extra pike in store, and the inhabitants—they were mostly Catholics—ripe for treachery.

Philip's own burghers gave him plenty to worry about. Had his coming been delayed any longer, they would, he believed, have gone over to the enemy: so weary were they of the war, so disheartened by Elizabeth's vacillation and the hopeless confusion in their own government since the death of William of Orange. Immediately he was involved in the web of misunderstandings and maladjustments which invariably impedes the joint action of two nations of differing customs and languages, whose common cause is barely sufficient to counteract their innate antipathy for one another: and the long months in which the Flushingers had had the unpaid, half-ragged and disorderly English soldiers on their hands can have done nothing but aggravate their annoyance.

By the terms of the English occupation they had been promised that they should be "as custom free as English born subjects." Philip accordingly issued certificates to their merchants and took the additional precaution of writing to Walsingham to make sure that these should be properly respected. But one man was, nevertheless, "miserabli spoild"; so Philip had to write again, demanding the punishment of the stupid and corrupt Jacks-in-office who were responsible. It is small wonder that at times he considered himself to be "among the worst humourd people."

But he had his father's gift of seeing what of right there was on the side of those who were opposed to him, and he dealt with them with a tact and patience that were inexhaustible. In making such changes as he thought necessary he moved with cautious deliberation. When it came to strengthening his garrison, he quietly incorporated the fresh levies in the depleted organizations of which it was already composed, lest the sight of additional companies should excite the jealous fears of his burghers. When Monsieur Gelee, at whose house he had his lodging, desired to go to England, Philip made sure that Walsingham would provide a cordial welcome for the influential citizen. He cultivated the acquaintance of Count Hohenloe, the German commander, who was a veteran in the Dutch service, and he did not neglect that of Sainte-Aldegonde, who, much blamed and suspected for his surrender of Antwerp, was living in retirement near by. Elizabeth wished to have the gallant nobleman arrested and tried by court martial as a traitor. But Philip, who had met him some years before, kept a high opinion of him, though he watched him, as he said, with "a suspiciows ey."

The eighteen-year-old Count Maurice of Nassau, the son of William of Orange, hailed the new Governor's arrival with affectionate delight. Not only had Philip been much liked and admired by the young man's father, but his stepmother had been Philip's friend since his Paris days when, as Louise de Teligny, she had barely escaped death in the St. Bartholomew's massacre. William of Orange had married her not long after the death of Charlotte of Bourbon. Now, twice widowed by Catholic assassins, she was living in the "Prinsenhuis" at Flushing with her infant son, and was eager to secure Philip's support of the rights of her stepchildren. Maurice had lately been made Stadholder in the place of his father; he was also lord of the cantankerous Flushingers by hereditary right; and his cordial co-operation was undoubtedly of the greatest assistance to Philip in establishing and maintaining relations of mutual respect and confidence with these "people of a froward and perverse disposition." For this Philip did succeed in doing, as one of his most experienced captains afterwards bore witness.

The same policy of untiring devotion to his duties and thoughtful consideration for the difficulties of others won him loyal obedience and willing co-operation from his subordinates and the other officers with whom he was associated, and this in spite of the fact that not a few of them had years of hard service to set against his brief experience of war in Ireland and might naturally have regarded him as a mere interloper. The conflict of authority which was bound to follow the appointment of the Earl of Leicester to supersede Sir John Norris as Commander-in-Chief had created at Flushing, as well as at other places, a situation that might have been disastrous for a less tactful commander than Sir Henry Sidney's son.

Davison, who had been in charge there for a short time, awaiting Philip's arrival, had garrisoned the Fort of Rammekins with the company of Philip's friend Captain Huntley; and Norris, with the professional soldier's resentment of civilian interference in military matters, had sent Huntley a peremptory order to relinquish the place to Captain Edward Norris, Sir John's brother. Here were all the materials for a very unpleasant garrison row. But Philip smoothed matters over by placing his brother Robert in command of the fort and sending Norris back to England with a letter to Walsingham, in which he praised the Captain's work at Flushing and recommended him as a horseman who might wisely be appointed to the command of cavalry which he longed for.

To Colonel Morgan, a veteran soldier of fortune in the Netherlands service, Philip did a good turn by letting Davison know that the valiant Welshman's Dutch regiment had received only twelve hundred guilders in the past three months: so disorganized had the administration of the States become. He found time also to write to his father-in-law in behalf of Morgan's nephew, who was off on Drake's voyage and stood in danger of losing his inheritance from his father through the action of greedy creditors. And all this was in the midst of his cares about his garrison and worries over his personal finances. The inexperience of his subordinates and his own incomplete equipment had laid a heavy burden upon his private purse: even a promise that he was to have his house "free of exises" was not fulfilled. But the course which he took yielded such returns that he could soon begin leaving his post to execute the various special missions with which Leicester entrusted him, and within two months he could write to Davison that he thanked God all was well at Flushing and his garrison in good order. Doubtless it would have remained so, if the soldiers had been paid with anything like regularity.

At first the joyful expectation of Leicester's arrival was of great assistance to him. "Your Lordeshippe's coming," he wrote to the Earl, "is heer longed for as Messias is of the Jews." When, on the 10th of December, Leicester actually arrived, his disembarkation at Flushing was celebrated with such a firing of salutes as must have strained those shaky gun-carriages on the ramparts. Well past fifty years of age, bulky, red-faced and bald, he came magnificently attended and attired with a splendour that astonished the natives. But in doing so he was hardly the vain fool which it has been the fashion to call him.

It had been very well for William the Silent to sit over his beer with his burgesses, as Fulke Greville saw him do, in a gown worse than that "of a mean-born student of our Inns of Court" and a woollen knit waistcoat like those "our ordinary barge-watermen row us in." William was one of their own, tried and tested by nearly two decades of adversity; Leicester was a foreigner, the personal representative of his queen, to be sure, but a queen of whose intentions the Dutch had good reason to be suspicious. Moreover, it was not an age in which the equivalent of a morning-coat and a bow tie worn with a wing-collar would have been accepted as the proper travelling costume of a plenipotentiary; nor would half a dozen secretaries have been regarded as an adequate suite.

In the sixteenth century a man's greatness was gauged by the gorgeousness of his apparel and the brilliance and number of his attendants. The parsimonious Elizabeth herself spent lavishly for the splendour of her court and valued her servants in proportion to the sums of their own money which they laid out to give their functions a handsome setting. When Leicester wished to praise Davison to her, he did not forget to say that her ambassador lived like a gentleman and "chargeably every way."

That Leicester had, also, to compete in men's minds with their recent memories of the Duke of Anjou and his companies of guardsmen, French and Swiss, is made plain by the fact that the Englishmen about him judged the warmth of his reception by comparing it with that accorded to the Duke four years earlier. Those jewels in Leicester's ears, which have been so often represented by historians as the measure of the man, were simply the new fashion. Raleigh wore the like, and so did the hard-fighting Count Hohenloe and many another gentleman of worth and valour. So it seems unlikely that they were taken as signs of a fatal foppery by the Dutch of 1586 any more than the monocles which distorted the faces of so many officers of the British Expeditionary Force seriously impaired the confidence of their French allies in 1914.

The Earl's suite was so numerous that at Middelburg his gentlemen fell to "soche leapinge over tables, strivinge and disorder" in their struggle for places at a state dinner "that divers glasses were broken etc," and my lord "thereupon gave order, that all his gentlemen shoulde gōe oute of the howse." The young Earl of Essex, the beautiful Penelope's brother, was among the distinguished company. So were Lord North, Lord Audley, Lord Willoughby, Sir William Russell and Philip's youngest brother, Thomas, who was beginning at sixteen that career—so undistinguished for a Sidney—in which he was to gain a certain reputation as a fighting soldier, win a colonelcy, and make a rich marriage.

Musters, pageants and banquets graced the Earl's progress through the country. From Middelburg by Dordrecht and Rotterdam he and his gallant retinue made their way to Delft through such a series of gastronomic encounters as must have made them almost rejoice in their short rations when they lay for some days wind-bound and fog-bound on those inland waters. Pigs that were served standing on their feet, pheasants in their feathers, pies with the heads and necks of swans arising through the crust, sugar-works most brave and sumptuous, challenged their prowess as trenchermen for three hours and a half at a sitting. Detachments of six hundred to eight hundred musketeers escorted them from town to town and formed guards of honour at the landings. A thousand pikemen, "tall able personages," lined the great market-place of Delft, to which the Earl paid the highest compliment an Englishman can pay and called it "an other London almost for bewty and fairness. . . . Ther was such noyse," he reported, "in crying, 'God save Queen Elizabeth' as yf she had ben in Chepesyde."

He saw all things through rose-tinted spectacles, did Leicester, these early days. Or so he chose to report them to Burghley and Walsingham. The Dutch town-militia were the ablest, the people the kindest he ever saw anywhere. Count Hohenloe, who was the husband of one of the daughters of William of Orange, he took to be "surely a wise and gallant gentleman and a right soldier . . . a right Almayn . . . free of his purse and of his drynk." And if in the latter he soon showed himself altogether too free, he also showed signs of mending his ways. Louis William of Nassau so governed Friesland that the Earl wished every province had such another. Even Paul Buys, the former Advocate of Holland, whom he hoped to hang for a traitor before the half-year was out, now seemed to him to excel in skill and judgment.

Among the few who did not win his approval and confidence at this time was Philip's new friend, Count Maurice of Nassau. To him the Earl attributed "a sullen deep witt" and a less than lukewarm support of the English alliance. Maurice had some associations with those opposed to it, which his brother-in-law Hohenloe attacked with characteristic alcoholic violence; and when Leicester's popularity began to wane, the young man saw a good deal of the suspected Sainte-Aldegonde. But there was no need for Leicester to reassure himself, as he did, with the consideration that the house of Nassau was poor and the young Prince had no one but Elizabeth to look to. Maurice was always a sound patriot. Philip Sidney never doubted it, however long Leicester remained uncertain.

The Earl's solemn reception at The Hague was spiced for him by a sound snubbing which was accorded to an emissary of the King of France. He was assured by the renegade Archbishop of Cologne, who had seen good reason for embracing the cause of the Reformed Religion in the beauty of Agnes Mansfield, that Queen Elizabeth's dispatch of Drake to the West Indies and her army to the Netherlands had aroused the German Protestant princes of Germany to support the King of Navarre, and that the King of Denmark was encouraging their enterprise. And these heartening tidings were in the main confirmed by a letter from Walsingham, who added that even in Italy the new English policy had produced a certain effect among those who feared the growing power of Spain.

In this hopeful mood Leicester threw himself into his work with an energy, an industry and a singleness of purpose which seem wonderful in one whose reputation has come down to us as that of a vain, unscrupulous, self-seeking and shallow politician. Reflected in his letters from the Netherlands to Walsingham and Burghley, and in their replies, appears a conscientious gentleman and hard-working public servant, for whom no labour was too difficult, no hours too long, and no danger too great or too imminent. He had borrowed heavily on his estates for the means to live on the princely scale which his position demanded. He travelled continually about the country, which was his viceroyalty in all but name, inspecting the fortresses, encouraging the garrisons and inspiring confidence in an atmosphere that was thick with treachery, distrust and discord. There was no part of his charge to which he did not give his personal attention, as there was none but had need of it in the confusion which he found there.

He strove to establish a proper rate of exchange between the sound English money he brought with him and the chaotic coinage of the country, urged the creation of a monetary commission to establish financial order, and took measures to root out the thriving counterfeiters. For the stimulation of commerce and to draw from Spanish Flanders many "that occupie wollen occupacions" he commended certain Dutch proposals favouring the importation of English cloth and wool. He struggled against the dishonesty of the army treasurer and wrote repeatedly of the miseries of the English soldiers, who were so ragged after four months of neglect that they were ashamed to show themselves. Again and again he begged for an adequate force of pioneers and for miners to be raised for him in Cornwall and Devon. For he had a war of sieges before him, and the humblest soldier of the time considered the pick and shovel beneath his dignity and would hardly use them even for his own protection. The canals froze up, stopping all intercourse inland; foul weather and contrary winds cut off instructions from his home government for forty-two days; and he carried on as best he could.

From the beginning Elizabeth had made it plain to him that he would be furnished with but little straw for the bricks that would be expected of him. At the very start he

ROBERT DUDLEY, EARL OF LEICESTER

from the painting in the National Portrait Gallery

was denied the customary allowances for his staff, a thing hitherto unheard of in Tudor military administration. His letters from Walsingham and Burghley were heavy with reminders of the Queen's displeasure at "all thinges that mynister matter of charges." Not a military man, he was well aware of his need of an able and experienced chief-of-staff. Sir John Norris, gallant and capable though he was, was unfitted for the post, both because he might yield to some feeling of jealousy against his successor, and because he was hand in glove with the army treasurer, who was his uncle.

The Earl wrote again and again, begging for some suitable professional soldier to be sent out to fill the place. He would have had Sir William Pelham, if he could. But upon Pelham, who had been Lieutenant-General of the Ordnance, the Queen had fastened the responsibility for that shortage of two hundred bronze cannon. Unless he made it good, she swore, he should serve in the Low Countries as no better than a private gentleman, if he served there at all. And when Leicester tried asking for Lord Grey de Wilton, who had sufficient rank to replace him as commander-in-chief, if one of the many plots to assassinate him should be successful, he got no better result.

Worst of all, his cautious, captious and jealous sovereign refused him what he needed most: namely, the title and powers of "Absolute Governor," which the United Netherlands were eager to bestow upon him. The exigencies of the situation demanded it; but vainly had her most honest and far-seeing advisers urged her, vainly had the Dutch deputies besought her to permit him to accept it. Still hoping for peace and cherishing the belief that, so long as her representative bore no titles but those of commander-in-chief and "advisor" to the rebellious provinces, she could at any moment withdraw from the struggle, she stubbornly refused the entanglement which such a high-sounding designation would involve. She had forbidden Leicester to assume it, and he did not again ask her leave to do so. But in an evil hour for himself, for the cause and for his nephew Philip Sidney, he accepted it without consulting her.

The pressure to which he was subjected before he yielded was enormous. On New Year's Day the Chancellor Leoninus and the Deputies of the States waited upon him with a herald and trumpets, ready to proclaim him the moment they had his consent. They returned again with "an act sett downe in writing by them all" to make it clear how perfectly the Queen's interests would be protected. If William Shakespeare was indeed a member of the Earl's troupe of players at this time, as has often been imagined, here to the life was Cæsar's refusal of the crown. Captains, magistrates, and governors of towns added their persuasions. Davison, who did not know that the Queen had expressly forbidden the Earl to accept, advised him to do so.

Philip Sidney's advice to him may be gathered from a letter which he wrote to Davison some months later: "I was ever of the opinion he shold accept it without delai, becaws of the necessity, without sending to her Majesty becows of not forcing her in a manner to be furdre engaged than she wold, which had been a peece of an undutiful dutifulnes." And Leicester was able to draw up excellent reasons on his own account: the Netherlands must have a governor or succumb to their present confusion; any governor other than he would control the English forces, or try to; and as governor he could make sure both that the States did not conclude a separate peace and that they would use all their power to prevent an invasion of England.

There was only one answer to all these reasons. It was conclusive; but even Leicester, well as he knew her, may be excused for not foreseeing that Elizabeth's jealous fury at one whom she immediately chose to regard as a disobedient and presumptuous servant would endure so long that it would undermine his authority in the States and alienate from him many of the persons who had been eager to place him in power. So, on January 25th, at The Hague, with solemn ceremonies and in the presence of a distinguished gathering of Dutch and English he took the oath as Supreme and Absolute Governor of the United Provinces and was invested with such powers as had been exercised by the governors in the time of Charles V.

Davison was sent off to the Queen, primed with oral and laden with written explanations of her lieutenant-general's action, but unfortunately the Queen had heard of it before he arrived. Her anger blazed. A subject of hers to be styled "Absolute"! A creature of hers to allow himself to be addressed as "Excellency"! Her fury swept the carefully-prepared speeches from Davison's lips, reduced him to tears, to disavowing his own share in the business. Not a word would she hear in Leicester's defence. She dispatched Sir Thomas Heneage to the Netherlands with her command that the Earl publicly resign his new authority. Who would believe, otherwise, that he had assumed it without her sanction? "How contemptuously we conceave ourselfe to have been used by you, you shall by this bearer understand," she wrote to him. As for Philip, she talked of relieving him of his command as a punishment for his part in the affair.

Nor was her first rage allowed to consume itself by its own violence. It came to her ears in a lying story that her old enemy the Countess Lettice was going out to queen it at The Hague with such a train of ladies and gentlewomen, rich coaches, litters and side-saddles as would surpass Her Majesty's own splendour, and her wrath flamed afresh. In vain Leicester offered to resign the post altogether and come home. If the Queen desired only a general in the Netherlands, he reminded those about her, Sir John Norris was a far better one than he and was already there when the Earl was sent out. In vain he pointed out that since his "acceptation" the States had doubled his allowance and that he had already spent in the Queen's service eleven thousand pounds of his own money, supporting a force of six hundred crack cavalry and keeping such state that his household cost him a thousand pounds a month. In vain, too, were his reports of the capital which the enemy were making of the Queen's loud repudiation of his action.

From the first Alexander Farnese, who had lately become Duke of Parma, had circulated the rumour that Leicester's real mission was to negotiate a peace, of which the terms would be highly advantageous to Spain. He had even prepared and furnished sumptuously a house at Brussels, which became known as the English House, so general was the expectation that Leicester would occupy it while the terms of the treaty were being considered. Now, the Earl reported, the Duke "feeds himself with great jollity" on accounts of the Queen's dissatisfaction with her commander-in-chief; and the Spanish propaganda began seriously to undermine the confidence and resolution of the Dutch. But neither these considerations, nor the Earl's friends at court, nor ministers of state who saw the national safety endangered by their sovereign's unreasonable anger against him could persuade her to view his action in a less unfavourable light. His brother Ambrose of Warwick wrote him that he was never so honoured among good people as now, but that the Queen was not to be trusted by him, even on her oath, and if she persisted in her anger, he had better go to the remotest part of Christendom than return to England.

A friend tried telling her that the Earl was ill. She so far relented as to promise to send him her own physician, but she would not receive his letters. She would not endure it, she said, that "her man" should alter the commission she had given him "upon his owne fancyes." Walsingham incurred her displeasure by defending him. Only when Burghley threatened to resign did she change her attitude. It was the end of March before Raleigh could write to the Earl that she was, "thanks be to God, well pacified, and yow are agayne her 'sweet Robyn.' "

But such happy endings often fail to include the minor characters, who have been innocent or unwilling participants in the quarrels of the great. This one left poor Philip quite out in the cold. As late as July Walsingham informed Leicester that the Queen was "verry apt uppon every lyght occasyon to Fynde fault" with Sir Philip. Philip, however, wasted little time on regrets for his part in the squabble. The duties of his command were pressing and numerous, and every moment which he could snatch from them was devoted either to the special missions on which the Earl employed him or to other matters involving the general interests of the alliance.

Fulke Greville in that late-written memoir of his said that Leicester took Philip to the Netherlands, despising his youth as a counsellor and "bearing a hand over him as a forward young man," but that soon he and all his stars were glad to fetch light from him. In fact the Earl must have been quick to change his mind. Almost from the beginning Philip was sent about the country wherever his intelligence, tact and obvious sincerity were most needed; and his letters to his commander were filled with advice and recommendations such as no man so sensitive as he would ever have offered, had he not felt sure of their welcome.

He did not hesitate to urge repeatedly even so important an appointment as that of Roger Williams to be Sergeant-Major over all the cavalry, or to report the idleness, lack of equipment and extravagance of Leicester's band "of very handsome men" at Rotterdam. He touched upon Count Hohenloe's "late drunken folly," patched up a serious quarrel between the Earl and that truculent and bibulous soldier, defended the Zeeland regiment's claim to higher pay, warned his uncle that the Dutch government was perpetrating such abuses under the cloak of Leicester's name as they would never have dared to do without it, and exhorted him to "be not discowraged with the Queenes discontentmentes."

The Hague, Rotterdam, Amsterdam and Utrecht saw him come and go upon his general's business. When there was open mutiny at Bergen-op-Zoom, he was sent thither twice. The loyalty of the garrison of Scottish troops seemed doubtful to Roger Williams; so Philip recommended that they be replaced by Welshmen at that important post. In March he made a flying visit to Germany to encourage the Protestant princes in their preparations to support the King of Navarre. And he kept in close touch with the widowed Princess of Orange and thus with the party that remained devoted to the fortunes of her late husband's house.

Thanks to her influence and to Count Maurice's affectionate admiration of him, he could send for their young liege lord and count upon his co-operation when he became involved with the inhabitants of Flushing in matters which his authority did not give him the power to settle. But he had to wrestle single-handed with those complications which always occur when the troops of one country come to defend another against a common enemy. The foreign soldier, imbued with the notion that he is the altruistic saviour of a people too feeble and timid to protect itself, is prone to feel that it is unreasonable that he should be expected to pay for anything, while the inhabitants, burdened and bored by the sudden influx of the alien and arrogant military, see no reason why they should not make what profit they can to recompense them for their discomfort.

In this, as well as in other ways, Philip's cornet of horse added considerably to his vexations. He had made himself personally responsible for their raising and equipment. "For the furnishing of my bande of horsemen," he wrote to his cousin Fynche, he had become "a begger unto many of my good frendes for horses." He was fain to borrow armour until that which he had ordered could be delivered. And while he was waiting to have them mustered into the Queen's service, the burghers who were lodging some of them dealt "so courteously" as to "arrest my horses . . . till I paid them two-hundred florins for the charges as they pretended."

A continual strain upon the mutual good feeling of the

allies, moreover, were the orders against trading with the enemy. Parma's sources of supply were so meagre that these prohibitions were of great importance for the success of the war. But their provisions were not well understood. "It may pleas your Eccelency," Philip begged of Leicester, "to send presently awai a placard of the prohibition and punishment of them that vittail the enemy, for yet there is nothing published." But the fact was that nobody really wished to forgo so profitable a business. Each ally enforced the rules rigidly only against the other and winked at infractions by its own merchants. While the English were protesting loudly against the Hollanders' and Zeelanders' commerce with Calais as trade with the enemy under the thinnest of disguises, certain cruisers out of Flushing captured an English ship with a cargo of lead consigned ostensibly to France; and Philip had to write "A Messieurs Messieurs du Conseil commiz des Estatz de Zelande," suggesting to them with consummate delicacy a way of settling the affair, which would still save everybody's face.

While his time and attention were thus occupied, he did not cease to long for action in the field or to keep himself informed about matters of a more purely military nature. Parma, untroubled by anything which Leicester had so far been able to do to interfere with him, was besieging Grave, the strongest of the towns that held the line of the Meuse for the United Netherlands and formed part of the barrier that closed to him a rich source of supplies in Germany. His garrison at Steenberg between Bergen-op-Zoom and Rotterdam was a thorn in the side of the Anglo-Dutch position. Early in February Philip outlined a plan for an attack upon Steenberg, by which he undertook "uppon my lyfe either to win it or to make the enemy rais his seeg from Grave or, which I most hope, both." Military experts in both of the allied armies gave their approval to the project, but a sudden thaw ruined the terrain for active operations, and he was thrown back upon the problems of his garrison and mediation in the continual quarrels and misunderstandings of his superiors and associates.

Recklessly he pledged his personal credit for the former and by steady self-control and courageous frankness strove to assuage the latter. Count Hohenloe became very angry because he was passed over in the choice of a colonel for the Zeeland regiment, an appointment which Davison unsolicited had obtained for Philip and which Philip had innocently accepted. Hohenloe objected that such a place ought not to be given to a foreigner. Roger Williams, whose record in the Dutch service was at least as brilliant as the Count's, retorted that Hohenloe was no less a foreigner than Philip. The Count circulated a petition against the practice of giving Dutch regiments to officers of any other nation. The dispute reached even to the ears of the Queen and she held it against Philip's reputation, although the "right Almayn" immediately collected the same signatures on a paper stating that the subscribers to the former one had been moved by no feeling against Sir Philip Sidney personally.

Worse than this tempest in the military tea-pot were the strained relations between Leicester and Davison, because anyone who meddled with them came under the direct fire of the Queen's displeasure. The Earl held it against Davison that he had neither properly stated nor supported his acceptance of the governorship before the Queen. The Earl, on the other hand, had placed Davison in a hopelessly false position by not telling him that the Queen had expressly forbidden the acceptance. To the mortified Ambassador, Philip wrote frankly that he thought he ought to have done better in the business, that he ought to have explained the necessity for Leicester's action and made it clear that the title did not mean "absolut as her Majesty took it." As for the favourable opinion which Philip himself had expressed to the Earl, he added boldly that he would "for no caws" deny it "and therefore yow shall have my handwryting to prove I am no acuser of yow."

That was no way to get on with Elizabeth, of course. But he wrote as stoutly not only to Walsingham but to Burghley as well, reiterating the shortcomings, mismanagement and corruption of the military administration and dwelling upon the disastrous consequences if these were not corrected. Doubtless he did himself little harm at court when he reminded his father-in-law that the soldiers could not be allowed to starve for want of money. Walsingham would see to that. But Burghley with his own son's career to further had no cause to shelter Philip from the Queen's dislike; yet to Burghley Philip did not stick at writing that Sir Thomas Heneage "hath with as much honesty in my opinion done as much hurt as any man this twelvemonth hath done with naughtiness."

He went on, moreover, to tell the Lord High Treasurer that, if the soldiers were not paid, especially in the cautionary towns, there would be "some terrible accident"; and the memory of the Spanish Fury at Antwerp, where the soldiery had taken their pay in pillage, rape and massacre, was fresh enough in men's minds to make it unnecessary for him to explain what he meant by the phrase. He hoped to God, he added, that when Her Majesty found out the truth about Leicester's governorship, she would not overthrow a cause "so behoveful and costly unto her." But that was beyond his office, he concluded: "I onely cry for Flushing." It was the case of his honest father in Ireland over again, and the Queen liked Sir Philip Sidney's forthrightness as little as she had liked Sir Henry's.

To the burden of the Queen's disfavour was now added the prickly annoyance of having certain letters go astray. He had entrusted them to a certain William, the Earl's "jesting plaier," and "the knave," who may have been the Will Kemp that morris-danced from London, "by little, red-roofed Sudbury," down to Norwich, or who more improbably may have been William Shakespeare himself, had delivered the whole packet to Lady Leicester. It contained a letter from

Philip to his wife, and also one to his father-in-law, in which he strongly recommended that Lady Leicester be kept at home. The Countess Lettice was not the sort of woman whom mere seals would keep from reading anything she wished to read; and, out of favour at court though she might be, she was resourceful and enterprising enough to make plenty of trouble for anyone whom she caught interfering with her plans. The anxiety with which Philip wrote to learn whether these letters had reached their proper destination was by no means groundless.

In March the post of commander at Bergen-op-Zoom was offered to him, in addition to his other duties. He was greatly tempted to accept it. Its nearness to the enemy made it attractive; and in the street leading from the Steenberg gate to the great square stood the palace of the marquises of Bergen-op-Zoom, with a groined and vaulted passage opening into the courtyard, an arcade and a large fruit and flower garden behind. "A very fair hows" in an excellent air, Philip told his father-in-law wistfully. He had destined it for his wife, but considering Elizabeth's doubtful policy, the danger that lack of pay might cause a mutiny at Flushing in his absence, and "how apt the Queen is to interpret everything to my disadvantage," he relinquished the appointment to the "vaillant and frank" Lord Willoughby, who acknowledged the favour to Walsingham as coming to him "by the singular love of your honourable son-in-law."

By this time, also, he had begun to doubt the wisdom of having his wife join him at all. "For if yow run a strange cource," he warned her father, "I mai take such a one heer as will not be fitt for any of the femenin gender." In this war, which daily demanded such great sacrifices of him he now saw the fruition of all that he had been dreaming and striving for since those dreadful August days in Paris had burnt into his young mind the fear and hatred of the nefarious partnership of Rome and Spain. "Me Thinkes," he went on to explain, "I see the great work indeed in hand.

. . . If her Majesty wear the fowntain I woold fear . . . that we shold wax dry, but she is but a means whom God useth and I know not whether I am deceaved but I am faithfully persuaded that if she shold withdraw her self other springes woold ryse to help this action."

If the Queen would not pay her soldiers, she must lose her garrisons, he continued. He had given the Council plain warning of that. The decision now rested with them. There would be "a sore war" the coming summer, and victory, which should have been easy, had been made doubtful by "these disgraces." But, having performed his own duties beyond the possibility of cavil, he would not, in any event, "to hastily to despair of Gods work." As for his personal difficulties, his father-in-law must not add them to his own. "I had before cast my count of danger, want and disgrace, and before God, Sir, it is trew that in my hart the love of the caws doth so far overballance them all that with Gods grace thei shall never make me weery of my resolution." He thought "a wise and constant man ought never to greeve, while he doth play, as a man may say, his own part truly tho others be out. But if himself leave his hold because other mariners be idle he will hardly forgive himself his own fault. For me I cannot promise of my own course . . . because I know there is a higher power that must uphold me or else I shall fall, but certainly I trust I shall not by other mens wants be drawn from my self."

It is the crusading note sounded upon no uncertain trumpet. If England should fail the cause, if her queen should be allowed to succeed in her underhand efforts for a separate peace, Sir Philip Sidney's knightly pennon—though no more than that of a gentleman volunteer—should fly beside whatever Protestant banner, Navarre's or Casimir's or young Maurice of Nassau's, still was flaunted against those whom he called "the abusers of the World."

CHAPTER XIV

"ÆS TRIPLEX"

IT WAS WELL FOR PHILIP THAT HE HAD PUT ON THE TRIPLE armour of resolution, integrity and faith. For shortly there fell upon him a blow which must have been the more terrible both for its unexpectedness and because it came neither through the fortune of war nor by the devious practices of the court. The spring of 1586 opened, indeed, in a way that seemed to justify those high hopes with which the Earl of Leicester had taken up his task.

Martin Schenk, a fire-eating freebooter who had deserted from the Dutch cause some years before and had been serving the Spaniards with conspicuous success, again changed sides and captured the strong and important fortress of Werl in Westphalia for the United Netherlands. An attempt to betray Ostend was frustrated, and a conspiracy scotched at Deventer. Miserable as was the state of the English soldiers, that of the Spanish was worse. They, too, were mutinous for want of pay, hungry and shoeless in the icy mud of the Flanders winter. Famine reigned in the subjugated provinces. "I know not to what saint to devote myself," wrote the discouraged Duke of Parma to his sovereign, whose parsimony could match that of the Queen of England herself. Leicester wrote home of hopes for a brief and brilliant campaign that should culminate in the capture of Antwerp and Bruges.

Early in April Count Hohenloe and Sir John Norris, defeating the enemy in a bitter fight amid torrents of rain, succeeded in throwing a year's provisions and a reinforcement of five hundred men into beleaguered Grave. Hohenloe had demonstrated his devotion to the English Queen to such an extent that the Earl advised her to reward his abstinence with a gold chain or her picture on a tablet worth two hundred pounds. The Count had also showed tact and discretion by hushing up the true report that in the battle before Grave five hundred English of the "oldest Flemish trayning ran flatly and shamfully away." Lord North wrote home in high spirits that, if May proved to be like April, it would put water in the Duke of Parma's wine.

Walsingham and Burghley sent good news from England. The Irish contingent, which Leicester had asked for, was going out to him. The Master of Gray had offered to lead over some four thousand or five thousand Scots. The great fleet, which Philip II had already begun to assemble at Lisbon, would "prove nothing this year," for Drake's successes in the West Indies had caused the bankers of Genoa to draw their purse-strings tight against the King of Spain.

The grateful burghers gave the Earl a triumph at Amsterdam. At Utrecht he kept St. George's Day with a splendour appropriate to such fair auguries. Six knights, four barons, the Council of the States, the Earl of Essex, the deposed Archbishop of Cologne and Don Antonio of Portugal rode before him in solemn procession to the Dome. Next came the officers of the Earl's household with white staves in their hands, then Portcullis Herald in a rich coat of the arms of England, and then "my lord most princelike" in his robes of the Order of the Garter, accompanied by the principal citizens of the town and followed by his own guard, "which were a fifty of halbarders in scarlet cloakes, guarded with purple and white velvet."

After a sermon by Master Knewstubs, his chaplain, whose discourse can hardly have proclaimed the Earl's adherence to the evangelical faith more clearly than the mere sound of the parson's name, the distinguished company moved on to the house that formerly belonged to the Knights of Rhodes; and there in "the very great hall, richly hung with tapestrie" Leicester knighted Martin Schenk, whose wounds were still fresh from the storming of Werl. A great feast followed, "most princelike and abundant," then dancing, vaulting, tumbling and "the forces of Hercules," which last "gave great delight to the strangers, for they had not seen it before." After a sumptuous supper there was jousting, and the day ended with a magnificent collation of "sugar meates for the men-at-arms and the ladies."

Amid all this viceregal splendour the Earl was at great pains to emphasize the subordinate nature of his position. In the church "the queenes maiesties state . . . was erected on the right hand," while his own stall was on the left and "by certaine degrees lower." An empty throne likewise dominated the banquet hall, where the Earl occupied a stool of comparative humility, while the baked meats shaped like lions and dragons, the peacocks, swans, pheasants and turkeycocks, "in their natural feathers spread as in their greatest pride," succeeded each other upon the board. It was well that he was thus careful. For the sun of royal favour, though it had begun to shine upon him once again, did so but fitfully. In answer to his complaints that the Council did not reply to his letters, Walsingham wrote him that the Queen had taken and kept to herself the whole direction of affairs in the Low Countries as well as "sooche advyce as she receyvethe underhand," so that "the lords knowe not what to wryte or to advyce."

Suddenly she began once more to insist that Leicester must renounce the governorship; and when Burghley protested against this, "she grewe so passyonat in the matter as she forbad him to argue any more. Suerly," wrote the harassed Principal Secretary, "there is somme trecherye amongest owreselves, for I cannot thinke that she woold doe this out of her owne heade." Thomas Morgan, the Queen of Scots' agent at Paris, could have confirmed his suspicions, for he assured his royal mistress that Leicester's force was honeycombed with treachery.

Elizabeth kept Sir Thomas Heneage lingering on at his honest blundering and presently demanded that he tell her the "flegmaticall reasons" for which he allowed the Earl to delay the renunciation of his office. "Jesus," she wrote to the unhappy Heneage, "what availeth witt when yt failes the ownar at greatest nede?" Burghley said that this matter of the governorship had caused him more trouble with the Queen than any other since he had been a member of her Council. A month after St. George's Day he and Walsingham were still urging upon her the necessity of recognizing it, and urging in vain, though her refusal kept the Master of Gray from joining the Anglo-Dutch forces and thereby committing James of Scotland to the war on the side of the allies.

To defray the expenses of the relief of Grave, Leicester had been compelled to borrow an additional four thousand pounds on his personal credit. For "not one groate . . . noe not one groate" was to be got for the purpose in any other way, although from the beginning he had urged the formation of a field army as the only means of obtaining a decision and had hoped to "wander" with two thousand horse and four thousand or five thousand foot "about Easter." But the States were quite content with a war of sieges and less and less disposed to join forces in the open with an ally whose soldiers' pay was three months in arrears and whose commander-in-chief had lost the confidence of his sovereign.

Early in May, however, the situation became such that offensive operations were the only remedy with which to meet it, cost what they might. The winter's reports of the condition of Parma's troops had been true, but with the coming of spring and the prospect of fighting again under the leader whom they adored his soldiers had sprung to arms with delight. The Duke had undertaken the siege of Grave in person and, since a freakish cannon-ball "tooke away the hinder part of his horse" from under him, was in no mood to be balked of the capture of the place. With the courageous determination to relieve it, although Parma's army considerably outnumbered any force which Leicester could hope to assemble, the Earl fixed his headquarters at Arnhem on the north bank of the Rhine, where the Romans had cut a channel from that river to the Yssel, and managed to get together there five thousand foot and fifteen hundred horse.

To Arnhem hurried Philip, glad, doubtless, to exchange his courteous bickerings with the States about the arming and the debts of English soldiers, the apprehension of deserters, the arrest of Amias of Lyme, "the father of all counterfeiters," and the exposure of worthless secret agents, for the dangers and glory of fighting in the field. And at Arnhem the blow fell upon him in the news that his dearly loved father had died of a swift and sudden illness on the fifth of May.

Travelling by barge between Bewdley and Worcester, Sir Henry Sidney had taken a cold which ended in his death a few days later. His heart, enclosed in a leaden urn, was placed near the monument of his little daughter Ambrosia in the oratory of Ludlow church—a thing that would have pleased him, for no man ever loved his children more dearly or with greater sympathy and understanding. Seven score horsemen escorted his body by way of Chipping-Norton, Oxford and Kingston to Penshurst, where it was buried in the parish church. Sir William Dethick, Garter King-of-Arms, presided over the funeral pomps. But he rather spoiled the occasion by beating the officiating clergyman: behaviour which does not strengthen for posterity the effect of his vilification of Robert Cook, Clarenceux King-of-Arms, who had had a hand in drawing up Sir Henry's "pedigrew" almost twenty years before.

When one remembers the complete and affectionate understanding that existed between Philip and his father, their frequent co-operation and mutual dependence, it becomes easy to realize how deep must have been Philip's sorrow and how devastating his sense of loss. He must have been harassed, too, by anxiety for his mother. Poor Lady Sidney had of late years lived chiefly at her house at Paul's Wharf, where she could enjoy the society of her daughter and her sister when they were at their town houses not far away. Now, widowed and with all three of her sons at the wars, she lay there, dangerously ill. Philip applied for leave to go home to see to the settling of his father's estate; and surely he was justified in doing so, if family affairs are ever a justification for a soldier's request for leave in the face of the enemy. But Elizabeth, who in her tantrums could threaten to relieve him of his command, was too prudent to do a kindness to an old and devoted friend at the risk involved in leaving Flushing without its governor; and Philip's application was refused.

The refusal did nothing to diminish his energetic efforts for the cause. He wrote to Walsingham from the camp at Arnhem, asking to have "the serviceable horses which were my father's" sent over for use in his cornet, "which, thowgh, alreadie, it be in the feild, full and faire, yet wold I have those to supplie the wannt, of some such as I wold take owt to serve my private use that whether I be ther, or no, yet my cornett maie alwaies be full as owght." Having taken precautions against the prying eyes of enemies, that letters might "come maidenly" to him, he continued to urge upon his father-in-law those things which he believed to be best for the service. He begged that the garrisons of the cautionary towns might be the first to receive their pay, on account of "the great importance of the places and the churlishnes of the peoples humours especialli Flushing." He recommended his cousin Sir Richard Dyer, who had gone home to bring over five hundred men. He even was willing to give Leicester's bête noire, the treasurer, the benefit of a doubt and, having in "dyvers waies been much beholding" to him, asked Walsingham to see that the man was not condemned on the Earl's charges "till yow see matters proved."

For Philip, though he now believed himself to be a

soldier in a holy war, was still the fair-minded gentleman, and his humour and tolerance seldom failed to temper his zeal. He recommended to his father-in-law a physician who had healed Roger Williams of a dangerous sickness in three days, although the man was "an Anabaptist in Religion, which is pitti for in conversation he is honest"; and even at the close of the letter in which he stated the belief that the cause was God's cause he could add lightly that a certain good-for-nothing was "worst for the sownd of the harkabus." Of Doctor Bartholomew Clerk he wrote, "we need no clearkes," and of Paul Buys that he "hath so many busses in his head, such as you shall find he will be to God and man about one pitch."

When it became clear that he was not to get leave to go home, his wife came over to join him. From Utrecht late in June he wrote happily to her father, "I am presently going toward Flushing whence I heer that your daughter is very well and merry." Thus from time to time the young husband and wife were able to snatch a few days or a few hours of life together out of the small number that remained of those which fate had allotted to him. But he was now almost continually on the move. He had been so indeed for the past six or seven weeks, although the military operations of the allies had been as far as possible from yielding any success.

At the end of May Grave, with its abundant stores, its strong walls and valiant garrison, had surrendered after a brief defence. On June 19th Schenk's city of Venlo surrendered, and Parma's way was open to the Rhine, where only Neuss and Rheinberg barred his road to the plentiful supplies of neutral Germany. In vain had Leicester threatened Nymingen, marched into Batavia and, disregarding Burghley's advice against matching his sixty-five hundred with the eight thousand veterans of the foremost general in Europe, attempted to lure him from his purpose. In vain had Schenk and Roger Williams with thirty of Schenk's men and a hundred and thirty English cut their way into the besieging army around Venlo, reached Parma's tent and killed his secretary and personal guards in a wild midnight camisado. The want of money, the Queen's refusal to recognize the Earl's title as Governor, and her continual underhand efforts for a separate peace had done their deadly work.

Even in August, when the discovery of the Babington conspiracy had frightened her into a more sensible attitude towards the situation, Philip wrote home, deploring that "we do still make camps and streight again mar them for want of meanes." Leicester had constantly to protest against the "pedlers and merchantes" who were allowed to "be seking and paultringe in so weighty a cause. . . . Such instruments," he pointed out, "must lay open all our councels. . . . The doings for this peace is as particularly knowen here, as with them that hath the managing thereof." The fall of Grave was a staggering blow, for which it was cold comfort to learn that the pusillanimity of the governor of the place rather than the skill and valour of the enemy was responsible.

Philip, the Earl of Essex and Count Hohenloe were among the members of the court martial that tried the wretched young man. They found him guilty, but recommended clemency, urging his inexperience and that he had been influenced by a mistress who favoured the Spanish cause. Both Hohenloe and Norris begged for his life. But Leicester was indignant that a town should be given up when its walls were still unbreached, its provisions ample and its garrison furious at being so betrayed. Unfortunately for the culprits, while his case was under consideration, the news arrived that Venlo had surrendered without even enduring a bombardment. "Indeed there is noe more made of giuing upp a towne then to forsake a mans howse," the Earl wrote to Burghley in explaining the necessity for making an example. He had the governor and the two officers who had supported his decision beheaded, "for that thei were all gentlemen and captens." Only these circumstances saved them from hanging.

But although those headless corpses might encourage others to make a more stubborn resistance, they could do nothing to stop the steady thunder of Parma's forty-five great siege-guns which, cooled with milk and vinegar, were soon battering incessantly at the walls of Neuss. The Earl pawned his plate for the means to assemble a force which should have marched to the relief of the town; but the money which might have financed such an operation was still going into the pockets of the treasurer who, as John Norris's uncle, could profit by the circumstance that his nephew's mother was Elizabeth's "own Crow"; and for mere want of funds Leicester had to send back to their stations the troops he had collected at so great a personal sacrifice.

Hohenloe and Robert Sidney had a successful brush with a cornet of horse out of Breda, driving off some cattle that belonged to the town, and making a prisoner of a certain Captain Welch of the Spanish service, whom Leicester would have hanged if Philip had not interceded for the life of the unlucky soldier of fortune. Lord Willoughby captured a number of wagons from a convoy intended for the provisioning of Antwerp. But it was Philip's good fortune to let in the first strong sunbeam of victory upon the gloom that brooded over the cause of the allies during that summer.

Leicester, meanwhile, had not unnaturally conceived so great a suspicion of the Dutch that he would rely upon the loyalty of no town that was not held by an English garrison, and when Count Maurice wrote to him, suggesting a certain bold project and stipulating that only Philip should be consulted about it, the Earl warned his nephew to be on the watch for treachery in the business. But Philip knew that there was no guile in his young friend, though he was an intimate of Sainte-Aldegonde, and the upshot of their consultations was that on a Tuesday night early in July five hundred English soldiers in boats, under the command of

MARY SIDNEY

from the painting attributed to Marc Gheeraedts, in the National Portrait Gallery

Lord Willoughby, met with Philip and a like number from his Zeeland regiment "before Flushing, upon the water, that it might be less noted." Silently they rowed up the Scheldt to within a league of the town of Axel, whose Spanish garrison guarded the approaches to Antwerp and Bruges. Disembarking there, they found young Maurice, with his copy of Cæsar's *Commentaries* in his pocket as usual, Sir Christopher Hatton's son as one of his captains, and several companies of Netherlands soldiers awaiting them. A column was formed and the advance upon the town began.

War was not new to Philip. In Ireland the short, fierce onslaughts of kerns and galloglasses had taught him the necessity for outposts and scouts, and he had learned that first essential of successful soldiering, the art of keeping the body fit and the mind clear amid the fatigues and hardships of life in the field. With this foundation of practical experience his constant study of military matters had taught him much. During the past few weeks he had ridden with Roger Williams on more than one reconnaissance and foray, and that veteran of more than thirty years of mixed fighting had advanced his education by precept mixed now and then with swift and bloody practice. But now, for the first time, he commanded in what, for that age and that war, could be called a major operation.

Behind him, as the troops advanced, glowed in their hundreds the sparks of the burning matches of his musketeers. From the sloped staves of his pikemen the tassels swung limp in the midnight damp. The murky, lowland starlight on pike-head and morion, burgonet and corselet, turned the long column into a great glimmering snake. From it arose no unnecessary sound, for he had put in force the old Roman rule of silence on the march. About a mile from the town the force, which numbered all told about two thousand, was halted, final dispositions were made, and Philip, like any hero of Plutarch, made the soldiers a speech. Probably, indeed, he made them several speeches, for the column must have been something between four hundred and eight hundred yards in length. Moreover, though he doubtless dwelt upon love of country and the sins of Spain and Rome, he would have been untrue to his father's example and his own natural wisdom if he had not explained to each division the part especially assigned to it in his plan of attack.

When they advanced once more, a forlorn hope of forty men with scaling-ladders marched ahead of the advance guard. Everything went according to plan. The moat surrounding the place proved to be too deep for wading, but the dauntless forty swam across, dragging their ladders with them. They planted them on the farther side, scaled the walls, slew the drowsy guard, flung open the gate and let the draw-bridge fall. Over it rushed Maurice's Dutchmen under Colonel Pyron, followed by Willoughby's English; and while the garrison, five hundred or six hundred in number, suddenly awakened and scantily armed, fought stubbornly to the last man, Philip occupied the market-place with his Zeelanders, ready to stabilize the conflict, should any accident of darkness and confusion turn it against him.

His conduct here shows a sober devotion to sound military principles which has not been well remembered by those who would read in the headlong and chivalrous valour of his end a character too easily swept away by the love of martial glory. Lieutenant-General Sir Philip Sidney, the commander, saw his duty far otherwise than Sir Philip Sidney, the gentleman volunteer who had no responsibilities for the time being and whose only means of assailing the enemy was by his physical prowess.

The whole exploit cost the allied forces not a single life, and only one man was wounded. Four outlying works or sconces were also taken. Colonel Pyron and a force of eight hundred troops were left to hold the place, and upon Prince Maurice's authority as Stadholder the dykes were cut, flooding the adjacent farmlands. The resulting loss in crops and cattle to the wretched inhabitants was estimated at two million florins, but the act was not one of wanton destruction, for this territory was one of the few sources of supply that were easily accessible for the subjugated provinces. Leicester, who had come over to Bergen-op-Zoom with five hundred men, as though Steenberg or Breda were his objective, and who had not slept for two nights in his anxiety about the attempt, wrote delightedly to Walsingham of how "your sonne Philip" had "notably handled" it. Even Sir Thomas Cecil, though he strove to minimize Philip's part in it, had to admit that "this victory hath happened in good time to make us lift up our heads."

Thomas had lately been writing to his father that so far only the weakness of the Spaniards had saved the English from catastrophe: so divided were they among themselves and so at loggerheads, from the Earl downwards, with their allies. Leicester's own letters tell the same story, while Pelham, money; money, Pelham, made a steady refrain for his complaints. For he was still without a chief-of-staff and the behaviour of many of his unpaid soldiers was as abominable as the condition of all of them was deplorable. "The cockney kind of bringing up" of the young men sent over—"your gallant bludd and ruffin men the worst"—promised to cause "as many frayes with bludgeons and bucklers as anie in London," he reported.

The wild, half-naked rascals of the Irish contingent, making nothing of ditches and farmyard walls with the long stilts with which they had supplied themselves, inflicted upon the peasants the horrors of warfare as it was waged in their native country. The ragged clothes and shrunken bodies of the older soldiers frightened all heart and courage out of the newly-arrived recruits. Everywhere there were desertions to the coast or, worse still, to the enemy, though the nooses of the provost-marshals were continually occupied in making horrible examples of those who were captured and brought back to their commands. "Divers I hanged," wrote Leicester bitterly, "and I assure you theie could have bine content all to have bine hanged rather than tarry." He expected, he said, "the fowlest mutiny that ever was made, both of our men and these country souldiers," and wondered that "theie doe not rather kill us all then runn away."

Burghley wrote back, suggesting that Parma's progress could be more than offset if he were completely cut off from the sea by controlling the commerce on the Ems and the capture of the Channel ports that were still held for Spain. But his words fell upon deaf ears. Leicester was too old to grasp the new doctrine of Sea Power and could see no other means to victory than the defeat of the Spanish army in the field. Not so Philip. To him the vision of Drake and the other great English seamen of his time was as his own. With his Axel laurels still fresh upon his helmet he got permission to make an attempt upon Gravelines, where, according to the report of one of his spies, the inhabitants would fling open the gates the moment he appeared before them.

But the luck of Axel does not often befall a commander twice. Fortunately he did not expect it. He regarded the enterprise with wholesome suspicion from the first, and when the conspirators failed to deliver the promised hostages, he so organized his advance-guard that, although it was ambushed by the garrison inside the open gate, he was able to draw off his men under the protection of the fire from his ships with a loss of only forty-four of their number. This failure brought him no blame. The attempt had been worth the making, and it was to his credit that his prudence and caution had kept it from being disastrous.

At home, meanwhile, there had been a change for the better. "Forced thereto by mere necessytye upon the dyscoverye of some matter of importance in the hyest degree thorrowghe my traveyl and cost," Walsingham informed Leicester, the Queen was now favourable to supporting her general's operations in the Netherlands. The cause of her change of mind was still such a secret that he begged the Earl to "make this letter an heretyke after you have read the same"; but the fact was that Her Majesty's astute principal secretary was now hot on the trail of the Babington conspiracy. Philip's man Pooley, whom he had left at home, had been playing the sedulous stool pigeon to the not too clever young men who plotted to kill the Queen. Before long it became clear that arrangements were again all but complete for a Catholic rising in England and an invasion of the country by a Spanish army from the Netherlands, and that persistent rumours of the building of flat-boats at Antwerp and of the collection of war material in the abbeys along the Channel coast were thus to be accounted for.

Elizabeth, convinced at last that Parma had been making a fool of her in her irregular negotiations for a separate peace, allowed Sir William Pelham to join the expeditionary force in the capacity in which Leicester desired to employ him. She even addressed her much abused commander-in-chief as "Rob" in a letter that breathed nothing but affectionate confidence except for a hint that the Norrises must be well treated. But the change came too late. The wisest in the States were ready to give up the struggle: so little faith had they left in her. It did more harm than good, when the sturdy burghers of Utrecht, furious at the activity of Paul Buys against the English, laid him by the heels. His papers were spirited away before they could be used against him. The States grew less and less willing to acknowledge that "absolute" authority which they had been so eager to confer upon the Earl six months before, more and more niggardly in their supply of money to him.

He was reduced to asking that Lord Buckhurst or some other member of the Queen's Council be sent over to assure them of the Queen's confidence in him and of the honesty of her intentions toward them. And while he sat with his hands bound in an empty purse, Neuss was taken and destroyed amid all the barbarities which it was customary to inflict upon a city that was carried by assault. In such circumstances it can hardly have soothed him to have Burghley tell him that it now looked as if the Queen had been right all along in her fear lest the whole charge of the Netherlands adventure should fall upon her.

Pelham's coming, which he had so long and earnestly desired, proved, as might have been expected, anything but an unmixed blessing. He was a veteran of the Scottish, French and Irish wars; but at his appointment to be Lord Marshal of the Field—the equivalent of the modern chief-of-staff—John Norris, with his many years of Low Countries service, chose to consider himself insulted. He asserted that, as Colonel-General of the infantry he had been reduced to fifth place in the establishment, and "he stomachs greatlie the marshal," was Leicester's report of him.

Sir Thomas Cecil, whom the Earl suspected of acting with his father's approval, was not alone among the English officers to join Sir John's brothers in supporting his quarrel. Over the irregularities of the army treasurer, Leicester had written to Walsingham that Norris was the equal of the late Earl of Sussex, his old enemy and the Sidneys'. Relations became so strained between Norris and Pelham that, in the opinion of their commander, a row between a couple of their lackeys would be enough to set the two factions at each other's throats. The lines of antagonism ran so intricately between Englishman and Englishman, Englishman and Dutchman, Dutchman and Englishman and German soldier of fortune, that even the diplomatic and generally-popular Sir Philip Sidney found himself not only involved in the quarrel but involved in it on the side of one of his uncle's opponents against Count Hohenloe, who was at this time one of the Earl's chief supporters.

At Gertruydenberg, of which he was the governor, the Count gave a supper one August evening to celebrate his return from some small raid into enemy territory. The guests were a distinguished company: the new Lord Marshal Sir William Pelham, Count Louis William of Nassau, the Earl of Essex, Lord Willoughby, Roger Williams, Sir Philip Sidney, his brother Robert and, by bad luck, Edward Norris, whom Philip had brought along in the hope of arriving in time for the expedition, and at the sight of whom their host's brow clouded ominously.

However much Hohenloe continued to deserve the English Queen's approval by his abstinence, it was still not for nothing that the English nicknamed him Count Hallock after a heady Spanish wine. In his cups there was no mad or murderous impulse on which he was incapable of acting. Supper was hardly over before he began to devote himself to the flagon with his usual ardour; and Sir William Pelham, who seems to have been determined that his countrymen should not be outdone in drinking any more than in anything else by a foreigner, plied his officers with round after round of toasts.

"The health of my Lord Norris and of my lady your mother," he called out to Edward Norris over a great glass brimming with wine. Norris replied ungraciously: he was not in the habit of drinking deep; Mr. Sidney could testify that he had drunk no wine for a week for his health's sake; he had no intention of getting drunk to please Sir William Pelham; but if drink he must, at least let him have a smaller glass. Supplied with one, he emptied it to the Earl of Essex, who in his turn drank to Count Hohenloe, proposing as he did so, "A Norris's father."

"An 'orse's father—an 'orse's father?" grumbled the Count, coming out of a drunken reverie. "I never drink to horses or to their fathers either." No amount of explanation could make him change his decision or his words. So the ceremony, so foolish and dangerous with tempers at the snapping-point around the table, went on without him. Again and in the same great glass Pelham pledged the badgered young man. Norris at first returned only a sulky silence, then, when the Marshal insisted, told him that he presumed upon his military rank. High words flew back and forth, but not unmingled with maudlin courtesies on Pelham's part, whereupon Philip was quick to intervene for peace. Norris, indeed, rose to his feet in reply to Philip's persuasion and, saying that he would overlook the wrong the Lord Marshal had done him, had the great glass at his lips, when Hohenloe seized the heavy cover of a vase of silver-gilt, hurled it at Norris's head and, as Norris staggered backward with his forehead streaming with blood, whipped out his dagger and sprang forward to finish him with it.

Philip with some others dragged the drunken madman from the room. They carried Norris to a place of safety outside the town. His forehead was cut to the bone; his feelings were more deeply wounded still; and presently Philip bore a challenge from Captain Norris to Count Hohenloe. Leicester did his utmost to prevent the duel and succeeded in delaying it for so long that it was never fought. But by doing this he brought down upon himself the anger of both parties. "Would God I were rid of this place!" he exclaimed over this last vexation; and small wonder, for he had just begun to get upon a working basis with Sir John once more; he was planning shortly to take the field again; and the affair caused such bitter feeling against Hohenloe among the English troops that the Earl was afraid to have the Count, who was one of his principal officers, appear before them.

Of the troubles whose combined weight bowed the shoulders of his uncle, Philip at Flushing had his full share. The shortage of munitions both in the town and at the Fort of Rammekins had reached the danger-point in the middle of August. The Dutch refused to supply them, both because they regarded the defence of the places as the Queen's affair and because, as Philip fairly stated in an urgent letter to the Lords of the Council, they had need of more than all they had to supply posts nearer to the enemy. But so desperate did he consider the situation that he sent Mr. Burnham, one of his officers, to present the case orally. If the Queen should think that he would squander her stores, let her appoint an officer to guard them "until the last point of extremity," which he thought would very likely be reached quite soon. To Walsingham and Burghley he wrote on the same day to the same purpose, striving to enlist the support of the latter by telling him that Sir Thomas Cecil was in similar straits at Brill.

From a reading between the lines it becomes clear that an uprising of the inhabitants was what he most feared as he wrote: "the people by thes crossed fortunes crossly disposed." If Flushing and Brill "shold be lost none of the rest wold hold a dai"; and there was nothing would keep the people in better order "then that thei see we are strong." But before he went to bed that night he had had such additional cause for alarm that he joined Captain White to Burnham's mission and dispatched a second letter to his father-in-law.

The soldiers, who in spite of his efforts had not been paid for another four months—"a thing unsupportable in this place"—had made a demonstration by which "we wear at a fair plunge to have lost all. . . . I did never think our nation had been so apt to go to the Enemy as I fynd them." Loyal Englishman and fair-minded gentleman that he was, this outbreak must have hurt his pride beyond measure. For to "make her Majesty sure of this yle" against English soldiers who were only protesting against outrageous neglect by their home government he was compelled to move in a company of Dutch infantry and to keep another at hand to overawe them.

In the midst of such distractions came the news that his mother had died, leaving the world, it was said, "most confidently, and to God (no doubt) most gloriously." Philip's sorrow for her death must have been mitigated by the thought that her many years of ill health and the long months of her suffering were at last ended. She was buried beside her husband in Penshurst church, but there could now be not even a hope of leave for Philip to see her body placed there. Parma had been battering the walls of Rheinberg, that last obstacle between him and Germany, for some weeks; and though Schenk and Colonel Morgan with twelve hundred English troops were joined in the defence of it, Parma's sieges were likely to end in only one way unless he was strenuously interfered with.

Before the end of August Leicester was in the field again; and Philip went to join him and assume in person the command of his cornet of horse and his regiment of Zeelanders. There was need of every horse and man to swell the little army of the allies, though at home, as the Earl commented bitterly, they expected him to lead out ten thousand Englishmen. Actually, what with desertions, the poor equipment of the levies which had been sent him recently, and the necessity of garrisoning with English troops every important town, lest it should "shutt the gates against us" and "seeke so to be at his owne libertie, that he maie deall as the world shall goe," he could assemble only seven thousand foot and two thousand horse, counting all the nationalities under his banner.

Made up of English, Welsh and Dutch regulars, Irish kerns, Scottish and German mercenaries, his force was typical of those armies with which English generals fought for the balance of power in Europe from that time to the day of Waterloo. But as one of the first to try the efficacy of the mixture Leicester may be excused for lacking any great confidence in it. It was not even numerically strong enough to march to the relief of Rheinberg. The Earl believed, however, that if he attacked Doesburg and Zutphen, thus threatening the enemy's hold on the line of the Yssel, Parma would have to break up his siege and come to their defence.

Arnhem was again the place of assembly, and there the Earl reviewed his troops. For all their shortcomings they must have made a gallant show. The pikemen in Spanish morions, breast-plates and back-pieces of steel, stood in solid squares ten files deep. In front of each company stood its captain, armed with sword and "fair, gilt partisan," and its ensign with the company colours, a red cross on a white field,

THE
COVNTESSE
OF PEMBROKES
ARCADIA,

WRITTEN BY SIR PHILIPPE
SIDNEI.

LONDON
Printed for William Ponſonbie.
Anno Domini, 1590.

TITLE-PAGE OF THE FIRST EDITION OF *ARCADIA*

On it is the Sidney coat of arms, emblazoned with the eight quarterings borne by Sir Philip, and surmounted by the crest, a porcupine statant. Above is a photograph of a tilting-helmet at Penshurst, bearing this crest.

by courtesy of Lord De L'Isle and Dudley

with streamers of the principal colours of the captain's arms flying from the head of the staff. Above the men bristled their eighteen-foot pikes, the massed steel heads reflecting the sunlight in broad flashes of brilliant red and blue.

The Spaniards still called the pike "la señora y reyna de las armas." A solid square of their pikemen with weapons levelled could stand the charge of horsemen like a rock. But rocklike, too, was the deficiency in mobility of that formation. So on the flanks formed the "shot," the musketeers, in steel morions also, but with coats of quilted leather and bandoleers from which hung their powder-charges in leather-covered cases of horn. They stood with matches burning and the long barrels of their heavy muskets sloped upwards in the breast-high iron crotches of iron-shod rests of ash-wood. Their work was to skirmish, to break the opposing ranks by their fire, and to seek safety behind the pikes when the hostile cavalry swept down upon them in a charge.

The horsemen were resplendent in steel from head to knee. Lance, sword and pistols were their weapons. Their saddles were plated in part with steel. At the head of each cornet, which was the equivalent of an ensign or company of foot, floated its colours in the shape of a three-foot swallow-tail, or a square if its captain was a knight-banneret.

The artillery of the period did not contribute greatly to the pageantry of a review. The improvements in the musket and the arquebus had driven from the battle-field the light mobile guns that marched with the French infantry in the Italian wars at the beginning of the century, advancing with them to the attack and unlimbering in the modern manner. Philip's friend, young Maurice of Nassau, had yet to devise those improvements which, perfected by Gustavus Adolphus, were to make field-guns an important factor in the battles of the Thirty Years' War. Leicester had an excellent siege-train, however, and it was doubtless present on this occasion, with its master of ordnance and his lieutenants, its master-gunners, wagon-masters, trench-masters and cannoneers.

After the review, since the day was Sunday, the troops were formed in hollow squares and the chaplains preached to them, good rousing sermons, no doubt, in the spirit of "the sword of the Lord and of Gideon."

Doesburg was the Earl's first objective. It barred his approach to Zutphen, but it was not a strong place. The moat, though a double one, was only three feet deep. The walls were only of brick and crumbled rapidly under the fire of the allied artillery, which went into action within a day after the Earl's arrival before the town: so swift and excellent were the means of transportation afforded by the canals and rivers of the country. But the garrison was brave and resolute and was supported by the goodwill of the inhabitants; and almost immediately appeared another instance of how much better was Leicester's advice than the judgment of those at home, to whom he offered it.

Those pioneers and Cornish miners whom he had asked for so many months before had never been sent to him. Dutch peasants had to be pressed into service for digging the trenches and erecting the emplacements for the batteries. These people, who had no strong walls to protect them, were only desirous of keeping out of a struggle in which they suffered about equally from the armies of both sides, and they did the work with as little spirit, as grudgingly and as badly as might have been expected, dropping their tools and fleeing for cover at every shot from the walls of the town. Thoroughly disgusted with them, Sir William Pelham, who had commanded the pioneers at the siege of Leith, stormed up to headquarters, just as Leicester was going to bed, to tell him "what beastly pioneers the Dutchmen were."

Whatever Leicester's faults, a want of energy was not one of them. Weary as he was, he set off with his angry chief-of-staff to see for himself. The night was very dark; soon they had lost their way like a couple of subalterns on the Western Front in 1914; and presently by a gleam of starlight they found themselves at the very gate of the town. A caliver blazed from the wall above them, and the Lord Marshal dropped with a bullet in his belly. He thought himself as good as dead and thanked God "verie cheerfully" that he had stood between his commander and the enemy's gun. But he actually suffered little inconvenience from his wound, although the surgeons dared not attempt to extract the bullet, was soon going about his duties as usual, and did not die of it until the following year.

The veteran Roger Williams was wounded also. Dashing about with a great, gay plume of feathers on his morion, supervising the construction of parallels and approaches and directing the fire of the batteries, he got a bullet through the arm. But the great guns went steadily on with their work. In vain did the garrison strive to fill the breaches in the walls with mattresses, logs of wood and tubs filled with earth, and strew the sloping rubbish with spike-studded planks. The blood of the besiegers was up. From Norris to the youngest lieutenant the officers quarrelled for the honour of leading the assault; and when the garrison saw the storming parties formed, one of English, the other of Dutch and Scottish, and both straining for the race to see which should be first to scale the walls, they accepted the Earl's liberal terms of surrender.

They were too late, however, to save the town from all the penalties of its resistance. Philip Sidney, his brother Robert, the Earl of Essex and other officers used the flat of their swords to drive the infuriated and rapacious soldiery from the pillage, which their commander-in-chief had expressly forbidden. So outrageous was the behaviour of the wild Irish that Sir John Norris rounded upon Sir William Stanley, their leader, demanding that he restrain them, and an old quarrel dating from their years in the Irish wars flamed afresh between the two men. But in spite of all efforts to prevent it the town was sacked.

The Earl was delighted by his success, as well he might be. For the first time in nine years, he exulted, a town had been captured for the States by regular investment and bombardment. Parma, advancing to the rescue of the place, had found himself too late and, lest Zutphen should fall also, broke up the siege of Rheinberg, bridged the Rhine at Wesel and with all speed pressed forward towards the threatened city with an army which, since he had to guard his communications, was now weaker than his opponent's.

It was no small triumph for Leicester thus to have snatched the initiative from the foremost general of his time. He could, moreover, await Parma's approach with confidence. As he settled down before Zutphen, captured Doesburg covered his right flank, Deventer his left; and although the latter place was still a hotbed of sedition, the possession of it by the allies restricted Parma to the use of land transport in any attempt that he might make to relieve or provision Zutphen.

Zutphen, however, was very strong. Since that winter Sunday fourteen years before, when from the tortured population had gone up one long-drawn wail of agony, its defences had been greatly amplified. Two years before the Earl's attack it had foiled the best efforts of Count Hohenloe with eleven thousand foot and three thousand horse in a siege of eleven months. The lofty brick tower of its Church of St. Walberga looked out over an encircling wall strengthened with round towers and bastions. The river Berkel filled its moat and, entering beneath an ancient water-gate with machicolated towers, flowed through the city and out again to the Yssel. A small fort guarded the eastern gate and the road to Germany. Sconces on the western bank of the broad, placid river and on an island just below the town made the approach to it from that side still more difficult. Reinforcements thrown into it in the nick of time brought the garrison up to about two thousand men. Tassis, the Lieutenant-Governor of Gelderland, commanded the forts. Verugo, whose rise from stable-boy to Governor of Friesland had disgusted Schenk to the point of leaving the Spanish service, was in command of the town.

Parma himself slipped in one night at the beginning of the siege. He loved occasionally to diversify the duties of commander-in-chief by disguising himself and collecting information on his own account. He could hear the furious pick-and-shovel work of the enemy bent upon repeating here the swift and daring attack which had made such short work of Doesburg. A raiding-party brought in a Scottish officer who told him that the besiegers numbered fifteen thousand. But what he saw assured him that Zutphen was not likely to yield except to starvation; and when he slipped away to his army again before daylight, he carried with him the comfortable knowledge that Leicester had neglected to block the eastern road, by which he could throw much-needed provisions into the place. The season favoured him. It was already September; and with the coming of the autumnal rains the ground occupied by the allied army would become no better than a lake.

Leicester had established his camp on the west side of the river and opened his attack upon the outworks that covered the approach to the town on that side. South of the place a bridge of boats connected him with the eastern bank. There, on Gibbet Hill, the single eminence—and that a low one—to break the monotony of the great plain with its windmills, farm-houses, straight, poplar-lined highways and clumps of willows, which stretched away for miles on every side, Sir John Norris established and fortified his camp. It was the post of honour, for it flanked within easy striking distance the only route by which the town could be provisioned; and the Earl's appointment of Norris to the command of it bears witness to the improved relations that now existed between him and the fiery Colonel-General of his infantry. There, too, Sir Philip Sidney and Count William of Nassau had their stations and made their quarters as snug as possible. For, as Leicester wrote home, "Winter is come to us here already."

In spite of the demands which his military duties made upon him in these days, Philip did not cease to do what he could for the cause in general and for the good of the service among the troops in the Netherlands. He wrote in Latin to his learned friend Lipsius to assure him that he was doing his best for that object of Leicester's detestation, Paul Buys. He interested himself in the appointment of a new governor for Brill in place of Sir Thomas Cecil, who was going home on account of ill health. Lord Burgh was Cecil's second-in-command and everyway fitted to succeed him. But there was a good deal of intriguing for the place; and when Leicester seemed inclined to shilly-shally about the appointment, Philip wrote off to Walsingham that Burgh would be disgraced if he were superseded by some other. Even in the darkness of the early morning, when he was arming himself for his last battle, he snatched the time to write what seems to have been his last letter to his well-loved father-in-law and next to the last he ever wrote. It seems singularly appropriate that this should have been a commendation of an old servant of the Queen and a request that Walsingham should assist the good old man in his suit for Her Majesty's support.

The siege well begun, Leicester took Philip and Robert and their cornets of horse to Deventer for a few days. Disquieting news had come up-river from that nest of perpetual privy conspiracy and rebellion; and when the Earl returned to his camp, he left the two troops of cavalry behind him to stiffen the garrison. Exciting news awaited him before Zutphen. The capture of a Spanish mounted messenger, who was attempting to steal into the beleaguered town, had revealed the fact that early next morning the Duke of Parma would attempt to provision the place with a great convoy of wagons. Actually, moreover, the Duke was sending along with it almost half of his available troops to ensure the success of the operation. But, if the messenger knew this, he did not tell it. Leicester accordingly counted on having to deal with no more than an escort of the usual strength: nor can he be fairly blamed for this mistaken estimate of the situation, for the presence of the veterans Norris and Pelham in the ensuing action seems to indicate that they were well aware of his arrangements. His error must be charged to the slackness of his scouts, but for that the blame should be placed upon his chief-of-staff. He assigned to Sir John Norris with only two hundred cavalry the task of halting and capturing the convoy and posted Stanley with three hundred of his highly mobile Irish infantry at Warnfeld church, about a mile and a half outside the city, to support him.

Pelham went along to see the fun, apparently, for he left off his steel thigh-pieces. Or perhaps their weight would have dragged down the front of his corselet till it chafed that raw belly wound of his. Leicester with his customary energy rose long before daylight and trotted across the bridge of boats to watch the encounter; and with him in the pure spirit of chivalry rode, as simple volunteers, a group of England's noblest and most valiant gentlemen. Essex, Audley, Willoughby, North, Russell, the Norrises, young Hatton, Perrot, and the two Sidneys, every one of them an accomplished performer in the tilt-yard and at the barriers, they rode encased in plate of proof and armed with lance and battle-axe like so many heroes out of Froissart, each bent upon some deed of knightly prowess for the honour of his queen. Lord North wore but one boot because he could not bear the weight of the other upon a wounded knee. Philip, free now from the responsibilities of command, forgetful of old Languet's warning against knight-errantry, and scorning to be better protected than the Lord Marshal, unstrapped his cuisses and flung them from him in the gallant gesture that was to cost him his life.

Through darkness and morning fog so thick that they could not see five yards before them the little troop groped their way to the rendezvous where Norris and his two hundred horse awaited the enemy's approach. There they halted and strained their ears to catch above the stamp and shiver of their impatient steeds, the creak of stirrup-leathers, and the clink of scabbard and battle-axe on spurred heel and steel-plated saddle-bow, some sound of the advancing convoy. They heard it soon: the ring of many iron-shod hoofs upon the roadway, the thud and shuffle of marching infantry, and all the rumble, squeaks and clankings of a wagon-train in motion. Then the fog lifted with the swiftness of a curtain, and the little force of English found itself confronting five hundred enemy horsemen and three thousand of the matchless infantry of Spain.

CHAPTER XV

"A CUP OF COLD WATER"

WHAT FOLLOWED HAS HAD ITS COUNTERPART IN MANY an English battle since, when blood and reckless bravery have had to compensate for lack of brains and foresight and sound military judgment. The charge of the Heavy Brigade at Balaklava was like it; so were the charges of the Twenty-first Lancers at Omdurman in 1898 and of the Ninth Lancers at Andregnies in Flanders in the August of 1914. At Zutphen, as at those other places, the spirit of sportsmanship, of the tournament, of the hunting-field and the polo-field, were pitted against the cold, mathematical formulæ of professional warfare.

It has been suggested that the traitorous counsel of Rowland York caused Leicester to permit what was a useless sacrifice. Perhaps Sir William Stanley, whose duty it should have been to obstruct the highway and place outposts to warn him of the numbers of the approaching foe, was not unwilling to see Zutphen well provisioned. The next year had hardly begun when those two went over to the enemy, yielding Deventer and the Zutphen forts without a blow. But the Earl, for all the odds against him, may have thought that he had a chance of success; and there is no record that either of the veterans, Pelham and Norris, raised his voice against the attempt. Granted a couple of successful charges by his armoured cavalry; a few wagons drawn crosswise of the road, overturned and their horses slain; and he might hope to delay the convoy until the arrival of the reinforcements which he immediately sent for.

If Stanley had been negligent with sinister purpose, he

was more than ready to stake his life like any loyal soldier upon the consequences. For when Sir John Norris called out to him, proposing that they forget their quarrel and, if need be, die side by side in their queen's service, he answered:

"If you see me not serve my prince with faithful courage now, account me for ever a coward. Living or dying I will stand or lie by you in friendship."

One can imagine the young Earl of Essex already standing in his stirrups, his lance uplifted high above his head in the signal for the charge. As General of the Horse it was his privilege to lead the onset.

"Follow me, good fellows," he shouted, "for the honour of England and of England's Queen!" It was an age of stately language, even on the battle-field—or, at least, of stately reporting of the language used there. Whatever he said, two hundred and sixty lances were levelled at the word, two hundred and sixty pairs of spurs thrust home. The Italian mounted arquebusiers on their small, active horses, and the Albanian mercenary light cavalry of the Spanish vanguard were swept away by the charge of the steel-clad cavaliers. Essex, his lance in splinters on the foremost foeman, swung his curtal-axe upon the thin Italian morions. Willoughby's lance sent Crescia, the Albanian captain, rolling in the ditch. Count Hannibal Gonzaga, the general of the enemy cavalry, fell, mortally wounded. The Marquis del Vasto was commander-in-chief of the Spanish force. Sixty years before, his grandfather had caused a tent to be erected over the dying Bayard, the last of the heroes of Chivalry. Now, on the field where their great imitator was to receive his death-wound, only a timely pike-thrust saved the Marquis from the wielder of an English battle-axe.

Only the muskets of the Spanish infantry checked the onslaught. Before their volley the English wheeled away. It cost them but a few men and a few more horses, and they re-formed and charged again, old Pelham with no armour but his cuirass and helmet, Russell's battle-axe swinging like that of Essex, swords clashing on pike-staves, clanging on breastplate and morion, thrusting deep between gorget and corselet. So deadly was the press that Willoughby's basses were torn from his legs before Philip and some others could cut him free. Right through the pikemen they burst at last. Philip's horse dropped dead beneath him; a trooper dismounted and gave him his. Stanley's horse carried seven bullets out of the action. A third time they re-formed, a third time charged, riding through and through the enemy infantry. The heavy Spanish bullets rattled on their armour, but for the most part rebounded from it.

Now, however, they encountered musketeers entrenched. An hour and a half had gone by since the rising fog had showed the enemies to each other; and in spite of every effort of the English, the convoy had not ceased to advance. The hireling drivers had fled at the first attack, but the Spaniards, imbued with the professional soldier's single-minded devotion to his mission, had whipped, goaded and dragged the wagons onward, while their comrades fought to keep open the road before them.

By this time they had reached a certain redoubt near the eastern gate of the town, which, as Parma had noted with satisfaction some days before, the English had evacuated. It was close enough for the great-guns on the city walls to add their fire to the action. From the gate two thousand of the garrison began to issue forth. The musketeers of the escort occupied the redoubt; and against their volleys, aimed at leisure from this protection, even the steel-clad English cavaliers were helpless, their horses dangerously vulnerable. Several of these fell dead or hopelessly wounded.

A bullet struck Philip in the left leg, just where his discarded cuisses should have protected him. His borrowed troop-horse wheeled, swung in a wide arc and ran, while he could for the time do little more than keep his saddle. In his pain—for the thigh-bone was shattered—the only thought of which he was capable was that he must not allow the sight of his fall to discourage his comrades. A trooper helped him to bring his horse under control. But with the same thought uppermost in his mind he refused to allow the man to lead it; nor would he let them lift him down and place him upon a litter. A flask of water was handed him to slake the raging thirst that comes from such a wound as his, but he passed it to a dying soldier whose eyes were fixed upon it with desperate longing.

"Thy necessity is even greater than mine," he said graciously and pledged him in what the man left of its contents.

Leicester accompanied him part way in the agonizing ride of a mile and a half back to his tent on Gibbet Hill, and afterwards wrote for Elizabeth's eyes a touching account of Philip's steady talk the while, which was solely concerned with the war and the cause of the Queen and her allies. Russell, in tears, threw his arms about his wounded friend, telling him that none had ever served so valiantly or been so honourably wounded.

There was ample opportunity for these condolences. In the face of the sortie from the town the Earl had broken off the action; and although his reinforcements had not arrived, there was no pursuit. The three hundred Irish infantry at Warnfeld church covered his withdrawal; but in any event the hard-bitten Spaniards were little likely to forget that their business was to get those wagons into the town as quickly and with as little fighting as possible. The hope of glory in an unnecessary combat has small appeal for veterans such as they; and the affair had cost them all too dearly as it was.

They had, in fact, lost about two hundred men killed, among whom were Gonzaga and two or three others, whose handsome dress, although the English were unable to identify them, marked them as men of importance. Crescia was a prisoner. Three cavalry standards had been taken, of which two were sent as trophies to the Queen. "The other a knave cutt in pieces," Leicester reported disgustedly.

The English loss in killed had been but twelve or thirteen of the horsemen and of the foot twenty-two. All in all it is small wonder that the Earl wrote home somewhat enthusiastically, calling it "the most notable encounter that hath been in our time." And when one remembers the prestige of the Spanish armies of that day and their enormous numerical superiority on that field, he seems hardly to have been guilty of exaggeration. He knighted young Henry Umpton and William Hatton on the scene of their exploits. They had served in the front rank of the infantry rather than miss the fight altogether. He did the like for John Wingfield, Henry Norris and Goodyear, the captain of his bodyguard, and made bannerets of Essex, Willoughby, Audley and North.

Meanwhile poor Philip, who, it seems, had richly earned a similar promotion—and none would have prized it more than he—was undergoing the tortures of the surgery of the time with a fortitude that called forth general admiration. Let them not fail in thoroughness, he urged, as the surgeons probed upwards along the course of the bullet amid fragments of the shattered thigh-bone. He could better endure the rigours of the examination now than in the weakness that was sure to follow, he reminded them.

That afternoon Leicester's own barge conveyed him up the river to Arnhem. He was comfortably established there in the house of a Mademoiselle Gruithueissens. Doctor James and five other surgeons attended him; and although the bullet could not be found, he soon seemed to be improving steadily. Leicester, who visited him as often as he could snatch the opportunity to do so, wrote frequently to Walsingham of hopes which every day grew stronger. The patient slept and rested well and had "a good stomach to eat." Presently both surgeons and physicians considered that "his worst days be past." All England rejoiced at the news, and the Queen in some contrition for her recent attitude toward him wrote to him in her own hand a letter full of sympathy and warm appreciation of his services.

He was in excellent spirits. His hurt, he said, was the ordinance of God by the hap of war: an attitude of mind which must have helped to make those first two weeks by no means the unhappiest of his life, though the position in which they forced him to lie caused such bed-sores that after the first week his shoulder-blades broke through the skin. His brothers, Robert and Thomas, were able to visit him frequently, and they cheered him with the best of news from the front. Acting for once against the advice of his military advisers, Leicester had attacked and taken the Zutphen forts on the island and west of the river after bitter fighting.

Philip must have thrilled to hear of the exploit of Edward Stanley, Sir William's brother. Dressed all in yellow, save for his corselet, the young man had hauled himself up the breach by means of the pike with which an enemy was thrusting at him, and with his sword had cleared the parapet so that his men could follow him. Better yet for the ears of the affectionate elder brother, young Robert had so borne himself on that day that he, too, had received the reward of knighthood. They could tell him also of riding over to Parma's camp at Lockem along with Sir William Russell, Roger Williams and other gallants and five hundred horse to tempt the Spaniard out to combat in the good old-fashioned way, "but there would none of his gallants come forth."

Philip's wife, heavy with the hope and promise that she might soon give him a son and heir, came up from Flushing to nurse him. He passed the time by writing to Bellier, the translator of Philo, a long letter in Latin of such purity that it was shown to the Queen. Like his dying friend Essex in Ireland years before, he composed a poem and had it set to music. It has long been lost; but whether it was like Walter Devereux's plaintive and religious death-song may fairly be questioned, since it was written while there were good hopes of his recovery. He called it "La Cuisse Rompue," and he would have been like his father's son if he had squeezed a quirky jest out of his misfortune.

He did not, however, neglect to take those precautions which the dangerous nature of his wound demanded. Praising God that, although sore wounded in body, he was whole in mind, he proceeded with great care and foresight to make his will. He appointed his "most dear and loving wife, Dame Frances Sidney," his executrix, with his uncles, the Earls of Leicester, Warwick and Huntingdon, his brother-in-law Pembroke, and Walsingham, his father-in-law, as supervisors to assist her. She was made residuary legatee and given a life interest in one-half of all his lands and revenues. If the child which she was carrying should prove not to be a son, Robert was to have the other half as well as the reversion of this. If Robert should die without heirs, then Thomas and his heirs were to inherit Robert's share. A provision of five thousand pounds for little Elizabeth Sidney was made a charge upon Robert's share, and so was a like amount for another daughter, should the unborn child be a girl. But there must be no usury about the investment of these sums.

To Thomas he gave lands of the value of a hundred pounds a year, to his beloved sister Mary his "best jewel beset with diamonds." For friends, servants and dependents his affectionate and generous nature broke forth in small legacies, presents and keepsakes innumerable: his books to Dyer and Greville; to Edward Wotton yearly a buck from Penshurst park; to Sir William Russell his best gilded armour; to the Queen a jewel of the value of a hundred pounds in remembrance of his "most loyal and bounden Duty"; while Leicester and Warwick were each to have a like amount. There were to be rings and jewels for his aunts of Huntingdon and Sussex, of Warwick and Leicester, and a hundred pounds each for his beloved parents-in-law for jewels or any other form of remembrance they might like to wear for him.

Every gentleman who came out to Flushing with him in November, every one who had joined him since, every servant—especially one that had "lain so long in misery" in the dungeons of Dunkirk—was generously remembered, as were also his surgeons and doctors and the numerous clergymen with whom he passed many hours in religious discussion. It seems as if he, who had always loved best in life the doing of services to others, was bound to make the most of this last opportunity to do so.

For the payment of the mountain of debts which he had piled up so recklessly in the service of Queen and Country, as well as the debts which his father had left behind him, he made special and, as he supposed, excellent provision. He instructed his brother Robert and Walsingham to sell enough of his lands to pay them and he begged that this be done with all possible speed.

But while he was thus busy with things temporal, he was not forgetful of things eternal. It was an age in which but few, either Protestant or Catholic, failed to seize the opportunity to make their peace with God at the approach of death; and Philip would have been the last to neglect to do this.

> It is not I that dye, I doe but leave an Inn,
> Where harbourd was with me all filthy kind of sinne.
> It is not I that dye, I doe but nowe begin
> Into eternal joyes by Fayth to enter in.
> Why mourne you then, my Parents, Freinds and Kin?
> Lament you when I loose, not when I winne.

So had he written, apparently during a severe illness in some earlier period of his life: one seems to catch in the verses the note of an adolescent piety. But his faith in Christianity and in the immortality of his soul had remained unshaken through the years since then. God moved through his instruments in a mysterious way, he felt, but the movements were the more godlike by reason of their very incomprehensibility. As for the teachings of Bruno and his kind, if the Scriptures and theologians had erred in astronomical matters, he found nothing in their errors to shake his faith in the teachings of Christ. Death was to him, as to millions before him and after, not the end of life but the portal by which he was to pass from one life to another and, he humbly hoped, a better one. Death was a part of life, dying a part of living, no mere passive experience to be endured, but a positive action which, like all actions according to his philosophy, must be performed in the best possible manner. He might have written as Jeremy Taylor wrote sixty-five years later, "to die willingly and nobly is the duty of a good and of a valiant man," though he was perhaps too kindly to have added as Taylor did, "and they that are not so are vicious and fools and cowards."

In the reassuring atmosphere of his apparent convalescence he found it pleasant to gather round him the numerous divines who had flocked to his bedside with the laudable desire to speed his soul to God, and to hold with them a symposium on the various conceptions of immortality, Egyptian, Greek, Jewish and Christian. But there came a morning when the subject assumed a deadly earnestness. Chancing to turn back his bed-clothes, he hastily replaced them and, with his accustomed courtesy, begged the watchers at his bedside to forgive the dreadful odour which had assailed his nostrils. They denied that they were aware of it; but from that moment he knew that his wound had become the seat of a fatal mortification.

The news spread through the army like the tidings of a defeat. Hohenloe, who had been shot through cheek and throat at the Zutphen forts, had had himself transported to Arnhem so that Philip might share the ministrations of his skilful personal surgeon, and when the man brought him the sad intelligence, the fierce old free lance turned on him in a fury. Forgetful of the Norris quarrel and that Philip had carried his antagonist's challenge:

"Away, villain," he croaked. "Never see my face again until thou bring better news of that man's recovery; for his redemption many such as I were happily lost."

Robert and Thomas hurried to their dying brother's bedside. To all three of them it must have seemed that death was striking thick and fast among that devoted family. The stress of these, their last hours together, was more than Philip could bear. He begged them to love his memory and to cherish his friends, whose faithfulness to him gave assurance of their reliability. Above all, he urged, let them govern their wills and affections by the will and word of their Creator, "in me beholding the end of this world and its vanities." Then he bade them farewell. That his wife might be spared the ordeal of watching beside him to the end he parted with her also at this time.

The Reverend George Gifford, who remained with him at his request through the long, agonizing hours that followed, wrote a most edifying record of them. Gifford, however, was so far inclined toward nonconformity that his place in the Church of England had become uncomfortable for him; and in our day, unfortunately, his account can hardly be read without impatience and annoyance; for in the modern mind his pious phraseology is chiefly associated with hypocrisy and cant. Now it was that Philip gave orders that his *Arcadia* should be burnt. Now he said that he had walked "a vague course" and that everything in his former life had been "vain, vain, vain." He acknowledged his guilt, wrote Gifford, and thanked God for giving him time to repent.

It may be, in these long days and nights of pain, with no spiritual comforters save the Calvinistic Dutch ministers and English chaplains of the Knewstubs type—those specialists in the wrath of God, to whom the sacrifice of Christ appeared to be so ineffectual—that he did actually fall into that horror of great darkness which was so unlike the happy and confident faith he had shared with his mother and father.

Or it may be only that we have in what seem to us the sanctimonious phrases of Gifford no more than the distorted reflection of thoughts that were perfectly natural in one of his beliefs. Certainly few men, and still fewer young men, have looked death in the face deliberately without being struck with the littleness of what they have accomplished as compared with what they meant to do and might have done. And Gifford, with the narrow morality of his creed and the weakness of his kind for snatching a brand from the burning on every death-bed, may well have given the colour of his own theology to much that was spoken in a quite different spirit.

At all events Philip was not so lost to a sense of the innocent beauties of this world but he had the musicians in to play and sing his song of "The Broken Thigh" once more. Nor was the last hope of recovery dead within him, for he wrote in Latin with his own hand a desperate appeal to his old friend, Johan Wyer, physician to the Duke of Cleves:

"My Wyer: Come. Come. I am in danger of my life and I need you. Alive or dead I shall not be ungrateful. I can write no more, only vehemently beg you to make haste. Farewell. Thy Ph. Sidney."

Once more his thoughts turned lovingly towards his friends and those who had served him. He rallied his failing strength to add a codicil to his will to benefit certain of them, giving to Leicester "my best hangings for one chamber and the best Piece of Plate I have"; to Essex his best sword; to Willoughby his next best; additional bequests to apothecary and surgeons among others; twenty pounds to Gifford; and rings to Sir George Digby and Sir Henry Goodyear, who witnessed his signature on the instrument.

But with the weakness of approaching death fears began to haunt him. He who had taken life so zestfully—its very reverses with a certain gusto—so that he was remarkable even in that zestful time—was now oppressed by thoughts of the wretchedness of man's lot upon this earth, saw him as "a poor worm" and had to call upon the full strength of his faith that God's providence must be good. And he said to Gifford, "I do with trembling heart most humbly entreat the Lord that the pangs of death may not be so grievous as to take away my understanding."

Gifford, who had never left him for a moment, and whose heart, like that of many religious men, was much kinder than his systematic theology, assured him that, though his understanding should fail, his faith would abide and would suffice with God. To this Philip's reply was a gesture that gives us in one flash an understanding of his charm. "With a cheerful and smiling countenance," the clergyman recorded, he "put forth his hand and clapped me softly on the cheeks." Then lifting up his hands and eyes, he cried, "I would not change my joy for the empire of the world."

Towards morning his speech failed him, but when it "seemed as if all natural heat and life were almost utterly gone out of him" and Gifford asked him to make some sign if he understood him, "he did lift up his hand and stretched it forth on high . . . which caused the beholders to cry out with joy that his understanding should be still so perfect." In his clouding mind was there a faint memory of the dying Roland at Roncevaux, his gauntlet lifted high above his head in defiance of that last enemy, death itself?

Weakness had closed his eyes. But, "that we might see that his heart still prayed, he raised both his hands and set them together on his breast, and held them upwards after the manner of those which make humble petitions; and so his hands did remain, and even so stiff that they would have so continued standing up, being once so set, but that we took the one from the other." William Temple, his secretary, held him in his arms till the last, faint breathing ceased. It was Monday morning, the seventeenth of October. In six weeks and two days more he would have been thirty-two years old.

SIR PHILIP SIDNEY

from the miniature by Isaac Oliver, in Windsor Castle

by gracious permission of His Majesty the King

They brought his body by water from Arnhem down to Flushing. There it lay in state for eight days, honoured by the burghers, who were eloquent in their regret for the loss of their governor and in sympathy for his widow. Of the English he alone had won the confidence of the Dutch. Leicester and Hohenloe were at loggerheads again, and there was no one to renew the good understanding between them as Philip had done more than once. The Council of the States begged for the honour of burying their English champion in their own hard-won soil: they would spend a half-ton of gold, if need were, to give him a worthy resting-place. But England could not relinquish the body of one of her most brilliant sons.

In column of threes, their arms reversed and ensigns trailing, drums muffled and fifers breathing softly through their instruments, the Flushing garrison of twelve hundred men escorted his coffin from his house to the shore. There his pinnace, all in black even to the sails and cordage, and hung about with festoons of black cloth and escutcheons of his arms, awaited it. A great velvet pall covered it. Behind it followed the mourning burghers of the town. The musketeers fired a triple volley; the great guns on the ramparts, whose carriages and emplacements had been among the earliest cares of his governorship, thundered twice in farewell; and for the last time—and, as always, with high honour—Sir Philip Sidney returned to his native land.

There the mourning for him was spontaneous and general, and all the more intense because the Netherlands had been cut off from England by storms for more than twenty days, so that the news of his death was the first to come after Leicester's report that there was good hope of his recovery. "I go no whither," wrote Fulke Greville to Archibald Douglas. At court and in the city alike the wearing of "any bright or gaudy apparel" was considered bad form for several months. "Her Majesty and the whole realm beside do suffer no small loss," Lord Buckhurst told Leicester. In her grief the Queen forgot details of public business, a most uncommon thing with her. She lashed out at Charles Blount, Penelope Rich's early and abiding flame, who had slipped off without her permission to see service abroad. He would never be satisfied, she told him, until he got himself "knocked on the head like that inconsiderate fellow Sidney." It was like her to mask in roughness the depth of her grief.

Meanwhile the autumnal rains and the approach of winter had put an end to the campaign in the Low Countries. The Earl of Essex and many another well-born young officer were going home on leave. Deventer was garrisoned in such force that its possession seemed to be secure; the Zutphen forts were strongly held; and Leicester, in happy ignorance of the intended treachery of Stanley and York, only delayed his departure until he could turn over his vexatious duties to Lord Grey de Wilton. He had Philip's young widow with him: "your sorrowfull daughter and mine," as he wrote to her father, "so wonderfully overthrowen thorow hir longe care since the beginning of her husbandes hurt" that, although she longed to leave the country, she was still too weak to travel with her unborn child. Two months later he wrote again, this time from Greenwich, anxiously begging to be told how "my daughter doth amend." For the journey home after those weeks of fatigue and sorrow had been too much for poor, young Dame Frances; and her child—a boy indeed, but still-born—had come to an untimely birth.

They carried Philip's body ashore at the Tower Wharf on the 5th of November and conveyed it to the near-by Minories, his old headquarters in the Ordnance. There it rested for more than three months, while Walsingham strove to bring such order out of the confusion of Philip's affairs that a funeral appropriate for one of his fame and position might be given him without ruining the many poor creditors whom he had left behind him. His "goods," Walsingham wrote to Leicester on November 6th, would not pay a third of his debts. A thorough examination of his estate revealed a situation even more unsatisfactory.

Since he had not been allowed to come home at the time of his father's death, Philip had made his will in ignorance of how small a part of the lands which he inherited was free of entail; and now the lawyers advised his father-in-law that only the lands held in fee simple were available both for the payment of debts and for the many annuities which his will had established as well. To give satisfactory title to purchasers of the rest would be something too difficult to attempt.

Dame Frances, with a grief-stricken young widow's generous eagerness that her husband's last wishes should be carried out to the letter, offered to waive her jointure; but that did not meet the requirements of the case. Robert Sidney appears to have treated it with the typical aristocratic negligence as to the prompt payment of debts; and so many years later that Frances was married to her third husband there was still in the courts a suit between her and Robert, that had its origin in Philip's will. Leicester, since he had mortgaged even his plate in the Queen's service, must be excused for not coming to the rescue. The Queen herself was indifferent, as might have been expected.

Finally Walsingham, moved by his inherited tradition of mercantile honour, paid six thousand pounds out of his own pocket. He counted it as nothing, he said, compared with the loss of "the gentleman, whoe was my chefe worldly comforte," and it wrung his heart that "a gentleman that hath lyved so unspotted a reputatyon, and had so great care to see all men satisfyed, should be so exposed to the owtcry of his creditors." But in so doing, as he wrote to Leicester, he reduced himself to "a most harde and desperat state." Burghley in a letter of condolence to him expressed his anxiety for the consequences of such magnanimous probity. His finances, indeed, never recovered from the strain thus put upon them; and he went to his own grave a few years later so poor that he was buried at night, lest he should be shamed by the meanness of his obsequies.

It was a Monday in the midst of the February of 1587 before all the arrangements for Philip's funeral were complete. William Shakespeare came to town that winter. Perhaps he stood in the crowds that thronged the streets from the Minories to St. Paul's Cathedral to see the stately cortège pass. Perhaps he could remember that on a day at Kenilworth twelve years before there had been pointed out to him the long, pale, handsome face of young Mr. Philip Sidney, the Earl of Leicester's nephew and heir, with his shining auburn locks and graceful height set off by the suit of black Venetian velvet which he had lately brought home with him from his foreign travels. Perhaps he already knew enough about the young dead hero to have it occur to him that here was the working model for a newer and better version of that old play about the tragic Prince of Denmark. At worst it is a harmless diversion to believe so.

Two-and-thirty poor men—one for each year of Philip's life—led the procession, followed by the sergeants of his infantry in the Netherlands with halberds reversed. Behind them came the drums muffled and draped in black, the softly playing fifes and an ensign trailing his colours, which were rolled but yet displayed the Queen's supremely ironical motto: "*Semper eadem.*" Foot soldiers, mounted officers of his cornet, trumpeters, a guidon trailed and a coroneted baton reversed came next; then his standard, which displayed St. George's Cross and the Sidney crest on a wreath: a blue porcupine with golden collar, chain and quills, between three lions' heads erased, and on the border his motto, at once so humble and so proud: "*Vix ea nostra voco.*"

Sixty of his gentlemen and yeomen servants, his physician and surgeon and the steward of his house led the way for sixty squires and knights, his kindred and his friends. His brothers-in-arms were among these: Unton and William Hatton, Perrot, Edward Waterhouse his father's secretary,

William Herbert his own, and Francis Drake. After the preacher and chaplains came his pennon, his horse for the field, ridden by a page who trailed a broken lance, his tournament horse in armour, whose rider bore a battle-axe reversed, then the great banner of his arms, and after it the heralds—Portcullis, Blue Mantle, Rouge Dragon, Richmond and Somerset—carrying the emblems of his knighthood: the spurs, the gauntlets, the helmet with its porcupine crest, the sword and the shield, and the surcoat of arms displayed upon a staff.

Robert Cook, Clarenceux King-of-Arms, who was marshal of the ceremonies, followed, and immediately after him came the corpse, preceded by its ushers and borne, beneath a black velvet pall set with escutcheons, by fourteen of Philip's yeomen. Four gentlemen of his near kindred carried bannerols in front of it and behind it. His dear friends Thomas Dudley, Fulke Greville, Edward Wotton and Edward Dyer held the corners of the pall.

Behind the coffin, as chief mourner, walked Robert Sidney. Thomas followed with six others; and after them, all on horseback, rode four earls and two barons: his uncles of Huntingdon and Leicester, his brother-in-law of Pembroke, Essex, Willoughby and North; then a delegate from each of the States of the United Netherlands, the Lord Mayor of London, the Aldermen, the sword-bearer and the recorder and the sheriffs all in purple. A hundred and twenty of the Grocers Company, of which Philip had received the freedom, followed in their livery; and three hundred of the city trainbands, musketeers, small-shot, halberdiers and pikemen, closed the column with weapons trailing.

Through the narrow, crowded streets of the old, mediæval city, beneath the projecting upper stories of the high, timbered houses, here past a mutilated cross and there a desecrated shrine, and under many a grotesque gargoyle and rain-spout and the pendent signs of ale-houses, the procession wound its way into the packed churchyard of the

Cathedral. The Yeomen of the Guard kept the great west door. In the centre of the choir, ready to receive the corpse, stood "a hearse" hung with black and bearing the inscription, "*Beati mortui qui in Domino moriuntur.*" The grave was beneath the choir aisle, and there John Aubrey saw the leaden coffin amid the ruins of the Great Fire eighty years later. In the churchyard the soldiers fired a double volley to give Sir Philip Sidney a soldier's farewell.

All in all it was such a funeral as Philip himself might have planned for his dearest brother-in-arms, for Essex or Willoughby or Maurice of Nassau, had he survived them. Its sombre splendours would have delighted that pageant-loving soul of his; and he would have loved it the better because men accorded him such honours as his fairly earned deserts. "*Hardly do I call these things ours*" ran his motto. But that he meant by it no half-mystic renunciation of earthly goods and pleasures the context in Ovid, from which he chose it, clearly shows:

> For ancestry and noble birth and all that we have not ourselves accomplished:
> Hardly do I call these things ours.

And few men placed as he was have more nearly succeeded in living up to the standard which they have set for themselves. Few have presumed less upon inherited position, or relied less upon such great expectations as his heirship to the Earl of Leicester seemed to promise him. Few have striven harder than he did to make themselves distinguished by their own efforts, and few have desired distinction from purer motives. What was said of his father in Fulke Greville's recondite phraseology was equally true of him: that he "sought not to make an end of the State in himself, but to plant his own ends in the prosperity of his country." No office or employment in the government attracted him save as an opportunity to serve his country and the cause of religious freedom as that was understood in his time.

The world went on without him, as it always has done, and as it must do, though it lose its best. Dame Frances married his good friend Essex, bore him a son who became the Parliamentary general of the Civil Wars, buried him when his hare-brained ambition forced Elizabeth to send him to the block, and found a third husband in an Earl of Clanricarde. The fair Penelope, after playing a double game for years and then living in open adultery with her Charles, finally divorced the uncouth Rich and became her lover's Countess of Devonshire by a marriage that cost her her respectability at the hypocritical court of James I. Philip's little daughter Elizabeth grew up to marry an Earl of Rutland at fifteen and died childless at the age of twenty-seven.

It fell to Robert to harvest most of Philip's planting. He went on diplomatic missions to Scotland in 1588 and to France in 1593 and was Governor of Flushing from 1588 to 1603, when James I made him Baron Sidney of Penshurst and he settled down in that lovely spot to lead the gracious life which his protégé and friend Ben Jonson recorded in grateful verses. King James made him Viscount Lisle two years later and Earl of Leicester in 1618. His uncle Robert's wealth had already come to him, for the Countess Lettice's son lived but a few years and her husband survived his distinguished nephew just long enough to command the troops collected at Tilbury to resist the great Armada.

The Countess Mary devoted herself to the rescue of her *Arcadia* and other of her beloved brother's works from the mutilating presses of piratical publishers and became the patroness of the poets whom he had befriended. Spenser celebrated her attainments as Urania in "Colin Clout's Come Home Again" and as Clorinda in *Astrophel,* in which he mourned the loss of the brilliant friend to whose encouragement he owed so much. To her son William fell the privileges which would have so greatly delighted his uncle Philip, the friendship of Shakespeare and of Donne and the opportunity to be of service to Massinger and Jonson.

But, short though Philip's life had been, he had died with his work accomplished. In the changing world into which he had been born he had been one of the leaders among those who guided his country on to the path it was thenceforth to follow. None saw more clearly than he that the centre of conflict for European supremacy had shifted never to return to Continental battle-fields and that from his time onward these would but register the decrees of fate wrought out in distant lands and on the sea. Plassey and Quebec, Aboukir and Trafalgar and Jutland were implicit in his conclusions.

Four days after his death the commissioners arrived at Fotheringay Castle to place the Queen of Scots on trial for her life. Two days after his funeral she stripped off her black dress in the great Chamber of Presence and stood forth all in red from head to foot to face her executioner. From that moment the time was past for subterfuges, half-piratical privateering, secret subsidies and faint-hearted military adventuring on the Continent. To that policy of "practicing" Philip's life, by a strange but not infrequent irony of human existence, was a sacrifice; and still his queen might hesitate, still strive to double and draw back. But now the current of events had become too strong for her. The issue, which Philip had seen plainly since that dreadful St. Bartholomew's Day at Paris fourteen years before—a free England or a world dominated by Spain; a Europe made safe for Protestantism or a Papal supremacy subservient to Spanish policy—could no longer be avoided. Within six months Drake was in Cadiz harbour, "singeing the King of Spain's beard" with the flames of ten thousand tons of shipping which had been assembled for the conquest of England. Within less than two years Philip's old garrison at Flushing was taking part in the destruction of the Great Armada. Within two years his brother Thomas was winning glory with an English expedition on the soil of Spain itself.

It was for his personal character, however, that he was

most admired by his contemporaries. All over Europe scholars and statesmen poured out their grief for him in elegies and private letters. No one seems to have known him or even seen him without treasuring the memory of the briefest contact with him. In the next century old men told with pride how in their boyhood they had watched him pause in his hunting to jot down in his "table book . . . his notions as they came into his head." Doctor Thomas Thornton, who lived to be Vice-Chancellor of the University of Oxford, directed that his tomb should be adorned with the statement that he had been tutor to Sir Philip Sidney. Lodovic Bryskett delighted to recall his journey with him into Italy. King James of Scotland and Sir Walter Raleigh were among the distinguished company that wrote sonnets on his death. And "Black John Norris," tough veteran fighter though he was, paid him the soldierly compliment of wearing no armour but his cuirass when he headed an attack in Spain.

More than a quarter of a century went by. Elizabeth was long dead, and on her throne sat James of Scotland, who quaked at sight of a naked sword and had no liking for any "men of war." Burghley, Walsingham, nearly all the great men of Philip's time were gone. Drake had found his grave in Nombre-de-Dios Bay. Raleigh, a prisoner in the Tower, was to be offered up a few years later as a sacrifice to Spain. The Navy was neglected. The Dutch had become the great maritime power of the world, and Barbary pirates preyed upon the coast of England. In these years, when things had changed so sadly from what they were in the spacious decades which he had shared with the friend of his youth, Fulke Greville, now Lord Brooke, wrote his *Life of the Renowned Sir Philip Sidney;* "to the end," he said, "that in the tribute I owe him our Nation may see a Sea-mark, raised upon their native coast above the level of any private Pharos abroad." There was need of such a monument to remind the English of their former glory; and Philip's name was still a name of power.

Fulke Greville, Servant to Queen Elizabeth, Councellor
to King James, and Frend to S[r] Philip Sidney.

So Greville had written his epitaph, when in 1628 he fe
beneath the sword of a disappointed servant at the age o
seventy-four. And men can have felt no anticlimax in th
inscription, though forty-two years had passed since Philip'
death.

It was twenty-four years later still when Greville'
biography of his friend was printed. England had killed an
driven out her kings by that time: she called herself a Com
monwealth. But an enterprising publisher foresaw a marke
for the book. Cromwell was leading the country back to he
old position of power in the world, of which the Stuarts ha
defrauded her; his admiral Blake was fighting Tromp t
recapture from the Dutchmen the mastery of the sea; an
so woven into the legend of England's former greatness wa
the memory of Sir Philip Sidney that his conception of wha
her foreign policy ought to be was sure to find many eage
readers.

In the eighteenth century, when Chaucer had bee
polished by Dryden and Pope, when the inelegancies o
Shakespeare were deplored and Doctor Johnson explained t
Miss Hannah More the reason why Milton had written "suc
poor Sonnets," the writings of Sidney lost the power t
edify and entertain, and have never recovered it. But th
memory of his personality was not forgotten. In the nine-
teenth, Shelley used it to conjure with in his *Adonais,* and
Charles Lamb delighted in contemplating its reflection in
the *Arcadia.* Today the *Arcadia* rests on library shelves, un-
opened by any save those who seek for scholastic honours in
English. To such, and to the poets, is left the fervid record
of *Astrophel and Stella.* None but the historians has knowledge of Sidney's influence on the statecraft and diplomacy
of his time, or of his exploits in war. The legend of his personal fascination has long been lost. All that remains of him

in the general memory is a single episode: the mortally wounded soldier conquering pain and thirst to ease the dying agony of a humble comrade with a draught of water and a gracious word.

But that "cup of cold water," which most children still hear of in school, and which most of them still remember when all else they have heard about him has been forgotten, is the quintessence of the man: his innate desire to serve others, his will to be master of himself, his effort to do all things well. This has persisted, and persisted strangely in an age that mistakes gentleness for weakness and seldom recognizes strength which is not manifested in predatory self-seeking.

BIBLIOGRAPHY

WRITINGS OF THE SIDNEYS; AND OTHER RECORDS OF THEM, CHIEFLY CONTEMPORARY

Brief Lives, J. Aubrey. 1898.

Complete Works of Sir Philip Sidney, The, A. Feuillerat. 1922-1926.

Correspondence of Sir Philip Sidney and Hubert Languet, The, S. A. Pears. 1845.

Life of Sir Philip Sidney, The, Fulke Greville, Lord Brooke (N. Smith, ed.). 1907.

Penshurst Papers, The, Hist. Mss. Com., 77th Report, vol. I., 1925; introduction by C. L. Kingsford.

Scandal and Credulities of John Aubrey, The, John Collier, ed. 1931.

Sidney Papers, The, A. Collins. 1746.

State Papers, Dom., Eliz., CLIX.

OTHER RECORDS AND BOOKS OF THEIR TIME

Annals of the Reformation, J. Strype. 1824.

Annales, W. Camden. 1625.

Annales, J. Stow. 1615.

Book of the Courtier, B. Castiglione.

Chronicles, R. Holinshed. 1807-8.

Correspondance Inédité de Robert Dudley, Comte de Leycester, P. J. Blok, ed. 1911.

Correspondence of the Earl of Leicester, J. Bruce, ed. 1844.

Description of England, W. Harrison; in *Elizabethan England*, L. Withington, ed. 1889.

Diary of Henry Machyn, The, J. G. Nichols, ed. 1848.

English Garner, An: Voyages and Travels (vols. X and XI, C. R. Beazley, ed.).

Life and Times of Sir Peter Carew, Kt., The, J. Hooker. 1857.
Lives and Letters of the Devereux, Earls of Essex, The, Hon. W. B. Devereux, ed. 1853.
Old English Ballads, H. E. Rollins, ed. 1920.
Prince, The, N. Machiavelli. 1893.
Progresses and Public Processions of Queen Elizabeth, J. Nichols, ed. 1788.

MODERN BIOGRAPHIES OF SIR PHILIP SIDNEY

Life of Sir Philip Sidney, The, W. M. Wallace. 1915.
Memoirs of the Life and Writings of Sir Philip Sidney, T. Zouch. 1808.
Philip Sidney, E. M. Denkinger. 1932.
Sir Philip Sidney, Mona Wilson. 1931.
Sir Philip Sidney and the Arcadia, M. S. Goldman. 1934.
Sir Philip Sidney en France, A. W. Osborn. 1932.
Sir Philip Sidney, Type of English Chivalry, H. R. Fox-Bourne. 1891.

OTHER BIOGRAPHIES AND STUDIES

Alexandre Farnese, Prince de Parme, L. van der Essen. 1933-1935.
Edmund Campion, A Biography, R. Simpson. 1896.
Fighting Veres, The, C. R. Markham. 1888.
Henry of Navarre, H. D. Sedgwick. 1930.
Lady Jane Grey and Her Times, I. A. Taylor. 1908.
Life and Correspondence of Lodovic Bryskett, The, Plomer and Cross. 1927.
Life of Jane Dormer, Duchess of Feria, The, H. Clifford (J. Stevenson, ed.). 1887.
Life of John Dee, The, C. F. Smith. 1909.
Louise de Coligny, Jules Delaborde. 1890.
Mary I, Queen of England, J. M. Stone. 1901.
Modern Studies, O. Elton. 1907.
Mr. Secretary Walsingham, Conyers Read. (U.S.A.). 1925.
Nine-Days Queen, The, R. P. B. Davey. 1909.
Penelope Devereux as Sidney's Stella, H. H. Hudson. Huntington Library Bulletin, 1935.
Philip II, W. H. Prescott. 1855-1858.

Philip II of Spain, M. A. S. Hume. 1899.
Private Character of Queen Elizabeth, The, C. T. Chamberlin. 1922.
Queen Elizabeth, J. E. Neale. 1934.

MISCELLANEOUS

Annals of Shrewsbury School, G. W. Fisher. 1899.
Council in the Marches of Wales, The, C. A. J. Skeel. 1904.
Description of the Escorial, F. de los Santos. 1760.
Discovery of America, The, J. Fiske. 1902.
Drake and the Tudor Navy, J. S. Corbett. 1898.
English Novel in the Time of Shakespeare, The, J. J. Jusserand. 1895.
English Travelers of the Renaissance, C. Howard. 1914.
English Voyages, W. Raleigh. 1926.
Europe in the Sixteenth Century, A. H. Johnson. 1909.
Experiment in Autobiography, H. G. Wells. 1934.
Histoire de la Literature Française, G. Lanson. 1902.
Historical Guide to Penshurst, Hon. Mary Sidney.
History of England, The, J. A. Froude. 1870.
History of England, The, G. M. Trevelyan. 1928.
History of Shrewsbury School, The, 1889.
History of the United Netherlands, The, J. L. Motley. 1873.
Ireland under the Tudors, R. Bagwell. 1885-1890.
Literary Ghosts of London, E. B. Chancellor. 1933.
Navigable Rhine, The, E. Clapp. 1911.
Old Virginia and Her Neighbors, J. Fiske. 1902.
Penshurst, Home of the Sidneys, J. W. L. Petley.
Paris, H. Belloc. 1900.
Rise of the Dutch Republic, The, J. L. Motley. 1870.
Spanish Story of the Armada, The, J. A. Froude. 1892.
Spanish War, The, J. S. Corbett. 1898.
Touring in 1600, E. S. Bates. 1911.

INDEX

Abondius, 116, 145
Adonais, Percy Bysshe Shelley, 352
Aetheopica, Heliodorus, 243
Alasco, Albertus, 248, 268
Alba, Duchess of, 37
Alba, Duke of, 4, 7, 15, 17
Albret, Jeanne d', 110
Alençon, François, Duke of, 105, 145, 174
Allen, William, 259
Amadis of Gaul, 243
Amyot, Jacques, 129
Angus, Earl of, 265
Anjou, Duke of (*see* Henri III, King)
Anne of Austria, 99
Anne of Cleves, 21
Anne of Saxony, 158
Antonio, Don, of Portugal, 7, 175, 221, 235, 277, 305
Antwerp, battle of, 275, 282, 301
Araucana, Alonso de Ercilla, 192
Arcadia, Philip Sidney, 44, 55, 134, 191, 200, 242, 254, 340, 349, 352
Argyle, Countess of, 55
Argyle, Duke of, 68, 75, 77
Armada, Spanish, 4, 260, 350
Arthur, Prince (Henry VIII's elder brother), 52
Arundel, Earl of, 206, 259
Ascham, Roger, 21, 63, 122
Ashton, Thomas, 63, 69
Astrophel and Stella, Philip Sidney, 219-233, 352
Aubigné, Théodore Agrippa d', 192
Aubigny, Count d', 208
Aubrey, John, 160, 348
Audley, Lord, 289, 329, 335
Augustus I, Duke of Saxony, 115
Avila, General d', 132
Axel, battle of, 313

Bacon, Francis, 20, 204, 271
Bacon, Roger, 256
Baltinglass, Viscount, 150
Banosius, 116
Bartas, Sieur du, 192
Bayard, Chevalier, 332
Bedford, Earl of, 14, 15, 39, 153
Bedford, John, Duke of, 42
Bellier, Pierre, 336
Bergen-op-Zoom, 297
Blake, Admiral Robert, 352
Blount, Sir Charles, 73; affair with Penelope Devereux, 147, 217, 219, 233, 349; reprimanded by Queen Elizabeth, 344
Blount, Lady, 73
Boleyn, Anne, 20, 144, 158
Bonaparte, Napoleon, 242
Bond of Association, 271
Bonner, Bishop, 47
Bothwell, Earl of, 88
Bowes, Jerome, 154
Bragadino, Marcantonio, 121
Brahe, Tycho, 156
Brandon, Anne, 23
Brandon, Sir William, 23

"Broken Thigh, The," Philip Sidney, 341
Brooke, Lord (*see* Greville, Fulke)
Bruno, Giordano, 268
Bryskett, Lodovic, 103, 120, 125, 351
Buckhurst, Lord, 317, 343
Burbage, James, 195
Burgh, Lord, 328
Burghley, Lord (*see* Cecil, William)
Butler, Edward, 93
Butler, Samuel, 51
Butrech, Peter, 172
Buys, Paul, 290, 310, 317, 328

Camden, William, 84
Campion, Edmund, becomes Jesuit, 157; executed, 213; friendship for Philip Sidney, 84, 96, 259; junior proctor at St. John's, 84; quoted, 100
Canterbury Tales, Geoffrey Chaucer, 199
Caraffa, Don Cæsar, 135, 145
Carew, George (*see* Totnes, Earl of)
Carew, Sir Peter, 93, 95, 96
Carew, Richard, 83, 90, 237, 256
Carleill, Christopher, 274
Casimir, John, 155, 169, 173, 241
Castiglione, Baldassare, 203
Catechism, Calvin, 62
Cathay Company, 171
Catholics, 9, 32, 98, 100, 106, 208, 210, 317
Catiline's Conspiracies, Stephen Gosson, 195
Cecil, Anne, 87, 92, 176
Cecil, Sir Thomas, 276, 315, 318, 321; benefited by impropriations from Catholics, 215; knighted, 141; member of Parliament, 271; retires as Governor of Brill, 328
Cecil, Sir William, 25, 113, 122, 141, 180, 182, 244, 306; disapproves daughter's engagement to Philip Sidney, 91; escapes assassination, 105; favours Queen Elizabeth's marriage to Robert Dudley, 57; friendship for Sidney family, 86, 100, 138, 220, 301; suggests method of halting Parma's progress, 316; threatens to resign as Secretary of State, 296
Challoner, Sir Thomas, 133
Chancellor, Richard, 250
Charles, Archduke, of Austria, 50
Charles I, King, 244
Charles V, Emperor, 4, 8, 10, 31, 41, 45, 133, 282
Charles IX, King, 72, 105, 109, 126, 157
Charlotte, Princess, of Bourbon-Montpensier, 158, 234
Chastelard, Pierre de, 192
Chaucer, Geoffrey, 352
Chronicle, Hall and Grafton, 19
Churchill, Winston, 275
Clanricarde, Earl of, 148, 165, 254, 349
Claudio, Crison, 135
Clerk, Bartholomew, 310
Clinton, Edward Fiennes de (*see* Lincoln, Earl of)
Cobham, Lord, 37
Cokram, John, 138
Coligny, Gaspard de, 108, 110
Cologne, Archbishop of, 291, 305
Commentaries, Julius Cæsar, 62, 313
Como, Cardinal of, 272
Comus, John Milton, 51

Condé, Prince of, 58, 66, 91, 108, 112, 131
Coningsby, Thomas, 119, 125
Cook, Robert, 308, 347
Corbet, Sir Andrew, 69
Corbet, Robert, 69, 125
Corbet, Vincent, 125
Cornwallis, Sir Thomas, 212
Coryat, Thomas, 122
Council of Blood, 4
Countess of Pembroke's Arcadia, The, Philip Sidney (*see Arcadia*)
Courtier, The, Castiglione, 203, 216
Courtyer of Count Baldessar Castilio, The, translated by Sir Thomas Hoby, 203
Cox, Captain, 140
Crato, 116
Crescia, George, 3, 332
Crofts, James, 270
Cromwell, Oliver, 352
"Cuisse Rompue, La," Philip Sidney, 337

Darnley, Lord, 67, 88
Davis, John, 249
Davison, William, 262, 281, 287, 294, 300
Dee, John, 249
Defence of Poesie, Philip Sidney, 134, 196, 204, 243
Defence of the Earl of Leicester, Philip Sidney, 266
Deffense et illustration de la langue françoyse, Du Bellay and Ronsard, 191
De Legationibus Libri Tres, Gentilis, 263
De Occulta Philosophia, Cornelius Agrippa, 250
De Philosophia, Cicero, 21
Derby, Lord, 273
De Re Metallica, Georgius Agricola, 171
Desmond, Earl of, 74-81, 93, 100, 209, 239
Desmond, John, 209, 239
Dethick, Sir William, 308
Deventer, 331, 344
Devereux, Sir John, 42
Devereux, Penelope, 146, 217-233, 344; marriage to Lord Rich, 219; marriage to Charles Blount, 349; "Stella" of Philip Sidney's sonnets, 217
Devereux, Robert (*see* Essex, Earl of)
Devereux, Walter (*see* Essex, Earl of)
Devonshire, Countess of (*see* Devereux, Penelope)
Devonshire, Earl of (*see* Blount, Charles)
Dialogue between a Scholar, a Gentleman and a Lawyer, A, 266
Diana Enamorada, Montemayor, 200, 243
Digby, Sir George, 341
Digges, Muster-Master-General, of Flushing, 283
Discourse on Irish Affairs, Philip Sidney, 165
Discovery of the Gaping Gulf in Which England Is Like to Be Swallowed by Another French Marriage, John Stubbs, 185
Divers Voyages, Hakluyt, 242
Doesburg, battle of, 324
Doomsday Book, 42
Dormer, Jane (*see* Feria, Duchess of)
Dormer, Sir Robert, 31
Douglas, Archibald, 265, 343

Drake, Sir Francis, 4, 170, 236, 256, 264; at Philip Sidney's funeral, 347; atrocity against Scots, 144; expedition to Spain, 274, 277; fleet attacked by Spaniards, 94; in Cadiz harbor, 350; member of Parliament, 271; plundered Spanish ships and towns, 209; successes in West Indies, 305
Drurie, William, 144
Dryden, John, 352
Du Bellay, Guillaume, 191, 216
Dudley, Ambrose (*see* Warwick, Earl of)
Dudley, Edmund, 20
Dudley, Lord Guilford, 27, 34
Dudley, Sir Henry, 14, 42, 46
Dudley, John (*see* Northumberland, Duke of)
Dudley, Katherine, 25, 28, 97
Dudley, Lady (wife of Earl of Leicester), 56, 150
Dudley, Mary (*see* Sidney, Lady Mary)
Dudley, Lord Robert (*see* Leicester, Earl of)
Dudley, Thomas, 347
Du Plessis-Mornay (*see* Mornay, Philippe de)
Dyer, Sir Edward, 234, 251; arrested for fraud, 253; friendship with Hubert Languet, 173; friendship with Philip Sidney, 154, 205, 337, 347; sent to Netherlands by Queen Elizabeth, 262; travels in Duke of Anjou's retinue, 237; writes sonnet for Philip Sidney, 222
Dyer, Sir Richard, 309
Ecclesiastical Polity, Richard Hooker, 84
Ecluse, Charles de l', 145
Edinburgh, Treaty of, 51
Edward VI, King, 13, 20-29
Egmont, Count, 33
Elizabeth, Queen, 8-11, 29, 44, 112; appreciated by subjects, 137; character, 24, 100, 142, 178, 257, 292; childhood, 21; commands resignation of Leicester as Governor of Flushing, 295, 306; demonstration of loyalty to, 271; desires peace for England, 264; education, 21; enjoyed attractive men, 234; imprisoned, 36; indulges in wholesale cruelty, 98; intimacy with Leicester, 56, 59; involves France in hostilities with Spain, 105; Kenilworth visit, 139; marriage negotiations, 99, 182, 184, 206, 234, 237; negotiations with Parma for separate peace, 317; Oxford visit, 71; plots against life, 104, 258, 271, 317; refuses sovereignty of Netherlands, 275; smallpox victim, 59; succeeds to throne, 48
England, condition of army in Netherlands, 315, 322; conditions during Queen Mary's reign, 41; education in, 60; in danger of invasion, 255, 258, 273; London sights, 82; love of music, 62; military weapons, 62, 256; plagues, 59, 63, 69; religious unrest, 210; sends aid to Netherlands, 275; sports, 61; treaty with France, 105; typical army, 322; wars, 47, 58, 66, 274
Erasmus, Desiderius, 115

Ercilla, Alonso de, 192
Errington (Governor of Ostend), 284
Essex, Earl of (Robert Devereux), 146, 305, 319; in Netherlands War, 289, 325, 329, 332; knighted, 335; marriage to Frances Sidney, 254, 349
Essex, Earl of (Walter Devereux), 70, 145, 336; affection for Philip Sidney, 146; death, 149; Governor of Ireland, 142-151
Estienne, Henri, 115, 136
Euphues, John Lyly, 84, 200, 243

Faerie Queene, Edmund Spenser, 205
Fakenham, Abbot, 35
Fane, Sir Ralph, 43
Ferdinand II, King, 8
Feria, Duchess of, 198; at Queen Mary's deathbed, 14, 48; childhood companion of Edward VI, 22; favourite of Queen Mary, 14, 31; friendship with Queen of Scots, 57; marriage, 49
Feria, Duke of, 48, 49, 123, 154
Ferrers, Lord (*see* Essex, Earl of)
Ferrier, Arnaud du, 122
First Blast against the Monstrous Regiment of Women, John Knox, 48
Fitzgerald, Elizabeth (*see* Lincoln, Countess of)
Fitzmaurice (brother of Earl of Desmond), 93, 161, 167, 209
Fitzwilliam, Philippa, 119
Fitzwilliam, Sir William, 141
Flanders, battle of, 7
Florence, Duke of, 104
France, civil war threatens, 273; treaty with England, 105; wars, 10, 46, 50, 58
François II, King, 50, 57
François, Duke of Alençon, 104, 105
Frederick II, King, 291
Frederick III, Elector, 155
French King's Stratagem, 130
Frobisher, Sir Martin, 170, 249, 256, 264, 274
Fromond, Jane, 251
Fuller, Thomas, 195

Gammage, Barbara, 270
Gammage, John, 270
Gardiner, Bishop, 32
Gelee, Sir Jacques, 286
Gembloux, battle of, 169
Gentilis, Alberico, 260, 263
Germany, 291, 298
Gerrard, Chancellor, 150
Ghent, Treaty of, 169
Gifford, Reverend George, 340
Gilbert, Adrian, 269
Gilbert, Sir Humphrey, 235, 242, 264; death, 248, 253; in Ireland, 96; recalled by Queen Elizabeth from Dutch service, 131
Gloria de l' Cavallo, La, 135
Gomez, Don Ruy, 15
Gonzaga, Count Hannibal, 3, 332
Goodyear, Sir Henry, 335, 341
Gosson, Stephen, 194
Gratulationes Valdensis, Gabriel Harvey, 194
Grave, battle of, 299, 305, 310
Gray, Patrick, 265, 305, 307
Grenville, Lady, 93
Grenville, Sir Richard, 96
Gresham, Sir Thomas, 51
Greville, Fulke, at Oxford University, 83; attended Duke of Anjou

to Netherlands, 237; biographer of Philip Sidney, 351; entertains Giordano Bruno, 269; epitaph, 352; fights in Ireland, 234; friendship with Philip Sidney, 154, 205, 337, 347; member of Parliament, 271; on Royal Commission on the Navy, 256; quoted, 63, 108, 154, 168, 174, 181, 184, 277, 297, 348
Grey, Henry (*see* Suffolk, Duke of)
Grey, Jane, execution, 34; imprisoned, 30; successor to throne, 27
Grey, Lord, 51
Grey, Thomas, 119
Gruithueissens, Mademoiselle, 335
Guise, François, Duke of, 8, 110, 234, 259, 273
Guise, Henri, Duke of, 108
Gustavus I, King, 115
Gustavus Adolphus, King, 323

Hakluyt, Richard, 84, 242
Hales, Sir James, 174
Harrison, Reverend William, 62
Harvey, Gabriel, 194, 205
Hastings, Lord (*see* Huntingdon, Earl of)
Hatton, Sir Christopher, 177, 180, 194, 213
Hatton, William, 329, 335, 346
Hawkins, Sir John, 94, 104, 236, 249, 271
Heneage, Sir Thomas, 295, 301, 307
Henri II, King, 25, 50
Henri III, King, 126, 180, 192, 213, 263, 289; considered as husband for Queen Elizabeth, 99, 104, 174; death, 262; elected King of Poland, 121; expedition to Netherlands, 237; failure as sovereign of Netherlands, 261
Henri IV, King, 106, 112, 131, 172, 258, 261, 273
Henry VIII, King, 24, 52, 181
Herbert, Henry (*see* Pembroke, Earl of)
Herbert, Katherine, 270
Herbert, Philip, 270
Herbert, William, 160, 201, 347, 349
Hertford, Earl of (*see* Somerset, Duke of)
Heywood, John, 32
History of Ireland, Edmund Campion, 90, 100
Hoby, Sir Thomas, 203
Hohenloe, Count, 290, 297, 300, 318; devotion to Queen Elizabeth recognized, 305; in battles, 304, 312; veteran in Dutch service, 286; wounded, 339
Hooker, John, 96
Hooker, Richard, 84
Howard, Catherine, 21
Howard, Lady, of Effingham, 251
Howard, Lord (Charles), of Effingham, 237
Howard, Lord Henry, 181
Howard, Sir William, 36
Hudibras, Samuel Butler, 51
Huguenots, 106-113
Humphrey, Duke, of Gloucester, 43
Hunsdon, Baron, 237
Huntingdon, Countess of, 14, 217
Huntingdon, Earl of, 28, 97, 220, 347
Huntley, Captain, 287
Huss, John, 115
"Hymne de la Mort," Chastelard, 192

Il Cortegiano, Castiglione (*see Courtier, The*)
"In Dispraise of Courtly Life," Philip Sidney, 187, 205
Innsbruck, 8
Ireland, internal strife, 76, 86, 92, 143, 239; peace, 100; plague, 142; war, 149 (*see also* Sidney, Sir Henry)
Italy, moral atmosphere, 122; war with Turks, 121

James, Doctor, 335
James I, King (VI of Scotland), 234, 260, 265, 307, 349, 351
Jarnac, battle of, 99
Jerusalem Delivered, Torquato Tasso, 129
Jewell, Bishop, 73
John, Don, of Austria, 7, 97, 109, 132, 154, 169
Johnson, Samuel, 204, 254, 352
Jonson, Ben, 349
Julian the Apostate (school play), 68
Julius III, Pope, 44

Katherine of Aragon, 21, 31, 52
Kelly, Edward, 250, 252
Kepler, Johann, 156
Kitson, Lady, 211
Knewstubs, Master, 305
Knollys, Sir Francis, 75
Knollys, Lettice, 146, 175, 295, 301
Knox, John, 48, 58, 131

Lamb, Charles, 244, 352
Lane, Ralph, 264
Langside, battle of, 88
Languet, Hubert, 115-136, 144; death, 174, 214; influence on Philip Sidney, 158, 208, 267; letters to Philip Sidney, 116-136, 169-172, 181, 184, 190, 209; supervises Robert Sidney's education, 174, 187; visit to England, 173
Lee, Sir Henry, 154
Lee, Rowland, 52
Leicester, Earl of, 13, 29, 32, 45, 98, 103, 146, 251; attacked by Catholic party, 266; devotion to Queen Elizabeth, 91; finances Netherlands fighting, 307, 312, 345; godfather to William Herbert, 201; honoured by Queen Elizabeth, 49; influences Queen Elizabeth, 162, 195; in Netherlands, 276, 287-297, 310-335; intimacy with Elizabeth, 56, 180; loses confidence of Dutch, 317; marriage to Essex's widow, 151, 175; offered in marriage to Mary of Scotland, 67; outfits Philip Sidney for Oxford visit, 70; pleads for Queen's help in Netherlands, 315; takes Zutphen forts, 336; triumph at Amsterdam, 305
Leigh, George, 69
Leigh, Sir Henry, 207
Lennox, Earl of, 105, 208
Lepanto, 7, 121
L'Hôpital, Michel de, 108
Life of the Renowned Sir Philip Sidney, Fulke Greville, 351
Lincoln, Abraham, 242
Lincoln, Countess of, 103
Lincoln, Earl of, 103, 106
Lipsius, Justus, 328
Lisle, Viscount (*see* Sidney, Robert)
Lok, Michall, 242
Louis, Count, of Nassau, 115, 132

Louis (son of Elector Frederick III), 155
Louis William, Count, of Nassau, 290, 318
Lucy, Sir Thomas, 272
Lyly, John, 84, 200

MacDonnell (*see* Sorley Boy)
Machyn, diarist, 56
Maddox, Griffin, 103, 136
Malleus Maleficarum, John Dee, 252
Mansfield, Agnes, 291
Mar, Earl of, 265
March, Earl of (*see* Mortimer, Edmund)
Margot (King Charles I's sister), 106
Marshall, Thomas, 61, 69, 76, 196
Mary, Queen of Scots, 8, 33; attempts to meet Elizabeth, 57; becomes French queen, 50; executed, 350; marriage to Bothwell, 88; marriage to Darnley, 67; plots to win English throne, 104, 234, 273; seeks refuge with Queen Elizabeth, 88; son born, 73; son crowned king, 88; treatment in England, 131; widowed, 57
Mary of Guise, 51
Mary Tudor, 11, 13, 21, 33-38; conditions during early reign of, 41; coronation, 32; death, 48; false confinement, 40; marriage, 37; proclaimed Queen, 30; unpopularity, 41
Matthias, Archduke, 169, 235
Maurice, Count, of Nassau, 286, 291, 298, 312, 323
Maurice of Saxony, 8
Maximilian II, Emperor, 152
Mayenne, Duke of, 259
Medici, Cardinal de, 6
Medici, Catherine de, 57, 58, 105-113, 263
Melanchthon, Philip, 114, 115
Meleager, William Gager, 221
Mendoza, Don Diego de, 134, 159, 169, 176, 210, 259; arrival in England, 36; expelled from England for plotting, 17
Mercator, Gerard, 249
Mildmay, Sir Walter, 256
Milton, John, 51, 244, 352
Mollineux, E., 166, 193
Monas Hieroglyphica, John Dee, 252
Montaigne, Michel Eyquem de, 115, 153
Montcontour, battle of, 99
Montemayor, Jorge, 200
Moors, 4
More, Hannah, 352
More, Sir Thomas, 29, 132
Morgan, Colonel, 287, 322
Morgan, Thomas, 306
Mornay, Philippe de, 172
Morocco, battle of, 174
Mortimer, Edmund, 51
Morton, Earl of, 208, 212
Motley, John Lothrop, 173
Muscovy, Duke of, 45
Muscovy Company, 171, 250

Netherlands, aided by England, 275, 305; propose joint army with England, 262; shortage of munitions, 320; strained relations between factions, 318; war with Spain, 275, 304, 310-336
Neuss, battle of, 312, 317
Neville, Edmund, 272
Newport, Sir Henry, 69

Norfolk, Duke of, 88, 97, 100, 105
Norris, Captain Edward, 283, 287, 319
Norris, Sir Henry, 329, 335
Norris, Sir John, 185, 287, 295, 325, 327, 329, 331, 351; affair over appointment as chief-of-staff, 293, 318; fighting in Netherlands, 304; in Dutch service, 169; involved in atrocity against Scots, 144
Norris, Lady, 180
North, Lord, 289, 305, 329
Northumberland, Duchess of, 31, 33, 37; godmother to Philip Sidney, 15, 39
Northumberland, Duke of (John Dudley), 13, 14, 19-31, 37
Northumberland, Earl of, 259
La Noue, François de, 184
Nudigate, Sebastian, 31

Œuvres, Pierre de Ronsard, 192
Oge, Rorie, 143, 161, 165
O'Neil, Shane, 50, 55, 67, 74-79
O'Niel, James Mack, 45
Ormonde, Earl of, 93, 100, 163-167; disliked Philip Sidney, 241; feudal wars with Desmond, 74-79; return to England, 151
Ortelius, 249
Osorio, Doña Isabel de, 19
Oxford, Earl of, affectations, 140; marries Anne Cecil, 92; quarrel with Philip Sidney, 176-182, 241

Page, bookseller, 185
Pagenham, Sir Hugh, 22
Paget, Charles, 259
Palladio, Andrea, 122
Parker, Matthew, 53
Parma, Duke of, aims to capture Flushing, 282; circulates peace propaganda, 296; discouraged by condition of army in Netherlands, 304; offers peace terms to Netherlands, 262; on way to Rhine, 310, 312; siege of Grave, 307; siege of Rheinberg, 321, 326; Spanish commander in Netherlands, 185, 258, 264
Parr, Katherine, 21
Parry, William, 272
Paul IV, Pope, 44, 135
Paulet, A., 248
Pelham, Sir William, 257; appointment to Chief-of-Staff in Netherlands, 293, 315, 317; at Zutphen, 329, 331; quarrel with John Norris, 318; wounded, 325
Pembroke, Countess of, *Arcadia* written for, 191, 200; birth, 55; birth of second son, 270; maid-of-honour to Queen Elizabeth, 137; marriage, 160; patroness of poets, 160, 349
Pembroke, Earl of, 160, 172, 182, 347
Penchester, Sir Stephen, 42
Pepys, Samuel, 154, 280
Perrot, Sir John, 329, 346
Petty Navy Royal, John Dee, 250
Philip II, King, 3-19, 159, 282; attack on Protestants of Continent, 131; becomes King of Spain, 45; godfather to Philip Sidney, 39; heir to Portuguese throne, 175, 182, 209; leads army against France, 46; marriage proposal to Queen Elizabeth, 49; marriage to Elizabeth of France, 50; marriage to Mary Tudor, 32, 37; pleased by St. Bartholomew's Day atrocities,

112; seizes Portuguese throne, 235; teaches Queen Elizabeth a lesson, 274
Philip Louis, Count of Hanau, 125
Philip the Good, King, 282
Pibrac, Seigneur de, 127
Piers, Captain, 93
Pius V, Pope, 72
Poland, King of (*see* Henri III, King)
Pole, Cardinal, 37, 44
Pooley (servant of Philip Sidney), 267, 317
Pope, Alexander, 352
Potter, Gilbert, 29
Prince, The, Machiavelli, 204
Protestants, 99, 210
Pugliano, John Peter, 134
Pulteney, Sir John, 42
Pyron, Colonel, 314

Quadra, Bishop de, 37, 50, 56, 68

Raleigh, Sir Walter, 83, 256, 264, 270; attends Anjou to Netherlands, 237; fights in Ireland, 234; friendship with Philip Sidney, 177; leaves Oxford to fight in France, 90; wrote sonnet to Philip Sidney, 351
Ramus, 108
Ratcliffe, Henry (*see* Sussex, Earl of)
Ratcliffe, Thomas (*see* Sussex, Earl of)
Renard, Spanish Ambassador, 12, 31
Requesens, Luis de Zunigay, 7
Rheinberg, siege of, 321, 326
Rich, Lord, 219, 225
Richardson, Samuel, 244
Ridolfi, Roberto di, 104
Robert of Montgomery, 52
Ronsard, Pierre de, 191, 216
Ross, Bishop of, 99
Royal Commission on the Navy, 256
Rudolph II, Emperor, 16, 156
Russell, Lady, 144
Russell, Sir William, 289, 329, 332, 336
Rutland, Earl of, 259
Rymenant, battle of, 169

Safiye, Sultana, 121
St. Bartholomew, Massacre of, 111, 115, 127, 130
Saint-Quentin, battle of, 3, 7
Sainte-Aldegonde, 286, 291
St. Leger, Lady, 93
St. Leger, Sir Warham, 96
Sanders, Nicholas, 157
Santa Cruz, Marquis of, 7
Sarpi, Paolo, 129
Saville, Henry, 84
Schenk, Martin, 304, 306, 310, 322, 327
School of Abuse, The, Stephen Gosson, 194
Scotland, 51, 149
Ségur, François de, 257, 265
Semaines, Sieur du Bartas, 192
Seydenay, Baron de (*see* Sidney, Philip)
Seymour, Jane, 20
Seymour, Thomas (*see* Somerset, Duke of)
Shakespeare, William, 294, 301, 346
Sheffield, 237
Shepheardе's Calendar, Edmund Spenser, 194, 197, 206
Shelley, Percy Bysshe, 352
Shelley, Sir Richard, 123, 135
Shrewsbury, Lord, 11
Sidenie (Sidney), John de, 23

Sidne (Sidney), William de, 23
Sidney, Ambrosia, 137, 308
Sidney, Lady Anne, 22
Sidney, Elizabeth (aunt of Philip), 14
Sidney, Elizabeth (sister of Philip), 55, 80
Sidney, Elizabeth (daughter of Philip), 337, 349
Sidney, Frances (sister of Philip), 40, 42
Sidney, Frances (wife of Philip), joins husband at Flushing, 310; marriage to Earl of Essex, 349; marriage to Philip, 221, 242, 253; nurses Philip, 336, 344
Sidney, Sir Henry, 14; advice to Philip, 64; birth, 24; death, 308; difficulties in Ireland, 161-167; early years, 24; honoured by Queen Elizabeth, 49; hurt by Queen's ingratitude, 80; illness, 101; imposes conditions for governing Ireland, 239; knighted, 25; Lord Deputy of Ireland, 67, 141; loyalty to Queen Elizabeth, 178; makes peace with Scots, 143; marriage, 19; member of Privy Council, 141; opposes Queen's marriage to Anjou, 182; protests Queen's indifference to Ireland, 95; recalled from Ireland, 165; receives degree at Oxford, 85; return from Ireland, 100; seeks favour of Mary Tudor, 31; service in France, 59; service in Ireland, 42, 45, 68, 73-78, 81, 86, 94, 142-152; service in Wales, 52, 186
Sidney, Mabel, 14
Sidney, Lady Mary, 20-26, 270; daughter's death, 47; death, 321; financial straits, 138; illness, 309; lady-in-waiting to Queen Elizabeth, 49; marriage, 14, 19; retires from court, 186; smallpox victim, 59; sons born, 38, 59, 91
Sidney, Mary (*see* Pembroke, Countess of)
Sidney, Nicholas, 23
Sidney, Philip, 11, 14; aide-de-camp to Don Antonio, 235; ambassador to Emperor Rudolph II, 152-157; ambassador to France, 263, 268; ambassador to Prince of Orange, 158; ancestry, 53; appointed steward of bishopric, 202; at Cambridge, 101; at court, 144; at Oxford University, 83, 89; attends Duke of Anjou, 237; attitude toward money, 138; at University of Padua, 123; betrothal to Anne Cecil discussed, 91; birth, 38; birth of daughter, 277; character, 118, 129; childhood, 53; childhood homes, 42-44, 51, 269; christening, 15; colonel for Zeeland regiment, 300; commander in attack on Axel, 313; correspondence with Languet, 116-136; death, 342; death of father, 308; death of mother, 321; declines service to Don Antonio, 236; defence of poetry, 196; disapproves persecution of Catholics, 211; education, 60-73; experience in warfare, 147, 313; financial difficulties, 100, 185, 213, 344; friendship with Hubert Languet, 116 *passim;* funeral, 344, 346; godchild of Philip II, 15; Governor of Flush-

ing, 16, 276; heir to Warwick and Leicester, 144; honours Queen Elizabeth with pageant, 207; illness, 127, 136; influence on brother, 189; in Germany, 113, 136; in Italy, 119-133; in Paris, 106-113; in Poland, 133; interest in Scottish problem, 265; in Vienna, 115, 133; journey to Kenilworth, 139; knighted, 241; leads attack on Gravelines, 316; letter to Queen opposing her marriage to Anjou, 182; letter to Mollineux, 166; literary reputation, 191; loses Queen's favour, 297, 300; love for Penelope Devereux, 217-233; loyalty to Queen, 178; makes will, 337, 341; marriage negotiations, 242, 246, 247, 253; member of Parliament, 208, 271; military policy still pursued in England, 264; mourning for, 343; poetry, 203, 205, 216-233; political interests, 130; proficiency in games and sports, 134, 177, 204; quarrel with Earl of Oxford, 176, 180; refuses post as commander at Bergen-op-Zoom, 302; religious interests, 62, 155, 338; seeks government positions, 240, 245; seeks to marry sister of Prince of Orange, 171; summoned before Queen, 180; tour on Continent, 101-136; visit to Ireland, 73-78; visit to Wales, 85; wounded at Zutphen, 3, 333; writes masque for Queen, 193; writing preserved by sister Mary, 349

Sidney, Robert, 88, 135, 319, 336, 349; birth, 55; chief mourner at Philip's funeral, 347; education supervised by Languet, 174; fights in Netherlands, 281, 285, 312, 325, 329; Governor of Flushing, 349; honoured by James I, 349; marriage, 270; seeks government position, 239; travelled on limited allowance, 187

Sidney, Thomas, 238, 289, 336, 347

Sidney, Sir William, 22, 23, 35, 54

Siena, 8

Sigismund, Emperor, 43

Silva, Don Diego Guzman de, 68, 71, 80

Simier, Monsieur, 174, 180

Sixtus V, Pope, 4, 9

Smith, Sir Thomas, 47, 105, 140, 194

Socrates, 132

Soloman (Sultan's physician), 121

Somerset, Duke of, 21, 22, 27

Somerville (plotter against life of Queen Elizabeth), 258

Sorley Boy, 143

Spain, army in miserable state, 304; attack on English ships, 94, 274; defeat in Netherlands, 350; encourages Irish rebellion, 93; menace to other countries, 262, 291; plots against England, 97; wars, 68, 132, 209, 274

Spenser, Edmund, 101, 194, 205, 349

Stafford, Sir Edward, 242, 259, 273

Stanley, Edward, 336

Stanley, Sir William, 325, 329, 331, 334

Steenberg, 299

Steganographia, Abbot of Würzburg, 249

Stevenson, Robert Louis, 64

Story, Doctor, 157
Stradling, Sir Edward, 270
Stuart, Esme, 208
Stuart, Mary (*see* Mary, Queen of Scots)
Stubbs, John, 185
Stukeley, Thomas, 96, 167, 174
Sturm, Johann, 114, 188
Sturmeck, Jacob Sturm von, 114
Suffolk, Duchess of, 26
Suffolk, Duke of, 25, 30
Sussex, Earl of (Henry Ratcliffe), 42
Sussex, Earl of (Thomas Ratcliffe), 40, 42, 97, 138, 182, 241; considered as husband for Queen Elizabeth, 99; failure at governing Ireland, 67; godfather to Thomas Sidney, 91; tries to poison Shane O'Neil, 74
Synott, Grey, 149

Talbot, Gilbert, 206
Taming of the Shrew, The, William Shakespeare, 130
Tarleton, Richard, 195
Tassis, Lieutenant-Governor of Gelderland, 326
Tasso, Torquato, 129
Taylor, Jeremy, 339
Teligny, Louise de, 108, 286
Temple, William, 281, 342
Ten Reasons for Being a Catholic, Edmund Campion, 212
Thirty Years' War, 323
Thomond, Earl of, 164
Thornton, Thomas, 84, 351
Thou, President de, 192
Throgmorton, Francis, 258
Tintoretto, 121
Tomasin, Mistress (Queen Elizabeth's dwarf), 251
Tortures in sixteenth-century Europe, 136
Totnes, Earl of, 84
Toxophilus, Roger Ascham, 61
Tragiques, Théodore Agrippa d'Aubigné, 192
Travel in sixteenth-century Europe, 119
Tremayne, Edward, 95
Troyes, Treaty of, 66
Tudor, Mary (*see* Mary Tudor)
Tuscany, Grand Duke of, 9

Umpton, Henry, 335
Underwood, Thomas, 243
Unfortunate Traveller, Thomas Nashe, 122
Upperosserie, Lord of, 163, 167

Vasto, Marquis del, 332
Vega, Garcilaso de la, 192
Venlo, surrender of, 311
Vere, Edward de (*see* Oxford, Earl of)
Veronese, Paulo, 122
Verugo, Governor of Friesland, 326
Vulcobius, 116

Walpole, Horace, 119
Walsingham, Sir Francis, 105, 142, 266, 296, 301, 316; ambassador resident at French court, 103; arranges Philip Sidney's funeral, 344; enemy of Philip II, 16; exiled self during reign of Mary Tudor, 107; favours war with Spain, 210; financial ruin, 284; friendship with Philip Sidney, 140, 161, 220; nicknamed by Queen Elizabeth, 180; pays Philip Sidney's debts, 345; rebukes Catherine de Medici for St.

Bartholomew's Day Massacres, 113
Walsingham, Frances (*see* Sidney, Frances)
Warwick, Countess of, 201
Warwick, Earl of (Ambrose Dudley), 14, 29, 98, 257, 296; backs Frobisher's voyage, 170; commands army in Le Havre, 59; godfather to William Herbert, 201; knighted, 66; opposition to Mary Tudor, 32; shared prison with Queen Elizabeth, 49
Warwick, Earl of (John Dudley) (*see* Northumberland, Duke of)
Waterhouse, Edward, 159, 162, 346
Watson, Very Reverend John, 113, 201
Wechel, Andreas, 115, 136
Welch, Captain, 312
Wentworth, William, 244
Werl, battle of, 304
White, Captain, 321
White, Henry, 188
Windsor, Lord, 206
William, Count, of Nassau, 328
William of Orange, 158, 185; assassination, 10, 208, 234, 238, 262, 271; correspondence with Philip Sidney, 171; insulted by Philip II, 17, 282; marriage, 158, 286
William the Silent (*see* William of Orange)
Williams, Roger, 262, 297, 319, 336; illness, 310; record in Dutch service, 300; teaches warfare to Philip Sidney, 313
Willoughby, Lord, 289, 319; fighting in Netherlands, 302, 312, 329, 333; honoured by Leicester, 335
Wilson, Thomas, 154
Wilton, Lord Grey de, 293, 344; defeats Papal expedition led by Fitzmaurice, 209, 234, 239; Lord Deputy of Ireland, 186
Winchester, Statute of, 61
Windsor, 237
Wingfield, John, 335
Worton, Edward, 134, 136, 267, 337, 347
Wotton, Sir Henry, 153
Wyatt, Sir Thomas, 33, 36, 154
Wyer, Johan, 341

York, Rowland, 331, 344

Zutphen, battle of, 326-336